RELIGIOUS DIFFERENCE
IN A SECULAR AGE

RELIGIOUS DIFFERENCE IN A SECULAR AGE

A Minority Report

SABA MAHMOOD

Princeton University Press

Princeton and Oxford

Requests for permission to reproduce material from this work should be sent to Permissions,
Princeton University Press
Published by Princeton University Press, 41 William Street, Princeton, New Jersey 08540
In the United Kingdom: Princeton University Press, 6 Oxford Street, Woodstock, Oxfordshire
OX20 1TW
press.princeton.edu
Cover art: Jamil Naqsh, Painting no. 25, oil on canvas, 30 × 24 inches. Courtesy of the artist.

Library of Congress Cataloging-in-Publication Data
Mahmood, Saba, [date]
    Religious difference in a secular age : a minority report / Saba Mahmood.
        pages   cm
    Includes bibliographical references and index.
    ISBN 978-0-691-15327-8 (hardcover : alk. paper)—ISBN 978-0-691-15328-5 (pbk. : alk.
paper)
    1. Religious minorities—Egypt.   2. Freedom of religion—Egypt.   3. Secularism—
Egypt.   I. Title.
    BL2460.M34 2015
    322′.10962—dc23   2015013177

British Library Cataloging-in-Publication Data is available
This book has been composed in Minion Pro
Printed on acid-free paper.∞
Printed in the United States of America
10 9 8 7 6 5 4 3 2 1

For Charles and Nameer

CONTENTS

ACKNOWLEDGMENTS

This book is based on research supported by the Carnegie Corporation's Islamic Scholars award and the Frederick Burkhardt Fellowship from the American Council of Learned Societies. The Burkhardt fellowship allowed me to take on a much more ambitious project than is usually possible for a second book. It afforded me the leisure of a year at the Center for Advanced Study in the Behavioral Sciences (Palo Alto), where I was able to explore scholarly debates in international law, Ottoman history, and minority rights. The American Academy in Berlin hosted me for six months, during which I wrote the bulk of this book on the beautiful premises of the Academy in Wannsee. Finally, a collaborative grant from the Henry R. Luce Initiative on Religion and International Affairs made it possible to engage with scholars from a wide variety of disciplines working on the issue of religious freedom. I especially want to acknowledge Toby Volkman, the director of Policy Initiatives at the Henry Luce Foundation, for her support.

In the course of writing this book I have accrued many personal debts, none of which I can adequately honor in this brief space. I start with my deepest thanks to friends who helped me understand the fraught condition of religious minorities in Egypt. Hossam Bahgat, the intrepid founder of the Egyptian Initiative for Personal Rights (EIPR), welcomed me into his organization and spent hours discussing the intricacies of his work with me. If not for him, and the gracious staff of the EIPR, this book would not have been born. I am grateful to Adel Ramadan for his patience and eloquence in explaining the ins and outs of Egyptian law to me, and to Yara Sallam—who is in prison as I write these lines—for her courage, care, and radiant smile. May you soon be free. I thank Magdi Guirguis for his invaluable insights into Coptic history. I also want to acknowledge Baha Mohamed, Muhammed Rajab, Nafissa Dessouky, Naseem Hashim, and Maikel Nabil for the research assistance they provided in Egypt. If not for the friendship and hospitality of Lamis al-Nakkash and Saif Eldin Hamdan, I could never have made Cairo my home; thank you for always being there.

The distance between research and writing is considerable; it requires conversations with friends and colleagues who push you to answer tough questions and explain what you assume to be obvious. I want to start by thanking Joan W. Scott, who not only read all the chapters at an early stage but also encouraged me to gather up the various threads of my argument and knit them together into one chapter, which now constitutes the introduction. If not for Joan's confidence in the project, I might have told this story differently. Wendy Brown read the entire manuscript before it went to the press and gave me invaluable suggestions for sharpening each turn of the argument. I am deeply grateful for this act of generosity. I want to thank Webb Keane for reviewing the book for Princeton University Press and for his meticulous comments on the manuscript. I am grateful to Samera Esmeir for her faith in the project and, despite her busy schedule, making time to read several chapters. A warm thanks to Judith Butler for reading the final version of my introduction with her customary wit and insight.

This book owes a huge intellectual debt to Talal Asad for opening up the questions that are at the center of this book. Talal also extended me his characteristic generosity and commented on the entire manuscript, pushing me to delve deeper into things that I had only hastily touched upon. I hope I was able to do justice to his instigations. This book has benefited enormously from conversations with Hussein Agrama, who has been thinking about these issues in relation to Talal's work for as long as I have. Many of the problems he writes about also animate *Religious Difference in a Secular Age*. I am immensely grateful for his deep engagement with this book, in particular his sharp comments on the political nuances of my argument that were, at times, unclear to me.

I want to thank Michael Gasper, Bruce Masters, and Wilson Chacko Jacob for reading the first two chapters and making sure that I did justice to the wide swath of historical material I discuss in this book. I am indebted to Aaron Jakes for sharing his archival savvy and introducing me to the 1923 constitutional records that became the basis of the second chapter. Thanks to Khaled Fahmy for his support while I was in Cairo, and to Kenneth Cuno for answering my initial queries about family law. To Sinan Antoon I owe a note of thanks for sitting down with me in Berlin to work through the gyrating prose of Egyptian constitutional debates while keeping us both smiling. Thanks to Ussama Makdisi for sharing his thoughts on Ottoman history and sectarianism. I am grateful to Michael Allan for convincing me to write on the novel *Azazeel*; much of what is in this chapter draws upon years of conversations with Mike and on his important work on literature and secularity. The chapter on family law benefited from conversations with Judith Surkis and her work on the topic in France. I would like to thank Peter Danchin for cowriting the article that became the basis of chapter 4 and for insightful discussions on the connections between the Bahai court rulings and international law. Finally, I would like to acknowledge Iftikhar Dadi's help in procuring the artwork for the cover of this book.

I am blessed to have an extraordinary set of friends who keep me invested in life and thinking. I want to thank Raka Ray for her immeasurable care that lightens up my spirits in ways that are hard to define. Whenever I have faltered, she has always been there. To Cori Hayden I owe my gratitude for her friendship and her presence in the corridors of Kroeber and Stinson. Jane Collier, a mentor and a friend, has always read my work with care and erudition; I remain indebted to her in more ways than one. My thanks to Anjali Arondekar, Colleen Lye, and Stephen Best for pushing me out of my anthropological habitus to think with them; and to David Goldberg for keeping matters on the edge. Ashok Bardhan, I owe you a debt for the skepticism you always inject into our conversations. Thanks to Mayanthi Fernando for not escaping to New York; to Behnaz Raufi for her laughter and care; and to Donald Moore and Jake Kosek for their unfailing camaraderie. And a warm thanks to Munis Faruqui, who has given me the invaluable gift of a pathway to the past: *shukriya dost.*

I am very fortunate to have an amazing group of students. A special thanks to Jean-Michel Landry and Candace Lukasik for their feedback on various chapters, and to Basit Iqbal for his edits and preparation of the index. My thanks to Mia Tong, who helped me prepare the bibliography as it was about to go to the press, and to Caroline McKusick, Behnaz Raufi, Hannah Jewel, and Rafi Arefin for their research assistance at various stages of this project.

I am grateful to Fred Appel at Princeton University Press for his early solicitation of the manuscript and for the care with which he has shepherded this project. A warm thanks to Anitra Grisales for her copyediting of the manuscript.

My final expression of gratitude is reserved for Charles and Nameer Hirschkind, to whom this book is dedicated. Much of what constitutes *Religious Difference in a Secular Age* owes to Charles's careful and erudite engagements over the years as I tried to make sense of what I wanted to say. Without Nameer's sharp intellect and joyful spirit, life would have been an impoverished version of what it turned out to be. Thank you both for being here, in spirit and mind.

***

Chapter 4 is a substantially revised version of a coauthored article that was published in the *South Atlantic Quarterly*. Chapter 5 is a modified version of an essay that appeared in *Comparative Literature*. Parts of chapters 1 and chapter 2 were published in abbreviated form in *Comparative Studies in Society and History*, and an earlier shorter version of chapter 3 appeared in *American Ethnologist*. I thank the publishers and journals for permitting me to use this material in this book.

NOTE ON TRANSLATION AND TRANSLITERATION

All translations from Arabic unless otherwise noted are mine. In transliterating Arabic words, I have followed a simplified version of the system outlined in the *International Journal of Middle Eastern Studies* (IJMES). Diacritical marks are used only to indicate the Arabic letters 'ayn (') and hamza ('). A hamza appearing at the beginning of a word is normally dropped, as is the *ta marbuta* at the end of a word. I have deferred to the transliterations used in standard bibliographic references, and to the styles chosen by authors for their own names, when these have appeared in English-language publications or websites.

RELIGIOUS DIFFERENCE
IN A SECULAR AGE

INTRODUCTION

Over the last few decades, the Middle East has emerged as the site of an unprecedented increase in violence between Muslims, Christians, and other religious minorities. While the mainstream Western media tends to present this as a product of primordial conflicts and Islam's inherent intolerance, even those critical of this interpretation nonetheless worry that the religious diversity that has characterized the region for centuries may be vanishing. This fear has only intensified following the recent exodus of Christians and Yazidis from countries like Syria and Iraq in the wake of the civil wars that have ravaged the two countries.[1] In this book I analyze the increasingly precarious situation of non-Muslim minorities in the modern Middle East, with a specific focus on Coptic Orthodox Christians and, to a lesser extent, Bahais in Egypt. While the Bahai faith is relatively new to Egypt, Coptic Orthodox Christians trace their history back to the first century, when Apostle Mark is said to have brought the faith to this land of Pharaohs and pagans. As the largest Christian minority in the Middle East, Coptic Christians have enjoyed a pride of place in Egyptian nationalist historiography for resisting British colonial occupation alongside Muslims.[2] Despite the wide recognition of their contributions to Egypt's anticolonial struggle, in the postcolonial period Coptic Christians have come to be treated as second-class citizens and have come to suffer various forms of social and political discrimination.

This book argues that modern secular governance has contributed to the exacerbation of religious tensions in postcolonial Egypt, hardening interfaith boundaries and polarizing religious differences. This claim will appear counterintuitive to many who

---

[1] Reports documenting this crisis can be found almost every day in the press. For three representative stories, see Daniel Brode, Roger Farhat, and Daniel Nisman, "Syria's Threatened Christians," *New York Times*, June 28, 2012, www.nytimes.com/2012/06/29/opinion/syrias-threatened-christians.html?_r=0; Jack Healey, "Exodus from North Signals Iraqi Christians' Slow Decline," *New York Times*, March 10, 2012, www.nytimes.com/2012/03/11/world/middleeast/exodus-from-north-signals-iraqi-christians-decline.html?pagewanted=all&_r=0; and Loveday Morris, "Desperate Iraqi Yazidis Flee into Syria," *Washington Post*, August 8, 2014, www.washingtonpost.com/world/middle_east/desperate-iraqi-yazidis-flee-into-syria-after-kurdish-forces-secure-escape-route/2014/08/08/817a17ad-233a-4ee9-935e-820eb53594e4_story.html.

[2] I will be using the terms *Copts* and *Coptic Christians* for followers of the Coptic Orthodox Church. Generally speaking, all Christian sects in Egypt are modified by the term *Coptic*—as in the Roman Catholic Coptic Church, the Armenian Coptic Church, and so on. Yet in Egyptian political and historical discourse, *Copts* (*al-Aqbat*) invariably refers to the adherents of Coptic Orthodox Christianity, hence my usage.

believe that secularism is a solution to the problem of religious strife rather than a force in its creation. Yet, as I hope to show, we cannot understand religious conflict in Egypt today without adequate attention to how modern secularism has transformed religious identity and interfaith relations. Secularism has an inescapable character that emanates, in part, from the structure of the modern liberal state, which promises to demolish religious hierarchies in order to create a body politic in which all its members are equal before the law. The secular ideal of religious equality, introduced in the nineteenth century, transformed relations between Muslims and non-Muslims, making it possible for the latter to imagine a future of civil and political equality. Despite this foundational promise, religious minorities continue to suffer various forms of discrimination in contemporary Egypt and other parts of the Middle East. While Islamic concepts and practices are crucial to the production of this inequality, I argue that the modern state and its political rationality have played a far more decisive role in transforming preexisting religious differences, producing new forms of communal polarization, and making religion more rather than less salient to minority and majority identities alike. Furthermore, I suggest that insomuch as secularism is characterized by a globally shared form of national-political structuration, the regulation of religious difference takes a modular form across geographical boundaries.

Two paradoxical features of this secular political rationality are particularly germane. First, its claim to religious neutrality notwithstanding, the modern state has become involved in the regulation and management of religious life to an unprecedented degree, thereby embroiling the state in substantive issues of religious doctrine and practice. Second, despite the commitment to leveling religious differences in the political sphere, modern secular governance transforms—and in some respects intensifies—preexisting interfaith inequalities, allowing them to flourish in society, and hence for religion to striate national identity and public norms. While these features characterize all modern states, in the case of non-Western polities such as Egypt they are often judged to be the signs of their incomplete secularization. My book challenges this diagnosis by asking us to attend to the structural paradoxes that haunt the secular project and how these paradoxes have helped shape the particular form that relations between Muslims and non-Muslims have taken in modern Egypt.

My analysis in this book is indebted to the burgeoning field of secular studies that has, over the past two decades, definitively challenged the conventional account of secularism as the separation between church and state, religion and law, and ecclesiastical and political authority.[3] Scholars from a variety of disciplines have argued

---

[3] Agrama, *Questioning Secularism*; Asad, *Formations of the Secular*; Bauberot, *Histoire de la laïcité en France*; Connolly, *Why I Am Not a Secularist*; Fernando, *The Republic Unsettled*; Fessenden, *Culture*

that modern secularism is far more than this minimalist formulation allows; it entails fundamental shifts in conceptions of self, time, space, ethics, and morality, as well as a reorganization of social, political, and religious life. The secular, in other words, is not the natural bedrock from which religion emerges, nor is it what remains when religion is taken away. Instead, it is itself a historical product with specific epistemological, political, and moral entailments—none of which can be adequately grasped through a nominal account of secularism as the modern state's retreat from religion. Roughly speaking, this emergent scholarship explores two distinct, albeit related, dimensions of the secular: political secularism and secularity. The former pertains to the modern state's relationship to, and regulation of, religion, while the latter refers to the set of concepts, norms, sensibilities, and dispositions that characterize secular societies and subjectivities.[4]

This book is primarily concerned with political secularism, particularly the modern state's production and regulation of religious differences in one region of the Middle East, and the effects of this intervention on the way religious identity has come to be lived for Muslims and non-Muslims alike. In the final chapter, however, I take up the question of secularity in terms of the proper attitudes, sensibilities, and reading practices that a modern believer is supposed to bring to the interpretation of sacred history and religious truth. Because these presuppositions are not so much found in the edicts and policies of the state but permeate culture at large, the final chapter tracks their imprint through a contentious debate over the publication of a historical novel about early Christianity in Egypt.

Following Talal Asad, I conceptualize political secularism as the modern state's sovereign power to reorganize substantive features of religious life, stipulating what religion is or ought to be, assigning its proper content, and disseminating concomitant subjectivities, ethical frameworks, and quotidian practices.[5] Secularism, in this understanding, is not simply the organizing structure for what are regularly taken to be a priori elements of social organization—public, private, political, religious—but a discursive operation of power that generates these very spheres, establishes their boundaries, and suffuses them with content, such that they come to acquire a natural quality for those living within its terms.

The state's sovereign power to define and regulate religious life is neither monolithic nor predetermined. Rather, it is shot through with a *generative* contradiction.

and Redemption; McLeod, *Secularization in Western Europe, 1848–1914*; Modern, *Secularism in Antebellum America*; Scott, *The Politics of the Veil*; Taylor, *A Secular Age*.
    [4] For an insightful discussion of how secularity and political secularism are related, see John Lardas Modern's engagement with Michael Warner in Modern, "Confused Parchments, Infinite Socialities."
    [5] Asad, "Trying to Understand French Secularism."

On the one hand, the liberal state claims to maintain a separation between church and state by relegating religion to the private sphere, that sacrosanct domain of religious belief and individual liberty. On the other hand, modern governmentality involves the state's intervention and regulation of many aspects of socioreligious life, dissolving the distinction between public and private and thereby contravening its first claim. This does not mean that the liberal state's ideological commitment to keep church and state apart is false or specious, or that secularism constrains religion rather than setting it free. Rather, the two propensities internal to secularism—the regulation of religious life and the construction of religion as a space free from state intervention—account for its phenomenal power to regenerate itself: any incursion of the state into religious life often engenders the demand for keeping church and state separate, thereby replenishing secularism's normative premise and promise. Consequently, the question of *how* and *where* to draw the line between religion and politics, between what is deemed public and private, acquires a particular salience in liberal polities and is constantly subject to legal and political contestation.[6]

A reader might object at this point that the model of secular liberal governance I outline above applies to Euro-Atlantic democracies, but not to Middle Eastern states that are best described as "authoritarian" because of their flagrant violation of individual freedoms and liberties. For some, this distinction means that Middle Eastern societies are inadequately secular, while for others it requires that a typology of secularism be developed so as to distinguish this authoritarian variant from the kind practiced in paradigmatically secular Euro-Atlantic societies.[7] While I understand the importance of attending to historically specific trajectories of secularism, I do believe that this way of casting the difference blinds us to common features of the secular project shared by Middle Eastern and Euro-Atlantic societies.

[6] This is evident in the interminable debates over questions such as: Does the French government's ban on Islamic headscarves in public schools violate a Muslim woman's right to religious freedom? Should the US government allow prayer in public schools, or fund religious programs in federal prisons? Can Germany allow Christian and Jewish religious symbols to be displayed publicly while banning Islamic ones, without violating its claim to secular neutrality? What should the proper role of Islam be in the new constitutions of Egypt and Tunisia (following the uprisings in 2011)? Do India's religion-based family laws violate the state's secular laws of general applicability?

[7] Among the scholars who make a categorical distinction between democratic and authoritarian secularism is Abdullahi an-Na'im: See an-Na'im, *Islam and the Secular State*, esp. chap. 5, "Turkey: Contradictions of Authoritarian Secularism." This distinction now permeates popular political discourse in the Middle East, as evident in the following remark made in 2007 by a leading member of the Muslim Brotherhood: "Labeling the Egyptian regime as 'secular' gives it unwarranted credit. In fact, the regime is neither secular nor Islamist. It is not liberal, conservative, or socialist for that matter. The only term that could accurately describe the Egyptian regime is 'authoritarian.'" Ibrahim El-Houdaiby, "Egypt's Two-Faced Regime: Not Secular, Not Islamic, Authoritarian," *World Politics Review*, March 30, 2007, www.worldpoliticsreview.com/articles/671/egypts-two-faced-regime-not-secular -not-islamic-authoritarian#.

To begin with, liberal and authoritarian states are not mutually exclusive entities. Authoritarian practices exist in paradigmatically liberal states, just as authoritarian regimes are held accountable in national and international courts for their violation of principles of liberal governance. Consider, for example, the series of executive decisions that have authorized torture, covert surveillance of the civilian population, and the suspension of individual liberties in the United States following the events of 9/11—all of which violate liberal norms of governance.[8] Furthermore, the hard distinction between liberal and authoritarian states does not acknowledge how liberal concepts and institutions, key among them the liberal ideal of legal and political equality for all citizens, have come to define a global norm from which no modern society is exempt. What distinguishes the secular dimension of the liberal project is an elaboration of the concept of equality in relation to religious difference—namely, the claim that all people ought to be treated equally regardless of religious affiliation. As an aspiration and a principle, religious equality signaled a sea change in how interfaith inequality was historically perceived: from a commonly accepted practice in the premodern period to a problem that requires a solution in the modern world. This aspiration is manifest in state reforms as well as the platforms of political parties and social movements; it provides the basis for a range of state laws and institutions that delimit the kind of religious claims one can make publicly. Even in the most repressive states, the variety of social movements fighting for religious equality attests to the global reach of this ideal and its promise.[9] I take this ideal and its attendant social imaginary to be a constitutive feature of political secularism, one that is shared across the Western and non-Western divide. The impossibility of its realization should not blind us to its power, its ongoing promise, and its constitutive contradictions.

In the course of writing this book, I stumbled upon the liberal-authoritarian distinction as I tried to parse the messy and overlapping histories of the Middle East and Euro-America. In chapter 4, for example, where I offer an analysis of the similar ways in which Egyptian and European courts sanction the customs and practices of religious minorities, the temptation was strong to mute this similarity and to force my material to conform with the liberal-authoritarian nomenclature. This is not surprising

---

[8] One might argue in response that the United States' respect for constitutional protections reigns in aggressive national-security practices in a manner that makes it quite distinct from authoritarian states. However, as Aziz Rana's work shows, the reverence for American constitutionalism emerged historically "in tandem with the national security state, functioning critically to reinforce and legitimate government power rather than simply to place limits on it." Rana, "Constitutionalism and the Foundations of the Security State."

[9] For example, in countries like Saudi Arabia and Israel, where the religious identity of the majority reigns supreme in the nations' laws, the ideal of religious equality continues to motivate a range of social struggles against religious supremacy.

since it exerts a tremendous force on our thinking and shapes the research questions that have become classic in the study of the Middle East.[10] For instance, even as scholars recognize the relative independence of the Egyptian judiciary over the long period of its postcolonial history, they regard it as an anomaly that requires an explanation, given the "authoritarianism" of the Egyptian state.[11] A classic question that guides numerous dissertations, books, and articles is "Why would an authoritarian regime allow an independent judiciary to develop and function?"[12] It is rare that we ask what this form of legality might teach us about the nature of modern law, the sovereign power of the state, and the constitutive relationship between the rule of law, its exemptions, and its failures.[13] A similar problem occurs in our approach to religious conflict: while in the Middle East it is analyzed under the rubric of "sectarianism," an understanding of the fate of Jews, Muslims, and other (racial or ethnic) minorities in Euro-America is understood to require a different analytical lens. In emphasizing these differences, we lose the opportunity to explore the structurally precarious position that minorities (religious, racial, and ethnic) have come to occupy in all modern societies, and how the modern state produces and conditions their precarity. The fact that the Egyptian state is obliged to respond to demands for religious equality, that its constitution pays homage to religious freedom, and that its courts entertain legal challenges to its discriminatory policies points to a set of liberal legal and political norms that it shares with Euro-Atlantic states that are regarded as secular exemplars.

A second objection to the characterization of Middle Eastern states as secular centers on the role Islam plays in the articulation of national identity and law, a role that clearly violates the principle of state neutrality toward religion (however formally and minimally conceived). Egypt seems to exemplify this problem. Not only does the

[10] There is a veritable industry of academic works on the authoritarianism of Middle Eastern states. See, for example, Diamond and Plattner, *Democratization and Authoritarianism in the Arab World*; and Platt, *Democracy and Authoritarianism in the Arab World*. For an earlier version of the argument about the exceptional character of Middle Eastern authoritarianism, see Waterbury, "Democracy without Democrats?"

[11] Since the military coup that brought General Sisi to power (in 2013), this image of the Egyptian judiciary as an impartial body has become unsustainable. As a number of recent commentators note, however, the regime has achieved judicial subservience to its goals by appointing a series of pliable and sympathetic judges who do not necessarily reflect the standpoint of the judiciary as a whole. See, for example, Nathan Brown, "Why Do Egyptian Courts Say the Darndest Things?," *Washington Post*, March 25, 2014, www.washingtonpost.com/blogs/monkey-cage/wp/2014/03/25/why-do-egyptian -courts-say-the-darndest-things/; and Ursula Lindsey, "Egypt's Judges Strike Back," *New Yorker*, March 26, 2014, www.newyorker.com/news/news-desk/egypts-judges-strike-back.

[12] See, for example, el-Ghobashy, "Constitutionalist Contention in Contemporary Egypt"; Ginsburg and Moustafa, *Rule by Law*; and Moustafa, *The Struggle for Constitutional Power*. While these works offer invaluable insights, the data presented often goes against the authoritarian-liberal dichotomy on which the analysis is premised.

[13] For an exception, see Esmeir, *Juridical Humanity*.

Egyptian state proclaim an Islamic identity, it also regards the shari'a as the principal source of law in the country (enshrined in the country's constitution since 1981). While most of Egypt's laws derive from French legal codes, Islamic concepts continue to permeate court decisions and political debates. For example, the Quranic concept of "People of the Book" (*ahl al-kitab*), referring to the Abrahamic religions, is used to extend state recognition to Christians and Jews, while members of other faiths (such as Bahais) are excluded.[14] This conjoining of citizenship and religiosity is further manifest in the existence of separate religion-based family laws for Christians, Muslims, and Jews instead of a shared civil law to which all citizens are equally subject regardless of their religious affiliation.

All these features of Egyptian political life seem to violate the norm of secular neutrality, a norm that Euro-Atlantic societies are supposed to exemplify. Such an understanding, however, overlooks the centrality of Christianity, increasingly glossed as "Judeo-Christian civilization," to the identity of Euro-Atlantic states, an inheritance that politicians, judges, and public intellectuals widely hail.[15] Consider, for example, the following passage from the well-known *Lautsi v. Italy* decision (2011) of the European Court of Human Rights (ECtHR) that upheld the right of Italian public schools to display the crucifix in classrooms:

> Looking beyond appearances it is possible to discern a thread linking the Christian revolution of two thousand years ago to the affirmation in Europe of the right to liberty of the person and to the key elements of the Enlightenment . . . namely, the liberty and freedom of every person, the declarations of the rights of man, and ultimately the modern secular state. . . . It can therefore be contended that in the present-day social reality the crucifix should be regarded not only as a symbol of a historical and cultural development, and therefore of the identity of our people, but also *as a symbol of a value system: liberty, equality, human dignity and religious toleration, and accordingly also of the secular nature of the state.*[16]

Note the simultaneously particularistic and universalistic nature of the claim here. While the theological and doctrinal predicates of Western Christianity made secularism

---

[14] As I explain in chapter 4, under various premodern Islamic empires, followers of non-Abrahamic religions were also granted state protection. The Egyptian government, however, refuses to extend similar recognition to Bahais.

[15] David Sorkin notes that the "Judeo-Christian tradition" is a term of post–World War II American coinage that had no equivalent in pre-Holocaust Europe. Sorkin, "Religious Minorities and the Making of Citizenship," 8.

[16] Italian Administrative Court's judgment, quoted in *Lautsi and Others v. Italy*, March 18, 2011, http://hudoc.echr.coe.int/sites/eng/pages/search.aspx?i=001-104040, para. 15, emphasis added.

possible, it is also the only religion capable of transcending its own historicity to spawn a truly universal model of secular governance.[17] This assessment is now widely echoed by contemporary Euro-American intellectuals such as Marcel Gauchet, Charles Taylor, and Slavoj Žižek.[18] The following comment by the much-celebrated secular liberal philosopher Jürgen Habermas captures the spirit of this valuation:

> Egalitarian universalism, from which sprang the ideals of freedom and social solidarity, of an autonomous conduct of life and emancipation, of the individual morality of conscience, human rights and democracy, is the direct heir to the Judaic ethic of justice and the Christian ethic of love. This legacy, substantially unchanged, has been the object of continual critical appropriation and reinterpretation. To this day, there is no alternative to it. And in light of the current challenges of a postnational constellation, we continue to draw on the substance of this heritage. Everything else is just idle postmodern talk.[19]

Remarkably, in one fell swoop the entire history of the development of secular institutions and democratic governance is attributed to the "Judeo-Christian" principles of justice and love. The old standoff between clerical and republican values, as well as the long history of anti-Semitism, is set aside to represent secularism as a unique achievement born of the conjoining of Christianity and Judaism. I cite this example not to highlight its historical inaccuracy but to draw attention to the centrality of Christianity within narratives of European identity. Statements such as these do not simply invoke a historical legacy in the abstract, but occur in a context where the Muslim presence in Europe is increasingly cast as a threat to Europe's civilizational identity. These claims, however, are not simply expressions of European prejudice. They are, I suggest, symptomatic of the fundamental centrality of Christian norms, values, and sensibilities (however Judaic they are made out to be) to European conceptions of what it means to be secular. Prejudice against European Muslims today (and European and non-European Jews of the past) is constitutive of, and emanates from, this self-understanding of Europe as essentially Christian and simultaneously secular in its cultural and political ethos. This is an argument I elucidate in the chapters that follow.

Far more importantly, for my purposes, the purported incommensurability of non-Western and Western secularism (the former deficient, the latter accomplished)

---

[17] On this point, see Hirschkind, "Religious Difference and Democratic Pluralism."

[18] See, for example, Gauchet, *Disenchantment of the World*; Taylor, *A Secular Age*; Žižek, *On Belief*. See also my response to Taylor's characterization of secularism as a unique achievement of "Latin Christendom" in Mahmood, "Can Secularism Be Other-Wise?"

[19] Habermas, *Time of Transitions*, 150–51, emphasis added.

fails to grasp how secularity structures the practice of religion in polities like Egypt. It overlooks the fundamental ways in which key aspects of the secular episteme cut across the Western and non-Western divide, such as the concept of empty homogenous time as a precondition for the politics of the nation-state.[20] It also fails to appreciate the shared history of the institutionalization of the modern state, whose political rationality is predicated upon the private-public distinction that, in turn, is foundational to the promise of civil and political equality. Under this arrangement, religion is relegated to the private sphere, which is also the legal and discursive domain of sexuality and the family, often entwining their moral and political fates. While religious morality has always been concerned with sexuality, as I will suggest in chapter 3, their delineation as quintessential elements of private life under secular modernity has created an explosive symbiosis between them that is historically unique. This is evident in how sexuality has come to serve as a flashpoint in a number of struggles over what it means to be religious or secular in the world, including in conflicts over gay marriage, the veil, contraception, HIV-AIDS, and abortion. In countries as diverse as Egypt, India, and Israel, this manifests in the exaggerated importance accorded to family law as the exemplary site for the preservation and reproduction of religious identity. Similarly, the distinction between religious *practice* (public) and religious *belief* (private), so consequential to European and Egyptian legal traditions, continues to justify state sanctions against minority religious symbols and practices in the public sphere. (The *Lautsi* decision I cite above is just one example of this; chapter 4 will present more.) We cannot make any of these related forms of secularity legible if we remain stubbornly entrapped within a logic of essential, often civilizationally weighted differences that keep the boundaries of the West and the non-West intact and stable.

These shared modalities of being secular notwithstanding, it is nonetheless important to attend to the historically specific forms of life into which secular concepts and institutions were inserted in the Middle East. In Egypt, for example, the political rationality of the modern state had to adjust to the legacy of Islamic political rule, which did not simply restrain the modern state's emancipatory project, but also inflected the way that project came to be interpreted and enacted. The fact that national sovereignty itself was predicated upon being able to claim a unique culture, religion, and language further entrenched the place of Islam in the making of Middle Eastern polities. As a result, one might say that premodern Islamic concepts of governance in a place like Egypt have rearticulated and transmogrified the principles, concepts, and institutions of political secularism, thereby giving them a specific form.

---

[20] For a discussion of the secular temporality that structures the historicity of the nation-state, see Anderson, *Imagined Communities*; and Chatterjee, "The Nation and Its Pasts."

How do we render such historical differences conceptually visible, while at the same time being attentive to the globally shared features of secularism? One strategy within postcolonial scholarship has been to argue for multiple secularisms, dislodging a Eurocentric account by showing other ways of being secular—one Protestant, another Islamic, Hindu, or Buddhist, each offering a unique trajectory of secularism. This position recalls the debates in the 1990s waged under the rubric of "multiple modernities," which was also meant to challenge Eurocentric accounts of capitalist modernity by drawing attention to the heterogeneous, local, and regional developments in the non-West.[21] Despite its popularity in the academy, a number of trenchant critics argued at the time that something important was lost in this purportedly pluralist account. Timothy Mitchell, for example, pointed out that "the language of alternative modernities" implied "an almost infinite play of possibilities, with no rigorous sense of what, if anything, gives imperial modernity its phenomenal power of replication and expansion."[22] He also suggested that the vocabulary of alternatives continued to imply "an underlying and fundamentally singular modernity," adapted to different cultural contexts, leaving undisturbed the epistemological hegemony of European forms of life and historical teleology.[23]

The call for "multiple secularisms" suffers from similar problems in that it constructs the history of the Middle East either as a deviation from Western models of secularism or as a local and regional story that adds little to its conceptual formulation. I treat secularism neither as a single formation that homogenously transforms all histories nor as a plurality expressed in local cultural forms. Rather, I suggest that secularism entails a form of national-political structuration organized around the problem of religious difference, a problem whose resolution takes strikingly similar forms across geographic contexts. In light of this, the critical issue is not so much to pluralize secularism as to conceptualize its variations in relation to a universalizing project, which, in the postcolonial context, also involves the ongoing subjugation of non-Western societies to various forms of Western domination.

This is no doubt a comparative enterprise, one that entails the analysis of how concepts travel across time and space in societies that are situated differently in a global matrix of power relations. Secularization in the postcolony is entwined with the history of power inequalities between the West and non-West, not least because

---

[21] Alfred Stepan, a strong proponent of the "multiple secularisms" approach, explicitly draws upon the "multiple modernities" argument of the 1990s. See Stepan, "The Multiple Secularisms of Modern Democratic and Non-Democratic Regimes." The notion of "multiple secularisms" is also espoused by a number of contributors to two edited volumes on the topic: Calhoun, Juergensmeyer, and Van-Antwerpen, *Rethinking Secularism*; and Jakobsen and Pelligrini, *Secularisms*.

[22] Mitchell, *Questions of Modernity*, xii.

[23] Ibid.

many of its signature concepts, institutions, and practices were introduced through (direct or indirect) colonial rule. Their ongoing exercise in the postcolonial period, as I hope to show in this book, continues to be beholden to this history of differential power. As Asad reminds us, the issue is not the Western or non-Western origins of these concepts but "the forms of life that articulate them, the powers they release or disable."[24] The question that follows therefore is how these secular concepts have transformed the self-understanding of people of the Middle East, opening certain avenues of action while foreclosing others.[25]

This book tracks the modern career of political secularism in Egypt through the institutionalization of five of its signature ideas: political and civil rights, religious liberty, minority rights, public order, and the legal distinction between public and private. This kind of work is, by necessity, recursive in that any attempt to track the Egyptian career of a secular concept or institution requires tracking its hegemonic footprints in the European landscape, not simply to register its deviations but to tame its liberatory and transcendent claims. Across the chapters of this book, I will explore different facets of the relationship between Egyptian and European articulations of secularism. In the epilogue, I gather up the diverse threads of this inquiry in order to highlight the implications of my analysis for how we might conceptualize secularism in both its unity and its dispersion. Briefly put, my argument is that even though religious minorities occupy a structurally precarious position in all modern nation-states, the particular shape this inequality takes—its modes of organization and articulation—is historically specific. Consequently, the means by which religious minorities wage a struggle against this inequality, as well as the paradoxes and contradictions such struggles generate, vary according to context (Egypt, France, Syria). While each chapter of this book elaborates a historically specific set of problems that Coptic Orthodox Christians and Bahais face in Egypt, I also show how these problems are derivative of a set of conundrums and paradoxes that the modern nation-state generates in its management of religious difference.

Religious Equality and Religious Difference

As I suggested, the inescapable quality of secularism in part emanates from the structure of the modern liberal state, which promises to demolish premodern forms of hierarchy in order to create a polity where all citizens are supposed to be formally equal in the eyes of the law. This promise, we might recall, was linked to a foundational

---

[24] Asad, *Formations of the Secular,* 17.
[25] For an illuminating discussion of this point, see ibid., 212–18.

critique of ascriptive inequality and a recalibration of particularistic forms of belonging. The modern political subject had to subordinate fealty to his religion, locale, and clan to loyalty to the nation-state.[26] In the nineteenth century, the liberatory promise of political and civil equality transformed how Christian subjects of Islamic empires came to understand themselves in relation to the state. No longer destined to remain unequal by virtue of their faith, membership in the modern polity promised to allow them to stand as equals with Muslims (see chapter 1).

A key dimension of this transformation was the legal and political elaboration of the public-private divide, which was an important source for elaborating other modern distinctions such as secular/religious, political/civil, and universal/parochial. When Coptic Christians, at the turn of the twentieth century, tried to find themselves in this abstract language of citizenship, their Christianity posed fundamental, if familiar, problems. Their enfranchisement was predicated upon their willingness to privatize their Christianity, precisely because their religious difference was deemed to be inconsequential to their public, political, and legal status. This circumscription of Coptic Christianity to the private domain went hand in hand with the enshrinement of Islam as the collective identity of the nation. Despite the citizenry's diverse allegiances, all Egyptians were expected to recognize Islam as essential to the formation of the nation in a way that other religions were not. As I recount in chapter 2, when the first Egyptian constitution was being forged in the 1920s, Coptic Christians struggled with this condition of their political enfranchisement. Despite protestations, Coptic representatives decided to accept this wager at the time, encapsulated in the legendary statement made by Makram Ebeid, a prominent Coptic leader, that he was a "Muslim by country and a Christian by religion"—the former public and the latter private. This assessment, as I will elaborate, continues to haunt the Coptic political struggle for equality today.

This earlier moment in the making of the Egyptian nation is often read as a tragic gamble that the Copts lost to Islamic forces, who hijacked the promise of equal citizenship. Yet it behooves us to think critically about the structural challenges Coptic Christians faced, not unlike other religious minorities, in the framework of the nation-state. The parallel with the Jewish question in Europe is instructive here. As historians of Europe tell us, Jewish emancipation over the long nineteenth century was predicated upon the privatization and individualization of Jewish religious life. This often entailed both the dissolution of their autonomy over various aspects of communal life *and* their assimilation into the cultural norms of European nations

---

[26] See Wendy Brown's excellent discussion of this historical process as it pertained to the articulation of Jewish difference in contrast to gender in nineteenth-century Europe: Brown, "Tolerance as Supplement."

rooted in Christian values and sensibilities.[27] Despite Jewish attempts to accommodate this demand, their difference from the identity of the nation did not simply disappear. The persistence of the "Jewish question" well into the twentieth century indicates that Jewish difference—particularly embodied in the practices and lifestyles of the unassimilated Jews—could not be successfully abstracted. It continued to pose a challenge to the norms of European nations, which were putatively universal and areligious but substantively Christian. The invention of the concept of "national minority" and the minority-rights regime instituted under the League of Nations during the interwar period were meant to recognize and redress the assimilative force of nationalist politics directed against European Jews and other groups whose religious, ethnic, and linguistic profile rendered them vulnerable (see chapter 1).

In the essay "On the Jewish Question," written in 1843, the young Karl Marx perceptively diagnosed the place accorded to religious difference within the political rationality of the modern liberal state.[28] Marx was responding to the dominant secular liberal view in circulation at the time, most eloquently captured by Bruno Bauer, that for Jews to be truly emancipated not only did they need to renounce Judaism, but the state also needed to depoliticize religion and make it irrelevant to the civil and political status of European citizens. Once religion was abolished from the sphere of politics, Bauer predicted, Jews would no longer stand in "religious opposition to the state"—a secular prescription that rings true to our ears to this day.[29] Conceding that the "depoliticization" of religion represented progress over the past, Marx argued that it was wrong to conclude, therefore, that religion had become irrelevant to the political life of the liberal democratic state (what he at times refers to as the "constitutional" or "political" state). While the liberal state had made religion marginal to the exercise of popular sovereignty, religious distinctions, not unlike "other distinctions established by birth, social rank, education, [and] occupation," were allowed to flourish in political states (including North America, which Bauer held up as a model). Their power to foster and proliferate social inequalities remained unchecked:[30] "Man emancipates himself *politically* from religion by expelling it from the sphere of public law to that of private law. Religion is no longer the spirit of the *state.* . . . [Instead] it has become the spirit of *civil society.* . . . It is no longer the essence of *community*, but the essence of *differentiation.* . . . The division of man into the *public person* and the *private person*, the *displacement* of religion from the state to civil society—all this is

---

[27] Katz, *Out of the Ghetto*; and Vital, *A People Apart*. On forms of communal autonomy that European Jews had to surrender, see Marcus, *The Jew in the Medieval World*, esp. 185–223. For my discussion of this point, see chapter 2.

[28] Marx, "On the Jewish Question."

[29] Ibid., 30.

[30] Ibid., 33.

not a stage in political emancipation but its consummation. Thus political emancipation does not abolish, and does not even strive to abolish man's *real* religiosity."[31] By sequestering religion in the private sphere, the political state in effect not only buries the inequalities that religion promotes but also *depoliticizes* them so that they appear natural and outside the sphere of politics. Note that, for Marx, the "*decomposition* of man into Jew and citizen, Protestant and citizen, religious man and citizen, is not . . . an evasion of political emancipation. It is *political emancipation itself*, the *political* mode of emancipation from religion."[32] Thus, even though religion is marginalized from the conduct of politics, it is simultaneously consecrated in the private sphere as a fundament of individual and collective identity in a liberal society.

Marx, as is well known, sought complete human emancipation of man as a "species-being," which would require the abolition of religion as well as the constitutional/political state. True human emancipation, argued Marx, would ensue only when man "has become a *species-being*; and when he has recognized and organized his own powers as *social* powers (*forces propres*) so that he no longer separates this social power from himself as *political* power."[33] Following Feuerbach, Marx understood religious consciousness as an attribute of the alienated and unemancipated subject who projected his own collective human powers onto an anthropomorphized divinity. Marx proposes in "On the Jewish Question" that religion and the political state work in analogous ways in that both are projections of human power that is alienated from itself: "The state is the intermediary between man and human liberty. Just as Christ is the intermediary to whom man attributes all his own divinity and all his religious *bonds*, so the state is the intermediary to which man confides all his non-divinity and all his *human freedom*."[34] For Marx, as Wendy Brown argues, man attributes to "the institutions of the church and the state powers that are not their own, powers that are actually human capacities and human effects that circuitously come to be invested in church and state. . . . Indeed, the power of these institutions is largely constituted by their systematic relations of *misrecognition* and *misinvestment*."[35] Marx's famous phrase "Religion is the opium of the masses" captures aptly the sense that religion, for him, is the ideological obfuscation of reality. Consequently, from this conception of religion, Marx argued against Bauer's secular prescription that man should free himself from religion; he suggested, instead, that this was not possible until man liberated himself materially, that is, until he owned and controlled the conditions of his existence.

---

[31] Ibid., 35.
[32] Ibid., 35–36.
[33] Ibid., 46.
[34] Ibid., 32.
[35] Brown, *Politics out of History*, 87, emphasis added.

Much of the recent literature on religion and secularism has challenged and re-thought this conception of religion as a distorted belief about the true nature of the world and human powers. Of particular importance is Asad's work, which shows that the concept of religion as belief is itself part of a normative secular framework in which religion is disinvested of its materiality.[36] This normative framework not only secures an ideational and subjectivist concept of religion at the expense of its material entailments, but also fails to apprehend how modern religiosity (whether as belief in transcendence, political identity, or state ideology) is enabled and spawned by the secular institutions that have become more, rather than less, enmeshed in its formulation and praxis. Indeed, if the religious and the secular are indelibly intertwined in the modern period, each conditioning the other, then the question is not so much how modern society can expunge religion from social life (as Marx envisioned) but how to account for its ongoing power and productivity in material and discursive terms. In what follows, I take up this charge by showing how religious difference has proliferated and metastasized in modern Egypt even as its raison d'etat secularized. I hope to show how the regulation of religion under secularism has not simply tamed its power but also transformed it, making it more, rather than less, important to the identity of the majority and minority populations. This process has resulted in the intensification of interreligious inequality and conflict, the valuation of certain aspects of religious life over others, and the increasingly precarious position of religious minorities in the polity.

Religious and Minority Rights in Egypt

This book is based on over fifteen months of fieldwork in Cairo, Egypt, conducted between 2008 and 2013. When I arrived in January 2008, I was planning to work on the secularization of Quranic hermeneutics in Egyptian scholarly, political, and public life. However, once there, my attention was captured by a more persistent problem that saturated the Egyptian media: the plight of religious minorities. Media networks circulated daily reports about skirmishes between Coptic Christians and Muslims, from minor incidents to more spectacular attacks on Christian monasteries, churches, and property. The struggle of Bahais, who compose less than 1 percent of the population, provoked a raging debate on prime-time television about whether the state should recognize their religion. These public discussions stood in contrast to

---

[36] Asad, "Thinking About Religion, Belief and Politics." It is interesting to note that the idea that religion is about belief in a transcendental reality is shared by champions and detractors of secularism alike.

the silence on the matter in the 1990s, when the media rarely acknowledged the existence of minorities, much less their problems, because of strict government censorship. My curiosity was piqued. Was this an old problem that could no longer be suppressed, or had relations across confessional lines deteriorated beyond repair in the preceding decade?

At the suggestion of friends, I sought help from one of the emergent but prominent legal aid organizations, the Egyptian Initiative for Personal Rights (EIPR, est. 2002). Unlike other secular human-rights organizations that tended to stay away from questions of interreligious strife, the EIPR was unique at the time in taking up cases on behalf of religious minorities, including Coptic Christians, Bahais, and Shi'a.[37] More importantly, the EIPR was also distinct in its thematization of the right to privacy—around which the organization was founded and named—and its focus on questions of religion and sexuality.[38] In addition to launching public campaigns, much of what the EIPR did was take the government to court for violating its own constitution and laws by intervening in religious life and stipulating substantive religious values. The organization was spectacularly successful in winning difficult cases—key among them the Bahais' right to have their religion recognized on government documents, despite the state ban on their faith (see my discussion of this case in chapter 4).

I spent a year working with the EIPR and following the debates it provoked in the media and among other human-rights activists in Egypt. Much of this book is indebted to the conversations I had with the EIPR's brilliant and dedicated staff and their insights into the social, legal, and political causes of religious discrimination in Egypt today. They also painstakingly taught me the landscape of international human-rights law, its simultaneous globality and parochialism, under the shadow of which they operated. This exposure to the potential and limits of the international human-rights regime inspired me to gain a better understanding of this tradition and its historical importance for the struggle of religious minorities. To my surprise, during the course of this fieldwork I came to learn that human-rights discourse had

---

[37] The case of Shi'a Muslims (less than 1 percent of the population) is somewhat distinct in Egypt when compared to Bahais and Coptic Christians. The geopolitical alliance between Egypt, the United States, and Saudi Arabia against the Shiite state of Iran and the Lebanese political group Hezbollah has led the Egyptian government to increasingly represent the Shi'a as foreign agents whose goal is to subvert Sunni Islam. As a result, many Egyptians now believe that Shi'ism is a heretical cult (rather than a historically legitimate branch of Islam) that must be purged from the social life of the country. Under emergency law, the State Security forces have arrested, interrogated, and tortured the Shi'a in Egypt as enemies of the state. See EIPR, "State Security Court Rejects Interior Ministry Appeal."

[38] The EIPR's work has since expanded to encompass other issues, including advocacy for economic justice, democratic and political rights, and the reform of the criminal justice system. For the full range of issues they now address, visit the website, http://eipr.org/en/.

powerful religious patrons, most prominently in the American evangelical movement. With help from the US State Department, evangelicals have mobilized a successful global campaign since the 1990s to "save persecuted Christians" in the Middle East (see chapter 2). For some Egyptians, the contemporary evangelical movement is reminiscent of nineteenth-century missionaries who also mobilized in the name of religious freedom and intervened in Egyptian domestic politics (see chapter 1). For others, the evangelical movement of today is categorically different from the missionaries of the past in that it aims not to convert Coptic Christians but to bring their plight to the global stage. This debate provoked me to explore how the earlier colonial and missionary promotion of the right to religious liberty informs the present discourse and campaigns, revealing the overlaps and departures between this earlier history and the present.

Over the course of my fieldwork, as I perused the carefully crafted legal briefs that the EIPR prepared on behalf of its clients, it became apparent to me that, in addition to national and human-rights law, another legal genealogy rooted in the Ottoman legacy of Islamic rule informed these court cases. The footprints of this legacy are legible in concepts such as "People of the Book" and the juridical autonomy granted to each state-recognized religious community over what is called family law. Though initially I was inclined to read this as nothing more than a holdover from the past, I eventually came to recognize the transmuted character of these earlier concepts and arrangements and the power they command in the life of Egypt's minorities today. Chapter 1 and chapter 3 are a product of this labor.

The struggle of religious minorities in Egypt today paradigmatically unfolds around the twin concepts of religious liberty and minority rights. While the former is enshrined in the Egyptian constitution, the latter is deeply contested. Both belong, however, to the semantic and conceptual field of civil and political rights. As I show in chapter 2, their meaning has always been deeply contested in the history of modern Egypt. In the current moment, for example, most secular activists conceive of religious liberty as an individual right consonant with the international discourse of human rights. For the Coptic Orthodox Church, in contrast, it is a group right—particularly the Church's right to administer the affairs of the Coptic community, to police religious conversions to Islam, and to maintain its autonomy over Coptic family law. For ordinary lay Copts, the individualized conception of religious liberty at times offers a release from ecclesiastical control over their lives; at others, the collective protections it offers represent a welcome respite from the assimilative thrust of the Islamic national project.

As I discuss in chapter 2, these tensions between different meanings of religious liberty are not simply local. They resonate with debates in international law during the interwar period about whether the individualized conception of religious liberty was adequate to protect a minority's way of life. As this earlier debate reveals, the issue for many European minorities was not so much freedom of conscience as it was a group's ability to establish and maintain social institutions that could, in turn, secure the passage of requisite traditions to future generations and the preservation of communal identity. If one example of this is the European Jews' attempts to push for such provisions in various minority treaties during the interwar years (see chapter 2), then the First Nations' efforts to preserve their collective autonomy over lands and resources in North America are another. The question of minority rights was thematized by liberal theorists of multiculturalism in the 1990s, such as Will Kymlicka, Charles Taylor, and Iris Young, who drew attention to the importance of communal identity to democratic pluralism, and advocated for group-differentiated rights for certain cultural groups, particularly Native peoples of North America. Their advocacy was always delimited, however, by liberalism's foundational concern for maximizing individual autonomy and freedom.[39] These theorists were primarily concerned with "cultural difference" and largely silent on the question of religious difference, often assuming religion to be a relatively minor attribute of "culture."[40]

While the current debate in Egypt shares some of the same concerns thematized in these earlier debates about minorities, it is also distinct in certain respects. Insomuch as religious difference is crucial to minority struggles in Egypt, it necessarily bears upon and engages questions of political secularism. The Egyptian debate on the status of minorities is also distinct in that it partakes in another genealogy, one rooted in the history of Islamic political thought and its place in the modern polity. Issues such as the proper relationship of the shari'a to Egypt's civil law, how to counterbalance the principle of civil and political equality with the Islamic identity of the state, and the place of religious minorities (such as Bahai and Shi'a) in the polity are heavily

---

[39] Kymlicka, for example, argued that group-differentiated minority rights should be made commensurate with the liberal principle of individual autonomy, which he identified as essential to the liberal concept of tolerance. See Kymlicka, *Multicultural Citizenship*. See also Young, *Justice and the Politics of Difference*.

[40] Religion, for example, is hardly mentioned in *Multicultural Citizenship*, Kymlicka's signature work on the topic. I suspect this is because when the multiculturalism debate peaked, the key challenge that the Euro-Atlantic states faced was how to assimilate immigrants into the cultural mainstream. In contrast, in the post-9/11 period, it is religion—particularly Islam—that poses a pressing national-security problem for these states. It is, therefore, not surprising that one of the leading theorists of multiculturalism, Charles Taylor, who had little to say about religious difference in his earlier ruminations on multiculturalism, has turned his attention to the problem of how religious diversity should be managed in a liberal polity. Compare, for example, Charles Taylor et al., *Multiculturalism and "The Politics of Recognition,"* with his more recent focus on religious diversity in Maclure and Taylor, *Secularism and Freedom of Conscience*.

debated and contested. The political theology of the Egyptian state therefore navigates between liberal and Islamic traditions, even if one commands a much greater force in this negotiation than the other.

Like religious liberty, the concept of a national minority is also deeply contested in Egypt today. When I first started working with the EIPR, I was struck by the fact that the term is not recognized legally, even though it saturates public debate. While both the Coptic Orthodox Church and the Egyptian government eschew the term, the fact that Copts command their own religion-based family law constitutes an example of group-differentiated rights often associated with minority politics. For many nationalist Copts, the term remains sullied by its colonial deployment, when the British used it to sow divisions between Muslims and Christians in order to secure their rule.[41] For these activists and intellectuals, the minority designation sets the Copts apart from the nation's identity, distancing them further from the ideal of universal equality and citizenship. The statement by Makram Ebeid quoted above ("I am a Muslim by country and a Christian by religion") is exemplary of this stance, and is often repeated with great national fervor. However, there is now a strongly dissenting view among Copts who call upon their coreligionists to embrace the designation "national minority" in order to make their subordination visible in a language that has traction in international and human-rights law. These voices draw upon an earlier moment in history, often ignored by nationalists, when, in the 1910s and 1920s, an important contingent of Copts tried to insist on their status as a minority in order to highlight the systemic religious discrimination they faced and to suggest political means of redress. In the early part of the twentieth century, these Coptic activists tried to cast the assignation of confessional community (*millet*/*ta'ifa*) aside in favor of using "nation" (*umma*) and "minority" (*aqalliyya*) to claim equality with Muslims. While I explore this point in detail in chapter 2, it is important to underscore how deeply contested any invocation of these concepts—religious liberty and minority rights—is because of their enmeshment in histories of colonial rule and missionary campaigns as well as in ongoing projects of Western hegemony in Egypt. In other words, Egypt's differential sovereignty in relation to Western power crucially determines the meaning and praxis of these concepts. This is manifest not only in the colonial history these concepts recall in the present, but in the significant power that human rights and international law command in settling domestic conflicts in Egypt today. In contrast, violations of minority rights and religious liberty in Euro-Atlantic societies are rarely if ever adjudicated on this terrain.

---

[41] For a review of this debate, see my discussion in chapter 2.

The fact that religious liberty and minority rights figure prominently in the struggle for religious equality in Egypt is not surprising: both work to highlight histories of subordination and provide the means for redress within the framework of the nation-state. Both concepts bring the issue of difference back into the disembodied language of civil and political rights. The demand for minority rights emerges when the hegemonic construction of the nation can no longer assimilate or incorporate its Others. Similarly, the call for religious liberty often marks a fissure from majoritarian religious norms that stand in for national culture. Both concepts are, in an important sense, diagnostic of the religious inequality that permeates the social life of a secular liberal polity, an inequality that constantly calls into question the undelivered promise of formal political equality. One might say that the concepts of religious liberty and minority rights are symptomatic of both the promise *and* the limits of political secularism: the former in its claim to make religion indifferent to the distribution of rights and freedoms, and the latter in its inability to eradicate parochial communal affiliations from the social and political identity of its citizens. This paradox, which is internal to political secularism, informs each chapter of this book.

Secular Objections

At this point, I would like to briefly address some common objections that readers may raise against my analysis of secularism. One might argue that I have painted too bleak a picture of secularism, in which it is nothing more than the exercise of state and (neo)colonial power, and that I have ignored its more promising and liberatory dimensions: the protection it extends to individuals and religious minorities to hold and practice their religious beliefs freely without state or social coercion; or its guarantee that a citizen's religious affiliation is inconsequential to her civil and political status in the eyes of the law; or that it allows believers and nonbelievers to speak their mind without fear of state or social discrimination. These are not negligible freedoms, as anyone who has been harassed for his or her religious (or nonreligious) beliefs knows full well. Furthermore, the history of religious persecution has taught us to be wary of fusing the identity of the state too closely with institutions of ecclesiastical power. If the Christian inquisition is an early example, then more recent ones from Saudi Arabia, Israel, and Iran should surely make us cautious about abandoning the principle of state neutrality toward religion.

While I appreciate the protections and freedoms that secularism might extend to religious dissenters and nonbelievers, I would also like to point out that political secularism is not *merely* the principle of state neutrality or the separation of church and state. It also entails the reordering and remaking of religious life and interconfessional relations in accord with specific norms, themselves foreign to the life of the religions and peoples it organizes. This dimension of political secularism—shot through as it is with paradoxes and instabilities—needs to be understood for the life worlds it creates, the forms of exclusion and violence it entails, the kinds of hierarchies it generates, and those it seeks to undermine. The two dimensions of political secularism—its regulatory impulse and its promise of freedom—are thoroughly intertwined, each necessary to the enactment of the other. A scholarly inquiry into this dual character, its limits, contradictions, and violence, should not be mistaken as a denunciation of secularism or as a call for its demise. Secularism is not something that can be done away with any more than modernity can be. It is an ineluctable aspect of our present condition, as both political imagination and epistemological limit. To critique a particular normative regime is not to reject or condemn it; rather, by analyzing its regulatory and productive dimensions, one only deprives it of innocence and neutrality so as to craft, perhaps, a different future.

One of the greatest difficulties in conceiving of liberal secularism as something other than the principle of state neutrality toward religion is that it puts into peril the possibility of civil and political equality, and thus the promise of a humanity freed from servitude to divine and clerical authority. Secularism temporalizes divine power, makes its transcendental claims immanent and worldly. To suggest that secular liberal politics is never free of religion threatens the hope that in the face of irredeemable religious strife there can be a neutral arbiter who can adjudicate the conflict by stepping outside the fray. It seems to me that to talk about secularism in today's world is to engage in what Quentin Skinner once called "evaluative-descriptive" speech acts, wherein to describe a political system is also to commend it by treating the normative claims of a given system as the grounds for assessing its superiority.[42] It is perhaps for this reason that when I have questioned the secular state's promise to deliver religious equality, I have been at times accused of infidelity to the principle itself, as if to interrogate secularism's promise is to reject the ideal. But the secularist hope that a truly secularized state *will* deliver us from religious conflict and prejudice is premised on a fundamental misunderstanding of what exactly the state is (or can be) neutral toward. As Marx argued, the secular liberal state does not simply *depoliticize* religion; it also embeds it within the social life of the polity by relegating it to the private sphere and civil society. This book tries to track this double movement in the social and political life of Egypt.

[42] Skinner, "Empirical Theorists of Democracy and Their Critics." See David Scott's discussion of this point in relation to liberal democracy, "Norms of Self-Determination."

Many critics of Egypt's discriminatory policies toward religious minorities argue that if the state were to be truly secularized—that is, if it became neutral in regard to its Islamic identity as well as those it governs—then it would eliminate interreligious conflict. While there is no doubt that this would improve the life of Egypt's religious minorities, it ignores the fact that the modern secular state is not simply a neutral arbiter of religious differences; it also produces and creates them. To think through *this* problem, one has to begin by recognizing the contradictions and inequalities that political secularism itself generates and the religious presumptions it embeds in the legal and political life of the nation. My suggestion is not that religious conflict is an inevitable or solely a product of secularism. But insomuch as secularism is one of the enabling conditions of religious conflict today, it behooves us to understand its paradoxical operations so as to mitigate its discriminatory effects.

It may be obvious to readers of the debate on secularism that this text eschews any use of the term *postsecular*, which has become fashionable these days in certain academic circles. This eschewal registers my basic disagreement with the assumptions this term entails. At the most fundamental level, the term *postsecular* expresses a sense of surprise that, despite the prediction that religion would wither away in modern society, it continues to be important to political and social life. Thus, in Jürgen Habermas's influential formulation of the term, despite "secularistic certainty that religion will disappear world-wide in the course of modernization," it continues to maintain "public influence and relevance."[43] This understanding, in its temporal accent on the *post-*, suggests that there is something unexpected and novel about the persistence of religion in the present. Yet, as much of the critical scholarship on the topic suggests, religion has been a constitutive feature of secularism throughout its modern history. There is nothing new about the copresence of the religious and the secular.

Perhaps most importantly, the term *postsecular* in its prosaic observation that religion is part of the secular present implicitly subscribes to a conventional theory of secularization that Charles Taylor aptly calls a "subtraction theory," wherein the secular is assumed to be that which remains after religion is taken away. The idea that secularism is devoid of religion is common among its champions and detractors alike. Christian fundamentalists and Islamists, for example, oppose secularism for undermining the place of religion in public life, and secularists champion it as an antidote to the rise of religious politics. Both subscribe to the same dichotomous view of religion and secularity, and hence fail to take stock of their mutual imbrication and interdependence. This anemic understanding of secularism (as the absence of religion) does not account for its substantive shape and form, the political and social

---

[43] Habermas, "Notes on a Post-Secular Society."

arrangements it engenders, and the ethical/moral commitments it normalizes. In this important sense, secularism is not simply another term for modernity; it is indexical of those social phenomena, institutions, and practices in which the distinction between the religious and the secular is recurrently salient and often contested.

A Comment on Method

Before I proceed, a few words about the kind of anthropology that lies at the heart of this book. As I mentioned, I could not have written *Religious Difference in a Secular Age* without conducting fieldwork with the EIPR and other minority-rights groups in Cairo. However, as I worked with these activists, I realized that the assumptions that informed their work were not simply "theirs" but belonged to a global political discourse that exerts an immense force on our collective imagination. The temporality and historicity of this discourse are quite distinct from the one that informed the actions of the Egyptian activists; the disjuncture between them was not always visible to the activists or me during the course of my fieldwork. Upon my return from Egypt, as I began the process of analysis and writing, I was compelled to dig beyond the ethnographic encounter to grasp fragments of the past congealed into the present, their temporal weight pressing into it. This process in turn required an engagement with historical materials from the eighteenth century to the present about which I knew little when I embarked upon this project. The book thus could not have been born without the ethnographic encounter, but also had to transcend it in order to make sense of *what* I encountered.

Even though *Religious Difference in a Secular Age* is not an ethnography in the classical sense, an anthropological mode of inquiry is crucial to this book's architecture.[44] In the chapters that follow, I track not the ideational life of a concept but its practical and material unfolding in a society that is historically distinct but also shares a global grammar of legal and political governance. Too often, anthropology is understood to be consubstantial with its method (participant observation and fieldwork) and a genre of writing (ethnography). Yet anthropology, in my view, is also a mode of analyzing distinct forms of life through a study of concepts internal to them, embedded and realized in social practice. To the extent that anthropology is a study of concepts in practice, the method of participant observation is a useful tool but should not be taken to stand in for anthropological analysis itself. In my view, "understanding" in anthropology implies not simply objectively recording how people in a given

---

[44] For some excellent ethnographies of Coptic Christian life, see Heo, "The Bodily Threat of Miracles" and "The Virgin Made Visible"; Guirgius, *Les Coptes d'Egypte*; and Shenoda, *Cultivating Mystery*.

society think or behave, but juxtaposing the constitutive concepts and practices of one form of life against another in order to ask a different set of questions, to decenter and rethink the normative frameworks by which we have come to apprehend life— whether one's own, another's, or those yet to be realized. It is this understanding of anthropology that animates this book.

Arc of the Book

This book is divided into two parts. In part 1, I track key shifts in the meaning and practice of the concepts of religious liberty and minority rights between the nineteenth and twentieth centuries as they traveled through Western Europe, the Middle East, and Egypt. In this part of the book, I attempt to establish a broad historical framework that I believe is necessary for analyzing the current interreligious conflict in Egypt. Part 2 of the book focuses on three sites of controversy about the proper place of religious minorities in the Egyptian polity: incidents of interreligious marriage and conversion; the civil and political status of Bahais in the face of a state prohibition on their faith; and the publication of an acclaimed novel about the early history of the Coptic Orthodox Church. The first two controversies elaborate key structural features of political secularism and its management of religious difference, while the last is a rumination on secularity, particularly the relationship between history and revelation. In what follows, I briefly delineate the central arguments of each chapter.

Chapter 1 begins with the period when the discourse of religious liberty and minority rights was first introduced into what now constitutes the modern Middle East as a means of extending European Christian power over the territories and populations ruled by the Ottoman Empire. As early as the sixteenth century, Christian European states had been successful in exacting concessions from the Ottomans to represent and protect Eastern Christians (as they were called at the time) living under Ottoman rule.[45] Initially granted as part of routine imperial policy, the European states' right to represent and protect Ottoman Christians took on a different cast as Ottoman power declined over the course of the nineteenth century. These concessions came to serve as a means of, and justification for, subverting Ottoman

[45] Eastern Christianity comprises four branches: Eastern Orthodox Church, Oriental Orthodox Church, the Nestorians, and the Eastern Catholic Church. Their followers span the territories of the Balkans, Eastern Europe, Asia Minor, the Middle East, Africa, India, and parts of the Far East; hence the name, Eastern Christians. Coptic Christianity is part of Oriental Orthodox Christianity, which includes the Syrian Orthodox, the Armenian Apostolic, the Ethiopian Orthodox, and the Indian Orthodox churches. This branch of Christianity broke with the Chalcedonian consensus in 451 AD, which is why its followers are also referred to as non-Chalcedonians. For more on this history, see chapter 5.

sovereignty over its Christian subjects and truncating its territorial boundaries. While Ottoman rule had been predicated on the norm of religious inequality, the Empire's slow and painful attempt at transforming itself into a republic led to the adoption of the concepts of religious liberty and minority rights. Parallel to the European experience, the implementation of these concepts aimed less at instituting interconfessional tolerance than at establishing the principle of state sovereignty and reorienting the parochial loyalties of its subjects to the emergent nation-state.

The history of the rise of the modern state in the Middle East is inextricable from the expansion of European colonial power into the region. An analysis of the development of secularism—its key concepts and institutions—in the region, therefore, needs to be situated within the framework of differential power relations that came to connect the Middle East to Europe. This is nowhere as evident as in the consolidation of the legal concept of minority in the late nineteenth century and early twentieth. As the second half of chapter 1 shows, British and French colonial powers made ubiquitous use of this new demographic identity in order to solve practical problems of colonial governance. Their divide-and-rule policy is well known in the scholarship on colonialism. Less known is the manner in which colonial powers subjected preexisting religious differences to a new grid of intelligibility. Under colonial rule, minority identity (bestowed by the state) became, paradoxically, sutured to a private attribute (religion), toward which the state claimed to be neutral. In contrast to scholars who tend to read this paradox as colonial hypocrisy, I suggest that it is diagnostic of the dual impetus internal to political secularism—namely, the modern state's disavowal of religion in its political calculus *and* its simultaneous reliance on religious categories to structure and regulate social life, thereby indelibly linking the private and public domains that the secular state aims to keep apart.

I continue my examination of religious liberty and minority rights in chapter 2, as I track their career in modern Egypt from the turn of the twentieth century until the present. I start with the 1920s, when the question of Coptic rights—and the term *minority* itself—was vigorously debated. When Egyptians drafted their first constitution in 1923 in anticipation of their independence from colonial rule, they faced a formidable challenge. How could the disembodied language of formal civil and political equality address the Muslim-Christian inequality that striated social life? Some Muslim and Coptic drafters of the constitution proposed that Copts should have proportionate representation in the parliament so as to secure Coptic interests that would otherwise be ignored. For others, to legislate minority participation within the parliament was tantamount to turning religious groups (*tawa'if diniyya*) into political groups (*tawa'if siyasiyya*). Ultimately, the proposal for Coptic proportional representation was rejected because of the secular assumption that to give religious minorities a political voice was to compromise the principle of state neutrality toward religion.

The debate over accommodating religious minorities within the political structure of the state in the 1920s appears tame when compared to the rancorous exchange that erupted between Copts and Muslims over the drafting of a new electoral law in 2012. Through a close reading of this recent debate, I offer some reflections on what has changed for the Copts since the early 1920s, when the political horizon for a Muslim-Coptic partnership seemed open. Key to the current state of affairs are the consolidation of militarized state rule and the (neo)liberalization of the economy, which has accelerated since the 1970s. The radical privatization of the economy, ironically, has made religion far more central to Egyptian public and political life than it was in the 1920s. The rise of the Islamist movement is the most notable face of this development, but the other side of economic privatization is the increasingly central role the Coptic Orthodox Church has come to play in the provision of social and welfare services to lay Copts. As a result, the Church stands as the sole political and social representative of Copts today, a position of unparalleled power in the history of Egypt. Rather than understand this as the failure of secularism to take hold in Egypt, I hope to show how these developments are part and parcel of the secularization of Egyptian society.

Chapter 3 focuses on the issue of interreligious marriage and conversion, which is a key site of incendiary violence between Muslims and Christians in Egypt. While this conflict is deeply gendered, Egypt's religion-based family laws and the inequitable regulation of religious conversion play a pernicious role. Egypt's granting of juridical autonomy to Christians and Jews ("People of the Book") over family affairs is often presented as a continuation of ancient shari'a norms. However, drawing upon the work of a range of historians, I argue that family law, as an autonomous juridical domain, is a modern invention that did not exist in the premodern period. It is predicated upon the public-private divide so foundational to the secular political order, and upon a modern conception of the family as a nuclear unit responsible for the reproduction of the society and the nation. Religion, sexuality, and the family are relegated to the private sphere under this system, thereby conjoining their legal and moral fates. As a result, family law has come to bear an inordinate weight in the reproduction and preservation of religious identity. The Coptic Orthodox Church, for example, views any state-mandated reform of family law as an unlawful incursion into its sphere of juridical and ecclesiastical autonomy; and Christian-Muslim conflict often unfolds over the terrain of interreligious marriage and romantic liaisons.[46]

---

[46] A very similar situation prevails in other countries with religion-based family-law regimes. See, for example, Yüksel, *Human Rights under State-Enforced Religious Family Laws in Israel, Egypt, and India*; and Agnes, "The Supreme Court, the Media, and the Uniform Civil Code Debate."

Through a careful analysis of some of the most well-known controversies over Coptic conversions to Islam between 2006 and 2012, in chapter 3 I develop an analytical framework for thinking about the explosive entwinement of religion, sexuality, and the family within Egyptian social life today. In a nutshell, I argue that interreligious conflicts of this kind are a product of the simultaneous privatization of religion and the family under modern secular governance, further exacerbating premodern patterns of confessional hierarchy and gender inequality.

If, indeed, family law is the means by which the Egyptian state acknowledges and regulates the presence of permissible religious difference in the polity, what is the status of those confessional groups that the state does *not* recognize? I take up this question in chapter 4, where I focus on the small Bahai minority through a close reading of Egyptian court cases dealing with their right to religious liberty and, by extension, their civil and political status in the polity. As I show, the Egyptian courts grant Bahais the right to hold their beliefs but use the concept of public order to deny them the right to manifest their beliefs in public, which, the courts argue, includes proclaiming their faith on government-issued documents. The legal grammar that the Egyptian courts use, particularly the secular concept of public order, bears strikingly familiarity with the jurisprudence of the European Court of Human Rights on religious minorities in a range of countries, including some that espouse a distinctly secular identity (France, Switzerland, and Turkey) and others that proclaim to be Christian (Italy and Greece). The analogous deployment of public order and religious liberty, as well as the majoritarian bias of the law, regardless of the national identity of the state (religious or secular), I argue, is instructive for explicating the shared legal grammar of political secularism that cuts across the Western and non-Western divide.

The final chapter is somewhat of a counterpoint to the book's focus on political secularism in that it takes up the question of how secularity conditions even the most polemical Christian-Muslim debates in Egypt today, key among them secular conceptions of temporality, history, and revelation. These assumptions were at play in the controversy that erupted over the publication of the novel *Azazeel* (2008), which won several literary awards and was translated into a number of languages. *Azazeel* is a piece of historical fiction located in the early history of Christianity in Egypt (319–431 AD) when the Christological debate split Christendom apart (between the Chalcedonians and the anti-Chalcedonians), a schism that eventually led to the consolidation of the Coptic Orthodox Church. The novel provoked an outcry among Coptic clerics, who charged that it defamed Christianity and misconstrued the doctrinal schism in order to legitimize an Islamic interpretation of Jesus Christ. While the Coptic Orthodox Church tried to get the novel banned, its secular readers (Christians and Muslims) and the author, Youssef Ziedan, asserted that the novel was an enlightened critique of religious violence and that the novel's protagonist, an ascetic Christian monk, was a symbol of the human quest for freedom and truth against ecclesiastical power.

Key to the novel's architecture is the author's claim that it is a historically accurate account of the Christological schism, a claim that the Coptic Orthodox Church countered with its own interpretation rooted in competing historical sources. Their conflicting versions of early Christian history notwithstanding, the clerics and the author shared the assumption that for revelation to be authoritative it had to be grounded in historically verifiable events. Both arguments relied on a secular conception of history as a repository of "real events" that occurred in calendrical (rather than sacral) time, unbound from eschatological events and temporality. It is this conception of history and temporality that provides the ground over which religious skeptics and enthusiasts alike argue about their interpretation of religious truth, a tradition of argument that belongs to the secularization of religion and scripture that dates back to the nineteenth century. In concluding this chapter, I reflect on the relationship between secularism and secularity, particularly the place a positivist notion of history occupies in settling what appear to be incommensurable religious worldviews.

Finally, I close the book with a short epilogue in which I reflect on the ideal of religious equality, its significance as a legal mandate versus as a human aspiration that characterizes our modern secular imaginary. I suggest that these two dimensions of religious equality are distinct, neither reducible to the other, and each requiring different kinds of social action. Insomuch as secularism reduces the ideal of religious equality to a politics of rights and recognition, it privileges the agency of the state, which is far from a neutral arbiter of religious differences. In such a context, I ask what social, ethical, and moral resources are available in a secular polity to realize interreligious equality, resources that do not reflect or serve the imperatives of the state.

PART I

Chapter 1

MINORITY RIGHTS AND RELIGIOUS LIBERTY:
ITINERARIES OF CONVERSION

This chapter provides an account of political secularism in the Middle East by tracking the career of two of its signature concepts—religious liberty and minority rights—across the nineteenth and early twentieth centuries. Less a chronological history than a genealogy, it seeks to capture key shifts in the meaning and praxis of these concepts in order to understand how relations between Muslims and non-Muslims were reconfigured in the modern period. Because I am interested in how religious difference has come to be regulated and remade under conditions of modern secular governance, I focus on the problem of religious minorities rather than groups defined by ethnic, linguistic, or other attributes. This chapter tracks broader international and regional developments that are crucial to how religious difference has come to be imagined and lived in modern Egypt. In doing so, I go back and forth between European and Middle Eastern history because I firmly believe that no analysis of secular political concepts and institutions in the latter is complete without simultaneously accounting for their evolution in the former. Consequently, this chapter does not so much offer an "indigenous genealogy" of the concepts of religious liberty and minority rights as it highlights the overlapping histories that have shaped their modern trajectory.

There are three historical shifts around which this chapter is organized. I start in the nineteenth century, when the concepts of religious liberty and minority rights gained traction in the region with the expansion of European power into the territories ruled by the Ottoman Empire. Christian European states systematically used the discourse of religious liberty and minority rights to undermine Ottoman sovereignty in the name of safeguarding the interests of "Eastern Christians," as they were called at the time. Eventually, a weakened Ottoman Empire adopted religious liberty and minority rights within its governing apparatus in order to shore up its territorial sovereignty and harness the fractious loyalties of diverse irredentist groups. The adoption of these legal concepts did not simply level old religious hierarchies but recalibrated them to a new calculus, opening up certain forms of political belonging for non-Muslims while closing others.

A second historical shift in the meaning of religious liberty and minority rights came about with the institutionalization of the nation-state as the globally dominant form premised on the principle of popular sovereignty and formal equality. From instruments of imperial patronage, religious liberty and minority rights became part of the broader vocabulary of civil and political rights. While in Europe, the transition from imperial to popular sovereignty was a fait accompli by the end of the nineteenth century, this was not the case in the Middle East; there, popular sovereignty had to be developed institutionally and discursively within the context of expanding missionary activity and (direct or indirect) colonial rule. International law, which was supposed to institute a global political order based on the doctrine of sovereignty, readily accommodated the exceptional nature of colonial and mandatory rule. As a result, the meaning and praxis of religious liberty and minority rights in the Middle East were forged in the context of differential sovereignty between Europe and the Middle East, a context that, as I hope to show in this book, remains relevant to how the minority issue is debated in Egypt today.

A third shift that I track in the concept of minority rights belongs to the interwar period. Under the auspices of the League of Nations, an authoritative definition of "national minority" was developed and a system of minority treaties was established to track infractions in countries that were, for the most part, subject to European power. This period in the League's history is instructive not only because it exemplifies the logic of differential sovereignty that attends rights discourse in international law, but also for its consistent thematization of an irresolvable tension located at the heart of the concept of *minority*: on the one hand, a minority is supposed to be an equal partner with the majority in the building of the nation; on the other hand, its difference (religious, racial, ethnic) poses an incipient threat to the identity of the nation that is grounded in the religious, linguistic, and cultural norms of the majority. Even though the League of Nations and its minority treaties system were dismantled, eventually replaced by the United Nations and its charter of human rights, contemporary struggles over minority rights continue to reenact this tension in various forms.

This chapter is also an argument for why the discourse on religious liberty and national minorities needs to be urgently rethought outside the framework of rights. It belongs, I want to suggest, to a far broader field of secular political praxis that secures the prerogative of the modern state to serve as the arbiter of religious differences, to remake and regulate religious life while proclaiming its sanctity, in the process fundamentally transforming how people perceive and negotiate religious identity and communal relations. Viewed from this perspective, religious liberty does not simply protect religious belief (or unbelief) from state intervention, but secures the distinction between public and private that is so foundational to secular political rule. Similarly, the legal concept of national minority does not simply signify a predetermined demographic group upon whom the modern state confers rights and obligations. Rather, its institutionalization also produces the kinds of subjects who can speak in its name, transforming how religious differences are lived, recognized, and contested. Perhaps if we can apprehend these dimensions of religious liberty and minority rights we may be able to appreciate the double-edged character of political secularism, which promises religious neutrality even as it remakes the fundamental contours of religious life.

Sovereignty and Religious Liberty

The signing of the Peace of Westphalia treaties in 1648 is often narrated as the foundational moment in the emergence of the concept of religious liberty; it not only brought an end to nearly one hundred years of religious warfare among Christians, but also created a political order in which subjects of a state were allowed to hold religious beliefs that were different from the ruler's. While some scholars view the Peace of Westphalia as an earlier moment in Europe's unfolding commitment to the virtue of religious tolerance, others see it as a far more pragmatic instrument that helped settle long-standing territorial disputes by granting formal independence to polities struggling to be free from the Holy Roman Empire (such as the Netherlands, Switzerland, Savoy, and Milan). In this latter understanding, the Peace of Westphalia is credited with establishing the principle (if not the practice) of state sovereignty, with the sovereign's right to control his territory and subjects free from outside intervention.[1] Writing forty years later, John Locke in his *Letter Concerning Toleration* (1689) made government conduct indifferent to religious truth far beyond the parameters of the Peace of Westphalia, further consecrating religious liberty as a foundational element of liberal political rationality and raison d'état. What I want to highlight here is that in European historiography, the birth of the concept of religious liberty is deeply intertwined with the establishment of the principle of state sovereignty, securing regional peace, and the creation of an intrastate protocol for handling what used to be called religious dissenters but later came to be regarded as "religious minorities."[2]

[1] Challenging the conventional story that the history of religious liberty in Europe and America is a progressive march toward increasing toleration, there is a significant body of scholarship that emphasizes the multiple, discontinuous, and competing trajectories since the principle was initially founded. See, for example, Bhuta, "Two Concepts of Religious Freedom"; Dunn, *The History of Political Theory*; Haefeli, *New Netherlands and the Dutch Origins*; Hunter, "Religious Freedom in Early Modern Germany."

[2] While the principle of nonintervention in sovereign states is associated with the Peace of Westphalia, it was in fact not institutionalized until well into the late eighteenth century. The term *Westphalian sovereignty* is therefore somewhat of a persisting misnomer. Krasner, *Sovereignty*, 20.

While this foundational relationship between religious liberty and state sovereignty in European history is widely acknowledged, far less appreciated are the exceptions this narrative enacted as the discourse of religious liberty traveled to non-European shores. Notably, the introduction of the principle of religious freedom to non-Western lands often violated the principle of state sovereignty, instead of consolidating it. Consider, for example, the repeated attempts by Christian European rulers to assert their right to protect Christian minorities within the Ottoman Empire, beginning in the seventeenth century and only escalating over time. As long as the Ottoman Empire was strong, it could accommodate these pressures without compromising its sovereignty; but once Ottoman power started to decline, it could not resist Western European incursions on behalf of Ottoman Christians.

As early as the sixteenth century, Ottoman rulers granted special privileges—known as "capitulations"—to Western European traders, ensuring a considerable degree of self-government in matters of criminal and civil jurisdiction as well as freedom of religion and worship. Capitulations were legal instruments that a range of empires employed at the time to give extraterritorial jurisdiction to subjects of another state in order to bolster trade and strategic relations.[3] Malcolm Evans, in his magisterial history of the global career of religious liberty, notes,

> [The capitulations] were originally bestowed at a time when the Western States were economically and politically inferior to Ottomans but, as the balance of power shifted in their favour, they became a potent means of furthering their strength and the enfeebled Empire was unable to resist. Within this framework, the role of the Western European States as protectors of the religious freedom of their subjects within the Ottoman domains easily elided into a claim entitling them to champion the liberties, religious and otherwise, of *all Christians in the Empire*.[4]

Over time, the capitulatory privileges came to apply to European missionaries and, eventually, to indigenous Ottoman Christian communities as well, who were placed under

---

[3] Capitulations were part of a world in which the principle of "territoriality" accommodated the principle of "personal law" (the law of the community to which a person belonged). As a result, states often allowed people to abide by their own communal laws even when they traveled across state boundaries and jurisdictions. Özsu, "The Ottoman Empire."

[4] Evans, *Religious Liberty*, 61–62, emphasis added. A key example of the treaties that accorded European Christian sovereigns the right to act as protectors of Ottoman Christians while the Ottoman Empire was still strong is the Treaty of 1615, signed between the Habsburgs and the Ottomans, which recognized Austrian interests in securing the freedom of Catholics to worship and repair churches. As Ottoman power declined, other treaties were signed, such as the Treaty of Kutschuk-Kainardji (signed in 1774) between Russia and the Ottoman Empire, which recognized the tsar's right to intercede on behalf of Orthodox Christians, and the Treaty of Passerowitz (signed in 1718), which granted the Austrian emperor the right to intercede on behalf of Roman Catholics residing in Ottoman territories. For the privileges accorded to French Catholics in Palestine, see Maïla, "The Arab Christians."

the protection of European Christian rulers. This amounted to a de facto revocation of Ottoman law in relation to many of its Christian subjects.[5] Notably, no parallel privileges existed for Ottomans in relation to non-Christian subjects of European empires.

As the nineteenth century progressed and the Ottoman Empire started to lose large portions of its Christian-dominated territories to breakaway states, the European powers deployed the claim of religious liberty for non-Muslim minorities to expedite this dissolution and secure their geopolitical interests in the region. The Treaties of Paris (signed in 1856) and Berlin (signed in 1878) both contained religious-liberty provisions for non-Muslims, which the Ottomans and the newly independent states were forced to adopt under European pressure.[6] The Treaty of Berlin, signed following the Russo-Turkish War, required that religious liberty be extended to minority subjects in the newly emergent states of Romania, Bulgaria, Montenegro, and Serbia. None of these states had the political power to negotiate similar terms from Europe. In the words of an influential scholar of the period, at the end of the nineteenth century the Ottomans "operated under severe constraints, the main constraint being the claim of Great Powers to be the protectors of Christians in the Ottoman Empire. This claim made the representatives of the Great Powers major actors in the domestic affairs of the Ottoman state."[7]

Religious Inequality under the Ottomans

The status of non-Muslims under Ottoman rule varied widely in part because of the empire's territorial scope and long duration. Not only did the Ottoman Empire rule over an immense diversity of faiths (including Judaism, various forms of Christianity, and heterodox Islamic sects) in a territory that extended across Asia, Europe, and Africa for over six hundred years, Ottoman policy also differed depending on the density of the non-Muslim population in a given region, the contracts negotiated at the time of Ottoman conquest, and the proximity of the conquered to the imperial center of the state. Historians, however, have tried to describe key features of Ottoman rule in regard to the status of non-Muslims. A striking feature of Ottoman rule was that it did not aim to politically transform difference into sameness (through

---

[5] For the abuse of the concessions granted to Europeans to extend the protégé system, see Sonyel, "The Protégé System in the Ottoman Empire"; and McEwan, "Catholic Copts, Riformati and the Capitulations."

[6] The Treaty of Paris was signed at the culmination of the Crimean War, which itself was precipitated by Russia's claim to speak on behalf of all Orthodox Christians living in Ottoman territories. Its ostensible aim was to recognize the territorial integrity of the Ottoman Empire and bring an end to foreign (particularly Russian) intercessions. In exchange the Ottomans passed the sweeping Hatt-i Hümayun decree, which dismantled distinctions based on religion.

[7] Deringil, *Conversion and Apostasy*, 25.

forced conversion or assimilation) but allowed diverse religious communities to exist contiguously within a system where Muslims occupied the highest status.[8] Thus, unlike Christian empires that forced nonbelievers to convert in order to save their souls, this was not a part of Ottoman imperial policy.[9] This distinctive feature of Ottoman rule has led one scholar to characterize it as the "empire of difference."[10] Under the pact of *dhimma* (literally, pledge of security), non-Muslims (*ahl al-dhimma*) were accorded state protection and the right to practice their religion, maintain their places of worship, and have communal courts as long as they recognized the supremacy and primacy of Islam.[11] Christians and Jews, as "People of the Book" (*ahl al-kitab*), a Quranic concept (9:29), had special status in comparison to non-Muslims who did not belong to the Abrahamic faiths.[12] The *ahl al-dhimma* communities were required to pay an additional poll tax (*jizya*), and Christians were regulated through sartorial markers and restrictions placed on the performance of religious rituals and church construction.[13]

In comparing the Ottoman treatment of religious minorities with the Christian empires of Europe during the Middle Ages, Benjamin Braude and Bernard Lewis note that, unlike the Jews in Europe, Jews and Christians under Muslim rule were not forced to live in ghettos and their movement and occupation were not restricted; while at times subject to violence, they were neither exiled nor killed for their faith.[14] Najwa al-Qattan's work shows that despite their lower legal status, when non-Muslims used Muslim courts (which they often did, particularly regarding issues of marriage and inheritance), they "had a fair chance of prevailing," even against Muslim adversaries.[15] For the modern reader it is hard not to translate these observations into a

---

[8] This system has been anachronistically described as a "millet system." But, as Benjamin Braude's work shows, it was only in the nineteenth century that the term *millet* came to denote "a non-Muslim protected community." Prior to this period, and sometimes even during the period of late Ottoman reforms, "*millet* could mean the exact opposite—the community of Islam in contradistinction to the non-Muslims under Islam's protection." Braude, "Foundation Myths of the *Millet* System."

[9] In comparing the Ottoman Empire to the Spanish *reconquista*, Deringil notes, "There was no formal Spanish equivalent of *dhimmi* (non-Muslim subject) status for the conquered Muslims" since the aim of the *reconquista* was to expel Islam from the Iberian Peninsula. Deringil, "There Is No Compulsion in Religion," 551.

[10] Barkey, *Empire of Difference*.

[11] The legal concept of *ahl al-dhimma* was developed in the ninth century and did not exist in early Islamic history. See Papaconstantinou, "Between Umma and Dhimma." For a discussion of the historical and regional variations in the implementation of the *dhimmi* system, see Emon, *Religious Pluralism and Islamic Law*.

[12] Emon, *Religious Pluralism and Islamic Law*, 73.

[13] These restrictions were similar to those imposed on non-Christians in other empires, such as the imposition of a poll tax on Jews under the Byzantine and Sassasin empires, or clothing restrictions imposed on Jews and Saracens under canon 68 of the Fourth Lateran Council in 1215. Ibid., 73, 132.

[14] Braude and Lewis, "Introduction," 6.

[15] al-Qattan, "*Dhimmis* in the Muslim Court."

calculus of greater or lesser tolerance, of equality versus persecution. Yet, as a number of historians argue, these terms are anachronous for describing the premodern Ottoman world, where *inequality* was the norm; just as women were unequal to men and slaves unequal to masters, non-Muslims were not equal to Muslims. The fundamental question that occupied Ottoman rulers was how to manage religious diversity while maintaining Islamic supremacy. As Anver Emon puts it, the pact of *dhimma* was a legal instrument for the political inclusion of non-Muslims into the empire as much as an expression of their lower doctrinal and legal status.[16] The freedom of worship granted to non-Muslims, therefore, did not mean that the Ottoman state was neutral in regard to religion or sought to treat its subjects equally; the universality of the truth of Islam was indeed presumed, as was the imperial sovereignty of the sultan over his subjects, even as "People of the Book" had a (limited) space of autonomy over their religious and legal affairs. In this sense, the Ottoman state was quite open-handed in proclaiming Islam's religious and political hegemony.

Consider, for example, the case of Coptic Orthodox Christians, who regard themselves as the indigenous inhabitants of Egypt. They suffered brutal repression for two hundred years at the hands of Byzantine emperors for their dissent at the Council of Chalcedon (451 AD). The Egyptian Church, as it was known then, broke with the Chalcedonian consensus and embraced instead its own version of hypostatic Christology (for a resonance of this history in the present, see chapter 5).[17] Over time, the Egyptian/Coptic Church developed a fiercely independent ecclesiastical structure and theology, as well as a strong sense of agonistic autonomy from the rest of Christendom (including Eastern Orthodox Christianity). With the arrival of Muslim conquerors in 639 AD and the subsequent consolidation of Muslim rule, the Copts went from being a persecuted community at the hands of Christian rulers to a subordinated group in relation to Muslims, who quickly gained a large number of converts in Egypt.[18] As "People of the Book," Coptic Orthodox Christians came to be governed under the system of *ahl al-dhimma* as a separate, protected, and unequal community in relation to Muslims.[19] Over the centuries, the Coptic condition varied dramatically

[16] Emon, *Religious Pluralism and Islamic Law*, 69.

[17] Strictly speaking, the Coptic Orthodox Church as we know it today is distinct from the Egyptian Church of the fifth century, which, as historians show, comprised multiplicitous theological strands. For a nuanced analysis of the historical process by which the Coptic Orthodox Church came to consolidate itself, see Papaconstantinou, "Historiography, Hagiography, and the Making"; and Mikhail, *From Byzantine to Islamic Egypt*.

[18] Some suggest that the Copts welcomed their Arab conquerors at the time because of fierce Byzantine persecution, while others contest this story. For the debate around Coptic reaction to Muslim conquest, see Davis, *The Early Coptic Papacy*.

[19] This system of rule for non-Muslims is often referred to as the "Pact of 'Umar" among Copts, and is supposed to date back to the conquest of Egypt under the second caliph, 'Umar ibn al-Khattab (634–644 AD). Historians suggest, however, that there is no evidence of its existence before the ninth

with the vicissitudes of the Islamic empires that ruled Egypt. The Mamluk era (1250–1517) is often cited as the worst, marked by a decline in the Coptic population, losses due to conversion to Islam, and its subjection to harassment.[20] When the Ottomans conquered Egypt in 1517, they continued to regard the Copts as *ahl al-dhimma* but were markedly less persecutorial than the Mamluks. Coptic Christians were allowed to select their religious leaders, administer religious courts, own property, and ascend to important positions within the bureaucratic and economic structure of the empire. Physical segregation based on religious affiliation and prohibitions on the public display of Christian religiosity continued.[21]

The relative improvement in the status of Coptic Orthodox Christians was in part a result of Egypt's peripheral location to the Ottoman Empire. Largely ruled through local proxies, the Sublime Porte's policies, as one historian suggests, "were open to arbitrary interpretation of regional and local rulers, and non-Muslims had to be prepared for both leniency and rigidity in their enforcement."[22] One unexpected consequence of this proxy rule was the emergence of a lay Coptic elite class, the archons (*arakhina* in Arabic), who gained prominence over the course of the eighteenth century by serving in the upper echelons of the Ottoman administrative and financial sector. This accorded them unprecedented power over ecclesiastical affairs, including the nomination of Coptic patriarchs and oversight of the Church's financial resources.[23] The center of gravity effectively shifted from clerics to lay elites, who came to play a significant role in mediating the relationship between the community and the state for 150 years.[24] According to Magdi Guirgis, Coptic laymen have not exerted this kind of influence over ecclesiastical affairs in any other period of Egyptian history, with the possible exception of the short-lived and highly contested experiment with the *Majlis al-Milli* (Coptic Communal Council, est. 1874; see chapter 2).[25] The archons' prominent role

century and that it was likely compiled from a variety of different legal sources. See Cohen, "What Was the Pact of 'Umar?"

[20] Armanios, *Coptic Christianity in Ottoman Egypt*.

[21] Behrens-Abouseif notes that these restrictions applied more to urban Copts than to those residing in rural areas, where the differences between Muslims and Christians were much less thematized and pronounced. Behrens-Abouseif, "Political Situation of the Copts," 186. Guirguis makes a similar argument in the opening pages of Guirguis and van Doorn-Harder, *The Emergence of the Modern Coptic Papacy*.

[22] Armanios, *Coptic Christianity in Ottoman Egypt*, 17.

[23] Guirguis and van Doorn-Harder, *The Emergence of the Modern Coptic Papacy*, 34–51. On the power of the archons, also see el-Leithy, *Coptic Culture and Conversion in Medieval Cairo*.

[24] According to Armanios, "By the seventeenth century, patriarchs were almost always elected by the highest lay leaders" instead of "electoral synods that included laity, bishops and priests." Armanios, *Coptic Christianity in Ottoman Egypt*, 34–35. This stands in contrast to the present, where the role of the Coptic laity has been progressively narrowed in the election of the Coptic patriarch, securely placed in the hands of the Holy Synod and clerical elite. For a discussion of contemporary opposition to this arrangement, see EIPR, "Dimuqratiyya al-'Iklirus!"

[25] Seikaly, "Coptic Communal Reform." Also see Guirguis and van Doorn-Harder, *The Emergence of the Modern Coptic Papacy*.

in the life of the Coptic community came to an abrupt end when Muhammad Ali rose to power in 1805. He introduced a number of secular reforms in Egypt, including dissolving the *dhimmi* system and granting political equality to non-Muslims.[26] Ironically, however, the story of Egypt's secularization is also the story of the consolidation of ecclesiastical power and the steady ascendance of the Coptic Orthodox Church as the sole representative of Copts.

Over the course of the nineteenth century, the Ottoman system of governance that was based on the twin principles of religious pluralism and inequality slowly dissolved. European campaigns waged on behalf of Christian minorities living in Ottoman territories played no small role in the eventual dissolution of the empire (in 1922).[27] These campaigns, however, also helped disseminate the ideals of religious equality, liberty, and minority rights among the rulers and ruled alike. In 1856 the Ottomans passed the sweeping Hatt-i Hümayun decree (right before the Treaty of Paris) that dismantled distinctions based on religion, language, and race, as well as forms of legal hierarchy, granting non-Muslims full civil and political rights.[28] Historians argue that such measures were not simply politically expedient ways for the Ottomans to yield to European pressure; rather, they were the crucial means for consolidating an increasingly fragmented polity and modernizing the state. As Bruce Masters points out, "Many in the generation of the [Ottoman] reformers genuinely wanted to transform the political landscape of the empire in order to create Ottoman citizens who could hold the line against the empire's dissolution."[29] Similarly, Donald Quataert suggests that granting political equality to Christians was a useful strategy to "bring Christians who had become protégés of foreign states back under the jurisdiction of the Ottoman state and its legal system."[30] One might say that at this point in history, the discourse of religious liberty and minority rights provided the grid of

[26] Guirguis and van Doorn-Harder, *The Emergence of the Modern Coptic Papacy*, 51. This was not the first time, though, that discriminatory practices against Coptic Christians were lifted. After his invasion of Egypt (1798–1801), Napoleon Bonaparte revoked "legal restrictions and discriminations against Christian minorities," which were reinstated and in place until the ascension of Muhammad Ali to power. Behrens-Abouseif, "The Political Situation of the Copts," 188.

[27] On this, see Deringil, *Conversion and Apostasy*, as well as Rodogno, *Against Massacre*.

[28] According to Bruce Masters, Hatt-i Hümayun "reiterated the principle [initially formulated in the Gülhane decree of 1839] that the sultan's subjects were equal, but went much further in outlining what that equality entailed. Freedom of the practice of religion was guaranteed. No distinction would be made on the basis of language, race, or religion among the sultan's subjects. Mixed tribunals, consisting of members of different religions, would replace shari'a courts for any commercial or criminal suits involving Muslims and non-Muslims. There would be no discrimination in admission to government schools or service. . . . Symbolic of the radical transformation in the relationship between the state and its non-Muslim subjects, the framers refrained from employing either *ahl al-dhimma* or *reaya* when referring to them in favor of a neutral neologism, *gayrimüslimler* (other than Muslims)." Masters, *Christians and Jews*, 138.

[29] Ibid., 137.

[30] Quataert, *The Ottoman Empire*, 66.

intelligibility for understanding, contesting, and making certain claims in the national and transnational geopolitical space against one's adversaries and with one's allies.

Saving Ottoman Christians

For the non-Muslims of the Ottoman Empire, the transformations ushered in by Hatt-i Hümayun were complicated. Despite the letter of the law, formal and informal discrimination against non-Muslims continued.[31] Furthermore, political equality came at a cost for non-Muslims in that their communal autonomy was drastically curtailed when they were subjected to the laws of the centralized state. As Kemal Karpat points out, this "stemmed not from the [Ottoman] government's express desire to curtail freedoms of its Christian subjects but from a logical and unavoidable incompatibility between the concept of a centralized unitary form of government and the idea of corporate autonomy which the reformed *millet*s desired to retain."[32] Political equality in the eyes of the law also meant that non-Muslims could now be recruited into the military and other forms of national service, which they actively resisted.[33] The European powers, for their part, eager to see the Ottoman reforms fail, continued to back "Ottoman Christians' complaints, [and] . . . allowed them to evade the provisions of the new laws and their responsibilities as citizens."[34]

The challenges involved in instituting political and civil equality for religious minorities in the late Ottoman Empire need to be understood in the framework of the rights that the modern secular state promised to its subjects and the privileges it withdrew. The parallels with the Jewish struggle in Europe are instructive. In charting the protracted history of Jewish emancipation in Europe, David Sorkin points out that even though "conditional tolerance" was extended to Jews as early as the eighteenth century, substantive political and civil equality remained elusive for them.[35] When it was granted in parts of Europe (in 1879 in France and 1871 in Germany), not unlike the case with non-Muslims of the Ottoman Empire, formal and informal discrimination against them did not end. Furthermore, in exchange for political equality, the Jews lost their corporate status and communal autonomy, not unlike the non-

---

[31] Masters, *Christians and Jews*, 130–68.
[32] Karpat, "*Millets* and Nationality," 165.
[33] Masters, *Christians and Jews*, 138.
[34] Rodogno, *Against Massacre*, 46.
[35] David Sorkin argues that it is only after state recognition was extended to Catholicism, Lutheranism, and Calvinism with the Peace of Westphalia that it slowly "began to spill over" to Jews and other dissenting Protestants in Western Europe. Ironically, it was Joseph II's "enlightened absolutism" that made this possible. His Edict of Toleration extended first to Lutherans, Calvinists, and the Orthodox (1781), was later applied to the Jews of Vienna, Silesia, Moravia, Hungary, and Galicia (1782–89), and came to serve as a model for similar edicts adopted in France. Sorkin, "Religious Minorities."

Muslims under Hatt-i Hümayun.[36] Jewish communal autonomy in Europe had meant variable things, including the right to have religious courts, the exercise of juridical autonomy (over personal status law and at times civil and criminal law), and the right to collective taxation and political bargaining.[37] As various historians of this period note, Jewish political integration into Europe was predicated upon the dissolution of various forms of Jewish self-government and their collective subjection to the centralized state and its national laws, which came to apply homogenously to all its subjects. This dissolution of communal autonomy was also meant to weaken religious ties, realigning Jewish fealty to the nation-state that now laid claim to the life and resources of all those it governed.[38]

In contrast to Western European Jewry's loss of communal autonomy in the nineteenth century, religious/*millet* identity was often strengthened by Ottoman reforms (*tanzimat*) (see my elaboration of the term *millet* below).[39] As the besieged state tried to incorporate religious minorities into its morphing political machinery, it encountered stiff resistance. This was especially true of Christian communities who had powerful European allies, which enabled them to resist collective inscription into the statist project, particularly in the wars the Ottomans were fighting against various encroaching powers (including Russia). The struggle between the crumbling Ottoman center and its dissenting Christian subjects not only resulted in the secession of Greece, Bulgaria, and Montenegro, among others, but also led to a series of massacres of Christians in Mount Lebanon and Syria (1860), Crete (1866 and 1896), and Armenia (1894–96). The European press and governments widely represented this conflict as an object lesson in the essential barbarity of the Ottomans, using their mistreatment of Christians as an excuse to stage "humanitarian interventions" on behalf of Christians and further truncating Ottoman sovereignty.[40] While the Armenian genocide received broad attention from Europeans, there was a deafening silence around the

[36] Sorkin shows that the process by which Jews were emancipated was checkered and piecemeal. Thus, even though Jews were granted political equality in 1790–91 in France, Napoleon "demoted the Jews of Alsace to a form of conditional emancipation in 1808 modeled on Joseph II's edict." Ibid., 9. Furthermore, in Britain, Jews "achieved civic and some political rights on an *ad hoc* basis either through the gradual removal of disabilities or the confirmation that they did not exist, often through court decisions that established unassailable precedents" (8).

[37] Katz, writing about eighteenth-century German Jewry, reports, "Personal matters like marriage, divorce, inheritance, and so forth came under the jurisdiction of Jewish institutions . . . [which] dealt with these matters on the basis of Jewish, that is Talmudic, law. Talmudic law also served as a source of authority for Jewish courts dealing with litigations between Jew and Jew." Katz, *Out of the Ghetto*, 19.

[38] See, for example, ibid., and Vital, *A People Apart.*

[39] See Davison, "*The Millets* as Agents of Change" and "The Advent of the Principle of Representation." I thank Bruce Masters for pointing me to these works.

[40] Despite the immense public outcry in European cities over the massacre of Armenian Christians between 1894 and 1896, European powers did not intervene to halt the genocide. For an interesting account why the Europeans desisted, see Rodogno, *Against Massacre*, 185–211.

massacres that the Belgian King Leopold II was committing in the Congo between 1891 and 1908, in which as many as eight to ten million Congolese died.[41] In commenting on the "humanitarian interventions" that European powers launched in the Ottoman territories during this period, Davide Rodogno notes that they chose to overlook "the fact that equality before the law and religious freedom in their own states, let alone colonies, did not exist. European diplomats and experts wanted the Ottoman government to legislate for equality and citizenship while, in a former Ottoman territory like Algeria, French authorities ruled in a far more intolerant, discriminating, and despotic way than the Ottomans had ever done."[42]

Despite its stated aim to uphold a political order grounded in the principle of mutual respect for state sovereignty, international law continued to authorize European violations of Ottoman sovereignty. Nineteenth-century European jurists decided to exclude the Ottoman state from membership in the "Society of Nations" (*la société des nations*) on the grounds that it was an "uncivilized" and "barbaric" polity, most clearly evidenced by the Ottoman mistreatment of its Christian subjects.[43] This was part of a broader European policy that excluded most if not all non-Western states from the ambit of international law. As Rodogno points out, while it was assumed that "uncivilized states" could offend European morals and values, "the opposite was not even contemplated as a working hypothesis."[44] Antony Anghie, in his analysis of the history of the emergence of international law, argues that this exclusion of non-Western states from *la société des nations* was enabled by a broader epistemological shift in international legal theory from *natural* law to *positive* law; the latter made a distinction between civilized and uncivilized states that the former had not. Anghie writes,

> The existence of a distinction between the civilized and uncivilized was so vehemently presupposed by positivist jurists, that the state of nature—and therefore naturalism—[became] epistemologically incoherent because it lack[ed] this central distinction. . . . In crude terms, in the naturalist world, law was given; in the positivist world, law was created by human societies and institutions. Once the connection between "law" and "institutions" had been established, it followed from this premise that jurists could focus on the character of institutions, a shift which facilitated the

---

[41] Not only did the international legal community and institutions at the time ignore the mounting evidence of the Congolese genocide, but prominent jurists actually defended King Leopold for abiding by the "humanitarian wishes of the Conference of Berlin." Koskenniemi, The *Gentle Civilizer of Nations*, 161.

[42] Rodogno, *Against Massacre*, 11.

[43] Ibid., 62–63. See also ibid., chaps. 1 and 2.

[44] Ibid., 55.

racialization of law by delimiting the notion of law to very specific European institutions.[45]

The "law of humanity" (*droits de l'humanité*), drafted to authorize humanitarian interventions against Christian massacres in the Ottoman territories, was premised on this structure of reasoning internal to international law.

Prominent secular jurists of the time, including Richard Cobden (1804–65), advocated European interventions on behalf of Ottoman Christians throughout the nineteenth and early twentieth centuries. Cobden argued that the principle of nonintervention applied only to European affairs and not to the Sublime Porte because it did not qualify as a member of the community of civilized nations. Similarly, John Stuart Mill categorically rejected even limited interference by a "civilized state" in the internal affairs of another, while he strongly supported the adoption of far more extensive and intrusive measures in the affairs of uncivilized nations in order to teach them enlightened behavior.[46] It is important to note that even as international law became secular in its language, rationale, and stipulations, it also came to root itself in Europe's unique Christian heritage, understood to be unparalleled in its humanism, especially when measured against the barbarity of Islam. As Rodogno shows, key legal and political figures argued that even though European humanitarian interventions had been secularized since they were undertaken at the time of the Crusades, Christian solidarity was so strong among Europeans that "*le droit des peuples* and *le droit de l'humanité*" were thought to accommodate "the old Christian ideal."[47] It was this sentiment of Christian fraternity that reinvigorated European support for Christian missions around the world in the mid-nineteenth century, even as the West came to understand itself as resolutely secular. Thus, just as France was issuing a fullthroated call to *laïcité* in the 1840s, it witnessed a Catholic revival that reignited popular French zeal to establish new missions in the Middle East.[48] Similarly, the United States and Britain at the time were undergoing their own Protestant awakening, which led to an expansion of Anglican and Presbyterian missions in the region. To be sure, there were important conflicts between the colonial administrators and missionaries, which have generated much historical debate among scholars of imperial France and Britain.

[45] Anghie, *Imperialism, Sovereignty, and the Making of International Law*, 55.
[46] Ibid., 50.
[47] Rodogno, *Against Massacre*, 62.
[48] Tejirian and Spector cite 1843 as a critical year when a renewed commitment to missionary work reemerges in France, evident in the establishment of Jesuit missionary schools in Syria, the reconstituted French mission in Mount Lebanon, and the Oeuvres des écoles d'Orient (est. 1855) that spearheaded the Catholic missionary enterprise. Tejirian and Spector, *Conflict, Conquest, and Conversion*, 98–99.

Nonetheless, from the point of view of those who were subjected to their transformative power, the interdependence of these two projects, as I show below, was enormously consequential to the articulation of religious identity and intrafaith relations.

Freedom to Proselytize

The largest expansion of Christian missionary activity in the Middle East was also the period of the consolidation of colonial rule in the region.[49] Europeans (Catholics, Anglicans, Episcopalians, and Lutherans) had dominated the missionary scene up to the end of the nineteenth century, when American Presbyterians began flooding the region to establish missions in Anatolia, Eastern and Central Turkey, Armenia, Persia, Iraq, Syria, Lebanon, and Egypt. The Protestant missionaries came armed with the Enlightenment critique of ecclesiastical authority, espousing a privatized conception of religion whose proper locus was the individual, his conscience, and personal experience.[50] Their call to religious liberty differed from the one issued by the Christian European rulers of the seventeenth century whose proper addressee was the collectivity of Eastern Christians who needed to be brought under the patronage of European sovereigns. In contrast, the Protestant missionaries conceived of religious liberty as an individual's right (indeed, a moral duty) to break from the weight of custom, tradition, and clerical authority to embrace the higher truth of an enlightened religion. Their individualized call to religious liberty was also a powerful antidote, or so they hoped, to local interdictions (Muslim, Christian, Jewish) against interreligious conversion.[51]

Despite inter-denominational rivalry, all Christian missionaries of the nineteenth century shared the belief that the Oriental churches represented a heretical and arcane form of Christianity that was in desperate need of redemption. The Protestant critique of ecclesiastical power easily accommodated Orientalist stereotypes that populated

---

[49] On this history of Christian missions in the Middle East, see ibid.

[50] This stood in contrast, for example, with the efforts of the Roman Catholic Church to lobby the Coptic patriarchs over the course of the sixteenth century to accept the Chalcedonian creed, denounce their heretical beliefs, and accede to the sovereignty of the Catholic pope. Even though the Coptic Church united with Rome briefly (from 1586 to 1601 AD), these efforts failed in large part because of the Catholic Church's arrogant attitude and ignorance of Coptic history and beliefs. See Hamilton, *The Copts and the West*, chaps. 3 and 6.

[51] If Muslim apostasy laws were one significant source of grievance for the missionaries, Jewish opposition to their projects was another. Arab Jews, for example, strongly opposed the recruitment of Jewish children in missionary schools. As a result, L'Alliance israélite universelle was founded in 1860 in Paris to provide Judaism-inflected education to the Jews living in the Middle East and the Balkans. By the end of the nineteenth century, their network of schools extended to Iraq, Morocco, Syria, Egypt, Iran, Libya, Lebanon, and Tunisia as well as Turkey and the Balkans. Tejirian and Spector, *Conflict, Conquest, and Conversion*, 149.

the European imaginary at the time (see chapter 5). Commenting on the American Presbyterians, Ussama Makdisi writes:

> From America the missionaries had come to save those whom they described as religiously "mingled" peoples of the East. Their awareness of what they believed to be the waning power of Islam, and what they regarded as the corruption of Eastern Christian churches, galvanized the missionaries. They believed themselves to be at the vanguard of the liberation of the world and the heirs to the Protestant Reformation.[52]

Orientalist and colonial scholarship was a key site for the reproduction of the missionary lore about the degenerate character of Eastern Orthodox Christians. Take, for example, the following remarks that the well-known lexicographer Edward William Lane made about Coptic Christians in his book *An Account of the Manners and Customs of Modern Egyptians*, published in 1836:

> One of the most remarkable traits in the character of Copts is their bigotry. They bear a bitter hatred to all other Christians; even exceeding that with which the Muslims regard the unbelievers in El-Islam. . . . They are, generally speaking, of a sullen temper, extremely avaricious, and abominable dissemblers; cringing or domineering according to the circumstances. . . . [They] are generally ignorant, deceitful, faithless, and abandoned to the pursuit of worldly gain, and to indulgence in sensual pleasures.[53]

Several decades later, Lord Cromer, who served as the British Consul-General (from 1883 to 1907) echoed Lane's judgment, differing only over the reasons for Coptic moral degeneracy:

> It is true that the Coptic Christian has remained stagnant, but there is this notable difference between the stagnation of the Moslem and that of the Copt. . . . The Copt . . . has remained immutable, or nearly so, not because he is a Copt, but because he is an Oriental, and because his religion, which admits of progress, has been surrounded by associations antagonistic to progress.[54]

The American Presbyterians, along with the Catholics and Anglicans, viewed Egyptian Christians as a damaged community that was both heroic for having survived Islamic rule and degenerate for having assimilated Muslim customs. As a result, in the words of Tejirian and Simon, "the Presbyterians joined the three-way competition for

---

[52] Makdisi, *Artillery of Heaven*, 3.
[53] Lane, *Account of the Manners and Customs*, 551.
[54] Quoted in Hamilton, *The Copts and the West*, 283, from Baring, *Modern Egypt*.

the Copts' souls."[55] The period of the British occupation of Egypt (1882–1918) was the heyday of missionary activity, during which American Presbyterians enjoyed the protection of British colonial authorities.[56] Notably, the Ottoman capitulations proved to be crucial for the European and American missionaries during this period, allowing them to buy property, travel along the Nile to proselytize, and build and run schools in which Christianity was openly taught to Muslim and non-Muslim children alike.[57] Thus the Ottoman capitulations were not simply a thing of the past but continued to have a transformative effect on non-Muslims and Muslims well into the early half of the twentieth century.

The consistent failure of the Protestant missionaries to gain converts from Christians and Muslims alike eventually prompted them to focus their energies on reforming the purportedly derelict and moribund character of Oriental/Eastern Christianity. Key to this reform was the inculcation of natives into a different understanding of religion that was privatized, individualized, and grounded in a personal experience of the divine. The individual's right to religious liberty was the most powerful expression and vector of this Protestant conception of religion, combining its various predicates in one pithy formulation: belief, conscience, and individual choice. It was bound up with the moral judgment that religion, in order to square with freedom and enlightenment, must be chosen freely by a rational, deliberate agent. The natives' stubborn hewing to their own faith was understood never as an act of will but as a product of either clerical coercion or servile cultural compulsion.[58]

The missionaries made ubiquitous use of international diplomacy and the colonial and foreign offices of Anglo-American governments to enforce their conception of religious liberty in the Middle East. As Sharkey notes, Andrew Watson, a founding figure of the American Presbyterian mission in Egypt, advocated for the adoption of religious liberty in forums as diverse as the League of Nations, the Paris Peace Conference, the US State Department, and the British Foreign Office.[59] His son, Charles R. Watson, a leading figure who helped establish the American University in Cairo, doubted the efficacy of Christian proselytization in Egypt but continued to promote religious liberty as an individual's right to freely choose his faith—particularly for "Egyptian Muslims to embrace Christianity and profess it in public."[60] In reflecting on this global campaign that Euro-American missionaries, educators, and colonial officials launched, it is hard to separate the religious elements of the campaign from

---

[55] Tejirian and Simon, *Conflict, Conquest, and Conversion*, 108.
[56] Sharkey, *American Evangelicals*, 30–31, 37.
[57] Ibid., 4.
[58] On this point, see Deringil, "There Is No Compulsion in Religion," 567.
[59] Sharkey, *American Evangelicals*, 161.
[60] Ibid., 5. On Charles Watson's changing position on Christian proselytization, see ibid., 156–62.

secular ones. Indeed, it is difficult to even imagine how one would secure such a separation epistemologically, politically, and historically.

Despite strident Anglo-American advocacy, the individualized concept of religious liberty failed to gain much traction among ordinary Muslims and Christians of the Middle East even as it became ensconced in the laws of the region. As anticolonial resistance mounted against the British in Egypt, for example, the issue for Muslim and Christian nationalists was how to secure the right to freedom *from* Christian evangelicalism rather than how to embrace its individualizing call.[61] By the 1930s, there was an organized backlash against the missionaries in Egypt; its most effective expression was found in the tracts the Muslim Brotherhood published against the missions, which often represented Christians tout court as agents of foreign powers. Eventually the power of the missions faded as European and American support for them declined; and as Egypt was decolonized, a whole host of restrictions and regulations were applied to them, including mandatory Islamic instruction in missionary schools.[62] In 1937, with the signing of the Montreux Convention, the legal and fiscal privileges that the missionaries had enjoyed in Egypt were also finally revoked.[63]

The transformative effect of the missionary project in the Middle East should be measured not in the number of converts they gained but by the dissemination of Protestant ideas about religion and education, which in turn fomented reform in the churches of the region, including in the Levant as well as in Turkey, Persia, and Iraq.[64] The Protestant belief that the Bible should be read in the vernacular in order to develop a personal relationship with God was crucial to the Bible's circulation in Arabic-language translation and to the adoption of Arabic in the rituals and liturgies of Middle Eastern churches. The schools and colleges the Anglo-European missionaries established are perhaps their next most important legacy, which produced a generation of national bourgeoisie and church leadership at the forefront of the anticolonial struggle. Historian Paul Sedra's work shows in great detail how the Coptic Orthodox Church in Egypt, under Protestant influence, came to adopt a series of educational reforms and a more service-oriented theology.[65] He also documents the role Protestant ideas played in fostering an elite Coptic consciousness that was highly critical

[61] To this day, the Coptic Orthodox Church conceives of religious liberty as a collective right of the Christian minority to protect itself against the corrosive effects of any kind of proselytization—Muslim, Catholic, or Protestant (see chapter 3).

[62] Sharkey, "Muslim Apostasy," 148.

[63] Under the auspices of the League of Nations, this agreement was signed between the governments of Egypt and several European countries (France, Britain, Spain, Belgium, and others). It abolished the extraterritorial legal privileges that were granted to foreigners in Egypt.

[64] Tejirian and Simon, *Conflict, Conquest, and Conversion.*

[65] Sedra, *From Mission to Modernity*; and Sedra, "John Lieder and His Mission in Egypt."

of ecclesiastical hierarchy and corruption.[66] It was this elite that led the first Coptic Communal Council, called Majlis al-Milli, created in 1874, to reform the Coptic Church and establish lay control over its endowments and clerical structure.[67] Although ecclesiastical authorities steadily stymied the Majlis's efforts, it was an important lay institution whose members played a leading role in the nationalist movement and in the drafting of the first constitution of Egypt (as I recount in the chapter that follows).

Human-Rights Missionaries

It is common to assume that Christian missions belong to a bygone past, their power replaced by secular values and norms in geopolitics. Yet it behooves us to think carefully about the entwinement of secular and Christian principles in international diplomacy. This entwinement is nowhere more apparent than in the making of Article 18 of the Universal Declaration of Human Rights (UDHR), which was formulated in the 1940s when Christian missions were in decline in the Middle East. The Article declares, "Everyone has the right to freedom of thought, conscience and religion; this right includes freedom to change his religion or belief, and freedom, either alone or in community with others and in public or private, to manifest his religion or belief in teaching, practice, worship and observance."[68] At surface, this article appears to prescribe no particular religious content and to accommodate all forms of belief (or unbelief). However, a careful study of the forces that helped shape Article 18 and the assumptions that underlie this much-revered text challenges its apparent neutrality. In a meticulously researched dissertation, Linde Lindkvist shows that the conception of religious liberty that Article 18 enshrines was the fruit of a successful campaign that American evangelicals and European missionaries mobilized in the mid-1940s.[69] While Locke's theory of the separation of temporal power from the question of salvation was an important precedent, the evangelicals and missionaries elevated to a human-right dictum the Protestant idea that religion is about the inviolable sphere

---

[66] The development of the "Sunday School Movement" from the 1920s to the 1940s was a consolidation of this trend led by Pope Shenouda III (d. 2012) in his early years as a bishop. On this, see also Hasan, *Christians versus Muslims*, 57–102.

[67] Sharkey similarly notes that it was no accident that the Majlis al-Milli "in its conception and scope . . . resembled the Evangelical Church's presbyterial structure." Sharkey, *American Evangelicals*, 45.

[68] Article 18 of the UDHR became the basis for the UN Declaration on the Elimination of All Forms of Intolerance and Discrimination based on Religion or Belief. For the tortured debate that accompanied its passage, see Evans, *Religious Liberty*, 194–226.

[69] Lindkvist, *Shrines and Souls*. See also the article based on the dissertation: Linkdvist, "The Politics of Article 18."

of human conscience (rather than collective forms of religious life).[70] Lindkvist documents the central role the American Federal Council of Churches and the International Missionary Council played in framing Article 18, setting up a Joint Committee on Religious Liberty (JCRL) whose explicit aim was to "work for an international charter of human rights that would have a satisfactory place for the protection of religion and conscience."[71] The United Presbyterian Church—the sponsor of American missions in Egypt and a member of the International Missionary Council—was a key player in drafting Article 18 of the UDHR.[72]

This coalition of evangelists and missionaries viewed Article 18 as central to their fight against "Soviet secularism" and "Orthodox Islam" as well as to their efforts to proselytize freely in the global south.[73] The emphasis Article 18 places on an individual's right to "change his religion or belief" was a victory for these evangelists, one that predictably elicited objections from members of Muslim states who had, indeed, been its primary target.[74] While this opposition is often cast as a clash between Western secular values and Islamic conservatism (particularly the prohibition on apostasy), Lindkvist argues that this interpretation ignores the fear many Muslim states expressed that Article 18 would open up their countries to Christian proselytization at a time when the missions were finally in decline.[75] The Muslim states in their statements focused on how Christian missionaries throughout history had used religious liberty to foment religious conflict and to facilitate projects of colonial and imperial intervention.

Article 18 of the UDHR is striking for its omission of any reference to the institutional conditions necessary for the preservation of collective aspects of religious life (such as religious schools, charities, and other associations). While Article 18 includes language such as "in community with others," the explicit object of protection is the individual and his or her conscience. No reference is made to religious groups deserving of protection. This omission is particularly consequential for religious minorities who, without collective and communal institutions, remain vulnerable to losing their distinct forms of life and to assimilation to majoritarian norms in a given

---

[70] Shorn of its evangelical moorings, conscience has become the defining feature of religious liberty, that which must be guaranteed through legal protection. On a strong argument for why this should be the case, see Leiter, *Why Tolerate Religion?*

[71] Lindkvist, "The Politics of Article 18," 440.

[72] Sharkey, "Muslim Apostasy," 139–66.

[73] Lindkvist, *Shrines and Souls*, 96–108. Two Christian figures who played a central role in shaping the wording of article 18 were Jacques Maritain (a French Catholic philosopher) and Charles Malik (a Lebanese Christian delegate on the Human Rights Commission). On their respective histories and views, see Lindkvist, *Shrines and Souls*; and Moyn, "From Communist to Muslim."

[74] See Mitoma, "Charles H. Malik and Human Rights."

[75] Lindkvist, *Shrines and Souls*, 130–36. Of the states that objected to the clause about freedom to change one's religion, only Saudi Arabia ultimately abstained in the final vote on Article 18. Iran, Egypt, and Pakistan voted for the Article, as did Syria, Yemen, Iraq, Afghanistan, and Lebanon.

polity.[76] Not surprisingly, it was the international jurist Hersch Lauterpacht, familiar with the plight of European Jews during the interwar years, who argued that equality was not reducible to "equal opportunities between individuals," but required a level playing field in which minority institutions and associational life had the same chance of flourishing as those of the majority.[77] Lauterpacht's attempts were robustly rebuffed, and Article 18 as we know it came to pass.[78]

While Article 18 of the UDHR is widely understood to be a secular accomplishment, as is clear from the history I recount above, it enshrines a particular conception of religiosity that is deemed normative and worthy of legal protection. It is therefore not a neutral instrument, as is often claimed, that can equally accommodate all conceptions of religion. Ways of being religious that do not fit this narrow conception either remain illegible or are not deemed worthy of its protection. Furthermore, the history of the passage of Article 18 elaborates the indelible ways in which the secular and the religious are intertwined, an entwinement that does not give the lie to secular neutrality but reveals its true character.

In wrapping up this section, I want to note that even though the narrative I have presented above is familiar to scholars of the Middle East, rarely does it serve as a resource for theoretical reflection on the shape secularism has taken in the region. For the most part, this history is used to demonstrate the incomplete character of secularism or its hijacked promise in Middle Eastern societies. In contrast, I have suggested that various aspects of this history are emblematic of key features of political secularism—such as the idea that religion is a matter of private belief and individual conscience, which now informs the constitutions of almost all Middle Eastern countries. The inhabitants of the region (Muslims and non-Muslims) clearly contest this notion, but their contestations are always located within this discursive frame against which another understanding of religion has to be polemically and rhetorically secured. Similarly, the history I recount above shows that the creation of a unitary and centralized form of government, as a fundamental feature of secularization, has brought religious life under the control of the modern state in a way that is historically unprecedented. One important consequence of this process is that all claims of reli-

---

[76] One would imagine that the Christian missionaries who helped draft Article 18 would have been sensitive to communal aspects of religious life. Yet history shows that they remained adamantly opposed to any accommodation of collective or group rights. Lindkvist, drawing on Samuel Moyn's work, argues that the ideology of "personalist humanism" was in part responsible for this. Lindkvist, *Shrines and Souls*, chap. 5; and Moyn, "Personalism, Community, and the Origins of Human Rights."

[77] Lindkvist, "The Politics of Article 18," 434.

[78] A very similar concern had informed the Jewish drafters of the initial version of the Polish Minority Treaty in 1919, which also lost to a thin, individualized conception of religious liberty that was ultimately more amenable to the eradication of Jewish communal life. See my discussion of this point later in this chapter.

gious identity are obliged to engage the state, its sovereign power now an indispensable feature of modern religious life.

In this section I have also charted key transformations in the concept of religious liberty. In the seventeenth century, when European Christian empires used it to claim Ottoman Christians as their brethren, it was primarily associated with communal affiliation. While its valence as a collective right did not entirely disappear, over the course of the nineteenth century, religious liberty came to take on an individualist cast—a formulation that is now enshrined not only in human-rights protocols but also in the national laws and constitutions of the Middle East. It sits in tension, however, with communal aspects of religious life and the rights and protections that this form of life can claim within a national polity. Thus, despite the individualist thrust of the language of political, civil, and human rights, struggles for collective rights persist into the present. Insomuch as liberal secularism enshrines the individual as the fundamental unit of political life, it continues to remain apathetic to communal aspirations. It is this tension, between individual and collective rights, that I analyze below.

What Is a National Minority?

The Versailles Peace Conference (1919) is narrated as a transformative moment in world history: with the dissolution of empires (the Ottoman, Habsburg, and Hohenzollern) that lost World War I, it heralded the creation of a new international order based on the nation-state. While that institutional form was already prevalent in Western Europe and North America, the victorious powers extended nation-state status to those that had broken away from the fallen empires. This privilege was denied, of course, to large parts of the world that were deemed unworthy of self-rule and thus brought under direct or indirect colonial rule. But, for the estimated sixty million people who were granted "a state of their own" in Central and Eastern Europe, this was a momentous development.[79] Despite this new international order, the Versailles peace treaties repeated the old pattern whereby the Allied powers' recognition of the newly independent states was conditional upon a pledge to uphold the rights of religious and ethnic minorities within their boundaries.[80] As was the case with

[79] Mazower, *Dark Continent*, 41.
[80] As Krasner notes, "The minority rights established after the First World War were set in peace treaties signed with Poland, Austria, Czechoslovakia, Yugoslavia, Bulgaria, and Romania in 1919, with Hungary and Greece in 1920, and with Turkey in 1923; in declarations made as conditions for admission to the League of Nations for Albania in 1921, Lithuania in 1922, and Latvia and Estonia in 1923, and Iraq in 1932." Krasner, *Sovereignty*, 90.

earlier treaties, none of the victorious Western powers (Britain, the United States, Italy, France, and Belgium) accepted similar provisions regarding their own minorities (the Welsh and Irish in Britain, Native Americans and blacks in the United States, the Bretons and Basques in France, and the multinational Tyrol in Italy). Despite having lost the war, Germany was not subject to these conditions because of the trust Western Europeans placed in their own capacity for tolerance.[81] Once the horror of the Holocaust unfolded almost two decades later, the irony of this judgment was not lost on those forced to accept minority stipulations in 1919.

The establishment of the nation-state as the dominant political form put into play a new rationale of governance that divided up the governed differently than did the empires. Instead of recognizing parallel and contiguous communities distinct by virtue of their confessional, denominational, or tribal affiliation, the nation-state sought to represent "the people," united by a shared history, culture, and territory. In this system, each individual qua citizen came to be tied to the state through a system of rights and obligations.[82] The terms *majority* and *minority* became a constitutional device for resolving differences that the ideology of nationalism sought to eliminate or assimilate. Since the Versailles Peace Conference, international law has used the concept of national minority to distinguish communities that can lay claim to membership in a national polity from populations that cannot, such as migrant workers or refugees.[83] Since 1919, minority has come to connote "an internationally sanctioned and politically consolidated category whose primary reference [is] to the nation state in which the minority [holds] citizenship, rather than the [group] to whom he/she 'racially' [or denominationally] belonged."[84] Notably, the new nomenclature of minority came to encompass not only religious but also racial, linguistic, and cultural differences. Religion thus became one among other features that was important to differentiating a group from the national majority.

The concept of national minority is built, however, on a fundamental tension. On the one hand, it signifies the membership of a minority group in a national polity; on the other hand, the minority group also represents an incipient threat to na-

---

[81] Jackson Preece, "Minority Rights in Europe," 82.

[82] In conventional accounts of nationalism, "civic nationalism" is often contrasted with "ethnic nationalism": the former, associated with Western Europe, is supposed to have created a homogenous and inclusive body politic, and the latter, linked with Eastern Europe, Asia, and Africa, is said to be riven with primordial differences. This image of Western European nationalism erases the long history of religious persecution that helped create the homogenous polities of the seventeenth-century (including the violence of Spanish Catholics against Muslims, Jews, and Protestants, of French Catholics against Huguenots and English Protestants, and of English Puritans against French and Irish Catholics). On this point, see Marx, *Faith in the Nation*; and Danchin, "The Emergence and Structure of Religious Freedom."

[83] See Jackson Preece, *National Minorities*, 14–30.

[84] Cowan, "Selective Scrutiny," 91n3.

tional unity, by virtue of its differences from the majority. This threat is intrinsic to the ideology of nationalism because the modern concept of nationhood regards linguistic, ethnic, and cultural characteristics as a legitimate basis for people's claims to self-determination and independent statehood. Under the auspices of the League of Nations (est. 1920) and the Permanent Court of International Justice (est. 1922), the Minority Treaties were instituted precisely to regulate this dual character of "national minorities." Minority-rights infractions committed by the newly created nation-states would be monitored, while irredentist movements that posed a threat to the status quo of the new system would be policed. One begins to get a sense of the magnitude of the problem that the Minority Treaties sought to manage when considering that more than twenty million people acquired the status of a "national minority" in Central and Eastern Europe alone.

Hannah Arendt was among the first to diagnose incisively the irreversible transformation that the globalization of national sovereignty had wrought in the meaning of the term *minority*:

> Minorities had existed before, but the minority as a permanent institution, the recognition that millions of people lived outside normal legal protection and needed an additional guarantee of their elementary rights from an outside body [the League of Nations], and the assumption that this state of affairs was not temporary but that Treaties were needed in order to establish a lasting modus vivendi—all this was something new, certainly on such a scale in European history. The Minority Treaties said in plain language what until then had been only implied in the working system of nation-states, namely, that only nationals could be citizens, only people of the same national origin could enjoy the full protection of legal institutions, that persons of different nationality needed some law of exception until or unless they were completely assimilated and divorced from their origin. . . . They thereby admitted . . . that the transformation of the state from an instrument of the law into an instrument of the nation had been completed; the nation had conquered the state, national interest had priority over law long before Hitler could pronounce "right is what is good for the German people."[85]

In international law, the definition of the term *minority* has proved to be elusive, despite the League of Nations's efforts.[86] It is unclear whether *minority* is an objective designation based on the presence of certain religious, racial, ethnic, linguistic, and religious

---

[85] Arendt, "The Decline of the Nation-State," 275.
[86] See the discussion of this issue in Jackson Preece, *National Minorities*, chap. 2, esp. 14–29. See also Rehman, "Raising the Conceptual Issues."

markers or a subjective one that registers a group's sense of discrimination based on these characteristics. The fact that there are groups who exhibit signs of difference from the national culture, or suffer from discrimination, but do not claim the term poses difficulties for international law. The jurist J. A. Laponce, for example, in an earlier book on the topic, writes that "a minority is a group of people who, because of a common racial, linguistic or national heritage which singles them out from the politically dominant cultural group, fear that they may either be prevented from integrating themselves in the national community of their choice or be obliged to do so at the expense of their identity."[87] Similarly, in his book on the topic, Inis Claude notes,

> The fundamentally subjective nature of the concept of the nation prevents a precise statement of the scope of our problem. Racial, religious, or linguistic differentiations may be treated as useful clues to the existence of national minorities, but *not as infallible indices*. We can only say that a national minority exists when a group of people within a state *exhibits the conviction* that it constitutes a nation, or a part of a nation, which is distinct from the national body to which the majority of the population of that state belongs, or when the majority element of the population of a state feels that it possesses a national character in which minority groups do not, and perhaps cannot, share. The *problem* of national minorities arises when such a situation exists within the conceptual framework of the national state.[88]

For both Claude and Laponce *minority* is not a demographic term but entails the subjective embrace of a group identity based on a shared sense of collective discrimination. The two entries in the *Encyclopedia of the Social Sciences* (1933 and 1968) also associate the term with a collective sense of economic, political, legal, and social disadvantage shared by a group.[89] These various attempts at defining the term link two disparate processes: the way a group comes to acquire a cohesive collective identity based on certain shared social characteristics, and the process by which the group becomes cognizant of its marginalization in a polity. *Minority* in this important sense is a *political* term in that it registers hierarchized difference (and not simply difference), despite the state's claim to ensure equality for all its citizens.

Given the ongoing ambiguity about who qualifies as a minority, the UN Special Rapporteur on the Protection of Minorities, Francesco Capotorti, tried to close the debate by offering the following definition in 1979: "[A] group numerically inferior

[87] Laponce, *The Protection of Minorities*, 6, cited in Jackson Preece, *National Minorities*, 24.

[88] Claude, *National Minorities*, 2, emphasis added.

[89] Seligman, *Encyclopedia of the Social Sciences*; and Sills, *International Encyclopedia of the Social Sciences*.

to the rest of the population of a State in a non-dominant position, whose members—being nationals of the State—possess ethnic, religious, or linguistic characteristics differing from those of the rest of the population and show, if only implicitly, a sense of solidarity, directed toward preserving their culture, traditions, religion, or language."[90] Despite this definition, often repeated in UN reports and human-rights protocols, questions persist. Do indigenous people, for instance, qualify as a minority, given that they face collective discrimination based on certain shared genealogical, linguistic, and tribal distinctions?[91] Similarly, do immigrants coming to Europe and America from former colonies who have gained citizenship status qualify as a national minority if they face discrimination based on their ethnic, racial, or religious identity? Answers to these questions depend not on clear definitions but on whether sovereign nation-states are willing to recognize the existence of minorities and grant them rights and liberties distinct from those accorded to the majority populace. This, in turn, often depends on how national belonging is defined and whether that definition is rooted in metaphors of blood, kinship, culture, or nature.[92] International bodies may force the UN definition on the so-called weak states but are helpless when it comes to convincing Western powers like Germany, France, Britain, and the United States to adopt it. France, which has coauthored all the major international treaties since the eighteenth century, continues to insist that no population living within its borders fits the description of the term as stated in the international conventions on civil and political rights.[93]

As is well known, the League of Nations spectacularly failed to curtail the rise of anti-Semitism and protect Europe's Jewish minority from genocide. Furthermore, the minority-rights regime provided the pretext for Hitler's invasion of Czechoslovakia to ostensibly protect the German-speaking minority in Sudetenland. The Euro-American Jewish diaspora had been gravely concerned with the tilt of European politics during the interwar years, before the national socialists ascended to power, and were at the forefront of advocating for minority rights. Their attempts were stymied for reasons that are instructive for understanding how inadequate the individualized conception of religious liberty is for protecting an endangered religious

---

[90] Quoted in van der Vyver, "Self-Determination and the Right to Secession," 251. Pursuant to this understanding, South African whites, despite being a numerical minority, do not qualify for this designation.

[91] See Kugelman on how the national minority debate is linked to UN protocols on indigenous rights: Kugelman, "Protection of Minorities and Indigenous Peoples." It is noteworthy that the debate on "national minorities" remains largely a European debate with little resonance in the United States, which continues to shun the term.

[92] There is a vast literature on this topic. For two contrastive treatments, see Brubaker, *Nations and Nationhood*; and Stevens, *Reproducing the State*.

[93] Berman, "The International Law of Nationalism," 40.

minority. The Polish Minority Treaty, passed after intense negotiations in 1919, exemplifies this inadequacy. The Treaty was a product of the labor of British and American Jewish groups who had pushed for proportional representation for Polish Jews at different levels of the government. They also sought communal control over the social, educational, and religious institutions that allowed the Jews to preserve their way of life, which was under the threat of dissolution.[94] These proposals were rejected on the grounds that this would turn the Jewish community into "a state within a state," a threat to Polish sovereignty itself. As a result, the Treaty erased all references to Jews as a nation in favor of "minority" so as to forestall any secessionist claims.[95] What the Polish Treaty did recognize, however, were individual liberties for Polish Jews; this included the free exercise of religion, provided that it did not violate the "public order and public morals" of the nation—a limitation that was enshrined in subsequent European and UN legal definitions of the right to religious liberty.[96] This condition establishes the sovereign prerogative of the state to intervene in the domain of religious practice (*forum externum*) while it sanctified privatized religious belief as a space (*forum internum*) free of coercion. It is important to note that however discredited the Polish Treaty seems from our present point of view for its failure to protect the Jews, its normative precepts and structural contradictions continue to animate the current legal and popular debates about national minorities in Europe and the Middle East. It is manifest in the legally consequential distinction that most national constitutions draw between interiorized belief, which is protected from state incursion, and the public domain of religious practice, which is subject to state regulation. I will return to this point in chapter 4, but suffice it to say that this distinction allows for the secular state to sanction religious *practice* while at the same time claiming to leave religious *belief* untouched.

The political fate of the European Jewry's struggle for equality is instructive for another reason, namely, the idea that only national self-determination could ensure the collective survival of a people. Carol Fink notes that there was a significant split at the end of World War I between Euro-American Jews who sought to secure rights for the Jewish diaspora dispersed across Europe as a "national minority" and Euro-American Zionists who insisted that without a nation-state "a minority without a territory remained

---

[94] Evans, *Religious Liberty*, 105. Even though there were other demographically significant minorities in Poland (such as the Ukrainians and Lithuanians), it was the Jewish problem in Central and Eastern Europe that was the motivating force behind the Polish Treaty. For a full discussion of the politics of this treaty, see ibid., chap. 4, 104–24; and Fink, *Defending the Rights of Others*, chap. 4, 101–32.

[95] For similar reasons, Polish Jews were denied the right to bring claims of discrimination to the League, a restriction that is enormously consequential when we consider the fact that very few Jewish appeals were made to the League before its dissolution in 1946. Evans, *Religious Liberty*, 120, 166.

[96] Ibid., 113.

perpetually vulnerable to exclusion, persecution and expulsion."[97] As the Nazi horror unfolded, it was the latter view that eventually prevailed, manifesting in the Zionist consensus that Jews from around the world had to be transferred to Palestine, where they were to become a majority and secure a state dedicated to preserving their collective interests.[98] Ironically, the Zionist solution to European anti-Semitism was enabled by the very discourse of majoritarian nationalism that had victimized the Jews. Mark Mazower astutely points out that this solution to Europe's "Jewish problem" was rooted in what had, by the end of World War II, become a widely accepted principle of "ethnic homogeneity as a desirable feature of national determination and international stability."[99]

Once again, Arendt is useful here for the prescience with which she predicted the victory of the nation over the state. As she put it, once "the whole question of human rights . . . was inextricably blended with the question of national emancipation," it followed naturally that "only the emancipated sovereignty of . . . one's own people [could] insure them."[100] Without citizenship or membership in a national community, human rights were meaningless, Arendt argued. The most tragic proof of this was the mass of stateless people, the "modern pariahs" created in the aftermath of World War I, who could not even qualify as a national minority because they "did not have a right to have rights."[101] This abject condition was a consequence of a world order in which membership in a nation-state had become a necessary condition for the realization of one's humanity. No international charter or institution (such as the Minority Treaties, the League of Nations, or later the Universal Declaration of Human Rights) could ensure this right.

If the Zionist founding of Israel as a Jewish state occupied one end of the political spectrum, then Third World people's struggles for self-determination against European colonialism marked the other end. In an important sense, both were distinct instantiations of how a people's hope for emancipation was linked to achieving national sovereignty. Those who could not lay claim to a homeland (or were prevented forcibly from doing so) were destined to inhabit the median status of "national minority." They

---

[97] Fink, *Defending the Rights of Others*, 45.

[98] At the end of World War II, population transfer was viewed as a legitimate strategy for consolidating the homogenous character of a nation-state. This was at play not only in the Jewish-only character of the state of Israel but also in the massive transfer of Germans (twelve million), Turks, Poles, Slovaks, Ukrainians, Hungarians, and Albanians to their "true motherlands." The policy of "population transfer" of the indigenous Palestinian population promoted by hardcore Zionists in Israel today belongs to this long genealogy of Jewish nationalism from the interwar period. On population transfer as a strategy of international law, see Berman, "But the Alternative Is Despair." On Eastern European population transfers, see Jackson Preece, "Minority Rights."

[99] Mazower, *No Enchanted Palace*, 141.

[100] Arendt, "The Decline of the Nation-State," 291.

[101] Ibid., 297.

were caught in the interminable struggle of having to fight the state for the guarantees and protections that might ensure their sustenance as a people and a community.

As historians of international law narrate it, minority rights were largely discarded and found no place in the Universal Declaration of Human Rights, which ennobled the individual. At the end of World War II, there was a sense that the emphasis on special protections for minorities had created greater tension, discord, and animosity rather than security for the communities they were meant to protect.[102] An important factor in the demise of the language of minority rights was the emergence of the United States as the dominant power. US national ideology eschewed any notion of community, collectivity, or group rights, instead celebrating the individual as the proper subject of humanity. In the discussion around the drafting of the UDHR, the US Under Secretary of State Summer Wells stated his country's distaste for minority rights explicitly: "In the kind of world for which we fight, there must cease to exist any need for the use of that accursed term 'racial or religious minority.'. . . Is it conceivable that the peoples of the United Nations can consent to the reestablishment of any system where human beings will still be regarded as belonging to such 'minorities?'"[103] Similarly, Eleanor Roosevelt, the UDHR's chief architect, argued that the declaration should not mention minorities. Ironically, even as the American architects of the UDHR championed individual equality as the basis of universal human rights, they refused to grant civil or political rights to African Americans who continued to suffer under the US apartheid regime of racial inequality. When the National Association for the Advancement of Colored People (NAACP) tried to use the UDHR to make its case for racial equality in the United Nations, Eleanor Roosevelt herself rebuffed it, declaring, "The minority question [does] not exist on the American continent."[104] The US State Department was successful in inserting a "national jurisdiction" clause in the UN charter that essentially made it impossible to intervene on behalf of American blacks in what was deemed to be an internal affair of the United States.[105] Though Cold War diplomacy is often cited as the reason why Eleanor Roosevelt blocked the NAACP's attempts, the US domestic-jurisdiction clause was consistent with the long history of Western powers claiming immunity from international law, even as they determined its scope, substance, and implementation elsewhere.

The discourse on the protection of religious and ethnic minorities languished for almost five decades during the Cold War until the fall of the Soviet Union in 1989,

---

[102] Mazower, *No Enchanted Place*, esp. chap. 3, 104–48; and Cowan, "The Success of Failure?"
[103] Quoted in Danchin, "The Emergence and Structure," 527.
[104] Ibid., 528. Quoted from the record of the Seventy Third Meeting, in 1948, of UN ESCOR, Committee on Human Rights.
[105] See Somers and Roberts, "Toward a New Sociology of Rights."

when it emerged once again with the creation of new republics and the displacement of peoples across state boundaries in a manner not seen since the end of World War II.[106] With the dissolution of political units such as Czechoslovakia, Yugoslavia, and the Soviet Union and the migration of large numbers of people to countries like Germany, Hungary, Turkey, and Austria, the threat of national minorities became relevant again to inter-European diplomacy. It is in this context that the UN General Assembly in 1992 passed the Declaration on the Rights of Persons Belonging to National or Ethnic, Religious, and Linguistic Minorities and the legally binding Article 27 of the International Covenant on Civil and Political Rights (ICCPR). Article 27 affirms the right of minorities not only to be protected against discrimination but also to be able to practice their distinct collective identity and participate in local decision-making procedures that affect them, provided they are compatible with national legislation.[107] As before, these minority rights were guaranteed by the successor states of Yugoslavia in return for European recognition in terms strongly reminiscent of the Treaty of Paris and the Treaty of Berlin, a reminder of how geopolitical inequality continues to structure minority-rights discourse today.[108]

The history I have presented here of minority rights and religious liberty is often read as geopolitical powers cynically using otherwise noble principles in service of realpolitik. Or as the subversion of a moral good that Western Europeans discovered for themselves and then slowly introduced to less enlightened cultures, sometimes through imperial force and sometimes through soft power (such as international diplomacy). Seen in this way, the principle itself—its logic, its aim, and its substantive meaning—remains unsullied by the impious intentions of the empires and states that sought to promote or subvert it. This manner of thinking needs to be rethought for at least two reasons. First, it is important to understand that when Western Europeans forced "weaker states" to recognize minority rights, they were not simply bringing their culture of tolerance to non-Western peoples and lands. If this were so, the

[106] Jackson Preece points to the marked absence of any provisions for national minorities in the texts produced by organizations as varied as the United Nations, Council of Europe, and Conference on Security and Cooperation in Europe (subsequently renamed the Organization for Security and Cooperation) during the Cold War period: "Not one of these organizations adopted a separate national minority rights text during the years 1945–1989. Furthermore, while these institutions all included within their various human rights instruments guarantees against discrimination on grounds of national affiliation or membership in a national minority group . . . they did not repeat or carry forward the League of Nations' efforts to provide minorities with language rights and a certain degree of cultural autonomy." Jackson Preece, *National Minorities*, 106.

[107] Article 27 reads: "In those States in which ethnic, religious or linguistic minorities exist, persons belonging to such minorities shall not be denied the right, in community with the other members of their group, to enjoy their own culture, to profess and practice their own religion, or to use their own language." Quoted in Krasner, *Sovereignty*, 99.

[108] For an excellent analysis of how minority-rights politics are lived and contested in Southeast Europe following the fall of the Soviet Union, see Cowan, "The Uncertain Political Limits."

European powers would have accepted similar provisions for their own minorities, which they refused to do throughout history. As this chapter shows, minority rights and religious liberty have been tied from their very inception to raison d'état, regional and national security, and geopolitics. Rather than see them as universally applicable moral principles, they are best understood as strategies of secular liberal governance aimed at regulating and managing difference (religious, racial, ethnic, cultural) in a national polity. Seen from this perspective, neither minority rights nor religious liberty signify a single essence or meaning—both have changed historically, in large part determined by the context of power relations within which they are inserted.

Second, it is also wrong to assume that religious liberty and minority rights are simply neutral legal instruments that protect certain groups or individuals from the exercise of state power and pervasive social inequality. People who are supposed to benefit from these protections are also transformed by virtue of their subjection to the calculus of state and geopolitical power in unique and unpredictable ways. For example, the shift from a group-based understanding of religious liberty to an individualist one in international legal discourse is more than a conceptual shift; it also affects the substantive meaning religion and politics as well as the kinds of subjects who can speak in its name. Similarly, recognizing a group as a minority transforms its self-understanding, its relationship to other religious communities and the state, and its standing in the eyes of the law. In order to fully elaborate this point, in what follows I turn to how the adoption of the category *national minority* has been transformative of religious identity in the Middle East.

From *Ta'ifa* to Minority

The process by which the religious demographics of the Middle East were made to fit the nomenclature of majority and minority identity was a slow and long process. In order to fully comprehend its scope, one must begin with the transformations wrought in the meanings of terms once used to signify group identity. The Ottoman term *ta'ifa* in the premodern period had denoted a social or economic group distinguished by religion, craft, or location; in the modern period, it came to signify primarily a religious group, as it still does today.[109] The Ottoman term *millet*, like the Arabic term *umma*, had been used throughout the sixteenth century to primarily refer to Muslims.[110] With the passage of nineteenth-century Ottoman reforms, its meaning shifted to refer to a non-Muslim community that enjoyed state protection.[111]

[109] Masters, *Christians and Jews*, 61.
[110] Strauss, "Ottomanisme et 'ottomanité,'" 20. I thank Michelle Campos for referring me to this work.
[111] Braude, "Foundation Myths of the *Millet* System," 69–100.

Importantly, this change indexes the shedding of the *ahl al-dhimma* system of governance with its connotation of Muslim supremacy and non-Muslim inferiority. Millet eventually became synonymous with the secular concept of the nation, similar to the way the term *umma* was resignified.[112] The Arabic term *aqalliyya* (literally, minority) is of recent coinage and refers not only to religious but also to ethnic and linguistic minorities, along the lines of the League of Nations definition.[113]

The transmutation of the multireligious Ottoman Empire into the Turkish Republic with a distinct Muslim majority population was a gradual and extended process during which the exact meaning of *minority* and *national identity* remained contested. As the Ottoman Empire lost large tracts of its Christian-populated areas in the latter half of the nineteenth century, a new demographic emerged that was overwhelmingly Muslim but ethnically and linguistically diverse. According to Howard Eissenstat, the emphasis on culture and religion slowly gave way to metaphors of blood in the early days of the Turkish Republic; eventually, "race took a greater role within discussions of national identity. . . . A broad and colorful national mythology was developed and propagated, 'proving' the racial unity and continuity of Anatolia."[114] Religious affiliation, however, was not entirely inconsequential to this new national self-image, and non-Muslims often remained excluded from the unifying metaphor of race.[115]

As the nineteenth century progressed, secessionist movements multiplied in the Ottoman Empire and religious dissent against the Sublime Porte came to be increasingly cast in nationalist terms. This was a fundamental shift in the relationship between the rulers and the ruled. Ottoman imperial rule had never claimed to represent the identity or interests of its majority or minority subjects, whereas the disparate secessionist movements in the Empire sought to establish states that reflected and represented the identity of "a nation" (*umma/millet*). The nation was a singular unit united by virtue of a shared history, religion, ethnicity, and language mapped onto a bounded territory called the "homeland" (*watan*). Given that communal identity under Ottoman rule was never coextensive with culture, language, or territory, this collectivity had to be invented anew. The transformation wrought in the identity of Greek Orthodox Christians exemplifies this process. As Benjamin White notes, Greek Orthodox Christians, defined as a religious *ta'ifa*, were spread throughout the Ottoman territories and many spoke Turkish as their language of everyday use. The movement to establish an independent Greece (est. 1832) created

---

[112] Strauss, "Ottomanisme et 'ottomanité,'" 21–23.

[113] Shami, "'Aqalliyya/Minority in Modern Egyptian Discourse."

[114] Eissenstat, "Metaphors of Race and Discourse," 250–51. See also Deringil, *The Well-Protected Domains*; and Salzman, "Citizens in Search of a State." I thank Kabir Tambar for pointing me to this literature.

[115] Minority Muslim identity continues to pose a challenge to the Sunni-dominant pluralism practiced in Turkey. See Tambar's excellent analysis of this issue in *The Reckoning of Pluralism*.

a far tighter association between the Greek Orthodox faith, Greek language, and a territorial homeland. The fact that a culturally homogenous citizenry had to be created by force is evident in the transfer of almost two million Greeks and Turks across national borders, an act that retrospectively produced the facticity of the nation-state of Greece and Turkey, each with a distinct Christian and Muslim majority. Selim Deringil charts a similar history across the Balkans, where secessionist movements led to the founding of a plethora of "national churches" that were supposed to substantiate claims of primordial belonging, thereby making it difficult to distinguish whether they were fighting wars of religion or national wars of liberation.[116] This history underscores my point that the process of secularization in the Middle East, far from eliminating religious difference, has subjected it to a new grid of intelligibility and a form of stratification that is compatible with the rationality of modern political rule.

The creation of modern nation-states in what is now called the Middle East, with its correspondent majority and minority demographics, was considerably fraught and varied. The breakup of the Ottoman Empire led to the creation of twenty-two Arab states, most of which were subjected to direct and indirect forms of colonial rule, primarily under the British and the French. Under colonial rule, religious differences did not disappear but intensified and proliferated. For example, during the French mandate period in Syria (1923–43), colonial administrators extended official recognition for the first time to the Druze, Ismailis, and 'Alawis as distinct Islamic sects (*tawa'if*, sing. *ta'ifa*), and they came to be regarded as "national minorities."[117] Under the Ottomans, these groups had no official status because the Sublime Porte did not recognize divisions internal to Islam. Similarly, in mandate Lebanon, the French extended formal recognition to the Shi'i/Jafari sect for the first time in 1926.[118] While these groups (the Druze, Shi'a, and 'Alawis) did have a distinct social profile before, the conferral of minority identity upon them meant something quite different: at times they were granted proportionate representation in governing bodies, at other times territorial autonomy, and at yet other times an equitable share of state resources. In almost all cases, however, once recognized by the state, a *ta'ifa* had the right to command juridical autonomy over their own religion-based family law. In cases where no such law existed, it was invented from scratch, amalgamating various practices, norms, and jurisdictions into one coherent whole supposedly rooted in the religious corpus

---

[116] Deringil, *Conversion and Apostasy*, 4.

[117] White, *The Emergence of Minorities in the Middle East*, 50–54. After World War I and the partitioning of the Ottoman Empire, the Mandate System was established under the League of Nations and gave the control of most of Ottoman Mesopotamia to the British and the rest of Ottoman Syria (modern Syria and Lebanon) to the French.

[118] Weiss, *In the Shadow of Sectarianism*, 125.

of each sect.[119] As White notes, it is only in the mandate period that the concept of religious community (sect/*ta'ifa*) comes to be attached to the community's right to command its distinct and autonomous religion-based family or personal status law. This association persists to this day in that when a religious community receives state recognition it must also be given autonomy over its own personal status law in countries like Egypt, Jordan, and Israel (see chapter 3).

In scholarship on the Middle East, the exacerbation of religious differences under colonial rule is often seen as evidence of its notorious divide-and-rule policy, which exploited confessional rivalries and consolidated communal fissures. While this view is not without merit, it overlooks the ways in which the colonial state also secularized native religious life by instituting the legal division between the public and the private; religion, like family and sexuality, were relegated to the latter, and politics to the former. As I will show in chapter 3, religion-based family law is a modern invention that did not exist in the premodern period; as such, it is a unique expression of the secular conjoining of religion, domesticity, and sexuality. The colonial state's claim that religion had to be separate from politics, therefore, was not an ideological farce; rather, it was a necessary step in the secularization of the Middle East. At times, as in the case of Syria, this process went hand in hand with extending state recognition to religious groups; at other times, as in the case of Lebanon, it went along with mapping religious identity onto other social distinctions (regional, economic, tribal), thereby investing it with new meaning. The consocial model of secularism that the Lebanese state eventually adopted created a patchwork of antagonistic religious communities that are united by virtue of their location within a bounded territory, but fractured by virtue of their autonomy over segments of sociopolitical power.[120] French policy in the settler-colonial state of Algeria was considerably different in that Muslim courts did not have the kind of autonomy that religious sects in Lebanon and Syria did; instead, Islamic law was subordinated to the French judicial system.[121] These varying arrangements of colonial and mandatory rule, therefore, exemplify not only the divide-and-rule policy of the French and the British, but also the double movement internal to political secularism: the simultaneous relegation of religion to the private domain *and* the amplification of religious differences.

In contrast to the Levant, the secularization of Egyptian religious life has followed a different trajectory, one that I track in chapter 2. Under British colonial rule, Egypt did not experience the proliferation of religious minorities (as in Syria) or the

---

[119] White, *The Emergence of Minorities in the Middle East*, 50. A very similar policy was instituted in Palestine under the British mandate. See Robson, *Colonialism and Christianity in Mandate Palestine*.

[120] For an excellent analysis, see Makdisi, *The Culture of Sectarianism*.

[121] See Christelow, "Transformation of the Muslim Court System."

Balkanization of religious differences (as in Lebanon). Egypt is distinct in that it has always had a large Sunni Muslim population and a significant Coptic Christian numerical minority. At the turn of the twentieth century, Egypt was religiously more diverse than it is today and included a range of small but politically significant communities of Jews as well as Armenian, Greek, and Syrian Christians. Coptic Orthodox Christians resented the British policy of favoring Armenian and Syrian Christians, who were regarded as outsiders, which suggests that by the 1920s there was a strong sense as to which minority was truly "of the nation."[122] Egyptian Jewry was regarded as a local *ta'ifa*, was part of the economic elite, and was a key player in the drafting of the first constitution of Egypt in 1923. It was with the establishment of the state of Israel in Palestine that Egyptian Jews came under attack and started to emigrate.[123] As chapter 2 will show, Coptic Orthodox Christians have been historically ambivalent about embracing the assignation "national minority" in part because, even though it accords them a special status, it sets them apart from the identity of the nation. The Coptic Orthodox Church continues to shun the term formally to this day, preferring the rubric of "People of the Book" because it allows them, as a state-recognized *ta'ifa*, to command juridical autonomy over Coptic family law and ecclesiastical resources.

It is commonplace to represent interreligious strife in the Middle East as a product of the failure of the secular project to take root in the region or of Islamic intolerance toward other faiths. Yet as is clear from the history I have presented in this chapter, the modern roots of religious strife belong equally to the history of secularization as to the legacy of Islamic rule. Many of the transformations I describe above are rendered as "local history" and seldom serve as the ground for theoretical reflection on the nature of the secular. The terms *global* and *local* mask the inequality of power relations between Euro-America and the Middle East, wherein "the global" stands for the former (universal and theoretically consequential) and "the local" for the latter (particular and theoretically inconsequential). The challenge is to think through the gap that opens up between universality and particularity, to force ourselves to rethink the globality of modern secular power through its non-Western itinerary.

---

[122] Behrens-Abouseif, "Political Situation of the Copts," 195.

[123] Joel Beinin describes the Jewish community in Egypt as primarily comprising Karaites and Rabbanites who practiced a Judeo-Arabic culture and lived primarily in Cairo and Alexandria. He argues that the rise of anti-Semitism in Egypt is a twentieth-century phenomenon that commences with the outbreak of the Arab-Israeli War in 1948 when Egyptian Jews and their property came under public attack. A significant portion of Egyptian Jews henceforth migrated to France, Israel, and the United States. Beinin, *The Dispersion of Egyptian Jewry*, 61. For a parallel history of Jews in Iraq, see Bashkin, *New Babylonians*.

Fateful Distinctions

In closing this chapter, I want to revisit the point I made about the precarious position that all minorities occupy within the context of the nation-state. While a minority's ability to flourish within a national polity depends on its integration into the national fabric, its assimilation often requires the attenuation, if not the abandonment, of values and practices that are fundamental to its identity. A minority's hewing to its customs and traditions sets it apart from majoritarian norms and can easily be perceived as a threat to national identity. Even though this tension is a generic feature of the minority condition, the possibilities open to any given minority will depend on its historical constitution, its place in the making of the nation as well as the particular ideology of national belonging embraced by a state. The Jewish experience in Europe has come to be treated as the paradigm through which the minority problem is elaborated; indeed, I have referred to it myself at various points in this chapter. Yet it is important to distinguish the Jewish experience from the plight of other minorities. The fact that Jews were dispersed throughout Europe made them quite distinct from minorities that are territorially consolidated. The creation of the state of Israel was meant to solve the diasporic problem for European Jewry, tragically at the expense of the Palestinians who have been turned into aliens in their own land. Territorially bound minorities are quite distinct from the European Jews in that they have often aspired to carve out their own homeland within the nation where they reside, an ambition that poses a very different kind of threat to state sovereignty. This is evident in the secessionist movements that split the Balkans and Yugoslavia and in the ongoing struggle of the Kurds in Turkey, Iran, and Iraq. Minorities that are not tied to a bounded territory pose a different kind of problem to state sovereignty, which requires a distinct form of political action. First Nations peoples of North America provide an interesting example in that they were once territorially sovereign, but European colonization and genocide have left them bereft of any substantive claim to sovereignty. In the few instances where they have been granted limited autonomy, their way of life has been ravaged to such an extent that they suffer a fate that is perhaps worse than that of other minorities. The term *minority*, therefore, congeals in itself different forms of marginalization and precarity that are historically distinct, which in turn determines the kind of political struggle a minority can pursue in order to ensure its collective survival and well-being. In the chapters that follow, I track the contours of various forms of minority politics (waged by Copts and Bahais) that pose different kinds of challenges to the secular-Islamic character of the Egyptian state.

Chapter 2

TO BE OR NOT TO BE A MINORITY?

When I was conducting fieldwork in 2008, I was often puzzled as to why the struggle for Coptic equality was seldom cast in terms of minority rights, and in the few instances when it was, it was denounced as an affront to national unity (*al-wahda al-wataniyya*). Unlike many parts of the world where minority rights are thematized in terms of the linguistic, ethnic, and religious identity of various demographic groups, in Egypt the term *minority* is deeply contested. The Coptic Orthodox Church regularly issues proclamations that Copts do not constitute a minority, echoing similar pronouncements of the Egyptian government. Human-rights activists working on behalf of Copts seldom frame their work in terms of a struggle for minority rights. This conspicuous avoidance of the term *minority* sits in stark contrast with the widely shared assessment among Copts that they suffer from various kinds of systemic discrimination. If in international legal discourse the term *minority* references a group's collective sense of marginalization at the hands of the national majority, then it is odd that many Coptic Christians go to great lengths to eschew the assignation. It was this conundrum that drove me to delve deeper into the historical roots of the profound ambivalence that surrounds the designation *minority* in Egypt today.

In this chapter, I analyze key moments in Egyptian history, from the colonial period to the present, when Muslims and Coptic Christians have debated the minority question. As I hope to show, even though there are developments unique to Egyptian history that have made Coptic Christians suspicious of the term *minority*, their ambivalence is also diagnostic of the structurally fraught place minority rights occupy in the topos of secular liberalism. The idea of group rights troubles liberalism's foundational belief that persistent forms of social discrimination are best addressed by treating all individuals equally in the eyes of the law regardless of one's race, class, religion, or gender. A range of liberal thinkers (Hegel, Rousseau, and Burke, among them) troubled by this valuation of the individual have emphasized instead one's embeddedness in, and dependence on, a set of social and historical conditions that are necessary for human flourishing. Multicultural theorists of the 1990s (such as Will

Kymlicka, Charles Taylor, and Iris Young) drew on this tradition of liberal thought to make a strong case for group-differentiated rights, taking North America as their primary site of intervention.[1] These theorists did not, however, abandon the liberal emphasis on the individual; instead, they made it the basis of their advocacy for group rights for cultural minorities. Will Kymlicka, for example, argued that individual autonomy *requires* the ability to maintain one's cultural institutions and ways of life because culture both expands the range of options an individual can choose from and makes the exercise of autonomy more meaningful.[2] This advocacy for group-differentiated rights drew wide reprobation from liberals who saw it as a weakening, if not dissolution, of liberalism's foundational commitment to individual autonomy.

Modern advocacy for minority rights—whether undertaken by theorists of multiculturalism or the League of Nations during the interwar years—derives from the basic realization that the liberal state cannot be neutral in regard to its national identity, which is rooted in the culture, religion, and language of the majority population. Because this majoritarian prejudice remains unacknowledged in the grammar of formal equality, theorists such as Iris Young argue that "justice requires that public policy actively compensate for the lack of recognition or the disadvantage that some members of the polity suffer because of their cultural membership by according cultural minorities special rights such as language rights, religious-based exemptions, representation rights and rights of self-government."[3]

A minority's struggle for equality, however, encounters a series of structural challenges that multicultural theorists have seldom addressed. For a minority to draw attention to its plight, it must necessarily highlight its difference from the identity of the nation, exacerbating the fissure that produces the group's exclusion in the first place.[4] Furthermore, a minority's demand for redress requires that the group's subordination be thematized in the laws of the nation-state (whether through affirmative action, proportionate representation, quotas, or special protections). This often elicits the majoritarian charge that the state is biased *toward* minorities, thereby contravening its commitment to treat all citizens equally.[5] While no doubt an expression of

[1] See, for example, Kymlicka, *Multicultural Citizenship*; Taylor et al., *Multiculturalism and "The Politics of Recognition"*; and Young, *Justice and the Politics of Difference*.

[2] See Kymlicka, *Multicultural Citizenship*, esp. chap. 5, "Freedom and Culture."

[3] Young, "A Multicultural Continuum," 48.

[4] This paradox haunts various struggles for civil and political equality where the question of difference is paramount, whether gender, racial, or sexual. For an insightful analysis of how this paradox emanates from the tension in liberalism between an abstract notion of the individual (as the bearer of rights) and a subjectivist one (as a distinct and unique being), see Scott, *Only Paradoxes to Offer*. For an elaboration of this paradox in the context of secular France, see Fernando, *The Republic Unsettled*.

[5] This is evident in the numerous challenges brought against affirmative action policies in the United States. Similarly, in India the government's extension of special protections to various minorities has come under fire for its "negative bias" against Hindus.

majoritarian supremacy, this accusation is also symptomatic of a system of governance that renounces difference politically even as it sustains it socially.

In what follows, I analyze how these secular liberal conundrums have informed the Coptic struggle for equality in Egypt from the early twentieth century to the present. The first half of the chapter focuses on the late colonial period (1911–23), when the Copts' status as a minority was vigorously debated publicly. An important cross-section of Coptic Christians at the time demanded proportionate representation in governing bodies so as to ensure that their collective interests were represented in the soon-to-be-sovereign Muslim-majority state. Egyptian secular nationalists (Muslims and Christians) rejected this proposal on the grounds that politics should be free of religion, and it found no place in the first constitution of Egypt. Even though Egyptian nationalist historiography represents this refusal as a high moment of Christian-Muslim unity, I read this debate as symptomatic of the classical dilemma at the heart of liberal secularism: how to banish religion from politics while at the same time devise laws to ameliorate religious inequality.

In the second half of the chapter, I turn to an analysis of Christian-Muslim relations in the postcolonial period (1952–present), during which confessional differences have become insuperable and the goal of Christian-Muslim equality a receding mirage. It is within this context of religious polarization that an important cross-section of Copts has begun to embrace the assignation *minority* to bring international attention to their plight. While the national context is crucial to understanding this reemergence of minority-rights discourse, equally important is an international shift since the events of 9/11 that has brought greater attention to the situation of Christians in the Middle East. I analyze this shift through a focus on some of the key geopolitical actors who are responsible for bringing the Coptic plight to the global stage, including the American evangelical movement and the US government. In summary, I hope to establish that while the Coptic-Muslim conflict in Egypt today is a national problem, it is also crucially shaped by the civilizational standoff between Christianity and Islam that, for many Egyptians, recalls the long history of missionary and colonial dominance in the region.

Minority: What's in a Term?

During fieldwork, when I inquired into the historical roots of the Egyptian rejection of the term *minority*, my interlocutors often pointed to the 1919 Revolution when Christians and Muslims heroically came together under the banner of the political party Hizb al-Wafd to oppose British colonial rule.[6] Egyptian nationalist historiog-

---

[6] The Wafd Party derived its name from the Arabic term for delegation, referring to a group of Egyptians who wanted to attend the 1919 Paris Peace Conference to demand Egyptian independence.

raphy narrates the 1919 Revolution as a watershed event when religious differences were set aside to envision a collective future in which citizenship, as opposed to religious affiliation or European patronage, would ensure equality for all Egyptians. In the minds of anticolonial nationalists at the time, the term *minority* was an exemplary device of the divide-and-rule policy that the British had pursued in the colonies. The British allocation of special seats to Christians, Jews, and Bedouins in the Legislative Assembly of 1913 was seen as evidence of this.[7] Egyptian historian Samira Bahr offers an influential and characteristic account of the 1919 Revolution in the following way:

> The Wafd was a united front comprised of Muslims and Copts that frustrated British political calculations, and the national movement was able to ward off impediments that sunk India in a sea of blood when Muslims and Hindus were at a crucial juncture in their struggle against colonialism. . . . The Egyptian people were [able to] harmoniously unite in a single joint front and this was embodied in the slogan, whose popularity is prevalent even now to a great extent, "Religion is for god and the nation for all."[8]

Many Christians and Muslims today continue to pay homage to this image of a united Egypt free from religious divisions, and it was powerfully invoked again during the protests in 2011 that overthrew the Mubarak regime.[9]

Despite the power of this nationalist narrative, a quick review of public debates in the decade preceding the 1919 Revolution reveals a far more fractured and contentious polity. Indeed, as early as March 1911, Coptic Christians had organized a public conference (known as the First Coptic Conference) that articulated a set of demands in the name of the "Coptic nation" (*al-umma al-qibtiyya*), including a new electoral law that would ensure Coptic representation in government bodies, equal distribution of public funds to support Coptic institutions (schools, monuments,

---

The arrest and exile of Saad Zaghloul, the leader of the Wafd Party, along with two other members, sparked protests that came to be called the 1919 Revolution. Order was restored only after Zaghloul was released and allowed to leave for Paris in April 1919. The Wafd played a leading role in drafting the 1923 constitution, and remained the most influential party throughout the 1930s. President Nasser dissolved it in 1952.

[7] This was the first time in the history of modern Egypt that a legislative assembly was founded on the principle of minority representation. Bishri, *al-Muslimun wa al-Aqbat*, 144–45.

[8] Bahr, *al-Aqbat fi al-Hayat al-Siyasiyya al-Masriyya*, 74.

[9] Samer Soliman (d. 2013), a leading Coptic activist-intellectual, summarized this sentiment in the following way to me: "You know the Copts have a long and prominent history in the making of modern Egypt. When people say that we had a revolution in 1952, I say no, that was the result of the revolution in 1919. Copts were leading figures in this revolution. It is not like the Maronites in Lebanon. They colluded with French colonialism. Copts did not collude with British colonialism because we have always thought of ourselves as Egyptians first. . . . The principle of unity as a nation is our only hope. We can't let go of this principle, it is only within the context of the nation-state that the point of unity becomes possible across differences." Personal interview, May 15, 2008, Cairo.

and courts), and for Sunday to be declared a national holiday.[10] The term *aqalliyya* (the Arabic equivalent for minority) had yet to gain traction, but the sense that *al-umma al-qibtiyya* conveyed was commensurate with the emergent meaning of the term *minority* in international legal discourse; it gave voice to a collective sense of disenfranchisement that demanded that the state address persistent forms of religious inequality.[11]

The British colonial office, the Egyptian monarch (the Khedive), and the Coptic Orthodox Church all opposed the Coptic Conference. The Church was locked in battle against the Coptic Communal Council (Majlis al-Milli), a group of influential Coptic elites who sought to establish greater lay control over Coptic communal affairs and who were at the forefront of the Coptic Conference.[12] Leading newspapers characterized it as "a plot against patriotism and Egyptian unity," dismissing the Coptic charge of discrimination by pointing to their overrepresentation in public-sector jobs.[13] As for the Coptic demand for proportionate representation in government bodies, an article published in the daily *al-Mu'ayyid* opined, "Egypt has been a Muslim country since the time of the Muslim conquest that established Muslim rule thirteen centuries ago. It is the right of the majority, currently comprising 92 percent of the population, that the ruler selected be an official representative of the [Muslim] caliph."[14] This statement was a fantasy at best, since not only was Egypt at this point under

[10] The immediate occasion for the Coptic Conference was the murder of Prime Minster Butrus Ghali, who was a Copt and appointed by the Khedive in cooperation with the British colonial office. For differing views on his murder, see Behrens-Abouseif, "Political Situation of the Copts," 197; and Seikaly, "Prime Minister and Assassin."

[11] It is striking that the term *aqalliyya* is not mentioned once in the subsequently published proceedings of the First Coptic Conference. Habib, *al-Mu'tamir al-Qibti al-Awwal*. The term *al-umma al-qibtiyya* had been in circulation since at least the late nineteenth century, as evident in the writings of Yacoub Nakhla Rufila, a leading Coptic reformer and author of the influential history of Copts *al-Tarikh al-Ummah al-Qibtiyya*.

[12] The Communal Council (Majlis al-Milli), established in 1874, comprised members from the Coptic aristocracy and landed elite. Their aim was to reform the ecclesiastical structure of the Church by limiting the role of the clergy in the adjudication of Coptic family law and the administration of Coptic charities and schools. The Coptic pope and the Holy Synod fiercely opposed the Council, and tried to disband it throughout the nineteenth century. It was not until the mid-twentieth century that the Church was successful in asserting its control over the Council (see below) and absorbing the membership into its clerical structure. For an insightful discussion of the struggle between Coptic clerics and laity, see Nakhla Rufila, *al-Tarikh al-Ummah al-Qibtiyya*; El-Khawaga, "The Laity at the Heart of the Coptic Clerical Reform"; and Seikaly, "Coptic Communal Reform."

[13] A quotation from Shaykh Ali Yusuf, the editor of *al-Mu'ayyid* and the leader of the Constitutional Reform Party. Ibrahim, *The Copts of Egypt*, 56. A number of Islamic writers in the past and the present contest this assessment. For example, Tariq al-Bishri, a leading Egyptian jurist and historian writes, "Despite the charge that the Coptic Conference was a cleaving apart of national unity, all or a majority of those who participated in it were devoted to its consolidation . . . [and] to serve the joint interest of the collective." Bishri, *al-Muslimun wa al-Aqbat*, 105.

[14] *al-Mu'ayyid*, "al-Mu'tamir al-Qibti wa Matalib al-Aqbat," April 3, 1911, 39. Other national newspapers that engaged in this debate were *al-Ahram*, *al-Watan*, *Masr*, *al-Istiqlal*, *Wadi al-Nil*, and *al-Akhbar*.

de facto British control, but the supposed "caliph" (an allusion to the Ottoman sultan) exerted no control over Egypt and the Ottoman Empire was on the brink of dissolution. Statements such as these buttressed the fear among Copts that Muslims fully intended to exploit their numerical advantage to uphold their premodern religious supremacy.

Copts responded to Muslim exclusionary claims with a version of their own grounded in a Herderesque mapping of lineage, blood, and territory that posited Copts as the direct descendants of the ancient pharaohs and Arab Muslims as foreign invaders. Responding to *al-Mu'ayyid*'s pronouncement, the Coptic newspaper *al-Watn* asserted, "The Copts *are* the true Egyptians. They are the real masters of the country. All those who have set their foot on Egyptian soil, be they Arabs, Turks, French, or British, are nothing but invaders. The originators of this nation are the Copts. . . . Whoever calls this country an Islamic country means to disregard the rights of the Copts and to abuse them in their own fatherland. Not one of them would accept such a thing."[15] This view was parasitical upon European theories of race and eugenics that French and British Egyptologists had popularized, theories that enjoyed a large following among Coptic separatists.[16] The early Egyptologists had represented Copts as an indigenous race that had suffered plunderous invasions over the centuries by various barbarous races that came from across the Sinai. Key among the intruders were the "Hebraic types," the purported ancestors of modern Arabs, who polluted the purity of the "ancient Egyptian race" through intermarriage and miscegenation.[17] This understanding of Egyptian history for some translated into a mandate to free their homeland from the control of Arab Muslims.

Even though this perspective enjoyed wide support among the Anglican Christian Missionary Society (CMS), it was opposed by the British Consul General at the time, Sir Eldon Gorst (1907–11). Gorst warned that Copts should not be treated as a racially distinct community and that the power of Coptic elites should not be underestimated.[18] This provoked an organized backlash against Gorst in the British press. Kyriakos Mikhail, a prominent Coptic journalist in London, mobilized a wide-ranging campaign, in concert with the Anglican Church and the CMS, to write telegrams and letters to British parliamentarians to garner support for the "Coptic

---

[15] Quoted in Behrens-Abouseif, "Political Situation of the Copts," 195–96, emphasis added.

[16] At the time, Egyptian secular nationalists (such as Taha Hussein and Salama Musa) also embraced the idea that ancient Egyptians were a race and regarded the pharaonic civilization as far more important to the constitution of Egyptians than the Islamic one. Sedra, "Copts and the Millet Partnership," 11.

[17] Bayly, "Representing Copts and Muhammadans," 172–73. See also Sedra, "Imagining an Imperial Race"; and Reid, *Whose Pharaohs?*

[18] Gorst had released a report that showed that even though Copts comprised only 7 percent of the population, they made up 30 percent of educated Egyptians and controlled 19 percent of the economy. Behrens-Abouseif, "Political Situation of the Copts," 198.

Question."[19] Mikhail argued that Copts had been able to preserve their racial purity because of their commitment to endogamy, keeping "their blood pure from admixture with semi-barbarous Arabs and savage Kurds . . . [who had introduced the] licentiousness of Mohammedan family life . . . in the country."[20] The characterization of Copts as a race even made it into the 1917 population census, where it remained until 1959, when it was replaced with the designation *ta'ifa*.[21]

While much of this history is known among scholars of Egypt, I want to reflect on its significance in light of the arguments and questions at the heart of this book. First, note that in modern Egypt, the demand for minority rights (or opposition to it) has always been entangled with the struggle for national sovereignty, and never autonomous of the concepts, practices, and policies that Western powers promoted. As the debate I have reviewed above shows, Western religious and secular discourses were crucial to the construction of the minority problem in Egypt. The political imaginary of Copts and Muslims alike at the turn of the twentieth century had become saturated with European depictions of Islam and Christianity. Just as the European discourse on race and eugenics undergirded the Coptic claim to racial purity, the Western portrayal of Islam as a barbaric and uncivilized religion was the foil against which declarations of Muslim glory were crafted. Similarly, the fact that the fate of "Eastern Christians" had been indelibly sutured to European beneficence since the eighteenth century was crucial to how Copts articulated their cause, how Muslims opposed it, and how Egyptian nationalists critiqued the granting of minority rights. In summary, none of these positions is comprehensible without an adequate appreciation of the power that the British colonial government, the missionaries, and European public opinion exerted in shaping the self-understanding of Egyptians and the field of political action within which they operated.

Second, I want to draw attention to the fact that the liberal and illiberal strains internal to nationalist ideology colored the self-understanding of Muslims and Christians and their perceptions of each other. Even though the discourse of national sovereignty produced the best ideals one associates with this age—self-determination, equality before the law, representative government—it also generated new forms of distinctions and exclusions, key among them Coptic assertions of racial purity as well as Muslim claims to majoritarian rule.[22] The ideology of national kinship that undergirded the

---

[19] Notably, the CMS was eventually successful in discrediting Gorst in the mind of the British public for his purported lack of sympathy for fellow Christians. See Bayly, "Representing Copts and Muhammadans." See the discussion of Mikhail's campaign in Ibrahim, *The Copts of Egypt*, 46–48.

[20] Quoted in Bayly, "Representing Copts and Muhammadans," 173.

[21] Shami, "*Aqalliyya*/Minority in Modern Egyptian Discourse," 160.

[22] The Muslim claim of majoritarian supremacy was quite distinct from the logic of Muslim-Christian inequality in the Ottoman Empire, where the state made no pretense to represent the people or to treat

promise of formal equality for all also produced forms of religio-cultural identity that were far more exclusionary than the hierarchies it sought to dismantle. Civil and political equality as the sovereign right of the people had yet to be debated legally in Egypt, but when it was discussed during the drafting of the first Egyptian constitution in 1923, it was built upon the duality of this modern prejudice and promise.

Can Minorities Be Represented?

When the British granted partial independence to Egypt in 1922, the first challenge Coptic Christians faced was how best to make the transition from a past in which they were unequal to Muslims to a present that made "citizenship" the measure of Muslim-Christian relations.[23] For the Copts who embraced the promise of civil and political equality, the challenge was how to forge a political future that would level past historical inequalities without reifying their difference from the Muslim majority. The designation *minority* seemed to open the door to the latter, while formal political equality threatened to bury past and present religious inequalities without adequate redress. The majoritarian tilt of a parliamentary form of government seemed susceptible to enshrining premodern Muslim privilege under a new secular regime.[24] In 1923 the Constitutional Committee considered two proposals that addressed the unequal status of national minorities. One option suggested that Christians, Jews, and Bedouins retain a certain degree of administrative control over their communal institutions. The other proposal advocated that minorities be granted proportionate representation in the parliament (*majlis al-nawab*), either through popular election or through executive or legislative appointment.[25] While the Jewish and Bedouin communities were part of the debate, it was Coptic Christians, as the largest and most powerful minority, who occupied center stage.

all religions equally. The discourse of popular sovereignty and representative government, while built upon the principle of equality for all citizens, also enables a majoritarian chauvinism that is historically unprecedented in its violence and exclusivity. On this point, see Mann, *The Dark Side of Democracy*.

[23] Despite formal independence granted to Egypt, the British continued to occupy Egypt militarily and to control its political, fiscal, and administrative affairs until 1952. The Egyptian monarchy (1922–52) collaborated with the British and opposed the anticolonial movement led by the Wafd Party. It was with the Free Officers coup in 1952 that British privileges were finally suspended, and the last British troops left in 1956.

[24] The Muslim minority in India had faced similar challenges, but was able to negotiate with the British to create independent electoral districts in the Muslim-majority areas. As is widely acknowledged, this provided the basis for the partition between India and Pakistan, each ruled by a decisive majority of Hindus and Muslims. For a comparative analysis of the situation of Copts in Egypt and Muslims in India under British rule, see Bayly, "Representing Copts and Muhammadans."

[25] There were also differences in the models proposed to secure proportionate representation in the parliament. For two popular ways of addressing the issue, one proposed by Tawfiq Doss and another by Mahmoud Azmi, see "Kayf Tamaththil al-Aqalliyyat fi al-Barlaman," *al-Watan*, April 25, 1922.

It is important to note at the outset that all the protagonists in the debate faced the impossible challenge of how to redress forms of religious hierarchy in a political and legal system that eschewed religious difference. On the one hand, civil and political equality in front of the law meant that the state had to be indifferent to the religious affiliation of its citizens; on the other hand, insomuch as religious differences and inequalities structured society, state law was called upon to manage and address them. How could a state that sought to eliminate religious inequality do so without making religious difference part of its political vocabulary? A second dilemma emanated from the circular relationship between the nation and the state. Was the state transcendent to the nation or constituted by it? If the state was constituted by the nation, then should its laws not reflect its cultural, religious, and ethnic particularity? The seemingly technical issue of proportionate minority representation in fact encompassed the far deeper question of how religious inequality could be redressed in a polity whose laws were supposed to be indifferent to religion.

The proposed Article 4 of the new constitution guaranteed equal rights to Egypt's religious, ethnic, and linguistic minorities (*al-aqalliyyat*), but it also granted them autonomy over their communal institutions.[26] As I suggested above, the ascendant view among Egyptian nationalists was that both the assignation *minority* and the idea of proportionate representation were colonial ploys. When the British tried to secure their status in the new constitution as the "official protectors" of Egypt's minorities, this impression was further entrenched. Abdel Latif al-Makabati, a prominent member of the Constitutional Committee, cast his objection to Article 4 in this way: "I am not in agreement that the text of our constitution should mention the existence of minorities. If the rights provided in this Article are already established in general for all Egyptian citizens, then such a provision may be used against us and present an opportunity for foreign intervention."[27] Similarly, the president of the Committee, Hussein Rushdie, resolutely declared, "In accord with the principles of the constitution, these minorities have come under the complete protection of the fundamental laws of Egypt. There is no place here for the special English measure for the protection of minorities, and it is not permissible for anyone to interfere in the internal affairs of Egypt."[28] Despite this widely shared sen-

---

[26] Article 4 reads, "Those who possess Egyptian citizenship and are from ethnic, religious, or linguistic minorities have the right in law and in reality to the same treatment and security as enjoyed by other Egyptian nationals. In particular they have the same rights as others to establish or administer or oversee their expenses in the running of charitable or religious or social organizations and schools or other educational institutions and the right to use in them their particular language and to practice their religious rites with freedom." Al-Sharif, *'Ala Hamish al-Dustur*, 16.

[27] Ibid., 16.

[28] Ibid. The Committee went even further and decreed that the British privilege to protect resident foreign nationals (Greeks, Armenians, and Italians) in place since the inception of colonial rule be annulled.

timent, it is noteworthy that the extraterritorial privileges Europeans enjoyed continued until their formal abolition with the passage of the Montreux Convention in 1937.

Tawfiq Doss, a prominent member of the Constitutional Committee who had played a leading role in the Coptic Conference in 1911, tried to detach the fate of the minorities from the colonial legacy and provided a nationalist interpretation. Doss advocated securing minority representation through popular elections (rather than executive appointment) proportionate to their percentage of the population.[29] He argued that the adoption of this measure would not further colonial intervention but safeguard against it.[30] If the government did not ensure that a certain number of minority candidates were included on the electoral list, Doss reasoned, then minority groups might come to feel, rightly or wrongly, that their rights had been violated, thereby opening a rift within the polity and encouraging European powers to intercede on behalf of minorities. It was in the national interest of Egypt to foreclose such an option by taking care of the issue internally. Having minority representatives within governmental bodies, argued Doss, was also a means of addressing their concerns when forming public policy, since the majority was not always aware of such issues and may overlook them, however unintentionally.[31]

Strikingly, the religious identity of the protagonists did not determine their support for or opposition to the principle of minority representation. The Jewish representative on the Constitutional Committee, Yusuf Qatawi Pasha, supported Doss, as did the Anglican Diocese of Egypt, the Coptic Communal Council (Majlis al-Milli), and *al-Jama'iyya al-Khayriyya al-Qibtiyya*, the leading Coptic welfare organization of the time.[32] The stance of the Coptic Orthodox Church's representative on the Constitutional Committee, Anba Yu'annis, remained ambiguous, but Coptic bishops from important dioceses in the country wrote letters supporting the idea of minority representation.[33] The most influential opposition to Doss's proposal came from secular Egyptians (Muslims and Copts).

[29] It is important to point out that the debate over proportionate representation had commenced well before the formation of the Constitutional Committee; the newspaper *al-Watan* had already been publishing articles debating its merits. The issue, however, received wide attention once Doss introduced the idea in the deliberations of the Committee and made his case in the press, which in turn provoked a wide public response. On this background, see al-Bishri, *al-Muslimun wa al-Aqbat*, 216.

[30] "Tamthil al-Aqalliyyat aydan fi Majlis al-Nuwab wa al-Shuyukh," *al-Watan*, May 10, 1922.

[31] al-Sharif, *'Ala Hamish al-Dustur*, 18–20.

[32] On Yusuf Qatawi Pasha's position on this issue, see "Ra'yi Ikhwan al-Isra'iliyyin al-Haqiqi fi Tamthil al-Aqalliyyat," *al-Watan*, June 6, 1922. Yusuf Qatawi Pasha (1861–1942) was a powerful and wealthy businessman, and served as the president of the Sephardic Jewish Community Council of Cairo from 1924 to 1942. Notably, when the state of Israel was established in 1948, the Sephardic Jewish Community Council of Cairo adopted an anti-Zionist position. See Beinin, *The Dispersion of Egyptian Jewry*, 45.

[33] See al-Bishri, *al-Muslimun wa al-Aqbat*, 218.

Abdul Hamid Badawi, a leading member of the Constitutional Committee, made a forceful argument for keeping religious distinctions out of politics, arguing, "The representative [*na'ib*] when in office should represent the nation rather than a particular entity or a sect."[34] Electing representatives because of their religious affiliation would not only violate the principle of state neutrality but lodge religious difference into the heart of politics. Badawi's belief accorded with the liberal conception of the citizen as an abstract individual, shorn of his or her particularity and equal to all before the law. But how was the law to address the historical inequalities that existed between Muslims and non-Muslims without compromising this abstract ideal? In responding to this question, Badawi posited a definitive break between the oppressive authoritarian past and a free democratic future in which religious differences were destined to become extinct:

> We all know that the system we inherited from the past was a monarchical system [*al-nizam al-amiri*] and we lived under the authority of the patron/father and [the vagaries of] his mercy and kindness. When the new period arrived, based on rights, . . . we began to live [in accord with it] and its tradition of mutual understanding and tolerance between the majority and minority. . . . Religious difference is weakening now even among us. And it won't be long before it will be erased from our social relations and all of its traces will be gone. . . . To institute special representation for the minorities is to institute a particular perspective that will cling to itself and lead to the proliferation of differences and divisions. . . . It would be impossible later to get rid of these divisions, which will [in the end] be against the natural progression [of society].[35]

Note how Badawi's statement echoes the assumptions of secularization theory, which predicted that religious distinctions in modern society would eventually become inconsequential as religion was individualized and privatized (that is, secularized). Insomuch as proportionate minority representation enshrines religion in politics, in Badawi's view this was tantamount to tampering with the natural flow of history and obstructing its telos. Other secular liberals of the time shared Badawi's position; key among them was Saad Zaghloul, the powerful leader of the 1919 Revolution and the Wafd Party, which enjoyed wide Coptic support.[36] Zaghloul made clear that it was *religious* difference—as opposed to other kinds of social differences—that

[34] al-Sharif, *'Ala Hamish al-Dustur*, 20.
[35] Ibid., 22–23.
[36] Zaghloul was a proponent of national equality for all Egyptians, captured in the famous statement that became the Wafd Party's platform: "Egypt belongs to Copts as well as Muslims. All have a right to the same freedom and the same privileges." Quoted in Wakin, *A Lonely Minority*, 17.

was destined for social extinction. While defining groups according to their social and material interests was useful because they pertained to law and economy, he argued that the "representation of groups divided by religion, but otherwise united in social and material interests, made no sense"; it would only sow religious sectarianism and factionalism.[37] William Weesa, another key Coptic figure in the Wafd Party, agreed with Zaghloul, declaring, "Copts are not a minority because they belong to no other nation than Egypt [like the Austrians in Germany or Armenians in Turkey], nor do they want a government that represents anyone but the Egyptian people, nor do they claim a language other than Arabic."[38] Ultimately, it was the Wafd Party's opposition that was most decisive in killing the proposal of minority representation in the 1923 constitution.[39]

Among those who articulated a trenchant critique of the new constitution's failure to redress religious inequalities was Mahmoud Azmi, a Muslim by birth who is known in Egyptian history for his *laïque* commitments.[40] Even though Azmi remained a strong advocate of the separation of religion and state throughout his life, he did not believe that Egyptian society was at a stage in its development where people would accept it. Azmi wrote a number of articles in prominent Egyptian dailies challenging the idea that religious distinctions were on the wane, pointing to the myriad ways in which religion mattered to all Egyptians. More importantly, he argued that, as the majority religion, Islam exerted an inordinate influence in the state's conduct, to the detriment of the minorities. A clear example of this was Article 149 of the constitution that declared Islam to be the religion of the state, which all members of the Constitutional Committee (Muslims and non-Muslims alike) had approved unanimously. Azmi contended that Article 149 had, in effect, secured a formal and enduring place for Islam in the state's structure, thereby transforming religious groups (*tawa'if diniyya*) into political groups (*tawa'if siyasiyya*).[41] Against Badawi, therefore, Azmi argued that, far from consecrating religious difference in politics, minority representation would combat the consequences of what was already an unfair system.

[37] al-Bishri, *al-Muslimun wa al-Aqbat*, 223.

[38] William Weesa, "al-Aqbat laysu Aqalliyya," *Jaridat Misr*, September 3, 1952, no. 15431, 1–4.

[39] When the Wafd Party's Coptic candidates won more seats than their share of the population in the 1924 and 1928 elections, this seemed to vindicate the decision from 1923 to reject the principle of proportionate minority representation. Never again in Egyptian history have Copts enjoyed this kind of popular electoral support, nor has any political party commanded comparable Coptic following.

[40] Mahmoud Azmi was trained in law in France, helped establish a number of key Egyptian newspapers and journals during his life, and was the official representative to the United Nations for the government of Gamal Abdel Nasser. Throughout his life he remained opposed to the idea of Islam as the state religion and advocated replacing religion-based family law with a uniform civil code. See Milad Hannah Zaki, "Mahmud Azmi: Qa'id Ma'rka Madda Din al-Dawla fi Dustur 1923," *al-Masry al-Youm*, May 3, 2012, www.almasryalyoum.com/node/815131.

[41] "Tamthil al-Aqalliyyat Aydan: Amr la Budda Minhu," *al-Watan*, May 11, 1922, no. 8210, 2.

The problem for Azmi was that Egyptian society was riven by religious inequalities, and failing to provide the legal means to address them in the 1923 constitution was to kill the nationalist project before it was born. The continuation of religion-based family laws in Egypt was an important marker of this problem. While he understood the persistence of these laws as an expression of the social importance of religion to Christians, Jews, and Muslims alike, he also saw family law as a way for the Egyptian state to perpetuate inequality between Muslims and non-Muslims—evident in the policy that allowed Muslim men to marry Christian women (in accord with the shari'a) while prohibiting the obverse. For Azmi, this amounted to a legally condoned violation of the sanctity of Christian family life that was foundational to their community.[42] Azmi believed that the ultimate solution to this problem lay in abolishing religion-based family laws altogether and instituting a secular code applied uniformly regardless of one's religious affiliation. Given that this idea was unacceptable to most Egyptians (Muslims and non-Muslims), he argued, a pragmatic interim solution was to give the minorities a guaranteed place in the parliament so that they could contest the prejudicial tilt of Islamic family law.

Among Azmi's most contentious interlocutors was a fellow secularist, Aziz Mirhim, a Copt who criticized Azmi for subscribing to a static understanding of Egyptian society as eternally mired in religiosity.[43] Instead, Mirhim prophesied, "The existence of majority and minority in Egypt, which are a product of history, will not survive for long and will disappear as was the case in Western countries. They will lose their place of importance among social and economic groups that are the basis of future political parties. It is incumbent upon our laws and our constitution to assist in this development and not impede it with backward ideas and depraved beliefs. *Religion is about belief and not about politics.*"[44] (Note how the last sentence succinctly paraphrases John Locke's prescription that religion belongs in the private domain while politics should deal with state and civic matters.) In response to Mirhim's accusation that Azmi had shed his secular ideals for pragmatic politics, Azmi shot back that he was no different from Coptic members of the Constitutional Committee who decided *not* to oppose Article 149 so as not to upset the Muslim majority.[45]

[42] Mahmoud Azmi, *Jaridat al-Istiqlal*, June 3, 1922.

[43] Mirhim presided over a meeting of 5000 Copts held on May 30, 1922, that issued a statement calling for a uniform secular civil law for all Egyptians. While agreeing with the goals of the statement, Azmi contended that Egyptian society was not ready yet for such a change. See al-Bishri, *al-Muslimun wa al-Aqbat*, 214.

[44] Aziz Mirhim, "Tamthil al-Aqalliyat: Radd 'ala Mahmud Azmi," *al-Ahram*, May 26, 1922, emphasis added. See also Aziz Mirhim, "Lajnat al-Dustur: Tasda'a Wahdat al-Umma," *al-Ahram*, May 11, 1922.

[45] Azmi, *Jaridat al-Istiqlal*. See also Bishri, *al-Muslimun wa al-Aqbat*, 213–15.

Taha Hussein, the leading secular intellectual of twentieth-century Arab thought, published a widely circulated article attacking Mahmoud Azmi's argument that minority representation was a necessary antidote to the dominance of Islam in Egyptian law. Hussein dismissed Article 149 ("Islam is the state religion") as nothing more than a "Platonic text" that had no effect on reality, its value merely symbolic and superficial.[46] As an Arab nationalist, Hussein believed that the elements that united all Egyptians (language, culture, and history) far outweighed what divided them (religion).[47] It was precisely this assessment that informed the legendary statement made by Makram Ebeid, a leading Coptic figure in the Wafd Party, that he was a Muslim by country and a Christian by religion.[48] Going against this regnant nationalist sentiment, Azmi pointedly challenged Hussein's casting of Article 149 as merely symbolic: "Why not then permit the constitution to contain the provision for minority representation as long as it too is understood to be a theoretical, figurative, and Platonic formulation destined to lose its significance with time?"[49]

As for Azmi's argument that the religion-based family laws of Egypt enshrined Muslim-Christian inequality, Taha Hussein contended that these laws would eventually be subsumed under a shared secular civil law; the role of religion would then be limited to ritually blessing marital unions, as was the case in the West. At one point in France, it had been impossible for Jews and Protestants to intermarry, Hussein contended, but just as this had changed with the passage of time in France, it would in Egypt as well. To base an entire political order on elements of a society that were destined to vanish was to will it into stagnation, Hussein concluded.[50] Hussein's arguments ventriloquize the secular certitude prevalent at the time that religion was destined to wither away in modern societies, a milestone that Europe had already reached but that non-Western societies had to judiciously strive to achieve. Note that in this view, like the nation-state, political secularism is teleological in that it projects its own future and assumes its inevitability. Liberals like Badawi and Hussein hoped that over time the nation would mimetically reproduce the state's forced indifference to religion. In so doing, they tried to depoliticize *religious inequalities* because doing otherwise would have called the telos of secularism into question.

---

[46] Taha Hussein, "al-Aqalliyya wa al-Akthariyya," *al-Ahram*, June 8, 1922, no. 13765, 1–2.

[47] This sentiment was widely shared among Arab nationalists of the Middle East at the time. For example, Christians in Syria, who had long-standing grievances against the Muslim majority, advocated for the adoption of the prophet Muhammad's birthday as a national holiday in an effort to unite Arabaphone communities against French colonial rule. White, *The Emergence of Minorities in the Middle East*, 52.

[48] Hasan, *Christians versus Muslims*, 39.

[49] Mahmoud Azmi, "al-Akthariyya wa al-Aqalliyya: Mawjudatan wa sa-tabqiyyan bi-Raghm al-Bara'a al-Bayaniyya," *al-Watan*, June 8, 1922, no. 8233, 2.

[50] Hussein, "al-Aqalliyya wa al-Akthariyya," 1–2.

Mahmoud Azmi was unique among his peers for recognizing the tension between the secular principle of state neutrality toward religion and the sociology of the nation that pulled in the opposite direction; for the former to take root, the hierarchy of religious differences had to be eliminated from Egyptian society. This, however, was not possible in Azmi's view, given Egypt's level of social development. While Azmi himself cast this as a sign of Egypt's incomplete secularization, it behooves us to ask whether this was a uniquely Egyptian problem, and to what extent it is a constitutive feature of the liberal secular state as such.

It is useful here to recall Marx's critique of the liberal democratic state that I discussed at some length in the introduction.[51] As Marx pointed out, the liberal (political/constitutional) state does not so much eliminate religion from its operative rationality as relocate it from "the sphere of public law to that of private law."[52] Under this arrangement, even though religion can no longer serve as the basis for political office, religious inequalities are allowed to proliferate unchecked in civil society (not unlike economic inequalities) and striate political conduct. Thus even as the liberal/political state *depoliticizes* religion, it also allows religion to define civic life and serve as the basis of interpersonal *differentiation*.[53] Marx's diagnosis of the double movement that characterizes all secular liberal polities helps us appreciate the impossible task that Egyptians like Azmi, Badawi, and Doss faced: they had to devise religiously neutral laws while at the same time attending to religion's ongoing striation of national and social life. Note that none of them challenged the sovereign state's prerogative to regulate religion in social and political life. By looking to the state to either preserve or eliminate religion from politics, they all conceded the foundational premise of political secularism.

Religious Difference in Postcolonial Egypt

Much has changed in Egypt since the 1923 constitutional debate, when the future seemed pregnant with possibilities. No one in contemporary Egypt dares to predict that religion will disappear from the social and political life of the country, nor is the proclamation "Islam is the state religion" viewed as merely symbolic, *pace* Taha Hussein. The legal status of Islam has been progressively elevated since the 1920s, and Islamic shari'a is now "the chief source" of Egyptian legislation (see chapter 4). Religious differences have become more entrenched and polarized in postcolonial Egypt,

[51] Marx, "On the Jewish Question."
[52] Ibid., 35.
[53] Ibid.

and the promise of political and civil equality is a receding mirage for Copts and Muslims alike. Most scholars tend to read this accentuation of religious identity as the failure of the secular project to take hold in Egypt, its promise hijacked by authoritarian rulers and religious conservatives. In what follows I will challenge this assessment by showing that the political and economic forces that have led to the current impasse cannot be described as religious in any simple sense. Rather, a variety of factors have colluded to exacerbate the majority-minority inequality located at the heart of the system of secular liberal governance. While Islamic concepts and practices have played a role, far more consequential is their realignment to fit a governing rationality that holds out the promise of abstract equality while at the same time allowing religious inequalities to flourish in the social life of the polity. Before I elaborate this argument, however, it is important to lay out some of the key transformations wrought in majority-minority relations since the 1923 constitutional debate.

Despite the sense that British rule was nearing its end in 1923, Egypt did not gain full independence until 1952. During this period, the anticolonial movement slowly began to fracture along confessional lines. The creation of Islamic political organizations, such as Shabab Muhammad and the Muslim Brotherhood in the 1930s and 1940s, was widely perceived by Copts as exclusionary; this, in turn, spawned parallel Christian organizations such as Jama'at al-Ummah al-Qibtiyyah. The latter's slogan, "God is our King, Egypt our country, the Gospels our law and the Cross our badge, and death for the sake of Christ our greatest hope," paralleled the Brotherhood's motto, "The Quran is our constitution, Arabic our language, and death in the way of God our greatest hope."[54] When Egypt gained full sovereignty, there were no Copts among the group of military officers ("the Free Officers") who ousted the British, in part because the army was overwhelmingly Muslim.[55]

Following the coup, Gamal Abdel Nasser, the first president of independent Egypt, created an administrative structure that did not draw upon the rank and file of the nationalist movement that had been at the forefront of the anticolonial struggle (most potently represented by the Wafd Party).[56] Instead, it was built around his charismatic personality and a small coterie of loyal insiders who were averse to sharing power and suppressed any form of political dissent. Nasser's intolerance of critics applied to Copts and Muslims alike; just as he banned the Wafd Party, he also brutally crushed the Muslim Brotherhood.[57] The Wafd had been consistently successful in electing

---

[54] Gorman, *Historians, State, and Politics*, 170.

[55] In 1951, only three Copts occupied positions of leadership in the army. Bishri, *al-Muslimun wa al-Aqbat*, 797.

[56] Ibid., 797–99.

[57] On Nasser's repression of the Muslim Brotherhood, see Mitchell, *The Society of the Muslim Brothers*.

Copts to public office from 1924 to 1942, but with its dissolution a singularly important avenue for Coptic participation in the political life of the country was shut down.
While Nasser paid homage to the idea of proportional representation by appointing
loyalist Copts to the parliament,[58] he systematically undermined the authority of the
Communal Council (Majlis al-Milli) that had sought to democratize the ecclesiastical
structure of the Coptic Orthodox Church. When Nasser shifted control of religious
endowments from the hands of Coptic laity to the Church and subjected membership
in the Communal Council to the pope's approval, he essentially enshrined the Coptic
Church as the main representative of the community.[59] Nasser's quasi-socialist program also had mixed results. On the one hand, it created a strong sense of national
identity by giving all Egyptians access to public goods and resources; on the other
hand, his agrarian and economic reforms weakened the power of the Coptic aristocracy, which had been a leading voice in the Community Council's attempt to reform
the Coptic Church.[60] Nasser was not a religious ideologue and his policies did not aim
to discriminate against Coptic Christians. His rule, however, had the overall effect of
silencing the plurality of Coptic voices that had been at the forefront of the nationalist
movement in the 1920s. In return, the Coptic Orthodox Church (under Pope Kyrol-
los VI) essentially guaranteed support for Nasser, while securing its interests through
a church-state entente.

After Nasser's death (in 1970), the two subsequent regimes reinforced many of the
trends he had institutionalized, thus indelibly linking religious difference to the issue
of citizenship. If Nasser's policies are credited with undermining the social power of
lay Coptic elites, then Anwar Sadat's regime (1970–81) is held responsible for confes-
sionalizing Egyptian politics. It is commonly acknowledged that in order to counter
the Nasserite legacy and leftist opposition, Sadat facilitated the rise of Islamist politics, which then quickly spun out of his control. Not only did Islamic political groups
become the most vociferous critics of Sadat's regime, but a group of Islamist soldiers
from his own army ended up killing him. Sadat is also known for his dramatic standoff with Pope Shenouda III (d. 2012), whom he summarily deposed as the head of the
Coptic Orthodox Church in 1981 and sent into rural exile, where the pope remained
until his return in 1983 under President Hosni Mubarak.

In contrast to Sadat, the Mubarak regime (1981–2011) resurrected the church-
state entente that Nasser had pioneered. This allowed the Coptic Orthodox Church

[58] Elsässer, *The Coptic Question in the Mubarak Era*, 79–81.
[59] On Nasser's circumscription of the Communal Council's authority, see Tadros, *Copts at the Crossroads*, 62–66. On paper, lay Copts are still supposed to elect the leadership of the Communal Council, but in effect it is the pope and his coterie of bishops who appoint the members. See Sedra, "Class Cleavages and Ethnic Conflict."
[60] Tadros, "Vicissitudes in the Entente."

(under Pope Shenouda III) to consolidate its control over the social and civic life of Copts while pledging its allegiance to Mubarak and his corrupt National Democratic Party.[61] Shenouda's papacy (1971–2012) is also credited with integrating Coptic laity into the ecclesiastical structure of the Church, and with creating a vast network of civic and communal organizations for Copts.[62] In 1999, when Mubarak was still in power, Paul Sedra described this arrangement aptly: "Shenouda is dependent upon Mubarak, the church hierarchy is dependent upon Shenouda, and the Coptic community is dependent upon the hierarchy for social services and political leadership."[63] Following a pattern that Nasser had set, Mubarak appointed Copts to the parliament (often with the approval of the Church), making a mockery of the principle of proportional minority representation. It is not surprising that when anti-Mubarak demonstrations broke out in January 2011, Pope Shenouda III urged his followers not to participate—a call that large numbers of Copts ignored as they joined the mobilization that overthrew the Mubarak regime.[64]

One of the fundamental shifts that Sadat's regime initiated and that Mubarak consolidated was the privatization of the economy and public goods. This had the unintended consequence of making religious institutions central to civic and social life in Egypt. While Sadat's presidency opened the Egyptian economy to private investment (foreign and domestic), Mubarak's administration essentially gutted public institutions (health, welfare, and education) under the tripartite agenda of economic liberalization, deregulation, and privatization.[65] It is in this context that Egypt witnessed the largest growth of religious nongovernmental organizations (NGOs)—both Christian and Islamic—that have come to provide the kind of services that in the past had been the purview of the state.[66]

Shenouda's papacy is widely known for having established a vast network of social services for Copts that, in effect, helped secure the Church's monopoly as the

---

[61] Under Pope Shenouda, the clergy mobilized parishes to secure the Coptic vote for National Democratic Party candidates.

[62] A key example of Shenouda's project is the "youth bishopric," created in the 1980s, to provide a vast infrastructure of support for Coptic youth in the fields of education, entertainment, and religious activities. See El-Khawaga, "The Laity at the Heart of the Coptic Clerical Reform," and "The Political Dynamics of the Copts."

[63] Sedra, "Class Cleavages and Ethnic Conflict," 228.

[64] Toward the end of Mubarak's reign, the entente between Mubarak and the Church had begun to show signs of tension. On this point, see Tadros, *Copts at the Crossroads*, chap. 4.

[65] The largest privatization of state-owned enterprises occurred between 1996 and 2000; it peaked again in 2005 under the rubric of "government reform." Dahi, "The Political Economy of the Egyptian and Arab Revolt," 47–53. For an overall account of this process, see Rutherford, *Egypt after Mubarak*.

[66] Few studies exist of this phenomenal transformation of Egyptian social life. For a rare and important sociological survey that documented the expansion of Muslim-Christian organizations, but has not been updated since its publication, see Abul Fattah, *al-Hala al-Diniyya fi Masr*.

sole representative of the Coptic community, with the figure of the pope as its icon and savior.[67] Across rural and urban Egypt, there are numerous Coptic community-development centers, vocational schools, and literacy and employment-assistance programs that provide poor and middle-class Copts with the kind of support that makes life possible when the state abandons its public mandate. Even in public universities, the great incubator of national solidarity, the Church provides the necessary infrastructure for Coptic students. All these services have tied Coptic Christians to the Church far more than the Egyptian state, which provides little, if any, support for its citizens. This trend has gone hand in hand with the simultaneous proliferation of Islamic NGOs across the country that provide parallel services to Muslims, with one key difference. Because there is no single ecclesiastical center akin to the Church, multiple Islamic networks compete for the allegiance of those they serve. In short, the cumulative effect of the *privatization* of the state is the *public* role the Church and the mosque have come to play in Egypt over the course of the past forty years.

No account of Egyptian communal strife is complete, however, without addressing the steady erosion of political and civil liberties for Muslims and Copts alike in the postcolonial period. A key marker of this erosion is the almost continuous rule of emergency law that has normalized a political culture of arbitrary arrests, imprisonment, and state torture against political and social dissidents.[68] Emergency rule, initially proclaimed under Nasser in 1958, has over time created a network of state security (*al-Mahakamat Amn al-Dawla*) and military courts (*al-Mahakim al-'Askariyya*) that regularly bypass civilian courts to prosecute a range of ordinary criminal offenses, forms of political and social activism, and, since the 1980s, even religious practices that the government deems threatening to public order.[69] Given this systemic violation of political and civil rights, it is not surprising that having the protection of a powerful institution like the Coptic Orthodox Church is crucial to surviving state violence. This, in turn, has only entrenched the Church's power and helped solidify the state-church entente in maintaining the status quo. One of the leading demands

[67] See el-Khawaga, "The Laity at the Heart of the Coptic Clerical Reform"; Hasan, *Christians versus Muslims*, 57–102; Sedra, "Class Cleavages and Ethnic Conflict"; and Guirguis and van Doorn-Harder, *Emergence of the Modern Coptic Papacy*, part 2.
[68] Emergency rule first emerged in the form of martial law in Egypt under the British in 1914. The 1923 constitution provided for its legality, and martial law was declared subsequently in 1948 (at the time of the Israel-Arab War) and again in 1952 (after the Free Officers revolution). It was in 1958 under Nasser that martial law gave way to emergency law and has remained in effect until now (with the exception of a short period between 1980 and 1981, and then again in 2012). See Reza, "Endless Emergency."
[69] For example, the small number of Egyptian Shi'a (less than 1 percent of the population) have been systematically arrested and tortured by the state security police for holding "heretical Islamic beliefs." For a report that documents these violations, see EIPR, "Freedom of Belief."

of the revolt in 2011 was the dissolution of emergency law and the state security and military courts, but since the uprising's collapse they remain powerfully in place.

The militarization and securitization of the Egyptian state have been discursively and strategically produced as a fight against "Islamic terrorism" since the 1980s, when Islamic militancy was at its historical peak. Despite having decisively defeated these groups in the early 1990s, the Mubarak regime continued to deploy anti-Islamist rhetoric as a means to suppress all forms of political dissent. With the events of 9/11 and the US-sponsored "global war on terror," the Egyptian security state received a boon in that it was able to render its domestic brutality as a service to its prime geopolitical patron.[70] Notably, the period between 2001 and 2011 marked not only the security state's most vicious entrenchment but also the accelerated privatization of Egyptian public resources, which were sold off at highly subsidized prices that even offended some sectors of the national bourgeoisie.[71] In this organized transfer of public wealth to private hands, the Egyptian military has been a key partner and beneficiary.[72] The protests in January 2011 that unseated Mubarak were in large part an outcry against the conditions of poverty and destitution in which most Egyptian now live. The same forces that had kept the dissenters in check for so many years, however, were quick to hijack this dissent.

The military coup that overthrew the first elected government of Mohammed Morsi (from the Muslim Brotherhood) in June 2013, with General Abdel Fatah al-Sisi at the helm, was also cast as a fight against "terrorism."[73] As the military killed over a thousand people who protested the coup and proceeded to ban the Muslim Brotherhood as a terrorist organization, arresting its leadership and seizing its assets, the Coptic Orthodox Church lined up to pledge its support for the new rulers.[74] Despite pockets of dissent among Coptic Christians against the military takeover, the Church played an old tune in its ongoing dance with Egypt's ruling class. When General Sisi ran his campaign for presidency in May 2014, the Church called upon its flock to cast

---

[70] The Egyptian military receives over $1.3 billion of annual aid from the US government. US Department of State, "Foreign Military Financing Account Summary."

[71] Dahi, "The Political Economy of the Egyptian and Arab Revolt," 51.

[72] A presidential decree (under Mubarak) in 1997 gave "the military the right to all undeveloped lands in the country, making it the largest landowner and developer in Egypt's history." *Cairo Observer*, "From Tahrir Square to Emaar Square," February 23, 2014, http://cairobserver.com/post/77533681187/from-tahrir-square-to-emaar-square.

[73] For a critical account of the military coup, see Esam al-Amin, "The Grand Scam: Spinning Egypt's Military Coup," *Counterpunch*, July 19–21, 2013, www.counterpunch.org/2013/07/19/the-grand-scam-spinning-egypts-military-coup/.

[74] On the massacre, see Kristin Chick, "Egyptian Authorities Pave Over Rabaa Massacre," *Christian Science Monitor*, November 14, 2013, www.csmonitor.com/World/Middle-East/2013/1114/Egyptian-authorities-pave-over-Rabaa-massacre.

their vote for Sisi as a service to Christianity.[75] This alliance between the state and the Church is highly unstable because Egypt's rulers are no more interested in giving Coptic Christians their due than Egyptian Muslims.

The panoply of prejudicial laws that govern non-Muslim religious life remains in place, enforced by the state police and security apparatus. Not only are Coptic Christians underrepresented at all levels of public office, but a range of soft and hard laws restrict the construction of new churches and prohibit conversion from Islam to Christianity, while Islamic family law continues to prevail in marriages across Christian sects (see chapter 3).[76] The situation is much more difficult for poor Copts than for the elite, whose wealth can buy them access and security.[77] Perhaps one of the most disturbing developments is the gradual increase in acts of violence committed against Coptic Christians over the last two decades.[78] While these attacks had been on the rise during Mubarak's rule, they have continued unabated under the current military junta that presents itself as the secular guarantor of national unity. As before, human-rights organizations charge that the national State Security Intelligence Services (SSI) and the police are complicit in these attacks, and the perpetrators of violence remain unprosecuted.[79] Perhaps most aggravating for a generation of young Copts is the way in which the Coptic Orthodox Church helps forestall legal investigation or prosecution of such crimes. Instead, in collusion with the government, Church officials force the victims to informally settle such conflicts through publicly staged "reconciliation meetings" (*jalsat al-sulh*) that allow the perpetrators to go free in exchange for issuing an apology.[80] The Coptic Church's collusion with the security state bodes ill for the

[75] On the Church's support for the military coup, see Georges Fahmi, *The Coptic Church and Politics in Egypt*, Carnegie Middle East Center, December 18, 2014, http://carnegie-mec.org/2014/12/18/coptic-church-and-politics-in-egypt.

[76] A large number of violent attacks on Copts involve the construction or rehabilitation of churches, which is strictly regulated by a law that dates back to Ottoman times and was later amended by the British in 1934. See Sharkey, *American Evangelicals*, 59.

[77] Islamists often exploit the existence of wealthy Copts to argue that there is no religious discrimination in Egypt. See, for example, the statements made by Muntasir al-Ziyat, an influential Islamist lawyer on a television show hosted by *al-Jazeera*. See "al-Mas'ala al-Qibtiyya wa Mustaqbal al-Ta'ayush al-Dini fi Masr," *al-Jazeera*, June 19, 2008, www.aljazeera.net/home/print/0353e88a-286d-4266-82c6-6094179ea26d/14c505e0-4151-4c12-836b-aaf76eaf41c7.

[78] The year before the uprising in January 2011, the EIPR reported that there had been a steady escalation in Muslim attacks on religious minorities, which the government systemically ignored by allowing the perpetrators to go unprosecuted and by failing to provide adequate police protection to the victims. EIPR, "Two Years of Sectarian Violence."

[79] See EIPR, "Taqrir al-Ta'ifiyya" and "Crimes in al-Amiriyya."

[80] The "Abu Fana controversy" is one example of this state-church collusion. In May 2008, a group of Muslims attacked the historic Abu Fana monastery in Upper Egypt over a land dispute in which one Muslim was killed, several monks were injured, and the buildings were desecrated. Despite public calls for an investigation, Pope Shenouda III entered into secret negotiations with the government over the land dispute in exchange for which all the accused were allowed to go free. Instead, a public "reconciliation meeting" was staged between Muslims and Christians of the town under the watchful eyes of the

future because any viable plan for Muslim-Christian coexistence cannot be forged without dismantling the governing regime.

We may easily understand the entrenchment of religious identity in postcolonial Egypt as an inevitable product of the slow and steady dissolution of the secular promise of the modern state to keep religion and politics separate. Yet such a diagnosis overlooks the central role secular political rationality and modern institutions have played in fomenting and exacerbating the confessional divide between Muslims and Christians. Few of the economic and political transformations I have described above—from the securitization of the state to the privatization of public goods—can be neatly aligned on either side of the religious-secular divide. The entrenchment of religion in Egypt is a product of the transformations wrought in institutions of modern governance, statecraft, and private capital. Even attempts to redress religious inequality—whether the appointment of Copts to the parliament or granting greater autonomy to the Church—have not only embroiled the state further in religious affairs of the country but also made the Church more rather than less important to Coptic life.

In narrating the history of postcolonial Egypt I find it striking that regardless of the kinds of policies pursued—from Nasser's quasi-socialist reforms to Sadat's policy of economic liberalization to Mubarak's securitization of the state—religious inequality has been a constant feature of Egyptian life. Even the period of the 1920s, upheld as the pinnacle of national unity, was not free of interreligious strife. I suggest that we need to understand this not simply as a result of specific policies that various regimes have pursued, but in terms of the enshrinement of religious inequality within the structure of the modern state and its operational logic. A double movement characterizes this logic: on the one hand, the modern state enshrines majoritarian values in the social and legal norms of the nation; on the other hand, it holds out the promise that the state *can* be a neutral arbiter of religious differences. This paradox characterizes not only Egypt but also other secular liberal polities (for an elaboration of this point, see chapter 4). How can secularism be called upon to solve the majority-minority conflict when it is partly responsible for its creation? Yet secularism's claim that it is the best solution to religious strife continues to hold sway. Despite the erosion of political and civil equality in Egypt, activists continue to call upon the state to make good on its mandate. This not only shows how state sovereignty has become the ineluctable condition of our political imagination but, more importantly, it also reentrenches the state's power, its prerogative to act as the arbiter of interreligious relations, embedding

clergy and government officials. See Reem Leila, "Abu Fana in Focus," *al-Ahram Weekly*, July 24–30, 2008, http://weekly.ahram.org.eg/2008/907/eg2.htm.

it further in domains of religious life. The circularity of this problem is not unique to Egypt, I want to suggest, but a defining feature of our secular age.

"But We Are a Minority"

It is within the double-edged context—of the confessionalization of Egyptian civic-public life and the increased marginalization of Copts—that over the last three decades many Copts have come to question their earlier resistance to self-identifying as a minority. To the extent that the assignation *minority* makes visible the marginalization of a group within a polity, it draws international and national attention to the Coptic Christian plight. Unlike in the 1990s, when any invocation of "minority rights" provoked nationalist invective, a subtle but definitive shift has been underway.[81] The recent Coptic advocacy for the assignation *minority* notwithstanding, it remains a contested term. For example, the current Pope Tawadros, like his predecessor, declared emphatically in 2013, "Copts are *not* a minority."[82] The Coptic clerical establishment, at least formally, prefers to speak in the name of "People of the Book," which allows the Church to claim autonomy over Coptic communal affairs (see chapter 3). For Coptic nationalists, the term *minority* reeks of the colonial legacy, and its association with international law makes minority rights a dubious instrument that compromises the sovereignty of the Egyptian state. In what follows, I track contemporary invocations and denunciations of the term in order to show that the challenges the framers of the 1923 constitution faced continue to be relevant today. These discussions are heavily indebted to how the minority question was formulated during the interwar period as well as the ability of Western powers to intervene and shape Christian-Muslim relations in Egypt. In this context, colonial experience is not a thing of the past but configures majority-minority relations in the present.

[81] Consider, for example, the wide condemnation leveled against the leading human-rights activist Saad Eddin Ibrahim in 1994 (by Pope Shenouda, the Mubarak government, and leading public figures) for organizing a conference entitled Minorities of the Arab World. At the time, Muhammad Hasanein Haykal, a prominent Nasserite political pundit, attacked the conference in a widely circulated article in *al-Ahram*, the title of which parroted the old consensus: "Copts are not a minority: Indeed they are a part of the block of human civilization that belongs to the Egyptian people," *al-Ahram*, April 22, 1994. Eleven years later, Haykal used the term *minority* himself to refer to Copts on his popular talk show on *al-Jazeera*, which provoked Saad Eddin Ibrahim to demand that Haykal issue a public apology to the minorities of the Middle East for his earlier stance. See Saad Eddin Ibrahim, "I'tizar lil-Aqalliyat fi-l-'Alam al-'Arabi," *Metransparent*, September 18, 2005, www.metransparent.com/old/texts/Sa'ad_eddin_ibrahim/Sa'ad_eddin_ibrahim_appologies_to_arab_minorities.htm. For an account of this controversy, see Makari, *Conflict and Cooperation*; and al-Gawhary, "Copts in the 'Egyptian Fabric,'" 21–22.

[82] 'Abd al-Mun'im Halawa, "al-Baba Tawadros: al-Dustur al-Jadid 'Unsuri wa al-Aqbat laysu Aqalliyya," *al-Balad*, February 5, 2013, www.el-balad.com/389604.

Consider, for example, Magdi Khalil, a shrill and polemical figure in the field of Coptic rights who contends that the Coptic elite's earlier rejection of the assignation *minority* was nothing more than a "product of the hatred and pressure from the majority."[83] In a series of articles and blog posts, he argues that Copts qualify as a national minority, per international and human-rights law, because they are distinct by virtue of their religion *and* ethnicity, which sets them apart from the majority population of Egypt (Muslim Arabs). The Coptic claim to being a minority, however, is not simply a demographic issue for Khalil; it highlights their subordinate status that needs to be redressed legally and politically.[84] The fact that Copts "objectively" qualify as a minority according to these standards is not enough, Khalil contends, since they also need to embrace this status *subjectively* in order to be eligible for international legal protection. Here Khalil's argument echoes the consensus among international jurists during the interwar period that the mere presence of ethnographic traits (religion, ethnicity, language, and so on) does not constitute a national minority; the group must also face discrimination because of these attributes (see chapter 1). Consequently, Khalil urges the Copts to embrace this assignation because it not only makes visible their historical marginalization but also helps mobilize the force of international law to bring about a change in Egyptian government policies. Under the Mubarak regime, Khalil was among the few Copts to call openly for international intervention in Egypt (modeled on the invasion of Iraq in 1992) on behalf of the Coptic minority. He insisted that this would not constitute a colonial intervention because it would abide by international law, which, in his estimation, serves no single geopolitical power.[85]

In contrast to Magdi Khalil is Samir Murqus, who remains a vocal champion of the vision of Egyptian national unity from 1919 and rejects the minority identity. He asserts, "It's reductive to define people according to race, sect, or number. Why not just be an Egyptian citizen? . . . This is the choice I've made: to try to recapture the nationalist sentiment of Egypt in 1919—one nation with many individual citizens."[86] In a series of books and articles, Murqus challenges the link activists draw between

---

[83] Magdi Khalil, "al-Dimuqratiyya wa Huquq al-Aqalliyyat . . . al-Aqbat Namuzajan," December 10, 2005, www.middleeasttransparent.com/old/texts/magdi_khalil/magdi_khalil_democracy.htm.

[84] Ibid.

[85] Ibid. Khalil distinguishes between international and colonial interventions using a theory of interests: the latter tend to be rooted in binary oppositional interests (colonizer versus the colonized), while the former represent the collective interests of several protagonists. With this distinction, Khalil proposes that international interventions (such as the US invasion of Iraq in 1992) are justified as long as they abide by international protocols, because "it is incumbent upon all member-states of the UN to holdup [sic] and protect its charters and conventions."

[86] Maggie Morgan, "Samir Morcos: The Mirror of the Copt," *al-Ahram Weekly*, June 23–29, 2005, http://weekly.ahram.org.eg/2005/748/profile.htm. I follow the Library of Congress in spelling his name as "Murqus." Murqus is often paired with Coptic thinkers such as William Suliman Qilada and Yunan Labib Rizk.

political equality and minority rights. Specifically addressing those who call on Copts to identify as a minority, he argues,

> [They believe] that they are bringing Egyptian consciousness to a new level that the framework of national community does not encompass. [They want to] present Muslims and Copts as a majority versus a minority, rather than citizens of the Egyptian nation. Despite the insistence by some that there is no contradiction between the concept of citizenship and minority, indeed there is a fundamental contradiction between the two: the concept of minority emanates from a divisive and fractious principle, whereas citizenship emanates from the principle of equality in rights, responsibilities, and participation in the creation and adoption of decisions at all levels, for all citizens, irrespective of differences in occupation, class, language, ethnicity, or religion. . . . [Thus] the thought of majority and minority does not help achieve equality.[87]

Note the similarity between the terms of debate today and those from 1923 that I recounted above. Despite the differences in their political positions, neither Murqus nor Khalil (like the Coptic Christians who argued for minority rights in the first constitution of Egypt) can escape their inscription as the Other of the nation. Even though Murqus claims that he speaks not as a Copt but as an Egyptian, in the eyes of his Muslim audience he remains a Copt. When called upon to assist in the democratic transition following the ouster of Mubarak in 2011, Murqus was widely understood to represent "Coptic interests" despite his repeated public insistence that he agreed to serve in this capacity as a citizen of Egypt, not as a Copt.[88] Khalil, on the other hand, emphasizes his Otherness from the identity of the nation precisely as a means to claim his equal status as an Egyptian citizen. Their dilemma is a familiar one in that the Copts' abject status in relation to the nation is also the condition for their political action.

The ongoing centrality of Western power to the realization of minority rights in countries like Egypt is the indispensable context in which Khalil's and Murqus's arguments unfold. Note how Magdi Khalil's call on Western powers and international institutions to intervene on behalf of Copts recalls almost two hundred years of history during which the fate of minorities—especially Christians—in the region had come to depend on such interventions. Given this historical precedent, arguments such as Khalil's cannot be understood as colonial in any simple sense, insomuch as they presuppose and reflect the historical reality of minority rights in the Middle

---

[87] Murqus, *al-Himaya wa al-A'qab*, 78.

[88] Murqus resigned from this position in November 2012, joining many others in protest of the Muslim Brotherhood's heavy-handed stacking of the Constitutional Committee and the parliament with Islamists. See Samir Murqus, "Dustur: Masr fi Ma'zaq," *Al-Shuruq*, October 22, 2012, www.shorouknews.com/columns/view.aspx?cdate=22102012&id=9881eeb5-edfc-4fa3-b040-ab2255eb9bc9.

East. For Copts like Murqus, the history of geopolitical inequality is equally relevant and serves as a starting point for any reflection on the status of Copts as a minority. Unlike Khalil, however, Murqus concludes that because the discourse of minority rights was used to subjugate national sovereignty to foreign rule, it cannot serve as the instrument for Coptic salvation. Any embrace of this principle necessarily entails the inscription of Copts in this long-standing colonialist project. While we may be tempted to side with one position over the other, it is impossible to deny that both arguments reflect how the inequality of power between the West and the non-West has continued to structure the fight for Christian-Muslim equality in Egypt.

Religious Liberty, Geopolitics, and Human Rights

While minority-rights discourse may have taken a number of different forms in Egypt, by the time I conducted fieldwork in 2008 religious liberty had emerged as its primary site of articulation and struggle. Public debate was saturated with a distinctly new vocabulary that was different from the terms used in the 1980s and 1990s: *huriyyat al-'aqida* (religious freedom), *huriyyat al-mu'taqid* (freedom of conscience), *izdira' al-adyan* (defamation of religion), and *fitna ta'ifiyya* (sectarian strife). Secular human-rights organizations that used to avoid taking on religious issues were involved in a number of campaigns and court cases on behalf of the Copts, Bahais, and the Shi'a, deploying both Egypt's constitutional guarantees and international human-rights conventions (such as Article 18 of the UDHR and Article 27 of the ICCPR). This ascendance of religious-liberty discourse in Egypt parallels the prominence given to the issue in the United Nations and international human-rights organizations over the same period.[89] Because Egypt is a signatory to the UN Human Rights Convention, this entitles its citizens to report violations to the Special Rapporteur on Freedom of Religion. Egyptian human-rights organizations, most notably the EIPR, have increasingly come to use this mechanism to bring international attention to the plight of Christians and Bahais in Egypt.[90]

What were the social and political conditions that allowed for religious-liberty discourse to gain traction in Egypt? How did Egyptian activists succeed in casting

---

[89] Even though the right to religious liberty was foundational to the UDHR, it was not until 1986 that the UN Commission on Human Rights created a separate post, "Special Rapporteur on Religious Intolerance" (resolution 1986/20), which later became the "Special Rapporteur on Freedom of Religion or Belief" (resolution 2000/261). See Evans, "Strengthening the Role of the Special Rapporteur"; and Wiener, "The Mandate of the Special Rapporteur."

[90] The EIPR has also fought cases on behalf of the religious liberty of Muslims, including the right of a Muslim woman to wear the face veil at the American University in Cairo, which had banned the practice. EIPR, "Supreme Administrative Court Outlaws Complete Ban on Niqab."

the issue of religious discrimination as a violation of religious liberty and, perhaps even more importantly, in having this claim be *heard*? What made this an effective political strategy?[91] I want to point to three distinct developments that are crucial to understanding this shift in the Egyptian political landscape: the implementation of the neoliberal paradigm of "good governance," under the auspices of international development agencies, which encompassed the promotion of human rights; the expansion of American evangelical activism on behalf of Middle East Christians; and the US government's passage of the American International Religious Freedom Act (IRFA). Note that none of these developments can be adequately described in exclusively religious or secular terms at the national or international level; in fact, the religious and the secular are intertwined both in the articulation of these developments and in the effects they have produced in the social and political life of Egyptians.

The 1990s are widely known as the decade of the "good governance" paradigm that international financial institutions promoted in Third World countries, linking the free-market economy to the rule of law and democracy. If the former entailed a de facto privatization of public goods, then the latter encompassed the advocacy of human rights, suturing two distinct discourses under a single project. According to Antony Anghie, "The concept of good governance . . . [was] used as a 'bridging concept' by institutions such as the [World] Bank to articulate a new relationship between human rights and development."[92] This helped achieve two discrete goals: it deflected criticism of the controversial economic policies the IMF and the World Bank were promoting; and it cast the restructuring of Third World political and public institutions as a necessary step toward realizing global human rights.[93] While problems of economic and political corruption in the Third World were subject to the disciplinary measures of "efficiency, transparency, and accountability," similar problems in Western Europe and the United States continued to be treated as issues of national and domestic reform.[94]

Egypt during the 1990s is a textbook case of the adoption of the "good governance" program that led to the unprecedented growth of human-rights activism in the country. As Tamir Moustafa points out, despite the policy of economic liberalization adopted in the 1970s under Sadat, Egypt had failed to attract foreign capital; in response, the government undertook a broad series of measures during the 1980s that

---

[91] As one of the lawyers who worked on Muslim-Christian cases remarked to me, "All kinds of neighborhood skirmishes between Coptic and Muslim neighbors are now cast in terms of religious violation. Even if the laundry drips from the balcony above from a Muslim household, it is immediately understood as a violation of religious liberty!" Personal interview, May 13, 2008.

[92] Anghie, *Imperialism, Sovereignty, and the Making of International Law*, 262.

[93] Ibid., 261.

[94] Ibid., 258.

aimed to reform judiciaries, discipline the public sector, and restructure government service and audit units.[95] This entailed the establishment of the Supreme Constitutional Court (SCC) in 1979 and the rehabilitation of administrative courts, both of which were accorded considerable judicial autonomy. In the ensuing decade, while the SCC instituted a privatization regime through a series of landmark rulings that secured optimal conditions for domestic and foreign capital, the rehabilitated administrative courts reined in state corruption and bureaucracy.[96] The restructured judiciary, however, did not challenge the constitutionality of the Mubarak regime and its repressive policies; instead, the SCC upheld the legality of the Emergency State Security Courts and refused to hear cases challenging the transfer of civilians to military courts.[97] Nonetheless, true to the "good governance" paradigm, the SCC created an expanded political space for civil-society activism, and the 1990s witnessed a steady expansion of human-rights organizations in Egypt.[98]

These organizations, buoyed by legal support from the SCC and material support from foreign governments and foundations, saw the reformed judiciary as an opportunity to use the nation's courts to challenge the government's violations of human rights as well as to reform existing public-interest legislation. Legal mobilization became a cornerstone of human-rights activism during the 1990s.[99] Moustafa notes that the Center for Human Rights Legal Aid (est. 1994) alone litigated as many as 1616 cases in 1996.[100] Linked with and supported by the network of international human-rights organizations and the United Nations, the Egyptian NGOs were able to score political victories that had been otherwise impossible to imagine under previous regimes. The proliferation of religious-liberty discourse belongs to this period of increased human-rights activism in Egypt. The government's attempts to shut down these NGOs notwithstanding, they continued to operate and subsequently played a key role in the uprising that toppled the Mubarak regime in January 2011.

---

[95] Moustafa, *The Struggle for Constitutional Power.*

[96] In regard to private property, the SCC limited the state's ability to nationalize private capital while giving more legal security to foreign and domestic capital to operate without constraints. At the same time, the SCC supported the expansion and protection of human rights and civic activity even as the Mubarak regime continuously tried to limit its scope. On the former, see ibid., 93–94; on the latter, see ibid., 182–88.

[97] Ibid., 232.

[98] Some of the leading human-rights organizations in Egypt were established between 1992 and 1999, including Nadim Center for the Management and Rehabilitation of Victims of Violence, Center for Human Rights Legal Aid, Center for Women's Legal Aid, Land Center for Human Rights, and Human Rights Center for the Assistance of Prisoners. Ibid., 147–49.

[99] In 1999, the Mubarak regime tried to curtail the work of human-rights NGOs by passing a restrictive law (153/1999) that was overturned by the SSC. Subsequently, the government resorted to the use of emergency state security and military courts in order to intimidate human-rights activists and contain their activity. Ibid., 182–92.

[100] Ibid., 145–54.

My aim in recounting this history is not to impugn the integrity of Egyptian human rights organizations or to paint them as tools of Western power. Indeed, those who toil in this field have had to put up with government threats while making the most of the space created by the "good governance" paradigm to squeeze slim, if important, victories. Rather, my aim in narrating this history is to spell out the conditions under which the discourse of religious liberty and minority rights became pursuable as a viable political strategy to criticize government conduct. One of the greatest ironies is that in order for human rights work to flourish in Egypt, the country had to be subjugated to the dictates of Euro-American power and capital, which had little to do with the domestic circumstances that created the amplification of religious inequality in Egypt in the first place. It is not surprising therefore that even though human rights activists were able to wrench a few important victories, the fundamental structure that holds up the edifice of religious inequality remains firmly in place.

If the rise of the human-rights movement provides one arc of the career of religious liberty in Egypt, then another is the ascendance of the American evangelical movement in the 1990s, which has taken on the global mandate of saving the "persecuted Church."[101] These "new evangelicals"—a term that often includes Episcopalians, Presbyterians, and Southern Baptists—share certain similarities with their colonial counterparts in their mobilization of ecumenical global networks and international diplomacy to achieve their ends. However, they are also distinct in that they are heir to two generations of American activists from the Cold War period who were foot soldiers in the fight against the "godless communism" of the Soviet Union and its satellite states. Casting religious liberty as a right to *have* religion, they provided a vocabulary to challenge the "totalitarian secularism" these states practiced.[102] After the collapse of the Soviet Union, their energies had been focused on Eastern Europe and Central Asia when 9/11 happened.[103] This seismic event gave these evangelicals a new enemy, radical Islam, which they have come to construe as the greatest threat since communism to the security and freedom of the United States. In this project, the evangelical movement found a willing partner in right-wing think tanks, initially established to serve the Cold War agenda, which had turned their attention to fighting the menace of fundamentalist Islam after 9/11.[104] The Hudson Institute is a case

[101] See Castelli, "Praying for the Persecuted Church"; and McAlister, "The Politics of Persecution."
[102] For this history, see Moyn, "From Communist to Muslim."
[103] Joshua Green, "God's Foreign Policy," *Washington Monthly*, November 2001, www.washington monthly.com/features/2001/0111.green.html.
[104] These think tanks include the Freedom House (established in 1941 by Wendell Wilkie and supported by Eleanor Roosevelt), the Hudson Institute (established in 1961 by Herman Kahn and the RAND Corporation), and the Institute for Religion and Democracy (a self-described Christian think tank established in 1981). For a discussion of their relationship to IRFA, see Castelli, "Praying for the Persecuted Church."

in point. Established in 1961 to fight communism, its website describes the Institute's newfound mandate in this way:

> Since 9/11, the link between our own security and freedom, between our national interests and our ideals, has never been clearer. Winning the War on Terror turns on the battles of ideas and at its heart is the principle of religious freedom. . . . During the Cold War, the Center focused on helping religious believers persecuted under Communism. Today, while it continues to press for religious freedom in the remnant communist states of China, North Korea and Vietnam, it is increasingly engaged in ensuring that American policymakers defend the principle of religious freedom and believers who are persecuted purely for their religious beliefs in the Muslim world.[105]

One of the signal achievements of this constellation of American evangelicals and Cold War think tanks was the passage of the International Religious Freedom Act by the US Congress in 1998, essentially allowing the US government to police violations of religious liberty globally.[106] The IRFA established the Office of International Religious Freedom in the US State Department and a special IRFA adviser to serve on the National Security Council. While IRFA's stated mandate is to censure religious persecution wherever it occurs in the world, it provides a special waiver to important geopolitical allies and economic partners of the US government. Thus Saudi Arabia, Israel, and China are often exempted from enforcement, while countries like Iran and Sudan are targeted.[107] As a number of scholars and journalists note, it was the new evangelicals who mobilized their grassroots base in support of the IRFA, giving it the shape and form that eventually came to pass.[108]

The chief architects of IRFA who galvanized American churches to help get it passed in the US Congress were Nina Shea, Paul Marshall, and Michael Horowitz.[109]

---

[105] This text comes from the following website for the Hudson Institute, which has since been removed, http://crf.hudson.org/index.cfm?fuseaction=about_detail. Similar language can, however, be found on the Institute's new website, www.hudson.org/policycenters/7-center-for-religious-freedom.

[106] Since the passage of the IRFA, Canada and a number of other European governments have taken on the mandate of promoting religious freedom around the world. For a critical analysis of this Euro-American campaign, see Hurd, *Beyond Religious Freedom*.

[107] Gunn, "Religion after 9-11." The initial bill was sponsored by House Representative Frank Wolf and Senator Arlen Specter (both Republicans) and its prime focus was on persecution of Christians. It was later combined with the Nickles-Lieberman bill to give the IRFA a somewhat broader scope in its concern for religious minorities.

[108] On the history of the evangelical mobilization in support of IRFA, see Castelli, "Praying for the Persecuted Church."

[109] On their background, see McAlister, "The Politics of Persecution." Both Shea and Marshall wrote two widely popular books that acquired the status of manifestos for this movement, which sketch in dramatic detail the plight of Christians in the Middle East, Eastern Europe, and Central Asia. Marshall

In their congressional testimonies supporting IRFA, they cast religious liberty as a unique American mandate, bequeathed by the founding fathers, that all Americans have a moral responsibility to follow. While religious freedom was their general rubric, it was Christian persecution that was (and continues to be) their main concern. "Christians are the Jews of the 21st Century," declared Michael Horowitz, a judgment Shea echoed when she testified in front of the Committee on Foreign Relations in support of IRFA. The twenty-first century, she asserted, is "the worst century for anti-Christian persecution in history."[110] The argument Shea and her supporters propound is rather simple and goes something like this: Islam is intolerant, opposed to the values of democracy and freedom, and an enemy of Christianity; the United States as a Christian and democratic nation must ally itself with Christians of the Middle East so as to fight fanatical Muslims. After the passage of the IRFA, both Republican and Democratic administrations appointed Shea to the United Nations Commission on Human Rights and the US Commission on International Religious Freedom (USCIRF)—a position she held until 2012, at which point she became a fellow at the Hudson Institute.[111]

The IRFA commands considerable force in a country like Egypt, which is overwhelmingly dependent on US economic and military aid in exchange for which it has served as a proxy for US strategic interests in the region. (After Israel, Egypt is the second-largest recipient of such aid.) Republican senators have in the past argued that US aid to Egypt should be made contingent upon its compliance with the IRFA protocols.[112] In Egypt, the IRFA has had a mixed reception. Human-rights organizations are wary of the IRFA: on the one hand, it helps garner international attention for their cause, but on the other hand, they also see it as a tool of the US government to secure their strategic interests in the region.[113] This impression has only strengthened

and Gilbert, *Their Blood Cries Out*; and Shea, *In the Lion's Den*. Michael Horowitz is a Jewish neoconservative who served as general counsel in the Reagan White House and sits on the boards of Campus Watch and Students for Academic Freedom, two watchdog organizations that police critics of Israel on US campuses.

[110] Green, "God's Foreign Policy"; and Castelli, "Praying for the Persecuted Church," 329. Horowitz had wanted the IRFA to focus exclusively on the persecution of Christians, a suggestion that did not make it into the Wolf-Specter Bill that provided the basis of the IRFA.

[111] Under Shea, the USCIRF was criticized and sued for discriminating against its Muslim employees. Sarah Wildman, "Muslim Woman Sues Religious Freedom Commission for Discrimination," *Daily Beast*, June 25, 2012, www.thedailybeast.com/articles/2012/06/25/muslim-woman-sues-religious-freedom-commission-for-discrimination.html.

[112] House Representative Frank Wolf, one of the initial drafters of the IRFA, in 2008 introduced Bill 1303, which threatened to make US aid to Egypt subject to compliance with Coptic demands for religious liberty. GovTrack, "H. Res. 1303 (110th): Calling on the Egyptian Government to Respect Human Rights and Freedoms of Religion and Expression in Egypt," www.govtrack.us/congress/billtext.xpd?bill=hr110–1303.

[113] For example, the delegation in 2001 of the US Commission on International Religious Freedom elicited wide condemnation, including from human-rights activists deeply suspicious of the US State

as US military and economic aid has continued to flow unabated into the country, despite the violence against religious minorities under the military junta that came into power in 2013. This, of course, is in accord with the exceptions built into the language of the IRFA that let important US strategic and economic allies off the hook regardless of their human-rights record.

Others see the IRFA as an imperial ploy that is reminiscent of the discourse of nineteenth-century missionaries. Samir Murqus exemplifies this view in his elaborately titled book *Protection and Punishment: The West and the Religious Question in the Middle East; From the Law of Patronage to the Law of Religious Freedom; A Special Study of the Copts; History, Citizenship, Concerns, and the Future.*[114] He argues that the IRFA is the most recent example in a long history of European interventions in Egyptian domestic affairs supposedly on behalf of Eastern Christians. Murqus recounts the record of European and American missionaries who, while denigrating Copts, also sought to convert them to what they perceived to be a superior form of Christianity. While acknowledging the differences between the IRFA and earlier projects of Christian proselytization, Murqus sees continuity in the effects these projects have produced in the lives of Egyptians, Muslims and Copts alike. In charting this history, Murqus argues that the IRFA is one among a series of historical violations of Egyptian sovereignty, which should be an affront not only to the Muslim citizens of Egypt but to Christians as well.

The IRFA enjoys wide support within the Coptic diaspora in the United States, who view it as an important tool for mobilizing their senators and congressional representatives to force the Egyptian government to change its policies toward Copts.[115] Known in Egypt as *aqbat al-mahgar* (the emigrated Copts), this is a diverse and fractious group that has spawned organizations all over Western Europe and North America in support of Coptic rights.[116] While these expatriates emigrated largely for socioeconomic reasons over the course of the twentieth century, since the 1980s they have become an important voice in Egypt in support of Coptic rights. Many of these

Department's motives. See Vickie Langhor, "Frosty Reception for US Religious Freedom Commission in Egypt," *Middle East Report Online*, March 29, 2001, www.merip.org/mero/mero032901.

[114] Murqus, *al-Himaya wa al-A'qab.*

[115] Currently, there are now over twenty organizations that are active on behalf of Egyptian Copts, most of them in the United States, Canada, Britain, France, Switzerland, and Australia. See Ziyan, *Aqbat al-Mahgar.*

[116] The three main US-based organizations are the American Coptic Union, headed by Rafique Iscandar (www.copts4freedom.com/english.htm); U.S. Copts Association, headed by Maikel Meunir (www.copts.com/english); and the Coptic Assembly of America (www.copticassembly.com/showcat .php?main_id=19), established in 2007. The American Coptic Association, founded by Shawky Karas, was a leading organization on Coptic issues until Karas's death in 2003. There are deep rivalries between these associations and their leadership, as well as considerable difference in how they view the Egyptian religious and political landscape.

groups are critical of the Coptic Orthodox Church for its collusion with the Egyptian government and its inability to foster change in government policies.[117] Despite these tensions between *aqbat al-mahgar* and the Coptic Orthodox Church, as I elaborate below, they have had a mutually transformative effect on each other.

In this section, I have tracked three distinct developments that have been crucial to the proliferation of the discourse on religious liberty in Egypt over the past ten years: the restructuring of the Egyptian economy under the "good governance" paradigm, which included judicial reform and the promotion of human rights; American evangelical campaigns on behalf of Middle Eastern Christians, especially Copts; and the passage of the IRFA. The fact that all of these developments presuppose Egypt's subordinate place in the geopolitical order suggests that the minority question in Egypt today continues to be beholden to Western power, as it was in the nineteenth century. To be sure, there are important differences between the past and present condition of minorities in Egypt. But it is striking that despite Egypt's sovereign status, the fate of the Christian minority and of religious liberty remains tethered to Western projects and designs. Analysis of key secular concepts and institutions in the postcolony, therefore, requires that we take into account how differential sovereignty has conditioned their praxis.

Copts Are an Ethnicity!

Despite the suspicions that attend the IRFA in Egypt, it is subjecting Coptic identity to a new set of demands, key among them the invitation to translate religious identity into ethnic, indigenous, and linguistic terms that are more legible markers of minority identity in international law. Ironically enough, it is the American evangelicals, with the force of the IRFA behind them, who are inciting this translation of religion into areligious forms of identity. Consider, for example, a controversial talk that a prominent Coptic monk, Bishop Thomas, delivered at the Hudson Institute in 2008. Bishop Thomas commands the diocese of al-Qussia and Mair in Upper Egypt, and is an influential figure both in the Coptic Orthodox Church and in European and American Christian networks.[118] Hosted by Nina Shea, the talk was addressed to the

---

[117] The American Coptic Union goes as far as to charge that Muslim fundamentalists and Egyptian security agents have infiltrated the entire hierarchy of the Coptic Orthodox Church, and that the Church accepts financial bribes from Saudi Arabia to assist the conversion of Copts to Islam. On their criticism of the Coptic Orthodox Church, see Tadros, *Copts at the Crossroads*, 74–76.

[118] Bishop Thomas is also the founder of the impressive and sprawling Anaphora Retreat Center outside of Cairo, which hosts Christian visitors from Europe and the United States in an environmentally friendly setting for meditation and prayers. See Anaphora Retreat, "Bishop Thomas," http://bishopthomas.wordpress.com/bishop-thomas/. For his position within the Church, see *St-Takla.org*,

American diplomatic and general public in Washington, DC, with the aim of showcasing the Coptic plight and the IRFA's ability to alleviate it. Casting Coptic religious difference in ethnic and linguistic terms, Bishop Thomas argued,

> The Copts have been always focused on Egypt; it's our identity, it's our nation, it's our land, it's our language, it's our culture. But when some of the Egyptians converted to Islam, their focus changed away from looking to their [own language and culture]. . . . Arabia became [their] main focus. . . . Are they really Copts or have they really become Arabs? . . . If you come to a Coptic person and tell him that he's an Arab, that's offensive. We are not Arabs, we are Egyptian. . . . I would not accept being "Arab" because ethnically I am not. Politically now, I am part of a country that was Arabized, and politically I belong to an Arab country but that doesn't make a person Arab.[119]

In this argument, conversion from Christianity to Islam is understood not as a change of religion but as the substitution of one ethnic identity (Coptic) with another (Arab). To give up the Coptic faith is also to lose one's ethnicity. In this logic, insomuch as Copts are indigenous to Egypt, Arabs and Muslims not only are foreign aliens but also betray the true identity of the nation. Given this chain of equivalences, Bishop Thomas concludes, "When you look at a Copt [today], you don't only see a Christian, you see an Egyptian who is trying to keep his identity versus another imported identity that is working on him." In the bishop's view, it is the Coptic Orthodox Church that is the primary custodian of ancient Egyptian heritage, in charge of "keeping [Coptic language and culture] in a very good nursery till the time would come when openness and good thinking would occur, when this country will come back to its own roots and lift it up. But until then we have to keep it in a nursery, in the church."[120]

Note that Bishop Thomas's views bear a striking similarity to those of Kyriakos Mikhail (discussed above in the chapter), who in 1911 also described Copts as the direct descendants of ancient Egyptians, locked in a battle for survival against Arab Muslims, who invaded their homeland in the seventh century.[121] However, in contrast to the earlier emphasis on the racial purity and superiority of Copts against the Arab

---

"H.G. Bishop Thomas, Bishop of El-Kousseya, Assiout, Egypt," http://st-takla.org/Saints/bishops/taa/thomas-kosia.html.

[119] See "Event Transcript: Coptic Bishop Thomas on Egypt's Christians: The Experience of the Middle East's Largest Christian Community during a Time of Rising Islamization," *Hudson*, July 18, 2008, www.xtome.org/docs/countries/egypt/July18%20Bishop%20Thomas%20Transcript%20-%20Final .pdf.

[120] Ibid.

[121] This view is common among a number of high-profile clerics in the Coptic Orthodox Church. See, for example, the remarks that Bishop Bishoy, the secretary for the Holy Synod since 1985, made in

Semites, a discourse that carries little force today, Bishop Thomas emphasizes the ethnic, cultural, and linguistic characteristics of Copts that set them apart from Arabs. As in the past, Coptic Orthodox Christianity's kinship with Western Christendom is relevant here, but the post-9/11 context gives it a new charge. The Arab Muslim victimization of native Copts stands in for Islam's essential tyranny and intolerance unleashed on the global stage, which Americans have now come to experience first-hand. What was previously a Coptic experience has now, following 9/11, become a shared one between the Copts and the American Christians whom Bishop Thomas is trying to recruit for his cause.

When Bishop Thomas's address reached Egypt, it created a raging debate in the media and the blogosphere. Samer Soliman (d. 2013) published a response titled "Note . . . 'I Am an Arab,' . . . and So Is the Bishop!" in the left-liberal newspaper *al-Badeel*. Soliman's article takes aim at the bishop's charge that Copts who speak Arabic betray their Coptic identity because they have adopted the language of foreign invaders (Arab Muslims).[122] The idea that Copts have their own distinct language (Coptic) has been promoted since the early twentieth century by a cross-section of clerics and intellectuals who have tried to resurrect it through various means.[123] Despite these efforts, Coptic language, which has roots in ancient Egyptian and is written in a combination of Greek and Demotic letters, has not been vernacularized and does not command a popular following today.[124] Even though the Church uses Coptic in its hymns and prayers, the Bible and the sermons are rendered in Arabic, which remains the primary language for the vast majority of Egyptian Copts. It is this gap between the bishop's claim and the reality of Coptic social life that forms the basis of Soliman's rejoinder:

> There is a mistake in the discourse of Bishop Thomas and the champions of pharaonic Egypt.[125] From a linguistic point of view, Egyptians are Arabs. . . . Arabization was a linguistic and cultural phenomenon and not an ethnic one. For this reason we can say that our use of Arabic does not make us Arabs, just as the use of English by Americans does not make them English. . . . Bishop

September 2010: "Copts are the original inhabitants of Egypt. We are interacting lovingly with guests [Arab Muslims] who descended upon us." Cited in Tadros, *Copts at the Crossroads*, 93.

[122] There were others who contested the bishop's claim that Copts are a distinct ethnicity. See, for example 'Abd al-'Azim Hamad, "al-Akhta' al-'Ilmiyya fi Muhadarat al-Anba Tumas," *al-Ahram*, August 11, 2008, www.ahram.org.eg/Archive/2008/8/11/OPIN3.HTM.

[123] Hasan, *Christian versus Muslims*, 205–6.

[124] By the medieval period, the patriarchs of the Coptic Church were already struggling to preserve the Coptic language while trying to make Christian pedagogy and prayers available to Christians who only spoke Arabic. Swanson, *The Coptic Papacy in Islamic Egypt*, 131.

[125] The phrase *champions of pharaonic Egypt* refers to those Egyptians who believe that Coptic Christians are the direct descendants of the ancient pharaohs.

> Thomas has the right, as do those who speak from a pharaonic
> point of view, to reveal what was done to Egypt during the his-
> tory of Arab Muslim rule. . . . But it is also important that Bishop
> Thomas consider the realities of the present and the necessities of
> the future. Today . . . Christian and Muslim Egyptians are Arab
> by language, and anyone who wants to put an end to his Arabi-
> zation will have to cut his tongue off with his own hand. It will
> not do for Bishop Thomas to claim that Copts are the primary
> reservoir of the Egyptian nation at the same time that he wants
> to do away with their language, regardless of the means by which
> it was adopted in the past. For Arabic is not just the language
> of the island of Arabia [from which Muhammad hailed] . . . but
> it is also the language of Nagib Mahfouz [an Egyptian novelist],
> Salama Musa [a leading Coptic nationalist in the 1920s], Fairuz
> [a famous Lebanese singer], and *rahbaniyya* [monasticism]; it is
> the language of the Bible as known by the Christians of Egypt.[126]

There were other responses from Copts committed to the old vision of *al-wahda al-wataniyya* (national unity) who accused the bishop of uncritically adopting the divisive discourse of the Coptic diaspora (*aqbat al-mahgar*) and ignoring the role Middle Eastern Christians had played in the fashioning of the pan-Arab project.[127] Yet there were many other Copts—Magdi Khalil among them—who defended Bishop Thomas for speaking a historical truth that has been politically silenced.[128] Reacting to the tide of criticism, the Coptic Orthodox Church distanced itself from the bishop's speech. Given how important a figure Bishop Thomas is within the Coptic Orthodox Church and to the overseas networks of North American and European churches, it was difficult to cast the bishop's remarks as marginal to the ecclesiastical establish-ment.[129] Many of the Coptic human-rights activists I was working with at the time chuckled when I asked about it, telling me there was nothing new in the bishop's statement. As one of them put it, "This is the dirty secret that we [Copts] all know, and many believe it; only Muslim Egyptians are shocked by it. What the bishop said in public is repeated in the churches all the time."

While Bishop Thomas's argument may have sounded foreign to many Egyptian ears, it was quite legible to his American audiences well schooled in minoritarian

---

[126] Samer Soliman, "Sajjal . . . Ana 'Arabi . . . wa Anba Tumas aydan," *al-Badeel*, August 24, 2008, 7.

[127] Kamal Zakhir Musa, "al-Mahgar wa al-Asqaf: Ma'zaq al-Muwatana," posted on MARED list-serve, August 8, 2008. See also Sara Aguzzoni, "Media Reports of Christians Converting to Islam," *Arab West Report*, Paper 6, March 2008, www.arabwestreport.info/ar/lsn-2008/lsbw-32/25-lmhjr-wlsqf-mzq-lmwtn.

[128] Majdi Khalil, "Mu'aqabat al-Aqbat 'ala Wataniyyathum," August 1, 2008, www.elaph.com/Web/ElaphWriter/2008/8/353107.htm.

[129] For a defense of Bishop Thomas's speech by the Christian youth of his al-Qussia and Meir dio-cese, see "Bayan Sadir min al-Shabab al-Masriyyin al-Taba'in li-Mataraniyya al-Qussia wa Meir," *Sawt al-Muhajir*, July 11, 2008, http://voiceofimmigrant.own0.com/t64-topic.

claims of ethnic and indigenous identity. It is not difficult to see how the performative demand of the political arena in which the bishop made his case (the Hudson Institute in Washington, DC) required him to amplify the differences between Copts and Muslims in order to capture the attention of a powerful ally who can finally make a difference in changing the Coptic situation.

The controversy surrounding the bishop's speech is illustrative of the dual predicament that haunts a minority's struggle for equality. On the one hand, Copts are no different than other minorities in that any attempt to draw attention to their plight inevitably sets them apart from the identity of the nation, enhancing the fractures that are internal to the body politic. On the other hand, the postcolonial nature of their predicament is apparent in that their call for Euro-American protection sets up an unstable synergy between the security this affords and the insecurity it engenders with respect to their relationship to the nation. Their dependence on supranational forms of support requires them to amplify their difference to a certain degree. This is not simply a case of the victim's hyperbole but a necessary feature of making their discrimination legible in terms of international law and Euro-American geopolitical interests. As Bishop Thomas's speech to the Hudson Institute makes clear, for the Coptic grievance to register in the theater of minority rights it must be made commensurate with the ethnic and cultural difference at the core of minority-rights discourse in Euro-America. While this commensuration may gain Copts foreign protection, it also sets them apart from Egypt's Arab and Muslim history, which in turn makes the project of finding ways of living together more difficult.

Proportional Representation Revisited

I want to close this chapter by reflecting on a recent moment in Egyptian history when the question of proportional representation for national minorities emerged again after the overthrow of the Mubarak regime in January 2011. The immediate occasion for its reemergence was a debate in the upper house of parliament (Majlis al-Shura) over how to devise a new electoral law that would capture the democratic spirit of the popular movement.[130] A year after a symbolic display of Christian-

---

[130] The authority of Majlis al-Shura at the time was in question because it was elected with a low voter turnout (7 percent) after a hastily called election by President Morsi. It was meant to replace Majlis al-Sha'b (the lower house of parliament), which was elected in January 2012 with wide (60 percent) voter participation but was dissolved six months later by the SCC. In the absence of Majlis al-Sha'b, Majlis al-Shura had legislative powers that many liberals saw as illegitimate, given that the house was stacked with Islamists. The SCC subsequently dissolved Majlis al-Shura on June 2, 2013, sending Egypt's political process into further disarray. "Update: Egypt Parliament Ruled Illegal, but to Stay On," *Aswat Masriya*, June 2, 2013, http://en.aswatmasriya.com/news/view.aspx?id=531e061a-5a78–4778-a1ce-fc

Muslim unity during the dramatic protests that overthrew Mubarak, the nation stood incontrovertibly divided between liberals, socialists, Islamists, Salafis, supporters of the old regime, and Coptic Christians who hailed from a wide political spectrum. The democratically elected government of Mohammed Morsi was still in power (deposed shortly thereafter in July 2013). A new constitution had just been passed through a popular referendum that was also contested by various political factions.[131] It was at this point when the question of proportional representation for minorities was raised again, not in relation to the constitution but to draft a new electoral law that many hoped would be more democratic than the one that had prevailed during the Mubarak era.

There were two proposed options on the table, crafted by a loose affiliation of Coptic political figures: (1) each political party would be required to float a certain number of minority candidates; (2) each electoral district would be required to nominate minority candidates proportionate to their percentage in the area. The debate that followed in Majlis al-Shura was raucously vicious and contrasted starkly with the genteel tenor of the constitutional debate in 1923. Opposition to these proposals came not only from far-right Islamists but also from Coptic Christians who were deeply divided over what it meant to be cast as a minority within the legal-political structure of the nation. Some of them suggested that such solutions were destined to reproduce the corrupt legacy of the Mubarak regime, which had used the "quota" system to handpick Coptic candidates who unquestioningly rubber-stamped its policies. A number of well-known Coptic nationalists issued a statement that rejected the idea of "affirmative action" (*al-tamiz al-'ijabi*) or "quota" as a violation of the "principle of citizenship" (*mabda' al-muwatana*).[132] One of them, Sami Fawzi, asked pointedly, if Copts had refused to accept the "quota solution" in 1923, then why would they embrace it now, when the country was even more divided along religious lines?[133] Fawzi, like others who signed the statement, argued that Copts needed to build a postrevolutionary Egypt together with Muslims as *citizens* rather than as religious partisans. This statement bore a striking similarity with the Constitutional Committee member

---

92f81b74ea. See Mohammad Maarouf, "Shura Council's Legislative Powers Are Worrying for Many," *Egypt Independent*, January 2, 2013, www.egyptindependent.com/news/shura-council-s-new-legislative-powers-are-worrying-many. For the legal challenges facing the new electoral law for Majlis al-Sha'b, see Nathan Brown, "Egypt's Constitution Swings into Action," *Foreign Policy*, March 27, 2013, http://carnegieendowment.org/2013/03/27/egypt-s-constitution-swings-into-action/fu3w.

[131] This constitution was annulled soon after General Sisi's ascension to power, and since then a new one has come to pass (in 2014) that bears striking similarity to the one passed under President Morsi. On the new constitution, see Grote, "Constitutional Developments in Egypt."

[132] They included prominent figures such as Samir Murqus, George Ishaq, Karima Kamal, and Samih Fawzi. See 'Emad Tomas, "Nushata' Aqbat fi Bayan lil-Umma Yarfidun 'Kuta' Tamthil al-Aqbat fi Majlis al-Nawab," *Copts United*, January 16, 2013, www.copts-united.com/Article.php?I=1385&A=82303.

[133] Ibid.

CHAPTER 2

Badawi's warning in 1923 that to adopt proportionate representation for religious minorities was tantamount to turning religious factions into political ones, thus consecrating religious difference at the heart of the polity.

Another group of Coptic Christians argued instead that setting aside seats for
minorities and women in the parliament (the "quota" option) was a temporary but
necessary measure, given the lack of adequate Coptic representation in politics over
the last sixty years.[134] Kamal Zakhir Musa, the founder of the Coptic movement for
clerical reform (*al-Tayyar al-'Almani lil-Islah al-Kanisa*), articulated a third position.
Zakhir distinguished between the executive or legislative appointment of Copts in
the parliament ("quota") and the proposal that political parties be required to float
a certain percentage of Coptic candidates. While the former, he argued, ran the risk
of serving the regime in power rather than the collective good, the latter required
Copts to compete for Muslim and Christian votes alike, thereby integrating them in
the political life of the nation.[135] In this latter model, Copts would be elected on the
basis of their public-service record rather than according to how well they served
their coreligionists. This, argued Zakhir, was the only way to bring Coptic Christians
out of their social and political isolation, making them an integral part of the national
fabric. Kamal Zakhir Musa's arguments closely echo those of Salama Musa, who, in
the 1920s, urged fellow Copts to become active in Egyptian political parties in order
to shape national projects; otherwise, he warned, given the majoritarian thrust of the
parliament, minority voices could be easily marginalized in the legislative sphere.[136]
Note that both men's views simultaneously articulate the hope that Coptic participation in politics might eventually level religious differences and the fear that majoritarian politics might well make this impossible.

Indeed this fear was borne out when the Muslim Brotherhood–affiliated Freedom and Justice Party declared that it would float two Coptic candidates from each
district in the parliamentary and municipal elections.[137] Given the long-standing
antagonism between the Brotherhood and Coptic Christians, this move took many
Copts by surprise. In a widely publicized move, Kamal Zakhir Musa changed his ear-

---

[134] This group included a number of prominent Coptic figures with divergent political views:
Maikel Meunir (the head of the American group Copts United), Mona Makram Ebeid (daughter of
Makram Ebeid, who had opposed the designation *minority* in 1923), Georgette Qallini (a former Coptic appointee to the Egyptian parliament under President Mubarak), and leading Coptic lawyers (such
as Mamduh Nakhla, Naguib Gibreel, and Rami Lakh). See Ahmed Shahin, "al-Aqbat 'ala Qawa'im
al-Ikhwan," *Oktober*, January 20, 2013, www.masress.com/october/134524.
[135] Kamal Zakhir Musa, "al-Fakh Alladhi Yantazir al-Aqbat," *al-Bawabah News*, January 20, 2013,
www.albawabhnews.com/7959.
[136] al-Bishri, *al-Muslimun wa al-Aqbat*, 220.
[137] It was surprising in part because the Brotherhood has historically rejected proportionate representation for minorities. See Shahin, "al-Aqbat 'ala Qawa'im al-Ikhwan."

lier endorsement of the principle on the grounds that it had turned into a ploy for the Brotherhood to garner Coptic votes, even as it sought to undercut Coptic social and political power.[138] Notably, the Brotherhood's position contrasted with that of the more right-wing Islamist Salafi political party (Hizb al-Bana' wa al-Tanmiyya), which rejected the idea of proportional minority representation outright for violating the principle of equality for all Egyptian citizens.[139] The party's representative in the parliament, Abbud al-Zumar, suggested instead that if Copts failed to secure any seats in the elections, minority candidates could be appointed by presidential decree.[140] Given the history of Salafi antagonism toward Egyptian Christians, al-Zumar's suggestion was widely seen as a hypocritical ploy to exclude Christians from participating in the electoral process. Far more fallacious, argued the Coptic activists I worked with, was the suggestion that the Salafis were concerned with the principle of citizenship equality when it was they who constantly sought to undermine Christians within Egyptian politics.

How should we read the debate in 2012 about proportionate representation against the one that took place in 1923? On the surface it appears that the earlier debate occurred almost exclusively within the classic framework of liberal secularism: how to engineer a system of governance that was neutral in regard to religion while at the same time allowing it to flourish in the social and civic life of the polity. Recall that religious differences, indeed religion itself, were projected to wither away at the time, and religiously neutral legislation was supposed to hasten their demise. In contrast, no one in the debate in 2012 prophesied that religion was destined to disappear from Egyptian society or that its demise could be socially or legally engineered. Rather, the religious affiliation of all political actors provided the basis from which various positions were argued, contested, and judged. Whereas before religious affiliation was one among a set of distinctions, by 2012 it had become the key distinction and a constitutive aspect of Egyptian citizenship.

Despite these differences, there is also a strong similarity in how proportional representation was debated in 1923 and 2012. Note that in both moments, Egyptian legislators struggled with the same problem: How can the state address substantive

---

[138] Musa, "al-Fakh alladhi Yantazir al-Aqbat."

[139] Hizb al-Bana' wa al-Tanmiyya is an affiliate of al-Gama'a al-Islamiyya, the radical Islamic group that led a militant insurgency against the Mubarak regime between 1992 and 1996. After a brutal crackdown against them that left the organization paralyzed, in 2000 the government and al-Gama'a al-Islamiyya agreed to a truce, at which point the group formally denounced violence.

[140] Wa'il al-Qamhawi, "al-Jama'a al-Islamiyya Tarfud Kutla al-Mar'a wa al-Aqbat fi al-Barlaman," al-Dustur, December 31, 2012, www.dostor.org/121423. al-Zumar was the founder of the Egyptian Islamic Jihad and was indicted for President Sadat's assassination in 1981. He was released after the uprising in January 2011 and subsequently contested elections as a Hizb al-Bana' wa al-Tanmiyya candidate.

religious inequalities without enshrining religious difference at the core of the nation's laws? Would the political thematization of Christianity not undercut the ideology of a nation united? Critics in both moments argued that proportional minority representation would jeopardize and compromise the principle of formal equality for all citizens. Egyptians from a variety of different political positions made this argument: from secular Muslims and Copts in 1923 to the Salafis and Coptic liberals in 2012. While some of these actors were criticized for their hypocritical deployment of the principle of abstract equality, others were condemned for their naïve nationalism. In reading these debates, it appears that the problematic place that religious minorities occupy in the Egyptian polity today is a continuation of the problems they faced in the 1920s. These problems are, in an important sense, internal to the edifice of liberal citizenship, which is purportedly abstract but in practice normatively majoritarian. Formal political and civil equality, as I have suggested, depoliticizes religion while simultaneously enshrining it as a unique attribute of civil society, where its social powers and hierarchies are allowed to thrive. As the developments described in this chapter demonstrate, since 1923 the deepening enshrinement of religion within social life has, paradoxically, endowed it with a new political significance in Egypt. I use the term *political* in the sense not only that religious identity has become an integral aspect of citizenship but also that the state is repeatedly called upon to redress its deleterious effects (through quotas, affirmative action, proportionate representation). This only embroils the state further in the religious field, contravening the principle of state neutrality.

The language of religious liberty and minority rights reintroduces the problem of difference into the purportedly neutral language of political belonging, drawing attention to the social and substantive inequalities that continue to permeate a polity. It is not surprising, therefore, that both religious liberty and minority rights occupy a prominent place within Egyptian political discourse today. Their reemergence should be understood as a sign not of the failure of political secularism in Egypt but of its ongoing promise. The Coptic-Muslim struggle is a window, I want to suggest, not only into Egypt's problems but also into those of the secular state and its embattled relationship with (religious) difference.

In this chapter, I have also argued that sociopolitical developments in Egypt from 1911 to 2012 cannot be characterized in accord with a secular-religious binary. The privatization of the state and the public sector since the 1970s, for example, is partly responsible for religious organizations (Muslim and Christian) taking on the pastoral functions of the state. While the Islamicization of Egyptian society is one face of this, the other is the ascendance of the Coptic Orthodox Church as the prime patron of Coptic Christians. Even though the current military rulers of Egypt cast themselves as the secular arbiters of a divided polity, they are incapable of suturing this religious fracture precisely because they remain wedded to the project of privatizing the state—a seemingly secular project that impacts conditions of religious inequality in the country. The pertinent question, therefore, is not so much if Egypt is truly secular (measured against an imagined Euro-American model), but what secularization as a sociological and historical project has meant in Egypt and how it has transformed the religious and political life of Egyptians.

Secularism in Egypt, however, is also infused with the legacy of Islamic rule and Oriental Orthodox Christianity, both of which are consequential to the shape that majority-minority relations have taken in the present. In the second half of the book, I turn to this legacy, in particular how it configures the Egyptian state's accommodation of religious difference in the domains of family, law, and cultural production. My exploration of the status of Bahais in Egypt in chapter 4 serves as an occasion to unpack key similarities and differences across European and non-European secular modes of governing religious difference.

PART II

Chapter 3

SECULARISM, FAMILY LAW, AND
GENDER INEQUALITY

Some of the most common issues that ignite Muslim-Christian violence in Egypt today involve rumors about interfaith romance or marriage, abducted women, and religious conversion.[1] All three figured prominently in a controversy that erupted in the working-class neighborhood of Imbaba in May 2011 (three months after the overthrow of the Mubarak regime) that left two churches burned, twelve people dead, and scores injured. It all started when a Muslim man came looking for his wife in Imbaba, where her Coptic family lived. He claimed she had converted to Islam the previous year, but then had suddenly disappeared.[2] The man alleged that her Coptic relatives had kidnapped her and were holding her against her will in the local church, which Coptic residents of the neighborhood and the police denied. When rumors began circulating that a group of Muslims was coming to attack the church, things degenerated quickly and an armed battle ensued between Muslims and Copts. The police stood by and did nothing to stave off the clash. The Coptic community was irate at the impunity with which the violence was allowed to unfold and at the police's failure to intervene or protect them.[3]

The rumors and allegations that provoked this incident follow a pattern that is by now familiar to observers of Coptic-Muslim strife. One year earlier, similar events unfolded when a woman named Camilia Shehata, the wife of a Coptic priest, disappeared from her home. Her husband charged that Muslims had abducted her, and then forced her to convert and marry a Muslim man. Copts took to the streets and demanded the government find Camilia and bring her back to the Coptic Orthodox

---

[1] The second major issue that often sparks violence against Coptic Christians is the building and restoration of churches, which the Egyptian government strictly regulates. For a discussion of Egyptian laws about church construction, see Jason Brownlee, "Violence against Copts," *Carnegie Endowment for International Peace*, http://carnegieendowment.org/2013/11/14/violence-against-copts-in-egypt/gtsf, 8–10.

[2] David Kirkpatrick, "Clashes in Cairo Leave 12 Dead and 2 Churches in Flames," *New York Times*, May 8, 2011, www.nytimes.com/2011/05/09/world/middleeast/09egypt.html.

[3] See the EIPR's report on this incident, "'Adala al-Shari'a."

Church. A few days later, the state security forces located her and handed her over to the Church, where she was immediately sequestered. The Church announced that Camilia had not converted to Islam but had left her home temporarily because of marital problems.[4] A number of human-rights and feminist organizations demanded that Camilia be allowed to make a public appearance and clarify her position, while various Islamist groups charged that the Coptic Church had abducted her.[5] As the pressure on the Church mounted, Camilia made an appearance on a Coptic satellite channel alongside her husband and son to announce that she had left home because of ongoing marital disputes, but neither had converted to Islam nor was being held captive.[6]

The ur-controversy, the paradigmatic reference in these events, centers on the figure of Wafa Qustuntin, also married to a Coptic priest from a small village in Beheira, who went missing in November 2004. Upon investigation, the security police reported that she had converted to Islam and was now living with a Muslim family in Cairo. Stories circulated that she had fallen in love with her Muslim colleague, who had convinced her to convert and elope. Protests broke out in her village and thousands of Copts occupied the Coptic Patriarchate in Cairo, shouting slogans such as "religious conversion cannot be coerced" and "stop the gangs of women kidnappers."[7] When the State Security Investigation Services (SSI) ignored the demonstrators' demands to "restore" Qustuntin to her family and the Church, riots broke out at the Patriarchate, injuring both Copts and police. The Coptic Pope Shenouda III went into isolation to protest the government's inaction. Finally, on presidential orders, on the night of December 8, 2004, the security police handed over Qustuntin to the Church, at which point, under tight security, Church officials took her into custody and sequestered her from the public. The Church emphatically denied Qustuntin's conversion to Islam, charging instead that her Muslim colleague had drugged her and forced her to convert, but once she came to her senses she reclaimed her faith. No one has heard from or seen Qustuntin since she was delivered to the Church in 2004.

---

[4] Yusuf Ramiz and Mahir Abdul Sabbur, "Camilia Ghabit 5 Ayyam wa Zaharit fi Amn al-Dawla wa Ikhtafit fi al-Kanisa," *al-Shorouk*, July 25, 2010, www.nmisr.com/vb/showthread.php?t=159129.

[5] See Amira Howeidy, "The Camilia Conundrum," *al-Ahram Weekly*, September 2–8, 2010, http://weekly.ahram.org.eg/2010/1014/eg8.htm.

[6] Some Copts charged that the unprecedented bombing of al-Qiddissin church in Alexandria in January 2011 was related to the Shehata controversy. Tadros, "Sectarianism and Its Discontents." After the Mubarak regime was overthrown in February 2011, it was revealed that the bombing was masterminded by the then minister of interior, Habib el-Adli, with the intent of blaming the Islamists and justifying a government crackdown on them. See Farag Ismail, "Ex-Minister Suspected behind Alex Church Bombing," *al-Arabiyya*, February 7, 2011, www.alarabiya.net/articles/2011/02/07/136723.html.

[7] Reem Nafie, "When the Social Becomes Political," *al-Ahram Weekly*, December 16–22, 2004, http://weekly.ahram.org.eg/2004/721/eg7.htm.

Four years later, when several Muslim clerics alleged in an incendiary fashion that the Church had killed Qustuntin, Church officials announced that she was alive and well, living a secluded life in the pope's home monastery in Wadi al-Nutrun, and would soon appear on Coptic television. To date, no such sightings have been reported.

Shortly after the Qustuntin incident, a number of commentators in the Egyptian press suggested that the core issue was Coptic family law, which since 1971 has banned Copts from divorcing or remarrying unless one of the spouses has committed adultery or changed his or her religion. This has served as an impetus for Coptic men and women to convert to Islam in order to escape difficult marital situations or to remarry.[8] That both Qustuntin and Shehata were married to Coptic priests with whom they reportedly had marital problems lent credence to this claim. According to Karima Kamal, a leading Coptic journalist and the author of an important book on the topic, "The explosion of the crisis of Wafa Qustuntin opened the door to [a public discussion of] issues pertaining to Copts, key among them the Copts' relationship with the state on the one hand and the Church on the other. But the most important issue [that came to the fore] was the predicament of Coptic divorce that has been going on for the past thirty years without any solution."[9] Kamal reports an increase in the number of Coptic divorcees who cite conversion to Islam (or another Christian denomination) as their reason for marital separation.[10] Notably, Coptic men's conversion to Islam is subject to a different calculus. Whereas Christian male converts to Islam can remain legally married to Christian women, when a Christian woman converts, her marriage is immediately annulled in both Muslim and Coptic family law.[11] Given this combination of laws, it is easy to see why many critics of the Coptic Church believe that Coptic women in difficult marital situations might be tempted to resort to conversion to have their marriages automatically dissolved.

The Qustuntin and Shehata controversies have also come to serve as flashpoints in how the broader Muslim-Christian conflict is framed regionally and internationally.

---

[8] Interdenominational marriages between spouses who are from different Christian sects (or different religions) are subject to Muslim family law. This practice was formally legalized in 1955 under Law 462. Berger, "Secularizing Interreligious Law."

[9] Kamal, *Talaq al-Aqbat*, 12.

[10] Ibid., 32. When a Coptic Christian woman or man converts to another Christian denomination in Egypt, his or her marriage is subject to Islamic family law, which allows divorce. Kamal and other scholars suggest that, given the Coptic Church's prohibition on divorce, a large number of Coptic women are using Islamic family-law provisions to initiate divorce proceedings against Coptic husbands. For example, an increasingly large number of Coptic Christian women have started to use the principle of *khul'* in Islamic family law (adopted in 2000), which allows a woman to file for divorce unilaterally. Since *khul'* can only be used if one of the two spouses is not a Coptic Orthodox Christian, this suggests that Coptic women are opting to convert either to Islam or to another Christian denomination to make use of this provision. See El-Alami, "Can the Islamic Device of *Khul'* Provide a Remedy"; and Kamal, *Talaq al-Aqbat*, 23.

[11] Berger, "Public Policy and Islamic Law."

In November 2010, claiming vengeance for the abduction of Camilia Shehata and Wafa Qustuntin, an al-Qaida affiliate bombed a prominent church in Baghdad that was packed with worshipers.[12] On the Euro-American side, a number of Christian evangelical and Coptic diaspora groups have organized a global campaign to save Coptic women from what they claim is a Muslim conspiracy to abduct these women and force them to convert to Islam. These groups are now lobbying the American government and the United Nations to indict the alleged gang of Muslim kidnappers under international human antitrafficking laws (see my discussion below).[13]

This gendered narrative of abductors (male) and abductees (female) seems emblematic of how women have often been treated as symbolic placeholders for broader struggles over cultural, identitarian, and territorial claims throughout history. The epic tales of Helen of Troy in the *Iliad* and Sita in *Ramayana* attest to the pivotal role that the figure of the abducted woman has played in settling moral and political battles. In the words of one historian, women might be the objects of these narratives (to be saved or repudiated), but they are seldom its subjects.[14] That women's bodies figure prominently in not only religious but also nationalist, ethnic, and racial conflicts strengthens the sense that the Coptic abduction stories fit this historical pattern. However, in what follows, I want to rethink this feminist wisdom because I believe it is inadequate for understanding the role that the secular state has played in the creation of interreligious conflicts of the kind I describe above. As I will argue, these abduction stories are symptomatic of the pernicious symbiosis created between religion and sexuality under modern secularism. The simultaneous relegation of religion, sexuality, and the family to the private sphere has tied up their regulative fates in such a way that struggles over religion often unfold over the terrain of gender and sexuality. Whereas this entwinement is apparent in a variety of global struggles (over gay marriage, abortion, contraception, and HIV/AIDS, for example), in Egypt it is instantiated in the institution of religion-based family law.

---

[12] "Qa'ida al-Iraq Ta'tabir al-Masihiyyin Ahdafan Mashru'a li-'Adam Afraj Kanisa Masriyya 'an Sayyiditayn," *Marebpress*, November 3, 2010, http://marebpress.net/news_details.php?sid=28568. This incident is at the center of Sinan Antoon's 2012 novel *Ya Maryam*. Set in Baghdad, the book narrates the transformation of Muslim-Christian relations in Iraq since the first American invasion in 1990 and the rise of violence against Iraqi Christians. Subsequently, in February 2015 the Islamic State brutally murdered a group of Copts in Libya allegedly in retaliation for Camilia Shehata's failed attempt to convert to Islam. See David Kirkpatrick and Rukmini Callimachi, "Islamic State Shows Beheading of Egyptian Christians in Libya," February 15, 2015, www.nytimes.com/2015/02/16/world/middleeast/islamic-state-video-beheadings-of-21-egyptian-christians.html.

[13] See, for example, the following report on the Atlantic Council's website: Jayson Carter, "Ebram Louis and the Contested Nature of Coptic Disappearances," *Atlantic Council*, October 29, 2013, www.atlanticcouncil.org/blogs/egyptsource/ebram-louis-and-the-contested-nature-of-coptic-disappearances.

[14] Mani, *Contentious Traditions*.

Permitting Muslims, Christians, and Jews to have their own separate family laws is one of the primary ways the Egyptian state has enshrined religious difference in its legal and political structure.[15] Ensconced in the state's distribution of rights and freedoms, religion-based family law is also the most salient expression of the state's recognition of non-Muslims in the polity. By granting juridical autonomy over family affairs to "People of the Book," the Egyptian state recognizes certain non-Muslim minorities (Jews and Christians) who deserve special privileges and protections that other religious groups (such as the Shi'a and the Bahais) are denied. Even though religion-based family law is often regarded as a continuation from the premodern past, in what follows I show that it is, in fact, a modern invention that belongs to a radically distinct political order—one that has little in common with the premodern arrangement from which it supposedly emanated.

Family law today is predicated upon the public-private divide—foundational to the modern secular political order—that relegates religion, family, and sexuality to the private sphere, thereby entwining their legal and moral fates. This has invested modern religious identity in the domain of sexuality and family relations in a manner that is historically unique. In this context, minority religious communities that have legal autonomy over family law tend to view any state attempt to reform family law as an illegitimate intervention into communal affairs.[16] Rather than interpret this resistance as an example of religious intransigence and patriarchy, we need to think critically about how modern secularism has perniciously linked religious, sexual, and domestic matters to the extent that the family has become the primal site for the reproduction of religious morality and identity, exacerbating earlier patterns of gender and religious hierarchy.

Some of the questions this chapter explores are: How are the religion-based personal status laws of Egypt and the broader Middle East similar to, and distinct from, the emergence of modern family law globally? How has the creation of modern religious family

[15] In practice, three Christian sects (Orthodox, Catholic, and Protestant) and two Jewish sects (the Karaites and Rabbanites) command their own religious-based family law in Egypt. The Christian sects comprise multiple denominations, each with its own family law. Bernard-Maugiron, "Divorce and Remarriage." There is no secular or civil marriage in Egypt (as there is, for example, in India, which also has religion-based family laws). For a comparative reading of religion-based family law in India, Egypt, and Israel, see Sezgin, *Human Rights*.

[16] The Qustuntin and Shehata controversies bear a striking resemblance to the Shahbano affair in India, which also has multiple religion-based family laws. In 1985, the Supreme Court of India ruled that Shahbano, a divorced Muslim woman, should be paid alimony by her ex-husband, a ruling that was contrary to Muslim family law but in accord with the Criminal Procedure Code of India. The Muslim minority immediately protested this ruling as an unfair incursion of the state into matters over which Muslims have autonomy, and the government decided to exempt Muslim women from the requirements of the Criminal Code. For an insightful analysis of this case, see Agnes, "The Supreme Court, the Media."

law transformed the self-understanding of majority and minority alike, shaping the Christian-Muslim conflict to take a particular form? How is this national struggle linked to global geopolitics? In what follows I take up these questions through the entwined histories of Muslim and Coptic family laws and their current manifestation in Egypt.

The Privatization of Religion and Family

The existence of religion-based family law in Egypt and other Middle Eastern countries (such as Lebanon, Israel, Morocco, and Jordan) is often seen as a surviving legacy from the era of Islamic empires. As one historian of the Middle East puts it, "The continued existence of differing personal status law for various communities . . . is . . . an example of the survival of an institution based on principles traceable from ancient times to the present."[17] Similarly, another writes, "The religious or community Courts, with their limited personal status jurisdiction, were necessarily preserved intact as an inviolable legacy of Islam and the millet system."[18] Those with a more diachronic view of history tend to argue that the religion-based family laws of the Middle East are a product of the partial secularization of Middle Eastern societies, wherein the scope of religious power came to be sequestered to the domain of the family while other aspects of social life were subject to civil law. Critics of colonialism charge that colonial rulers who secularized civil and criminal law but left family law intact did so with self-interested malfeasance in order to pacify what they perceived to be a religiously zealous population.[19] As a result of this colonial ambivalence, the argument goes, religion-based family law is an ossified and recalcitrant remnant that the secularizing and modernizing force of civil law has left untouched. The assumption is that *if* the colonial powers and modernizing states had done their duty, *if* these societies had gone through a complete process of secularization, then they would have abolished religion-based family laws, dissolving in the process the patriarchal norms of kinship grounded in religious doctrines. The persistence of religion-based family laws in the Middle East, in other words, is taken as a sign of the region's incomplete secularism.

This account is flawed for a number of reasons. Apart from the fact that it rehearses the exhausted trope of non-Western secularism as always lacking or inadequate, more importantly it fails to recognize that neither personal status law nor

[17] Liebesny, "Comparative Legal History," 41.

[18] Stephen Longrigg, quoted in Weiss, *In the Shadow of Sectarianism*, 98.

[19] An oft-cited example of the British policy of nonintervention in the religious life of its colonial subjects is the following statement made by Queen Victoria: "We do strictly charge and enjoin all those who may be in authority under us that they abstain from all interference with the religious belief or worship of any of our subjects on pain of our highest displeasure." Quoted in Kennedy, "Savigny's Family/Patrimony Distinction," 838.

the object to which it is applied—the family—has remained unchanged in this process.[20] As Talal Asad points out, the transmutation of religious law into family law was a product of the "secular formula for privatizing religion" that designated religion and family (and, by extension, sexuality) to the private sphere to be ruled by its own unique set of laws.[21] Thus the telescoping of the shari'a into family law did not simply curtail religion's reach; it also transformed the shari'a from a system of decentralized and locally administered norms and procedures to a codified system of rules and regulations administered by a centralized state. No longer administered by local *muftis* and *qadis* according to customary norms and moral knowledges, shari'a law was reduced to the domain of the family as a unit of socioeconomic production.[22] Religion-based family law under the auspices of the modern state is, therefore, not simply a tool for executing divine law; it becomes one of the central techniques of modern governance and sexual regulation, of which the family is a crucial part.

Furthermore, family law itself, as a distinct legal domain, is a modern invention that did not exist in its present form in the premodern period. Classical shari'a jurisprudence, for example, did not entail a separate domain called "family law."[23] As historians of the Middle East show, family law is a product of liberal legal reforms enacted in the nineteenth century that changed substantive notions of marriage, family, and kinship relations.[24] Importantly, what today is called personal status or family law, the supposed essence and core of a religious tradition, is an amalgam from a variety of customary and religious jurisdictions that had no distinct coherence in the premodern period. Judith Tucker, for example, argues that the Islamic judicial system, "with its diversity of schools, doctrines, courts, and jurists of both official position and unofficial standing, [had] eluded comprehensive state control." But with the passage of a range of reforms undertaken throughout the Middle East, "the state stepped up its regulation of the marital institution and self-consciously sought to bring the marriage practices of its citizens into sync with its vision of modernity. . . . In selecting a

[20] Michael Lambek argues that the concept of the family is analytically distinct from that of kinship. The latter does not map onto the public-private divide that the former assumes, and it encompasses social relations that are much more extensive than those included in the modern unit called "the family." Lambek, "Kinship, Modernity, and the Immodern."

[21] Asad, *Formations of the Secular*, 228.

[22] Ibid., 227.

[23] For example, Ibn 'Abidin's classical compendium of applied jurisprudence (*fiqh*) from the eighteenth century contains no section on family law. It does, however, have chapters on marriage, evidence, divorce, maintenance, custody, and the like. This material cuts across the modern categories and juridical boundaries of private and public, family and penal law. I thank Kenneth Cuno for pointing this out to me. Ibn 'Abidin, *Hashiyat Radd al-Muhtar 'ala Durr al-Mukhtar Sharh Tanwir al-Absar.*

[24] According to Kenneth Cuno, even though personal status law was not codified until after the First World War, the reforms enacted in 1856, 1880, and 1897, modeled on European law, significantly transformed not only the substance and application of Islamic law but also the conception of marital relations. Cuno, "Disobedient Wives," 4.

particular doctrine in response to each legal question, the framers of these codes were of course engaged in the fundamental transformation of Islamic law from a shari'a of vast textual complexity and interpretive possibilities to a modern legal code of fixed rules and penalties. In the process, they changed and standardized many of the practices and understandings of [the institution of] marriage."[25]

One important effect of this process is the historical transformation of the concept of the family, from a loose network of kin relations and affines to the nuclear family, with its attendant notions of conjugality, companionate marriage, and bourgeois love.[26] As it did elsewhere in the modern world, the family in the Middle East came to be associated with privacy, affect, nurturance, and reproduction—ideologically distinct from the individualistic and competitive rationality of the market. It is only in the nineteenth century that the Arabic terms *usra* and *'a'ila* came to signify the modern sense of the family as "a man and his wife and his children and those who are dependent on him from his paternal relatives," a meaning that was conspicuously absent in dictionaries of the earlier period.[27] Commenting on the contrast between thirteenth-century marriage contracts and early-modern ones in the Middle East, Amira Sonbol notes that the earlier contracts are striking in that "the family" is not conceptualized as a social unit responsible for the reproduction of society, and it is not necessarily linked to spouses and descendants as it came to be in the modern period.[28] Nineteenth-century procedural reforms of both the Muslim and the non-Muslim communal (*milli*) courts were crucial to establishing the secular legal distinction between the private and the public that relegated religion and the family to the former, while subjecting both to the sovereign control of the modern state.[29]

Paradoxically, even as the family was assigned to the private domain in the nineteenth century, it simultaneously was made central to the (re)production of the nation-state and became a key target for projects of social and political reform.[30] Hussein Agrama's work shows that the legal concept of public order, a key measure of the state's domestic sovereignty, has been used since it first emerged in nineteenth-

---

[25] Tucker, *Women, Family, and Gender in Islamic Law*, 70–71.

[26] Despite the long-standing practice of polygamy in Egypt, by the early twentieth century the nuclear family had become the norm. See Kholoussy, "Nationalization of Marriage in Monarchical Egypt"; and Cuno, "Ambiguous Modernization."

[27] Asad, *Formations of the Secular*, 231.

[28] Amira Sonbol argues that these contracts are striking in that they neither suggest that the purpose of marriage is to have a family nor imply that family comprises solely spouses and descendants. Sonbol, "History of Marriage Contracts in Egypt," 170.

[29] By the mid-twentieth century, the assertion that "the family is the foundation of state and society" had become the norm, enshrined in the 1956 Egyptian constitution as well as the 1948 Universal Declaration of Human Rights. Article 16(3) of the UDHR declares, "The family is the natural and fundamental group unit of society and is entitled to protection by society and the State."

[30] For Egypt, see Pollard, *Nurturing the Nation*.

century Egypt to reorganize the fundamentals of kinship relations in accord with the rationality of the secular liberal political order.[31] Despite relegating matrimonial relations to the domain of private law, public-order reasoning was and continues to be widely deployed to shape domestic relations in accord with priorities of the state. It is important to note that Western European societies have made just as much use of public order to create state-mandated marital arrangements. Ursula Vogel shows that even as marriage came to be normatively understood as a private contract between individuals (rather than a sacrament) in nineteenth-century Europe, the imperatives of public interest and public order "constituted the dominant mode in which [state] arrangements of marriage were explicated and justified."[32] Similarly, in contemporary France a range of legal cases involving sexual conduct, monogamy, interracial marriage, adoption, and parenting have been debated and adjudicated under the rubric of public order, turning what the law declares to be a matter of private conduct into decisive claims about state sovereignty, French national identity, and socioreligious norms.[33] Note the double movement these invocations of public order entail in that the state (whether exemplarily secular or incompletely so) can intervene in the private domain even as it hails privacy as a distinct and sacrosanct feature of modern polities.

It is often assumed that religion and family are linked because the latter is the paradigmatic site for the reproduction and preservation of moral values. This is understood to be the case in both non-Western and Western polities—hence the difficulty in subjecting issues such as domestic violence, contraception, and parenting to standard forms of rights adjudication. My analysis in this chapter challenges this assessment. I suggest instead that even though religion, gender, and sexuality have been historically intertwined, the exaggerated weight that the family commands in contemporary religious debates is an artifact of the state's relegation of both to the private juridical domain. What appears to be a natural affinity between "family values" and religious morality, in other words, is in fact a contingent effect of the privatization of religion and sexuality under modern secularism.

The Global Genealogy of Family Law

The religious basis of Middle Eastern family laws makes them distinct from secular civil codes that regulate marital relations in most Western liberal societies. While this is a consequential difference, one that I attend to below in the chapter, here I want

---

[31] Agrama, *Questioning Secularism*, 92–101.
[32] Vogel, "Private Contract and Public Institution."
[33] See Bowen, "Shari'a, State, and Social Norms"; and Surkis, "Hymenal Politics."

to point to their shared global genealogy, which is seldom acknowledged and which gives both religion-based *and* secular family-law codes a paradigmatically similar cast. Legal theorists Janet Halley and Kerry Rittich summarize the central features of this genealogy.[34] Using a comparative project across different legal traditions and histories, Halley and Rittich argue that modern family law emerged in the eighteenth century for the first time as an autonomous juridical domain distinct from other regulatory spheres, especially the law of contract: "the former housed a nuclear affective unit and the latter housed the individualist ethos of freedom of contract." While the contract was deemed to be "individualistic, market-driven, affectively cold, and free, the family [was] altruistic, morality-driven, affectively warm, and dutiful."[35] Halley and Rittich suggest that modern family law, in comparison with other juridical domains, exhibits "exceptional" qualities in at least two senses of the term. First, even though it purports to be descriptive (as an aggregate of people's customs), family law enfolds normative claims about cohabitation, marriage, sexuality, and a sexual division of labor that pertain to the domain of obligation, status, and affect (in contrast to the domain of rights, will, and rationality). The global adoption of family law, Halley and Rittich argue, institutionalizes the modern concept of the family as the sole provider of nurturance, biological reproduction, moral inculcation, and intimacy against the cold rationality and calculus of the market. Other historical and cultural practices of kinship came to be measured against this normative concept of the family, and were often subsumed by it. The history of the emergence of the modern family in the Middle East clearly fits this global genealogy. Neither those who want to uphold the religious foundation of family law nor those who champion its secularization can escape this global structure of family law and its normative imperatives.

Family law is exceptional in a second sense in that it is supposed to emanate from and express "the spirit of the people" and their traditions, particularity, and history. Insomuch as it is supposed to represent "the traditional, the national, the indigenous," family law is distinct from the law of the contract or the market, which is understood to be the "real domain of universality."[36] In Halley and Rittich's words, "It is in the nature of family law to become the same everywhere and in the nature of family law to differ from place to place."[37] Thus while the colonizers imposed their own forms of commercial, criminal, and procedural codes in the colonies, the family laws they devised were understood to emanate from the religious and customary laws of the

[34] Halley and Rittich, "Critical Directions in Comparative Family Law."
[35] Ibid., 758.
[36] Ibid., 754.
[37] Ibid., 771.

native peoples.[38] Given that religion was understood to embody the "true spirit" of the colonized people (recall the Orientalist construction of "the East" as essentially religious and spiritual), it is not surprising that family law came to be grounded in the religious traditions of the communities that the colonial powers ruled over for 150 years. Notably, just as family law was invented from fragments of various juridical and customary traditions, so was the univocality and unanimity of the religious traditions to which the newly formulated family law was supposed to correspond.[39] It follows, therefore, that defenders of religion-based family law consider it to be the essence of the religious tradition itself.

The fact that family law and personal status law are used interchangeably in Middle Eastern legal parlance suggests another important genealogy. In the Middle Ages, "personal status" referred to "the capacity and condition of the person" determined by one's membership in a tribe, group, or nation.[40] In the eighteenth century, personal status law came to be attached to the individual, and traveled with him beyond his place of domicile. It was opposed to "local law," which was territorially bound and applied to all persons residing in the areas of the statutory authority.[41] This legal dualism "mirrored effectively the two dominant competing ideas of international order existing at the time—the division of the world into peoples, and the division of the world into territories."[42] Because religious difference was the most salient aspect of the political organization of the Ottoman Empire, personal law pertained to one's confessional affiliation, a feature of the regime of legal pluralism that the Ottomans followed. With the global rise of the territorially bound nation-state, personal law that traveled with the individual was slowly abolished, giving way to a system of national laws that applied to all those residing within state borders.[43] Judith Surkis aptly describes this transformation: "With the unification of civil legislation for all citizens,

---

[38] In areas of the Middle East not under colonial rule, the same paradigm was adopted, albeit with local variations, through administrative reforms undertaken to modernize native legal systems. These reforms were not simply procedural but substantive in that they transformed the institutions and practices of kinship. On this point, see Cuno, "Ambiguous Modernization."

[39] Legal historian Philomena Tsoukala provides the most striking example of this by showing that when Greece became a nation-state (seceding from the Ottoman Empire in 1832) a unified family law, abstracted from a vast array of practices and jurisdictions, was invented that the Greek Orthodox Church then claimed as essential to its identity and doctrine. Tsoukala, "Marrying Family Law to the Nation."

[40] Mills, "The Private History of International Law."

[41] Mills suggests that "mixed status" was a third category that was created in order to accommodate the problem of multiple claims of foreign and regional legal systems that did not fit within personal or local law. Ibid. When Mixed Tribunals were established in Egypt in 1876 to parse out laws that pertained solely to Europeans, they were premised on this third category of "mixed status."

[42] Ibid., 12.

[43] The nonterritorial aspect of personal law, however, continues to function in the form of international private law even though the nation-state is the dominant conceptual unit of this legal universe.

legal personality became a feature and function of a citizen's nationality, rather than religion or domicile."[44]

The persistence of the personal law system in Egypt well into the twentieth century marks an exception to this global genealogy, one authorized by the colonial powers that exempted European residents and visitors from being subject to Egyptian domestic law. Thus even as Europeans dissolved the system of personal law (as that which traveled with the person beyond his domicile) in their own countries, they insisted on its applicability in the colonies and the protectorates over which they ruled. In doing so, they drew upon and expanded the special privileges that the Ottomans had granted to Europeans in the form of capitulations (since the seventeenth century).[45] Thus Europeans residing in the Middle East were able to command their own law in matters related to civil, criminal, and family matters. In Egypt, for example, the British and the French maintained their own consular courts, which had criminal jurisdiction over them. Even after the creation of Mixed Tribunals in 1876, aimed at standardizing the regulation of commercial and civil affairs,[46] issues related to the status and capacity of persons, matrimonial relations, inheritance, and trusteeship—all pertaining to "personal law" in the classical sense of the term—were handled differentially for native and foreign subjects.[47] It was only in 1937 with the signing of the Montreux Convention that the extraterritorial legal privileges granted to foreigners were finally abolished (see chapter 1).

The patchwork of modern family laws that exists in the Middle East today belongs to these transformations wrought in the meaning and scope of personal status law. In Western Europe, the consolidation of the nation-state required the dissolution of the communal autonomy of religious minorities in exchange for political and civil equality—most famously exemplified in the Jews having to renounce Talmudic law.[48] With the decline in the authority of canon law in Western Europe over the course of 150 years and due to considerable regional variation, marriage came to be seen as

---

[44] Surkis, "Code Switching."

[45] See Berger, "Conflicts Law and Public Policy."

[46] These Tribunals were created initially to secure European investments and loans. The Italian jurist Mancini's conflict of laws doctrine was crucial in the development of the Egyptian Mixed Courts. Berger, "Conflicts Law and Public Policy," 559. Mancini was a strong advocate of the personal law principle. He argued that aliens should have their own law in foreign lands, unless it violated the public order and sovereignty of the state they were residing in, at which point the territorial principle would supersede. Shreve and Buxbaum, *A Conflicts of Law Anthology*, 23–24. On Mixed Courts in Egypt, see Brown, *The Rule of Law in the Arab World*, 26–29.

[47] The extraterritorial character of personal status law still prevails in parts of the Middle East. For instance, when a marriage is contracted under another country's family law, Lebanon adjudicates it in accord with that law, even when the spouses are Lebanese citizens.

[48] On the transformation of family law in Europe, see Bonfield, "Developments in European Family Law."

contractual and regulated by secular civil codes that applied uniformly to all European subjects.[49] In contrast, while the communal autonomy of religious communities
was radically curtailed with the consolidation of the modern state in the Middle East,
state-recognized religious sects were allowed to keep a measure of juridical control
over what came to be called "family law." As I suggested in chapter 1, in many cases
where a religious group enjoyed no formal legal status under Ottoman rule, when
colonial powers granted it recognition they did so by creating a new religion-based
family law unique to the group (as was the case with the Druze, Ismailis, and 'Alawis
in Syria).[50] This invention was consistent with the logic Halley and Rittich trace in
that modern family law in the eyes of European jurists was supposed to reflect the
true spirit of the people and their traditions. One important long-term effect of this
invention is that religious identity has come to be invested in the domain of family
law, tying up matters of confession, gender, and sexuality in ways that appear to be
primordial but in effect are recent, contingent, and provisional.

Coptic Family Law and Minority Politics

While Egypt has as many as fifteen religion-based family laws (one for Muslims, two
for Jews, and twelve for different Christian denominations), it is Coptic family law
that is most consequential in defining Egyptian interreligious politics. Coptic personal status law is as much a product of the genealogy I have presented above as its
Muslim counterpart in Egypt. Following that trajectory, Coptic family law has also
institutionalized the modern concept of the family as a sociopolitical unit necessary
to the reproduction of national and communal life. Furthermore, the telescoping of
religious authority into the domain of personal status has invested Coptic religious
identity in family law to a degree that is historically unprecedented. These similarities notwithstanding, as the law of Egypt's largest minority, Coptic family law also
bears additional burdens. Unlike Islamic family law, which represents majoritarian
national identity, Coptic family law is exceptional in the distinct norms and mores it
embodies, and in its subjection to communal sovereignty—most potently symbolized
in the Coptic Orthodox Church. This arrangement pulls the national and communal projects in opposite directions, with Coptic family law seen as particularistic and

---

[49] Civil marriage was instituted in England in 1837, and became the norm in Germany in 1875. In
France, even though a civil code for marriage was adopted in 1791, Catholic proscription on divorce
was reinstituted in 1815 and remained in place for another seventy years. Bonfield, "Developments in
European Family Law."
[50] White, *The Emergence of Minorities in the Middle East*, amply documents this. See my discussion
of this point in chapter 2.

Islamic family law as national. While this tension is most apparent in polities like Egypt that have religion-based family-law regimes, it is also internal to the ideology of the nation-state itself insomuch as minority identity, by virtue of its religious, cultural, or ethnic difference from the majoritarian culture, represents a departure from majoritarian norms. A minority group's attempts to preserve its communal institutions exaggerate this line of fracture, often eliciting the charge that the minority tends to act as "a state within the state." Whether leveled against Native Americans in the United States, Muslims in India, France, and Britain, or the Kurds in Turkey, this charge is diagnostic of the precarious position that minorities occupy in modern national polities. The political struggle around Coptic family law in postcolonial Egypt is a unique expression of this structural problem.

Coptic family law is also distinct in that it is seen as the *sole* domain of communal *legal* autonomy. In Egypt, where the discourses and symbols of the Muslim majority saturate the nation-state and its public ethos, Coptic Christians feel that if not for control over family law, their assimilation to Islamic norms would be total. This sense is further intensified among Coptic Christians by the fact that, in Egypt, Islamic family law applies to interdenominational marriages between Christians, and inheritance and custody issues are subject to its edicts. As a result, for Coptic clerics and laity alike, Coptic personal status law has come to represent the essence and core of the religious tradition and its viability in the present. This attitude stands in contrast to the past; throughout the Ottoman period, for instance, Copts made wide use of shari'a courts in order to bypass the more restrictive laws of the Church.[51] While clerical authorities sought to curtail such practices, the Coptic Church has become far more aggressive in policing them in the modern period.[52]

Any effort on the part of the state to reform Coptic family law is seen as an incursion into the minority's right to command its ecclesiastical affairs and exercise its constitutionally guaranteed right to follow its own family law (now increasingly cast as an issue of religious freedom). Even though the *'ulama'* and Islamist groups have opposed Islamic family law reform, it has been executed through a series of executive decrees and legislative acts in postcolonial Egypt (in 1979, 1985, 2000, and 2004).[53]

---

[51] Afifi shows that under the Ottomans, many prominent Coptic Christian families opted for shari'a marriage contracts because it allowed them more flexibility (in terms of divorce and remarriage) than the Christian ones. Afifi, "Reflections on the Personal Laws." Jews and Christians continued to use shari'a courts well into the mid-1930s, despite the existence of Christian courts at the time. See Kholoussy, "Interfaith Unions and Non-Muslim Wives." See also Shaham, "Shopping for Legal Forums."

[52] Shaham, "Communal Identity, Political Islam, and Family Law."

[53] On the difficulties of reforming Muslim family law in the modern period, see Abu Odeh, "Modernizing Muslim Family Law."

In contrast, the Coptic Church's resistance to state-mandated reforms of Coptic family law has steadily increased since 1955, when communal courts were dissolved to create a national judicial system that included provisions related to the permissibility of divorce and remarriage.[54] This resistance reached a new apex in 1971 when Pope Shenouda III, shortly after his ascension to the papacy, prohibited Copts from divorcing or remarrying except under conditions of adultery or religious conversion, an edict that threw the Coptic community into disarray.[55]

Even though Pope Shenouda based his proscription on Biblical edicts (Mark 10:11, 12 and Matthew 19:3–9), as historian Tamer el-Leithy points out, this interpretation is quite novel in the history of Coptic religious law. Between the eleventh and thirteenth centuries, the Coptic Orthodox Church permitted Copts to divorce and remarry under a variety of circumstances.[56] This was done in part to deter Christian men from taking advantage of Islamic laws to dissolve marriages, remarry, and take multiple wives and concubines, and in part to increase the authority of the Church over lay Copts. The first full compendium of Coptic matrimonial laws, composed in the early part of the thirteenth century, not only expanded the grounds for divorce but also allowed Christians who had divorced and remarried to partake in the life of the Church, lest their ostracization "[push] them to convert to Islam."[57] In the mid-thirteenth century, Patriarch Cyril III (1235–43) commissioned the most influential compendium of Coptic law, *al-Majmu' al-Safawi* (1238), written by al-Safi ibn al-'Assal, a leading figure of the thirteenth-century Coptic renaissance. This volume drew upon a variety of legal sources, interpretive methods, and forms of religious reasoning from Islamic, Roman, and Byzantine traditions. Like its predecessor, it also revamped the older clerical prohibition on divorce, permitting it under twenty-eight different conditions.[58] *Al-Majmu' al-Safawi* became the basis of Pope Cyril III's *Nomocanon*, which remained the most influential source of Coptic law well into the

---

[54] The Coptic Orthodox Church presided over Christian courts until 1883, at which point this authority came to be invested in the Communal Council (Majlis al-Milli). In 1955, the Egyptian government unified the separate religious family-law courts under one national system wherein state-appointed, secularly trained judges came to apply religion-based family laws appropriate to the religious affiliation of the litigants. Notably, in response to Christian protests against the court unification in 1955, the Egyptian government granted Christian clergy the right to register and issue marriage licenses to spouses from the same denomination. On this history, see Sezgin, *Human Rights*, 119–26, 134.

[55] Papal decree number seven, issued to the Holy Synod on November 18, 1971. See Bernard-Maugiron, "Divorce and Remarriage of Orthodox Copts in Egypt"; and Kamal, *Talaq al-Aqbat*, 14.

[56] El-Leithy, *Coptic Culture and Conversion*.

[57] Ibid., 426.

[58] el-Leithy notes that Ibn al-'Assal does not use the Arabic term *talaq* for divorce, which is associated with Islamic law, but instead uses words such as *faskh* (rupture), *inhilal* (dissolution), and *firaq* (separation). *Talaq* in Islamic law was a male privilege, whereas in Coptic religious law, under certain conditions a marriage could be dissolved regardless of whether the spouses intended it. Ibid., 428.

latter part of the nineteenth century, when its central premises made their way into the code of personal status law from 1896 known as *al-Khulasa al-Qanuniyya al-Ahwal al-Shakhsiyya li-Kanisat al-Aqbat al-Urthuduksiyyin*, commissioned by Patriarch Cyril VI.[59] When the Coptic Communal Council (Majlis al-Milli) crafted a new Coptic family law in 1938, Copts were once again allowed to divorce and remarry under a number of circumstances.[60] The Egyptian state adopted the 1938 Code formally in 1955, when communal courts were dissolved to create a unified national judicial system.[61] Even though the Coptic Church and the Holy Synod protested the 1938 Code, Coptic family affairs were adjudicated in accord with its stipulations until 1971, when Pope Shenouda categorically declared that while "binding from a civil perspective, [it] did not oblige the Church to permit divorcees to remarry."[62] He condemned the 1938 Code as a heretical invention that "was written by Coptic Orthodox lay leaders who, seeking to satisfy their worldly desires and lust, invented novel grounds for the dissolution of marriage."[63]

Pope Shenouda's decree not only pitted ecclesiastical sovereignty against that of the state, but also created a crisis for thousands of Coptic Christians who had divorced under the 1938 Code but could no longer obtain permission to remarry from the Clerical Council for Family Affairs.[64] Many segments of the Coptic community, breaking with protocols of communal solidarity, criticized Shenouda's decree as catastrophic for the Copts. Karima Kamal, whom I quoted at the beginning of this chapter, characterizes the prohibition as a de facto invitation for Copts to abandon their religion or commit adultery in order to get out of unhappy marital situations. Some Coptic priests even defied papal orders to preside over the marriages of Coptic Christians who had procured divorces from national courts in accord with state law.[65] The papal prohibition also set into motion a black market of sorts, as local priests began charging a fee to provide marriage licenses that family-law courts would accept in accord with national legislation. Matters finally came to a head in 2002, when a Coptic

---

[59] Shaham, "Communal Identity, Political Islam, and Family Law."

[60] These conditions are laid out in ibid., 417–18.

[61] When the Communal Council issued the 1938 Code of Coptic family law, it included nine reasons for the dissolution of marriage, which the Holy Synod contested vehemently. Both Pope Macarius III and Pope Cyril VI registered their protest in 1945 and 1962, respectively, and the former declared that divorce was only allowed under conditions of adultery. Rowberry and Khalil, "A Brief History of Coptic Personal Status Law."

[62] Shaham, "Communal Identity, Political Islam, and Family Law," 413.

[63] Ibid., 415.

[64] Estimates for the number of Coptic divorcees affected by the pope's decision range between 70,000 and 160,000. See, for example, Sulayman, *Qawanin al-Ahwal al-Shakhsiyya lil-Masihiyyin*; and Kamal, *Talaq al-Aqbat*. For journalist reporting, see Muhsin Abd al-Radi, "al-Zawaj al-Thani lil-Aqbat Azma Tahtaj ila Hal," *Masress*, March 25, 2012, www.masress.com/elfagr/148343.

[65] Usama, *Masir al-Aqbat fi Misr*, 403–4, 407–9.

man brought a lawsuit against Pope Shenouda in a lower administrative court.[66] He challenged the Church's refusal to grant him a remarriage license on the basis of rights accorded to him under the 1938 Code.[67] The court ruled in favor of the plaintiff in 2006, but Shenouda refused to abide by it, stating, "We are only bound by the teachings of the Holy Bible. We cannot go against our conscience and comply with a court ruling which is a civilian ruling and not [an] ecclesiastical [one]."[68]

The Church appealed the lower court's decision in the Supreme Administrative Court (SAC) using two key arguments: (1) that family-law courts lack the jurisdiction to review Coptic applications for (re)marriage because marriage in Coptic Orthodox Christianity is neither "a civil nor an administrative matter, but *purely a religious one*"; and (2) that the Church's prohibition on divorce (and by extension remarriage) constitutes the *essence of Christianity*.[69] This appeal is illustrative of two key features of the religion-based family-law regime under modern secularism that I discussed earlier. Note that the Church's position amplifies the secular distinction between civil and religious jurisdictions, in doing so exacerbating the tension between church and state sovereignty. Furthermore, the Church's argument rhetorically renders the regulation of marital relations and, by extension, the papal prohibition on divorce as consubstantial with Christian doctrine. As the Church's legal counsel Nabil Jibril put it, "Can the Court oblige the al-Azhar grand Imam to make prayers six times a day instead of five? Why does the Court intervene in religious rituals of the Copts which stem from the Bible?"[70] In making this analogy, Jibril effectively elevates what has been a historically variable practice to an inviolable doctrinal and biblical edict. As I recount above, not only had the Coptic Church allowed Copts to divorce

---

[66] In administrative courts, citizens can challenge actions of the executive, the state bureaucracy, or public agencies on the grounds that they are mutually contradictory or violate the constitution. While the lower administrative courts deal with first-instance disputes, the Supreme Administrative Court examines appeals against the rulings of the lower courts.

[67] A number of Copts have filed similar cases against the Church, most famously the prominent Egyptian actress Hala Sidqi's husband. Sidqi had converted to Syrian Orthodox Christianity so she could divorce her husband, which allowed her to use the Islamic family-law provision of *khul'* that permits women to file for divorce without the husband's consent. Sidqi's husband filed a lawsuit against the Coptic Church for refusing him the permission to remarry; he won it in February 2007. See Bernard-Maugiron, "Divorce and Remarriage of Orthodox Copts."

[68] Sham, "Communal Identity, Political Islam, and Family Law," 419.

[69] In the appeal submitted to the SAC in May 2006, the Coptic Orthodox Church argued, "The obligation to obtain a marriage license is a basic foundation of the Christian faith that is not subject to interpretation [*ta'wil*] or substitution [*tabdil*]. This is an absolute principle [*hiya mas'ala qat'iyyat al-thubut*] and challenging it constitutes a violation of the essence of Christian belief." Bernard-Maugiron, "Divorce and Remarriage of Orthodox Copts," 367, emphasis added.

[70] Mary Abdelmassih, "Coptic Church Protests Court Ruling on Marriage License," *Assyrian International News Agency*, May 30, 2010, www.aina.org/news/2010053016089.htm. The spelling I use for "Nabil Jibril" in the text is more commonly used in the Egyptian press, but is different from the one Abdelmassih uses in this article.

and remarry under a variety of conditions in the premodern period, but this issue had never been represented as the core and essence of Christian doctrine. Its elevation to this historically unique status, I suggest, shows that by privatizing religious and family affairs political secularism does not simply accord them state protection (as is often believed). Rather, secular governance transforms both religion and kinship relations from within; amplifying certain doctrinal edicts and muting others, it accentuates religion's jurisprudential dimensions over other moral and ethical concerns.[71]

In a judgment delivered on March 1, 2008, the SAC rejected Pope Shenouda's appeal. The court acknowledged that even though it was within the jurisdiction of the religious leader (*al-ra'is al-dini*) to issue marriage licenses, he was obliged to conform to the Coptic Orthodox Personal Status Regulations adopted by the Coptic Community Council in 1938. It was the duty of the judiciary, argued the SAC, to "ensure respect for the goals and purposes of the law and to reach a balance between decisions related to *religious matters and the rights of citizens* guaranteed by the Constitution."[72] Given that the right to marry and form a family is constitutionally ensured and enshrined in the 1938 Code, the court argued that it was obliged to uphold the law. Pope Shenouda refused to abide by the court's decision, insisting that the state had no right to intervene in this issue because marriage is a matter of Christian doctrine over which the Church alone was sovereign. Note that in this exchange the Church and the Egyptian state *concur* that the family is the essential unit of social and communal reproduction. Where their disagreement lies is in the proper jurisdiction of civil versus religious authority, pitting the sovereignty of the state against that of the Church.

Three months after the SAC decision, the Coptic Church won a landmark victory by securing government approval to amend Coptic family law in accord with the papal decree.[73] Despite opposition from a wide cross-section of Copts, the Church used its political clout with the Coptic Communal Council and the Mubarak government to have the Personal Status Regulation for Coptic Orthodox Christians changed without so much as a discussion in the People's Assembly. This was an astounding achievement, and a powerful expression of two distinct developments in Egyptian

---

[71] This situation is not unique to Coptic Christianity. Evangelical opposition to homosexuality has come to be cast as a violation of core Pauline doctrine and mimics the same logic that I trace here. On this, see Warner, "Sex and Secularity."

[72] Bernard-Maugiron, "Divorce and Remarriage of Orthodox Copts," 366, emphasis added.

[73] For a full account of this amendment, see Bernard-Maugiron, "Divorce and Remarriage of Orthodox Copts," 369–73. Despite this amendment, thousands of Copts who procured a divorce under the 1938 Code continue to challenge in court the Church's refusal to grant them remarriage licenses. See Bishoy Ramzi, "Copts and Second Marriage: Religious or Legislative Conflict?," *Cairo Post*, April 2, 2014, http://thecairopost.com/news/104884/inside_egypt/copts-and-second-marriage-legislative-or-religious-conflict.

history: (1) the church-state entente, in place since the Nasser administration, which allows the Coptic Church to bypass Coptic critics of its policies; (2) the Church's cooptation of the Coptic Communal Council (Majlis al-Milli), once known for its stalwart opposition to the clerical prohibition on divorce and remarriage, by integrating the Council into its ecclesiastical structure. Under the current Pope Tawadros, once again the Church has pledged its support for the ruling junta of General Abdel Fattah al-Sisi on the assumption that this will help preserve its diktat more than if it were to make its case in the courts or before the public.[74]

The 2008 amendment of Coptic personal status law is noteworthy for expanding the meaning and scope of the term *adultery* beyond the sexual act of marital infidelity (*flagrante delicto*) to include a range of behaviors, inclinations, and thoughts that had, to date, fallen outside the Church's legal jurisdiction.[75] This interpretation is in accord with the general trend in postcolonial Coptic family law toward greater conservatism, often to the detriment of women's rights.[76] In the view of one legal historian, "At the same time that the reform of personal status law for Muslims [in Egypt] is gradually improving the status of women, non-Muslim family law is becoming increasingly restrictive, especially as regards divorce."[77] The amendment of Islamic family law in 2000 that grants Egyptian Muslim women the right to unilateral divorce (on the basis of the Islamic concept of *khul'*) is a case in point.[78]

Coptic family law's adoption of increasingly more restrictive laws on issues related to gender and marriage needs to be placed within the broader framework of the simultaneous privatization of religion and family affairs in the modern period. Once religious power was circumscribed under secularism, the family became the sole domain of religious authority and the primal site for its reproduction. It is, therefore, not surprising that religious morality has come to devolve upon the conduct of family affairs in a manner that is historically unique. The control of women's sexuality

---

[74] For dissension among Copts on this policy, see Leyla Doss, "A Civil Coptic Movement Struggles in Polarized Egypt," *Mada Masr*, May 12, 2014, http://madamasr.com/content/civil-coptic-movement-struggles-polarized-egypt.

[75] Bernard-Maugiron, "Divorce and Remarriage of Orthodox Copts," 370. For further elaboration of these conditions, see Maikel Faris, "Nanfarid bi-Nashr La'iha al-Ahwal al-Shakhsiyya lil-Aqbat al-Urthuduks al-Jadida," *al-Youm al-Sabi'a*, April 5, 2013, www1.youm7.com/News.asp?NewsID=1006356.

[76] For an analysis of the Church's shift to the right regarding issues of gender, see Armanios, "The 'Virtuous Woman.'"

[77] Bernard-Maugiron, "Divorce and Remarriage of Orthodox Copts," 385.

[78] Muslim women are given this right on the condition that they forfeit their right to financial support from the husband. For a review of this change in Islamic family law and the *'ulama's* intense opposition to it, see al-Sharmani, *Recent Reforms in Personal Status Laws and Women's Empowerment*, chap. 1. Christian women have also started to use the *khul'* provision to file for divorce, provided they have converted either to another Christian denomination or to Islam, in which case their marriage is subject to Islamic family law. See note 10 in this chapter.

has always been at the center of the institution of heterosexual marriage. Under the secular dispensation, this control has become the sine qua non of religious morality, exemplified in battles over family law and family values. For the Coptic Church this investment is further intensified because of the undue power that Islamic family law exerts on regulating Christian relations. The Coptic Church's retrenchment on the question of divorce and remarriage is not simply an example of its conservatism; it is also a window into how secularism has created a volatile cathexis between religion and sexuality.

The 2008 Coptic personal status law drew protests from a small but vociferous group of Copts who argued that with no recourse to dissolve unhappy marital arrangements, an increasing number of Copts would be forced to convert to Islam or other Christian denominations.[79] Its passage has also strengthened the resolve of some Coptic groups to push for reforming the Communal Council to weaken the clerical hold over Coptic family law.[80] To foreclose this possibility, the Coptic Church moved decisively in 2014 by successfully lobbying to have Article 3 added to the new constitution, which declares, "The canon principles of Christians and Jews [are] the main sources of legislation for their personal status laws, religious affairs, and the selection of their spiritual leaders."[81] By consecrating the Church as the sole authority over ecclesiastical and doctrinal affairs, Article 3 aims not only to limit state jurisdiction over the substantive content of Coptic family law, but also to exclude lay Coptic critics from having any say in the matter. Furthermore, insomuch as Article 3 only addresses the rights of "People of the Book," it upholds the reigning consensus between the Church and the Egyptian state that religious minorities other than Christians and Jews (such as the Bahais and the Shi'a) have no state recognition (see chapter 4).[82]

It is interesting to contrast the Coptic Orthodox Church's refusal to abide by the state-mandated Coptic personal status law in Egypt with the Church's position in the

---

[79] A new Coptic group called Coptic 38 was formed in opposition to the amended Coptic family law of 2008. It urges fellow Copts to "resign" from the Church in protest of its prohibition on divorce and remarriage. The group claims that as many as four thousand Copts have left the Church in response, and many others continue to convert in order to avoid the stipulations of Coptic family law. See "Coptic Christians Call for Divorce Law Relaxation," *al-Ahram Weekly*, April 23, 2012, http://english.ahram.org.eg/NewsContent/1/64/39993/Egypt/Politics-/Coptic-Christians-call-for-divorce-law-relaxation.aspx.

[80] Among those active on this front is Kamal Zakhir, head of al-Tayyar al-'Almani lil-Islah al-Kanisa, whose views I discuss in chapter 2.

[81] Article 3 was first included in the 2013 constitution passed under President Morsi (deposed in July 2013) of the Muslim Brotherhood, and was subsequently preserved in the 2014 constitution formulated under General Abdel Fattah al-Sisi. Despite long-standing tensions between the Coptic Church and the Brotherhood, it is noteworthy that both share the assumption that family law should be the purview of religious authorities because it represents the core of the faith.

[82] Insomuch as Jews are only a nominal minority in Egypt, for all practical purposes Article 3 of the new constitution pertains primarily to Christians.

Euro-American Coptic dioceses, where its members must follow secular civil codes that allow divorce and remarriage. Even though the edicts of the patriarch are supreme, practices in these dioceses vary considerably; numerous Coptic churches in the United States and Europe, for example, preside over marriages between divorcees. While the Coptic patriarchate might urge its followers to shun this practice, it cannot command its parishioners to flout the civil law of host countries. Nor can it accuse such states of discrimination for failing to adopt Coptic religious precepts in the adjudication of family relations because Euro-American governments usually do not allow such religious accommodations.[83] In contrast, a polity like Egypt, with a religion-based family-law system, cannot by definition be regarded as neutral because it proclaims religious difference as essential to its legal regime. Even in instances where Egyptian Islamic family law might actually help Copts sidestep the Church's interdictions, the fact that it is the law of another religious sect necessarily renders it partial. One might say that in the modern dispensation, secular law by virtue of its claim to universality necessarily appears neutral and, by contrast, religious law appears particular and partial.

It is easy to view the standoff between the Coptic Church and the state as a unique product of religion-based family-law regimes, and in some ways it clearly is. However, this conflict also partakes in a set of key conundrums that characterize all secular polities: What is the proper jurisdiction of the state versus that of religion? How should the modern state adjudicate conflicts between public policy and religious exemption? There is no axiomatic way to resolve these questions. Rather, they are often settled in a provisional and piecemeal fashion through courts and legislative action, not only in postcolonial societies like Egypt but also in those regarded as paradigmatically secular. In the United States this is manifest in the unending litigation around the granting of religious exemptions from state-mandated laws, whether they pertain to labor, education, the performance of prayer in public schools, or employers' compliance with healthcare laws.[84] The French government, despite its avowedly *laïque*

---

[83] There are exceptions to this rule, particularly in regard to Jewish family law that requires women who have procured a civil divorce to secure the husband's permission (called "get") before they can remarry. While European and North American family laws do not formally recognize this requirement, there are precedents in France, Germany, Belgium, and Canada, where courts have made allowances for it. See Shah et al., *Family, Religion, and Law*, 62. For an excellent analysis of the respect accorded to Jewish family-law provisions in Britain, see Malik, "Minorities and Law."

[84] Even though the First Amendment of the US constitution is supposed to guarantee a strict separation between state and religion, the Supreme Court has produced mixed jurisprudence on where the boundary between them lies. In the *Hosanna-Tabor v. EEOC* case (2012), the court dismissed a lawsuit filed by an employee of the Evangelical Lutheran Church for labor discrimination on the grounds that the application of the US labor laws would constitute an unlawful interference by the state in church affairs under the Free Exercise Clause. This contradicted an earlier judgment by the Supreme Court, *Employment Division v. Smith* (1990), which ruled that the state was within its rights to limit the free

character, regularly overrides public policy to accommodate religious exemptions to Catholics and Jews while refusing the same to Muslims.[85] In Germany, legal debates about banning circumcision, the construction of mosques, and the veil encounter the same question: where and how to draw the line between the jurisdiction of the state and that of religion. The religion-based family-law regime gives this problem a particular cast, which at first glance seems parochial, but is in fact an elaboration of a constitutive feature of political secularism.

Secularism and Gender Inequality

Religion-based family laws of the Middle East are often assumed to be inequitable to women in matters of divorce, custody, and inheritance because of their religious character. This in turn engenders the hope that if these laws were secularized they would yield greater gender equality. There is no doubt that both Muslim and Christian family laws have been historically unjust to women in the Middle East. It is, nonetheless, important to point out that the gender inequities enshrined in family law cannot be understood in religious terms alone. Historians have long noted that once the family became a cornerstone of the modern capitalist state, this created greater gender inequality, particularly in the institution of marriage.[86] This is reflected in the transformations wrought in Islamic marriage contracts in the Middle East. Muslim women, for example, used to be able to stipulate a variety of conditions (including the right to initiate divorce) during Mamluk and Ottoman times (the thirteenth to seventeenth centuries), a practice that became increasingly constrained with the institutionalization of family law under the modern state.[87] Women's ability to negotiate

exercise of religion when it contradicted the state's laws of "general applicability." For an insightful analysis of these competing interpretations of the First Amendment, see Sullivan, "The World That *Smith* Made"; and Danchin, "Religious Freedom."

[85] Fernando, *The Republic Unsettled.*

[86] Historically, modern capitalism institutes both a class and a sexual division of labor that renders women's economic activities at home obsolete, reducing their power and access to means of production. As economic production shifts outside the home, it becomes the provenance of men, while women's labor in the house is simultaneously devalued *and* hailed as necessary to the reproduction of morality, sentimentality, and the human race. The modern family is the primal site of this logic of reproduction and devaluation.

[87] Thus Judith Tucker argues, "By Mamluk times (thirteenth to fifteenth centuries), a variety of stipulations had become commonplace, such as allowing a wife to opt for divorce should her husband drink wine or fail to house and support her children from a previous marriage. In the Ottoman era, the technique of expanding a bride's rights through contractual stipulations continued apace: a woman might insert clauses into her contract that gave her the right of divorce if the husband did any number of things, including taking a second wife, changing their residence against her will, traveling more than once a year, moving permanently to a distant location, or beating her with enough force to leave marks." Tucker, *Women, Family, and Gender in Islamic Law,* 62.

was in part a product of the Islamic understanding of marriage as a contract (unlike Christianity, which regards it as a sacrament). Under Ottoman rule, Coptic Christians also took advantage of these marriage contracts by opting to use shari'a courts in order to bypass the Church's prohibition against divorce, polygamy, and remarriage. According to Amira Sonbol, "This type of contract was severely curtailed with the [modern] establishment . . . of personal status codes that made the inclusion of conditions to marriage contracts unrecognizable in court," while placing the wife in the sole custody of her husband and upholding the privileges the shari'a accorded him.[88] In refusing to recognize prenuptial conditions in marriage contracts, modern courts effectively foreclosed "the most important method by which a [woman] could control her marriage."[89]

The notion of spousal disobedience (*nushuz*) in the shari'a was not only expanded but also came to apply only to wives.[90] The Egyptian laws of 1897 and 1931 created an institution called the "house of obedience" (*bayt al-ta'a*), which allowed "a husband who had secured a decree of his wife's nushuz from the court" to have her forcibly returned, with the assistance of the police, to the marital home.[91] There was no scriptural support in the Quran or the hadith for this institution, nor were there any precedents in classical Islamic jurisprudence. This temporal stipulation for wifely obedience was part of the French Civil Code of 1804 (dissolved in France in 1938) on which the Ottoman Law of Family Rights of 1917 was based.[92] Importantly, the house of obedience provision also applied to Coptic Christians since it pertained not to a religious but to a state injunction, one that affected all citizens equally. (It was dissolved in 1967.) The creation of the house of obedience is an important marker of the kind of patriarchy that the nuclear family signified. "Home" was now the sole place of coitus, conjugality, and reproduction; and by denying women the right to return to their patrilineal home, the father's authority was resolutely replaced with the husband's.[93] The transformations wrought in the regulation of Coptic Christian

---

[88] Sonbol, "History of Marriage Contracts," 162.

[89] Ibid., 183.

[90] In classical shari'a, the concept of disobedience (*nushuz*) applied to both women and men. In modern family-law codes of the Middle East, *nushuz* became "exclusively a woman's liability, the result of failure to perform [a] variety of functions assigned to her by the law" in relation to her husband. Hallaq, *Shari'a*, 456.

[91] Tucker, *Women, Family, and Gender in Islamic Law*, 74.

[92] According to Wael Hallaq, the French Civil Code unambiguously stated, "The husband owes protection to his wife, the wife obedience to her husband." When the Ottoman Code of 1917 adopted this provision, in the name of marital equality it required "the husband to treat his wife kindly, but impos[ed] on her the obligation of obedience." Hallaq, *Shari'a*, 453.

[93] With few exceptions, even when women have greater rights through family-law reforms in the Middle East, the principle of male privilege remains sacrosanct. This is apparent, for example, in the law of primogeniture and male rights over the property and person of the wife and children. Ibid., 460–61.

marital relations from the premodern to the modern period, as I recount above, follow a similar pattern in that the conditions for the dissolution of marriage come to be increasingly restricted.

This scholarship on the history of Muslim and Christian personal status law forces us to reconsider the oft-repeated argument that secularizing it would lead to greater gender parity. Secularism is not synonymous with gender equality, and gender equity has not been achieved without a political struggle under various regimes of secular governance. This is just as true of paradigmatically secular Western societies as it is of non-Western ones often judged to be inadequately secular. Joan Scott, for example, argues that when the architects of French *laïcité* moved to separate church from state, "the equal status of women and men was not a primary concern."[94] The French law of 1905, "one of the exemplary laws of modern European secularism, . . . never mentioned gender at all."[95] Similarly, for almost a century none of the judgments related to the law of 1905 issued by the Conseil d'État, the highest administrative court in France, had anything to say about the "woman question."[96] The latter was, however, thematized in French republican thought in relation to the colonies, particularly in establishing the moral superiority of *laïcité* as a system of colonial rule over Muslim Algeria. Judith Surkis shows that family law was a key site of this articulation through which the distinction between citizens (French) and colonial subjects (Algerian), the barbarity of Muslim law and the impartiality of French civil law, was secured.[97] Viewed from this perspective, contemporary French panic over Islamic gender norms (including the Muslim headscarf) has a long history that remains invisible in national celebratory accounts of *laïcité*.[98] Rather than see colonial history as parallel to the development of secularism, I suggest that it is integral to the elaboration of the secular project—a project that is deeply imbued with gendered claims of European civilizational superiority.

Secularism is enormously consequential to how gender inequality is organized and reproduced in the modern period. According to Scott, the institutionalization of the public-private division enshrines sexual difference at the core of the secular political order, which then comes to serve as a matrix for organizing other hierarchical oppositions such as state and family, reason and sex, and politics and religion. Seen in this way, political secularism is not simply a neutral instrument in the management of gender and sexual differences but a means of instituting a distinct form of gender

---

[94] Scott, "Secularism and Gender Equality."
[95] Ibid., 31.
[96] Ibid., 32.
[97] Surkis, "Code Switching."
[98] Surkis, "Hymenal Politics."

inequality. This is consonant with the work of Carole Pateman, who, in her classic book *The Sexual Contract*, argues that the marriage contract is a unique instrument of modern patriarchy, one that simultaneously makes reproductive sex necessary to the constitution of the liberal political order even as it relegates marriage and family to the domain of privacy, which is declared to be inconsequential to politics.[99] Any attempt to think through conditions that propagate gender inequality must therefore countenance the patriarchy not only of religious traditions but also of modern secularism. To trust either one as inherently open or closed to gender parity is to misunderstand the fundamental centrality of gender inequality to both secular and religious dispensations. While the control of women's sexuality has always been important to religious morality, the creation of family law, as an autonomous juridical domain, has intensified this investment in unpredictable but consequential ways. The resistance feminists have encountered to instituting laws against domestic abuse and to legalizing abortion in Euro-America is rooted in the same public-private division that is at the heart of the resistance to reform religion-based family laws.

As Wendy Brown reminds us, the masculinist privilege that the liberal state enshrines is neither historically identical nor formulaic. Rather, it deploys distinct modalities of political power, each of which produces different kinds of effects and requires distinct analytical frameworks.[100] Of the four modalities she discusses, the two most pertinent to the analytical arc of this book are the juridical-legislative and the prerogative dimensions of state power: the former pertains to the state's legal and constitutional aspects, whereas the latter relates to the legitimate right of the state to arbitrarily intervene in and reorder human life.[101] Modern family law encompasses both modalities: it is the juridical expression of the liberal state's regulation of sexual and domestic relations, and it is also the vehicle for intervening and reordering the private sphere, which is supposed to be free from government interference in the liberal scheme. Both dimensions of state power, as I have suggested in this book, are crucial to the operation of political secularism.

The Politics of Religious Conversion

So far in the chapter I have focused on how the privatization of religion and family has created a volatile symbiosis between religious identity and family law in Egypt. In what follows, I want to examine the Egyptian state's asymmetrical regulation of interreligious

[99] Pateman, *The Sexual Contract*.
[100] Brown, "Finding the Man in the State," 175.
[101] The other two modalities Brown analyzes are the capitalist and bureaucratic dimensions of state power. Ibid., 175–93.

marriage and conversion, one result of which is that Christian-Muslim strife often unfolds on the terrain of gender and sexuality. As I will show, the Qustuntin and Shehata cases that I discussed at the beginning of the chapter are paradigmatic examples of this issue. Despite declaring that Christians have their own family law, the Egyptian government regards Islamic family law as the "general law" of the country.[102] This allows the government to uphold the shariʿa provision that permits a Muslim man to marry a Christian woman without changing his religion while requiring that a Christian man who weds a Muslim woman convert to Islam. In a society where the exchange of women is the organizing principle of kinship,[103] this law essentially makes Christian women available to Muslim men while prohibiting the obverse. A wide cross-section of Copts, lay and clerics alike, understand this law to be a violation of the sanctity of the Christian family, and view Coptic women's conversion to Islam as the channel through which their faith is being depleted. The fury surrounding Qustuntin's and Shehata's alleged conversions to Islam is an expression of the apprehension many Copts feel about this state of affairs, which is further exacerbated by the alleged increase in Coptic women converting to Islam following the papal prohibition on divorce.[104]

The other most discriminatory law pertains to the unequal regulation of Muslim-Christian religious conversion. At issue is the range of formal and informal bureaucratic and social norms that make it extremely difficult for a Muslim to convert to Christianity while facilitating the obverse. Even though Egyptian law does not formally prohibit religious conversion, when Muslims convert to Christianity (or another religion), the Ministry of Interior refuses to list their correct religious affiliation on their national identity cards, which are essential for the conduct of civil and political life (on this point, see chapter 4). This is a violation of Article 47(2) of the Civil Status Code, which allows Egyptian citizens to change their religious affiliation on state-issued documents, as well as a contravention of the right to religious liberty guaranteed in the Egyptian constitution.[105] Apart from the resistance that the converts face from governmental bodies, they also confront various forms of social harassment that effectively deter even those who have converted from coming forward publicly.[106]

---

[102] Berger, "Conflicts Law and Public Policy."

[103] Rubin, "The Traffic in Women."

[104] According to a report submitted to the New York Council of Churches, Coptic clerical sources suggested that 80 to 90 percent of the people who converted to Islam in 1999 were younger than twenty-five years old, and women made up 80 percent of the total. Sara Aguzzoni, "Media Reports of Christians Converting to Islam," *Arab West Report*, Paper 6, March 2008, www.arabwestreport.info/ar/lsn-2008/lsbw-32/25-lmhjr-wlsqf-mzq-lmwtn, section 2. See also Kamal, *Talaq al-Aqbat*.

[105] Berger, "Apostasy and Public Policy."

[106] For the first time in recent history, two Muslim converts to Christianity (Mohammed Hegazy and Maher al-Gohary) sued the Ministry of Interior (in 2007 and 2008, respectively) for violating

Given this situation, it is not surprising that Coptic Christians feel a high level of anxiety that their faith is under the threat of dissolution, an unease that, as I will discuss below, is deeply gendered.

The Egyptian policing of religious conversion is commonly understood to be a product of the Islamic prohibition against apostasy (a Muslim's renunciation of Islamic beliefs), which classical Islamic jurisprudence regarded as a crime that was, according to some schools, punishable by death. Historians note that there was much variation within and across premodern Islamic empires in how they treated and punished apostasy. Given that the Quran does not prescribe a worldly punishment for apostasy, Muslim jurists differed on the material consequences of the act. Deringil notes, for example, that the Ottomans seldom deployed the notion of apostasy to execute converts in premodern times.[107] However, this began to change in the modern period, as communal religious identity became the basis of a people's ability to claim political sovereignty; defection from one side to the other became consequential in a way that it was not in the earlier period. No longer a matter of religious truth, conversion became entangled in how national sovereignty was to be legitimated and defined.[108] The concept of apostasy also underwent a fundamental transformation when it was subjected to the authority of a centralized state and the calculus of majority-minority national demographics.[109] Modern penal codes, when they were first crafted, did not define apostasy as a crime in most Middle Eastern states. Baber Johansen points out that the demand for apostasy trials emerges in the 1980s and 1990s for the first time in the modern period as part of the larger popular demand to restore the shari'a.[110]

The policing of interreligious conversion in Egypt belongs to this political order, and should not be seen as a primordial interdiction against apostasy. In contemporary Egypt, even though apostasy is not litigable under statutory law, it is part of legal and

---

their rights under Article 47(2) of the Civil Status Law by refusing to grant them a national identity card with their correct religious affiliation. Despite the international support their cases garnered from human-rights and religious-freedom advocates, both lost their appeals. In its judgment against Hegazy, the Supreme Administrative Court opined that because "monotheistic religions were sent by God in a chronological order," one cannot convert to an "older religion." The judgment against Gohari stated that a Muslim's conversion was contrary to the shari'a and posed a threat to public order. On both cases, see the appeal submitted to the United Nations Office of the High Commissioner for Human Rights by the European Centre for Law and Justice on January 22, 2010, http://eclj.org/pdf/eclj_unsrrfecljhega zyapp_20100125.pdf.

[107] Deringil, "There Is No Compulsion in Religion," 556.

[108] Under the modern nation state, demography acquires a political salience that is historically unique. The ongoing contestation over the number of Copts reported in the Egyptian census is a case in point. See Pennington, "The Copts in Modern Egypt."

[109] Deringil, "There Is No Compulsion in Religion," 566–68.

[110] Johansen, "Apostasy as Objective and Depersonalized Fact."

popular discourse. When it surfaces in legal judgments, however, it does not entail the death penalty.[111] Prominent Islamic figures, such as Ali Gom'a, the former Grand Mufti of Egypt, regularly opine that although conversion from Islam is a religious sin, it is not subject to temporal punishment.[112] Changing one's religion, however, does have legal consequences because it impinges upon one's personal status law (marital status, inheritance, and custody rights). As a result, religious conversion cases are typically handled by family-law courts (or the Court of Cassation, which has appellate authority over civil and criminal courts). Due to the asymmetrical treatment of Christian-Muslim conversion, not surprisingly, these cases, with few notable exceptions, almost always involve Christian converts to Islam.[113]

Egypt's asymmetrical regulation of religious conversion is complexly entwined with its family-law regime. To begin with, Islamic family law, as the "general law" of the country, stands in a hierarchical relationship to the personal status laws of Christians and Jews. Unlike in other Middle Eastern countries (Jordan, Syria, Morocco), in Egypt marriage between two spouses from different Christian sects or religions is subject to Islamic family law (rather than the family law of one of the spouses).[114] All Egyptian churches are united in their opposition to this arrangement and over the years have attempted to create a unified Christian personal status law that is not subservient to Islamic family law.[115] These attempts have failed in large part because of the refusal of the Egyptian government to circumscribe the scope of Islamic family law,[116] but also because there are deep divisions between Egyptian churches regarding the permissibility of divorce; while the Catholic Church opposes the dissolution of

[111] Berger, "Apostasy and Public Policy," 722.

[112] Jonathan Spollen, "The Conversion Factor: The Egyptian Grand Mufti Has Thrown Fuel on One of the Country's Most Contentious Sectarian Issues: Religious Conversion," *Guardian*, July 27, 2007, www.theguardian.com/commentisfree/2007/jul/27/theconversionfactor.

[113] According to Maurits Berger, the great exception to this pattern was the case of Nasr Hamid Abu Zayd, a Muslim scholar who was accused of apostasy for his academic commentary on the Quran. Since apostasy is not a criminal offence, his case was brought to the Court of Cassation, which ruled him guilty and deemed his marriage to his Muslim wife invalid. The court argued, "Apostasy renders the marriage of the apostate null and void (*batil*), results in the separation (*tafriq*) of the spouses, and prevents the apostate from entering into a (new) marriage even with a non-Muslim." Berger, "Apostasy and Public Policy," 723.

[114] Law No. 462, which authorized this in 1955, also made it illegal for non-Muslims to opt to use Islamic family law when the spouses are from the same religion or Christian denomination, a practice that had been common until then. See Berger, "Secularizing Interreligious Law"; and Sezgin, *Human Rights*, 123.

[115] There have been repeated attempts to create a unified Christian family law (in 1980, 1999, 2013, and 2014), none of which has been adopted. For the proposal from 1999, see "Marriage, Politics, and Jerusalem," *al-Ahram Weekly*, April 1–7, 1999, http://weekly.ahram.org.eg/1999/423/intrview.htm.

[116] The proposal from 1980, unanimously approved by all the churches, was shelved by the government and never debated in the parliament. It adopted the Coptic Church's position on divorce and remarriage, allowing both only if one of the spouses had committed adultery or changed their religion. Sezgin, *Human Rights*, 147–48.

marriage under all circumstances, Anglicans and Protestants permit it.[117] When in November 2014 the Egyptian government finally released its proposal for a unified Christian family law that would allow Christian couples to secure divorce under a number of circumstances, Copts and Catholics strongly opposed it.[118] Given the lack of Christian consensus and the ongoing government intransigence, inter-denominational marriages continue to be adjudicated in accord with Islamic family-law precepts, exacerbating the asymmetry that defines majority-minority relations in Egypt.

This inequality has been subjected to a different set of pressures since the papal edict from 1971 led an increasing number of Coptic women and men to convert to Islam (or other Christian denominations) in order to dissolve their marriages. Combined with the state policy on conversion, this trend has heightened the anxiety among Copts that their community is being slowly depleted. Rather than change its stance on divorce in order to keep its followers from leaving the fold, the Church has chosen to fight on other fronts. These contentious dynamics came to the fore in the famous case of the "returnees" (*'a'idin*), a large group of Christian men who returned to their original faith after having converted to Islam in order to divorce their Coptic wives.[119] When they tried to have their second change of religion (from Islam to Christianity) registered on their national identity cards, the Ministry of Interior refused. The *'a'idin* then sued the Ministry of Interior in administrative courts for violating Article 47(2) of the Civil Status Law.[120] Though the Supreme Administrative Court ruled against the *'a'idin* in 2007, the following year it reversed itself and

---

[117] For example, the head of the Protestant Church, Dr. Samuel Habib, argued that "if the only ground for dissolution [of marriage] was adultery, Christians who wished to divorce their spouses would be inclined to convert to Islam or to change their church denomination, thereby making the application of Islamic law compulsory and consequently facilitating a new marriage for themselves." Shaham, "Communal Identity, Political Islam, and Family Law," 414.

[118] See Maikel Faris, "Nanfarid bi-Nashr Musawwida Qanun al-Ahwal al-Shakhsiyya al-Mawhid lil-Aqbat," *al-Youm al-Sabi'a*, November 12, 2014, www.youm7.com/news/newsprint?newid=1948942. For a discussion of the differences among the Egyptian churches regarding the government proposal, see 'Imad Khalil, "al-Kana'is Iyd Wahida didd Qanun al-Ahwal al-Shakhsiyya," *al-Masry al-Youm*, November 14, 2014, www.almasryalyoum.com/news/details/572242. The head of the Anglican Church in Egypt issued another demand for civil marriage in January 2015. See Karima Kamal, "Ra'is al-Ta'ifa al-Injiliyya: Matlub Tashri'a min al-Dawla lil-Zawaj al-Madani wa 'ala Kana'is la Ta'aridhu," *al-Masry al-Youm*, January 29, 2015, http://m.almasryalyoum.com/news/details/644977.

[119] When Copts divorce against the wishes of the Church or marry outside of it, they are often prevented from taking communion and are exorcised from the Coptic community. See Sezgin, *Human Rights*, 147.

[120] The *'a'idin* issue was hotly debated on Egyptian television. On one show, a Coptic man appeared publicly to declare that the reason he had converted to Islam was to sidestep the Church's prohibition on divorce. He criticized the Church for forcing him into such a position, and stated that he wanted to return to his faith now that he had solved his immediate problem. Many Coptic guests and callers to the show criticized the man for his instrumental use of religious conversion, but none demanded that the Coptic Church change its prohibition on divorce and remarriage. For an account of this show, see Gihan Shahine, "Fraud Not Freedom," *al-Ahram Weekly*, May 3–9, 2007, http://weekly.ahram.org.eg/2007/843/eg8.htm.

recognized the group's reconversion, provided that Islam was listed as their previous affiliation on the cards.[121] This judgment was widely criticized for exposing the litigants to potential harassment and abuse as well as the charge of apostasy. Subsequently, the Coptic Orthodox Church decided to mount a behind-the-scenes political campaign on behalf of the *'a'idin*. In the words of one advocate, Pope Shenouda made it clear to President Mubarak that "the Church wanted its sons back."[122] The campaign resulted in an unprecedented victory in 2011 when the SAC granted the *'a'idin* the right to have their religion listed as "Christianity," without qualifications.

In this judgment, the SAC argued, "In the interest of maintaining public order, the court prohibits the Ministry of Interior from refusing to list the returnees' religion as 'Christianity' because this will lead to social complications and to that which the shari'a rejects, such as the possible marriage of an apostate [*murtad*] to a Muslim woman, which is prohibited in the shari'a."[123] While granting the *'a'id's* request, this judgment leaves intact various elements of the church-state entente that has characterized postcolonial Egypt. First, note that the final judgment is grounded not in the litigants' right to change their faith but in the administrative consequences that such an act has for public order, which in turn is defined in accord with the shari'a. I will return to a detailed discussion of the notion of public order in the next chapter, but here I want to draw attention to the fact that even though apostasy is not a litigable crime in Egyptian law, the social consequences of the act are treated as significant to the state's ability to govern. Second, insomuch as the Coptic Church is just as committed to upholding the religion-based family-law regime as the Egyptian state is, the Church is also deeply invested in keeping the interdictions against interreligious marriage intact.[124] Where it differs is in its rejection of the principle that Islamic law, as the "general law" of the country, has precedence over Coptic family law.

The favorable outcome of the *'a'idin* case viewed in contrast to how Qustuntin and Shehata were treated demonstrates how deeply gendered the issue of interreligious conversion is in Egypt. Even though both were returned to their rightful patron as the "sons and daughters" of the Church, the male *'a'idin's* act was deemed to be their own

[121] Scott, *The Challenge of Political Islam*, 88–89.

[122] Personal communication with EIPR lawyer Adel Ramadan, July 5, 2008.

[123] SAC decision no. 19086, year 53 of the judicial calendar, issued on February 11, 2011. Quoted in Ibrahim, "al-Qadaya al-Khassa bi-Khanat al-Diyana wa al-Tahawwul bayn al-Adyan 2010–2012" (on file with the author). This was one among many of such decisions issued by the SAC in response to individual and group appeals.

[124] This is evident in the struggle the Coptic Church has waged to have the state-administered "oversight committee" (called *jalsat al-nush wa al-irshad*) reinstated since it was dissolved in 2008. This committee required that, when a Christian wished to convert to Islam, an official from both religious institutions be present to ensure that the conversion was not coerced. This institution dates back to Ottoman times, in place at least since the nineteenth century. Deringil, "There Is No Compulsion in Religion," 559–60.

in a way that Qustuntin and Shehata's were not. While the Coptic Church initially denounced the *'a'idin*'s decision to change their religion in order to bypass the papal ban on divorce, ultimately the clerics had to consider it valid so as to launch a legal battle to bring the men back into the communal fold. While a man's conversion to Islam is presumed to be a result of autonomous and individual will, the proper domain of civil rights, Qustuntin and Shehata's actions are seen as coerced, ultimately located within the ambit of the family, sequestered from civic life. Recall that the Church construed Qustuntin's purported conversion to Islam to be a product of Muslim coercion and manipulation, a construal that the Egyptian state adopted, and that now circulates globally to explain other Coptic women's conversions. In the case of Shehata, the Church never even conceded that she had converted, refusing to recognize her act even as an error in judgment, a refusal that Shehata herself reproduced when she appeared in public. It appears as though Islam deprives these women of agency whereas Coptic men's will and capacity to convert or reconvert remain their own. We will never know what Qustuntin and Shehata went through or what their intentions were. But the juxtaposition of the *'a'idin* controversy and their stories exemplifies the gendered nature of the family-law regime and the Christian-Muslim strife it provokes. It forces us to contend not simply with the injustice of these differential treatments, but also with how deeply nested gender, religion, and politics are in the Christian-Muslim conflict, at both the national level and, as I show below, the international level.

Gender, Coercion, and Geopolitics

Given this long history of the unequal regulation of Christian-Muslim conversion, combined with the new pressure on them to opt out of Christianity in order to obtain divorce, Copts have come to feel that their community is under duress. This collective anxiety is manifest in the belief, shared by many Copts, that there is a worldwide Muslim conspiracy to lure Coptic women (like Shehata and Qustuntin) to convert to Islam with false promises of romance and love. This claim is now globally circulated on evangelical media and among diasporic Coptic networks. The Qustuntin case is a watershed moment in this gendered saga; following her ordeal, there was a dramatic rise in newspaper stories about Christian families reporting missing daughters who were allegedly kidnapped by Muslim men.[125] Reports spiked again after the overthrow

---

[125] Arab-West, a nonpartisan US group that monitors Christian-Muslim relations in the Middle East, provides a wide sampling of Egyptian newspapers between 2004 and 2008 that reported the disappearance of Coptic girls from their homes. These newspapers include *Sawt al-Umma*, *al-Masry al-Youm*, *al-Dustur*, *al-Usbu'*, *Watani*, *al-Maydan*, *al-Kitiba Tibiya*, *al-Musawwir*, and *al-Sharq al-Awsat*. Aguzzoni, "Media Reports of Christians Converting to Islam."

of the Mubarak regime in 2011.[126] These allegations and counterallegations, while sensationalized in the Egyptian press, remain poorly investigated, and their veracity is hard to ascertain. In the absence of any reliable statistics from either the Ministry of Interior or the Coptic Orthodox Church, the rumor industry remains vibrant.

During my fieldwork with Coptic activists and intellectuals who were trenchant critics of the Coptic Church, I found that many of them believed these stories to be true, evidence of a devious Muslim plot to decrease the number of Christians living in the Middle East. Some of the evangelical and diasporic Coptic websites claim that as many as half a million Coptic girls have been kidnapped in Egypt.[127] These media outlets often cite testimonies from Coptic women and girls who went missing for a period of time, but returned to their families to claim that they had been abducted and forced to convert. An investigative report released in 2013 by the United States Commission on International Religious Freedom (USCIRF) states that these are "not kidnappings but cases of girls converting to Islam voluntarily to marry young Muslim men and then seeking to return to Christianity when the relationship failed. Some reported that the girls' families were shamed by the conversions of their daughters and resorted to claiming kidnapping to hide the situation."[128] In an earlier report, the USCIRF stated, "Well-respected human-rights groups were unable to verify such [charges] and found it extremely difficult to determine whether compulsion was used, as most cases involved a female Copt who converted to Islam when she married a male Muslim."[129]

Christian evangelical organizations and their diplomatic outlets are engaged in a global campaign that treats these allegations as facts requiring international action and intervention.[130] Christian Solidarity International (CSI), an evangelical organization devoted to saving persecuted Christians in Muslim-majority countries, released two reports (in 2009 and 2013), the former commissioned in partnership with the Coptic Foundation for Human Rights, which has wide appeal within the Coptic community in the diaspora and in Egypt.[131] The aim of these reports is twofold: (1) to

[126] See, for example, Alastair Beach, "Copts Alarmed by the Rise in Young Female Converts to Islam," al-Masry al-Youm, August 8, 2011, www.almasryalyoum.com/en/node/484562. The author notes that despite the escalation of such claims in post-Mubarak Egypt, even Coptic lawyers who register these complaints often remain skeptical about their accuracy.
[127] Aguzzoni, "Media Reports of Christians Converting to Islam," section 4.1.
[128] USCIRF, "USCIRF Annual Report 2013."
[129] US Department of State, "Egypt."
[130] For example, a report released by the American think tank Freedom House on violations of religious liberty in Egypt states, "There are credible reports from many areas of Egypt that militant Muslims kidnap or manipulate Christian girls into converting. This can even involve girls below the legal age in Egyptian law at which a person can change his or her religion." Center for Religious Freedom, Egypt's Endangered Christians 1999, 51.
[131] Clark and Ghaly, "Tell My Mother I Miss Her"; and Clark and Ghaly, "Disappearance, Forced Conversion and Forced Marriages." Both reports cite Coptic lawyers and well-known public figures in Egypt who support the reports' claims.

provide evidence of a clearly established pattern of deception, violence, sexual abuse, and the forced conversion of Coptic women in Egypt; and (2) to elevate the charge of Coptic women's abduction into "sexual slavery," which the US State Department (under its Trafficking Victims Protection Act) and the United Nations protocol on human trafficking regard as a crime.[132] In the preface to the report from 2009, John Eibner, the CEO of Christian Solidarity International, states, "Reports of Muslim men abducting and forcibly marrying and converting Coptic Christian women and girls have filtered out of Egypt with increasing frequency over the past decade. The emerging patterns of force, fraud and coercion correspond to definitions of human trafficking used by the United Nations and the U.S. Department of State, with the UN identifying it as a *crime against humanity.*"[133]

The characterization of Coptic women's conversion to Islam as a form of sexual slavery is crucial to the argumentative, rhetorical, and legal structure of the two reports. Given that many of the women converts to Islam are adults, the CSI made use of Article 3 of the UN trafficking protocol, which specifically addresses the blurred distinction between coercion and consent in the recruitment of individuals into sexual or labor servitude.[134] The UN "Protocol to Prevent, Suppress and Punish Trafficking in Persons, Especially Women and Children" (passed in December 2000) defines "human trafficking" as the recruitment of the victim "by means of the threat or use of force or other forms of coercion, of abduction, of fraud, of deception, of the abuse of power or of a position of vulnerability or of the giving or receiving of payments or benefits," and its definition of exploitation includes "the prostitution of others or other forms of sexual exploitation."[135] The second part of Article 3 further qualifies that an adult victim's consent is meaningless when it is secured by the aforementioned means.

The gender politics of the CSI reports are interesting to unpack for how they represent romantic liaisons between Christian women and Muslim men as relations of sexual coercion and instances of mixed marriages as evidence of "human trafficking." CSI argues, "Although some of the women consent to romance, they do not consent to the loss of identity, isolation, and forced conversion that follow. According to Article 3 of the UN Trafficking Protocol, consent is irrelevant in defining the crime as human trafficking if there are elements of force, fraud, and coercion, as there are in the cases

[132] The report from 2013 begins by acknowledging that human-rights organizations and the US State Department have been unable to verify these allegations, which it proceeds to characterize as a callous disregard for the "well-being of the victims."
[133] Clark and Ghaly, "The Disappearance, Forced Conversion and Forced Marriages," 2, emphasis added.
[134] This supplemented the UN Convention against Transnational Organized Crime. See United Nations, "Protocol to Prevent, Suppress and Punish Trafficking."
[135] Ibid. Exploitation in the protocol also includes the practice of forced labor, slavery, servitude, or the removal of organs.

documented in this report. Consent to an initial relationship, therefore, does not imply consent to subsequent instances of abuse, forced marriage or forced conversion . . . all of which are in the United Nation's definition of human trafficking."[136] The Egyptian-American Coptic activist Magdi Khalil, whose work I discussed in chapter 2, echoes this understanding in his statement to the CSI: "Abducting and converting Coptic girls to Islam is not only a result of the paranoid and racist incitation against the Copts, but it is an organized and pre-planned process by associations and organizations inside Egypt with domestic and Arab funding. . . . Coptic girls [are lured and seduced] through cunning, deceit and enticement."[137]

In addition to the UN protocols against human trafficking, the CSI reports also call upon the US government to take action against Egypt under the US Victims of Trafficking and Violence Protection Act of 2000, which focuses on "sex trade, slavery, and involuntary servitude."[138] According to sociologist Elizabeth Bernstein, the passage of this act was a product of years of Christian evangelical labor against sex work globally. These evangelicals succeeded in criminalizing sex work and in creating severe "criminal penalties for pimps and sexual clients [who were] portrayed as 'slaveholders.'" The spate of legislation that followed the passage of the 2000 protection act aims to "impose financial sanctions upon nations deemed to be taking insufficient steps to stem prostitution (understood to be self-identical with [human] trafficking and with slavery), and stipulate that internationally based NGOs that do not explicitly denounce prostitution as a violation of women's human rights [be] disqualified from federal funding."[139]

Citing the US Victims of Trafficking and Violence Protection Act of 2000, the CEO of CSI issued a public letter to President Obama urging him to take action against Egypt—the second-largest recipient of US aid. Playing on the post-9/11 sensibilities of its American audience, the CSI letter draws upon the widely available tropes of Muslim male violence, Islam's inherent misogyny, and the religion's lack of tolerance: "Trafficking of non-Muslim women and girls in Egypt is not simply an underworld criminal activity. This powerful report demonstrates that such violations of fundamental human rights are encouraged by the prevalence of *cultural norms* in Egypt—*often rooted in Islamic traditions*—that legitimize *violence against women and*

---

[136] Clark and Ghaly, "The Disappearance, Forced Conversion and Forced Marriages," 13. Of the twenty cases presented as evidence in the report, several do not fit the typology of coercion that the report constructs. In some instances, women and their family members give contradictory testimonies (in case 5, for instance), and in others, it is unclear why the Coptic women repudiated the relationships that they had with Muslim men.

[137] Clark and Ghaly, "Tell My Mother I Miss Her," 11.

[138] US Department of State, "Victims of Trafficking and Violence Protection Act of 2000."

[139] Bernstein, "The Sexual Politics of the 'New Abolitionism,'" 130.

non-Muslims."[140] The report from 2013 restates the CSI's demand for European and American governments to address "the deep seated Muslim and male supremacism [sic] that permeates large swaths of Egyptian society and provides the cultural context of the forcible marriages and conversions."[141] This narrative about the barbarity of Islam and its unparalleled misogyny has a long pedigree within Western Christian polemics. However, as I discuss in chapter 1 and chapter 5, during much of the history of Western Christendom, this narrative trope was also deployed to describe Coptic Christians, practitioners of a depraved form of Christianity. This characterization has shifted now so that Western Christendom has made a geopolitical alliance with "Eastern Christianity" and discovered their civilizational fraternity, painting Coptic Christians as victims of Islam's incomparable violence.

The portrayal of Coptic women as vulnerable subjects open to the predatory practices of Muslim men erases the role of the Church in this crisis. The difficulties that women such as Qustuntin and Shehata face in surviving unhappy domestic situations are strikingly absent from the CSI reports and the Coptic and evangelical media. The reported sequestration of Wafa Qustuntin in the pope's monastery (since 2004) is symbolic of the general erasure of the female convert's subjectivity from these campaigns, even as her actions serve as the pivot around which competing diagnoses of the Coptic crisis turn. The Church and its international evangelical allies cannot recognize Qustuntin's act as her own because to do so would complicate the claim that the primal source of minority Coptic suffering is Islam. A Coptic woman convert can only be represented as a pawn in the hands of her male Muslim oppressor. Her actions, in order to be truly hers, must first assent to this communal truth.

While rumors about Coptic women's abduction circulated in the past, what is new about the current moment is that women's religious conversion has become embedded in arguments for and against the right to religious liberty. In this framing, what is striking is that a Coptic woman's submission to the Coptic Church emerges as the paradigmatic act that secures the community's collective exercise of religious liberty. In such a context, a Coptic woman's conversion to Islam cannot be rendered in terms of *her* religious liberty precisely because she has become the bearer of *the community's* religious freedom. This paradoxical conjoining of her *submission* and the collectivity's *freedom* is not an expression of an essential religio-cultural patriarchy. Rather, it is a product of the secular dispensation in which minority identity has come to be vested

---

[140] Christian Solidarity International—USA, "Obama-Eibner Copts," *National American Coptic Assembly*, November 10, 2009, http://nacopts1.blogspot.com/2010/03/obama-eibner-copts.html, emphasis added.
[141] Clark and Ghaly, "Tell My Mother I Miss Her," 3.

in the regulation of the family, whose exemplary bearer is, after all, the woman. Note that minority and majority operate here not simply as legal categories but also as gendered ones insomuch as they mirror the hierarchical relationship between the coerced Coptic woman and the aggressive Muslim male.

It is interesting to compare the Coptic concern for Qustuntin against that expressed by the well-known Egyptian jurist Tariq al-Bishri, who has written extensively on Muslim-Christian relations in Egypt.[142] In his commentary on the Qustuntin affair, Bishri uses the case to reflect on what he describes as a fundamentally flawed and corrupt relationship between the Egyptian state and the Coptic Church. Bishri excoriates the Coptic Church for its hypocritical championing of the minority's religious liberty while at the same time violating Qustuntin's individual right to convert to Islam.[143] Criticizing Pope Shenouda's insistence that the state security police hunt down and bring Qustuntin back to the Church, Bishri writes, "The Church administration violated its own oft-repeated call to uphold freedom of religion and the right to [interreligious] conversion regardless of whether it is to or from Islam."[144] Note that even though Bishri's championing of Qustuntin's right to choose her faith secures his critique of the Church's power, he remains silent on the unjust laws that prevent Muslims from converting to Christianity while facilitating the obverse. It is this silence in Bishri's otherwise trenchant critique of the state-church entente that suggests that Qustuntin's actions are only legible to the extent that they expose the hypocritical duplicity of the Church and the dictatorial tendencies of the corrupt state. Her choice, to the extent that it is a choice at all, is intelligible only as a strike against the system.

While Coptic-Muslim inequality is a product of the peculiar way in which religious difference has been managed in Egypt, it is also important to realize that a constellation of global forces has played a constitutive role in transforming the terrain on which the Coptic question can be imagined, argued, and debated; key among these forces is the power of evangelical Christianity to define a new set of geopolitical agendas. It would be difficult to imagine this global force as "religious" in any simple sense, distinct from the operation of secular power, given how deeply imbricated the US State Department and various UN agencies are in the campaigns that I have outlined above. As such, the Coptic-Muslim struggle cannot be understood in culturalist terms alone. Rather, it provokes us to reflect on the consistencies and idiosyncrasies that the past and present of postcolonial societies represent in the making of the secular on a global and geopolitical scale.

[142] Tariq al-Bishri is also the author of several major studies on the Coptic question, including *al-Muslimun wa al-Aqbat*, *al-Jama'a al-Wataniyya*, and *al-Dawla wa al-Kanisa*.
[143] Al-Bishri, *al-Jama'a al-Wataniyya*.
[144] Ibid., 210.

Secularism and Sexuality

In this chapter, I have argued that one of the paradoxical consequences of the secularization of Middle Eastern societies is that just as religious authority becomes marginal to the conduct of civic and political affairs, it simultaneously acquires a privileged place in the regulation of family and sexual relations. This is a consequence of secularism's foundational public-private divide that relegates sexuality and religion to the latter while at the same time making both consequential to the former. The incorporation of premodern religious precepts into the legal structure of the modern state gives family law a primordial cast when in fact it represents a novel arrangement. This does not mean, of course, that premodern religiosity had no investment in the regulation of sexuality. It is to say that the pernicious entwining of religion and sexuality under modern conditions of secular governance has taken a unique form, which we cannot grasp if we simply chalk it up to religious traditionalism. Instead, it is important to analyze how the secular and religious elements that comprise family law have made interreligious coexistence a challenging prospect.

Since the publication of Michel Foucault's *History of Sexuality*, it has become widely accepted that the privatization of sexuality in the modern period has also been accompanied by its subjection to historically unparalleled forms of scrutiny, regulation, and discipline, crafted as a new object of knowledge, identity, and manipulation. The family, as a unit of economic and biopolitical reproduction, is a valorized site of this modern investment, and family law, by extension, is its juridical legibility. While much of the scholarly literature acknowledges the modernity of the institution of the family and its unique legal status, it is rarely analyzed as a necessary unit of political secularism. In this chapter, I have used the historical scholarship on the modern construction of the family as a lens through which to understand the trajectory of the secular project in Egypt, along with the endless struggle this has generated over how and where to draw the line between religion and state.

Religion-based family law in the Middle East is commonly regarded as evidence of the region's incomplete secularization. Such a judgment, I have argued, does not adequately grasp secularism as a shared modality of legal-political structuration that cuts across the Western and non-Western divide. The relegation of religion and family to the private sphere is a signal feature of this structuration, one that also links their regulative fates in modern society. The central role sexuality has come to play in the standoff between the religious and the secular in a variety of global struggles is diagnostic of this conjoining. This is evident in debates about the veil in Western Europe, gay marriage in the United States, and contraception and homosexuality in Africa, not to mention the exaggerated claim in France that gender equality and sexual liberty are synonymous with *laïcité*. The struggle over religion-based family law in Egypt and other Middle Eastern societies is part and parcel of this secular dispensation. Consequently, it is neither an expression of the essential religiosity of these societies nor a sign of their incomplete secularism. It is, however, a historically specific instantiation of a universalizing project that is often cast in civilizational terms.

Chapter 4

RELIGIOUS AND CIVIL INEQUALITY

In January 2008, when I first embarked on my field research for this book, I was surprised at the media attention devoted to an administrative court decision that had just granted Bahais the right to *not* have their religion listed on state-issued documents. While many human-rights activists declared this to be a victory for the Bahais, others condemned it as the state's endorsement of heresy. Even though I have been working in Egypt since 1995, I had never encountered any public discussion of the Bahai faith. A lawyer with the EIPR who had won a prominent legal victory for the Bahais told me that he too had never heard about their presence in Egypt until he started working on the case. Bahais were thrown into the media limelight in 2006 when an administrative court ruled that their religion could be listed on national identity cards, a decision that was widely contested. A vociferous debate ensued in the Egyptian media about the history of Bahais in the country, their divergence from the religions of "People of the Book," and whether the state should recognize their faith. These debates ranged from vitriol to more measured ruminations on how the Egyptian government should deal with a non-Abrahamic minority whose numbers were small when compared to the Coptic Orthodox Christians but whose status in the polity raised difficult questions for the distribution of religious and civil rights.

For many human-rights activists, the appearance of the Bahais on the Egyptian public scene was an invitation to expand the terms of the debate about the status of religious minorities beyond the Coptic question. As Soliman, a leading member of the activist group Egyptians against Religious Discrimination (Masriyun Didd al-Tamyiz al-Dini), put it to me,[1]

> You know, the Bahai issue is very important, even if their numbers are small in Egypt. When Egyptians talk of religion, we always talk about three religions, *ahl al-kitab* [People of the Book].

---

[1] This group, which goes by the acronym MARED, was formed in April 2008. It primarily comprises Christians and Muslims. Some members of the group view the Bahai faith as a deviant sect that diverts attention from the real challenge facing Egypt today, namely, Christian-Muslim coexistence.

> The existence of Bahais in Egypt raises the question of religions other than *ahl al-kitab*. You know they say that Bahais are *kuffar* [infidels, sing. *kafir*]. Well, yes, indeed, we want to accept this and deal with them as *kuffar*, who are fellow citizens and have the same rights as the rest of us. . . . You know, the Muslim Brothers want to reject the Bahais by calling them apostates [*murtaddin*]. But the Coptic Church is not sympathetic to them either because it wants to retain its privileged position as a religion of *ahl al-kitab*. So I think that the Bahai question is very crucial for thinking about [the problem of] religious discrimination [*al-tamyiz al-dini*] in Egypt. It forces us to go beyond religious arguments to the issue of citizenship equality.

Soliman was right to cast the issue in this way. The constitutionally guaranteed right to political and civil equality for Egyptian citizens stands in tension with the state policy of only extending recognition to "People of the Book," namely, Muslims, Christians, and Jews. It poses particular problems for Bahais, whose faith embraces the beliefs of a number of monotheistic and nonmonotheistic traditions and has, since 1960, been banned in Egypt. Bahais constitute less than 1 percent of the population, but their conflicted civil and political status is exemplary of the difficulties involved in negotiating between the secular civil-law tradition that informs most of Egyptian law and the Islamic concepts and practices that permeate the state's various legal and administrative bodies.

In this chapter, I examine the amalgam of secular and religious concepts that the Egyptian courts use to regulate the Bahais' religious difference. While the first half of the chapter focuses on Egyptian court rulings, in the second half I turn to an analysis of judgments from the European Court of Human Rights (ECtHR) that also pertain to the regulation of religious minorities in European societies. My aim in offering this comparative reading is to show how key secular concepts, when adopted into different religious and legal traditions, produce very similar kinds of effects: authorizing the state to pronounce on substantive religious content, and promoting majoritarian values and sensibilities at the expense of minority beliefs and practices. By analyzing the legal grammar involved in the regulation of religious difference, I hope to elaborate on secularism as a space of legal-political structuration that cuts across national contexts despite important differences.

The secular concept of "public order" and the distinction between private religious belief (*forum internum*) and its public manifestation (*forum externum*) are central to the corpus of jurisprudence I analyze in this chapter. As I will elaborate below, public order allows modern states to restrict basic rights of citizens when they are deemed to threaten the moral and legal cohesion of a given society. This legal concept is at the heart of the right to religious liberty that is enshrined in Egyptian and European law as well as in human-rights conventions. The Egyptian courts' use of these concepts may seem specious at first, smuggling substantive religious content into the neutral language of secular law. On closer inspection, however, the concept of public order is constitutively open to this seeming malfeasance in that it secures the right of sovereign power to intervene in a domain that is otherwise deemed private and immune from state interference. There are striking similarities between the jurisprudence of Egyptian courts and the jurisprudence of the ECtHR when it comes to religious minorities in countries as disparate as Turkey, France, Greece, Italy, the United Kingdom, and Switzerland. These convergences, I suggest, are instructive for thinking about the place of religious minorities, and by extension of religious difference, in modern secular governance across the Western and non-Western divide.

At the outset, let me state that I am fully aware that distinctly different models of religion-state accommodation prevail in Egypt and the European countries at the center of the ECtHR judgments. It is also clear that the ECtHR's arguments do not privilege references to, and interpretations of, religious principles in the way that Egyptian courts do. Similarly, many of the European states involved in the ECtHR rulings I discuss in this chapter espouse a secular identity that Egypt does not. It is precisely because of these differences that their analogous deployment of public order and religious liberty is so striking, challenging us to think analytically about what accounts for this resonance. In a nutshell, my argument is that the right to religious liberty and the concept of public order are important vectors of a secular political rationality that is beset with a characteristic set of questions and conundrums: How can the commitment to civil and political equality, which is indifferent to religion, be balanced with the regulation of religious difference in the social life of a polity? How is the state supposed to represent and preserve the values and traditions of the majority at the heart of national identity without discriminating against the minority? How is such discrimination to be judged, by whom, and on what grounds? How these questions are settled remains the prerogative of the sovereign state, which inevitably must make normative judgments about what religion is or ought to be and its proper place in the social life of a polity.

The Bahai Question

Founded in Iran in the mid-nineteenth century, the Bahai faith is of relatively recent origin. It drew its inspiration from the nineteenth-century millenarian Babi movement that expanded its scope under the leadership of Mirza Husayn Ali Nuri (1817–92), known as Baha'ullah, to incorporate teachings from a variety of faiths, including Islam, Judaism, Christianity, Zoroastrianism, and Buddhism.[2] Baha'ullah recorded the key principles of the Bahai faith in the *Holy Book* (*al-Kitab al-Aqdas*), which was composed in Arabic in the late nineteenth century and contains laws of worship and social relations, family law, and an administrative structure for adherents to the faith. Despite persecution in its early years, Bahaism has won converts throughout the Middle East, Asia, Europe, and the United States, and is currently estimated to have between six and seven million adherents globally. The Bahai administrative center (Universal House of Justice), located in Haifa, Israel, is responsible for the global welfare and order of the Bahai community. The Bahais also have an established office in the United Nations that works closely with its various programs (UNICEF, UNIFEM, and others). A leading historian of the Bahai faith, Juan Cole, points out that its administrative structure, initially designed to have elected representatives from Bahai communities worldwide, has become more secretive and punitive over time, as it has taken to purging dissenters and critics from within.[3]

Bahais have been living in Egypt since the 1860s, when a small number arrived to proselytize secretly and successfully converted some Muslims, Jews, and Christians.[4] Their numbers have remained small, even though in the 1920s they established a Bahai temple and petitioned the government to be recognized as an official religion with its own family law. Their fortune turned in the 1960s, however, as tensions between Egypt and Israel escalated and President Gamal Abdel Nasser passed a presidential decree (Law 263/1960) that dissolved Bahai institutions and criminalized their activities. This decree provided no religious or legal justification, and was understood primarily to be a result of Nasser's national-security policy toward Israel and the increasing animosity between the two states.[5] Since the Bahai administrative-spiritual center was located in Haifa, Nasser's government saw Bahais as potential collaborators with and informants for the state of Israel. Though Bahai communal and religious property was seized, most ordinary Bahais continued to practice their faith under the public radar.

After an initial failed attempt in 1975 to challenge the legality of the decree, the Bahais abandoned their efforts to persuade the Egyptian government to formally rec-

---

[2] After being banished first from Iran and later Baghdad, Baha'ullah finally settled in 1868 in Acre, part of Ottoman Syria, where he remained until his death. His son, Abdul Baha Abbas, subsequently took over his father's position and served as the leader of the movement from 1892 to 1921. His grandson, Shoghi Effendi, took over then, at which point an administrative system was put into place to regulate Bahai affairs internationally. Cole, *Modernity and the Millennium*.
[3] Cole, "The Baha'i Minority and Nationalism," 134–35.
[4] Pink, "A Post-Qur'anic Religion."
[5] Egypt and Israel formally went to war in 1967, but the animosities between the two states had already reached a climax in 1956 over Israeli access to the Suez Canal.

ognize their religion. It is not surprising, however, that Bahais periodically have to deal with the state's administrative bureaucracy, given that it rules over all aspects of a citizen's life, from the most intimate to the most public. Bahais primarily encounter the state's discriminatory powers when they have to acquire official documents from the Ministry of Interior (such as national identity cards, birth certificates, and passports) or settle custody and inheritance claims in family-law courts. All Egyptian citizens are required to identify their religion on these documents. Bahais' attempts to get their faith recorded have created a legal conundrum for the Egyptian state, as registering their religion on an official document amounts to a de facto recognition of their faith. But if the state does not allow them to officially identify as Bahai, then it forces them to list their religious identity as Muslim, Christian, or Jewish, which is a forgery—itself a crime.

In response to Bahai lawsuits, the Egyptian courts have produced a checkered jurisprudence, often invoking not only the presidential decree of 1960 but also Islamic shari'a, which in the courts' reasoning only recognizes "People of the Book" (*ahl al-kitab*), also referred to as "heavenly religions" (*al-adyan al-samawiyya*) and "recognized religions" (*mu'tarif biha*). This position, however, has no historical justification because there is no consensus in the shari'a on how to treat followers of non-Abrahamic religions. In premodern Islamic empires there were a variety of different arrangements regarding non-Muslims. While the populations living under Ottoman rule were primarily Muslim, Christian, and Jewish, in other parts of the world, Muslim rulers had to contend with a variety of faiths indigenous to the lands they conquered (such as Zoroastrianism, Hinduism, and Buddhism).[6] The Islamic empires could not afford to treat these religious groups as juridical nonentities, heretics, or simply infidels, but had to integrate them into the state's economic and governing structure. Despite the historical heterogeneity of shari'a norms, Egyptian courts of the modern period have refused to recognize the Bahai faith, basing their stance on a supposedly singular and unified interpretation of Islamic law regarding the status of non-Abrahamic religions within a Muslim polity.

It is often argued that a key legal hurdle to the Bahais' ability to challenge the Egyptian government's invocation of Islamic law is Article 2 of the Egyptian constitution, which stipulates, "The principles of Islamic shari'a are the main source of legislation." The introduction of Article 2 in 1971, which deemed shari'a to be "a"

---

[6] Anver Emon explains, for example, "When Muslims conquered Persia and encountered Zoroastrians, commanders allowed the local religious population there to reside peacefully in the empire and maintain their faith, as long as they paid the *jizya* [poll tax]. Likewise in India, when Muslims conquered that region, polytheists were allowed to pay the *jizya* and live a 'tolerated' existence under Muslim rule. . . . Although all these groups were able to live peacefully within the Muslim empire on condition of payment of *jizya*, the People of the Book were held in higher esteem than others." Emon, *Religious Pluralism and Islamic Law*, 73.

(rather than "the") source of Egyptian law, was a departure from Article 149 of the constitution (in place since 1923), which had loosely asserted, "Islam is the religion of the state," without clarifying what this meant in practice. It was in 1979 that President Anwar Sadat further modified Article 2 to declare that the shariʿa should be *the* main source of Egyptian legislation. Given that the shariʿa pertains only to personal status issues, while the rest of Egyptian laws derive from secular French codes, it is unclear how Article 2 should be implemented. The amendment was never followed by legislative or executive guidelines on how to interpret it or put it into effect. In the absence of these guidelines, the Supreme Constitutional Court (SCC) judges have had to come up with their own interpretation of Article 2. Clark Lombardi has attempted to map the rationale of the SCC jurisprudence on Article 2 since the amendment of 1979.[7] He shows that the SCC judgments consistently conform to the requirements of liberal legality in that they give the judges, who have no religious training, the supreme authority to pronounce on religious issues. The SCC judges invoke the principle of *ijtihad*, a form of Islamic legal reasoning, to resolve conflicting interpretations within the shariʿa or between existing secular laws and the shariʿa. Classically, only qualified religious scholars practiced *ijtihad*, but in the hands of the SCC it has become a tool for secularly trained judges to selectively interpret what they deem to be Islamic law. For the most part, the SCC rulings have tended to close the gap between secular laws and shariʿa precepts by privileging the former, through a casuistic reading of the latter using the principle of *ijtihad*. Thus, an important consequence of the Article 2 amendment is that it has increased the power of the secular courts to interpret Islamic principles in a way that buttresses the authority of the sovereign state and its exceptional powers.[8] Interpretations of Article 2 get even more ambiguous when we consider the fact that the administrative courts, which have litigated most of the Bahai cases, deal with challenges to legislative, executive, and administrative orders and conflicts between them.[9] None of these courts has any jurisdiction over the SCC's interpretation of Article 2 or its implementation. Given this situation, it is far from clear what it means to evoke Article 2 or "principles of shariʿa" in Egyptian courts today.

The viability of legislating the shariʿa in contemporary Muslim societies is fraught in another important sense. Scholars of Islamic jurisprudence argue that the life world

[7] See Lombardi, *State Law as Islamic Law*.

[8] Lombardi and Brown, "Do Constitutions Requiring Adherence to *Shariʿa*."

[9] The administrative court system in Egypt comprises three levels, beginning with the courts of first instance (*al-mahakim al-idariyya*), then moving to the appeals courts (*mahakim al-qadaʾ al-idari*), and finally ending at the Supreme Administrative Court (*al-mahkama al-idariyya al-ʿulya*). These courts are authorized to entertain challenges to executive, legislative, and administrative orders. While lower courts' decisions can be appealed in the Supreme Administrative Court, there is no further appeal from the latter's rulings.

that sustained key concepts and practices of the shariʻa no longer exists.[10] The shariʻa in the modern period has been radically transformed from what was once a context-bound and flexible tradition into a rigid system of codified rules largely confined to the domain of family law and administered by a centralized state.[11] Furthermore, many of the foundational assumptions of the shariʻa conflict with the predicates of modern governance and liberal legality that provide the metacontext for its practice. A clear example of this is manifest in Egyptian court rulings that pronounce on the civil and religious status of Bahais. On the one hand, the Egyptian constitution upholds the principle of formal equality between Muslims and non-Muslims; on the other hand, by invoking the classical concept of "People of the Book," Egyptian courts conjure a world in which Muslims were formally and substantively superior to non-Muslims under the system of *ahl al-dhimma*.[12] The two systems are markedly different in the model of governance upon which each is predicated. Citizenship is premised on the principle of *formal* political and civil equality, which is supposedly indifferent to the individual's religion, ethnicity, gender, and economic status. The "People of the Book" principle contradicts this logic in that it makes a citizen's religious affiliation consequential to the distribution of civil and political rights. Indeed, the Egyptian courts' varying and contradictory rulings may be seen as a product of these dueling principles. But are these contradictions unique to the Islamic character of the Egyptian state, or are similar paradoxes at play in self-avowedly secular legal traditions? This is a question that I take up in the second half of the chapter, where I compare the jurisprudence of the European Court of Human Rights with that of Egyptian courts. First, however, we need to understand how Egyptian courts have tried to square the religious *inequality* of Bahais with their civil and political *equality* in the eyes of the law.

Litigating Equality

Egyptian jurisprudence on the legality of the ban on the Bahai faith revolves around two distinct concepts: the Islamic concept of "People of the Book," and the secular concept of the right to religious liberty. The right to religious liberty is predicated upon a foundational distinction between the privacy of religious belief (*forum internum*) and the public expression of this belief (*forum externum*), a distinction found not only in Egyptian law but in various European constitutions and international legal protocols

---

[10] Hallaq, "Can the Shariʻa Be Restored?" and Hallaq, "What Is Shariʻa?"

[11] Messick, *The Calligraphic State.*

[12] As I discussed in chapter 1, "People of the Book" had a special legal status in various Islamic empires under the pact of *dhimma*, which obliged the state to protect their life, property, and right to worship in exchange for pledging loyalty to the sovereign and paying a special poll tax.

(such as the International Covenant on Civil and Political Rights, and the European Convention on Human Rights). In this formulation, while the privacy of religious belief is regarded as absolute, the state has a legitimate right to regulate and limit its manifestation in order to "protect public order, health or morals, or for the protection of the rights and freedoms of others."[13] The Egyptian courts have repeatedly invoked the concept of public order (al-nizam al-'am) to ban Bahai "communal forms"—temples, institutions, and the public performance of Bahai rites and rituals—while maintaining that Bahais are free to believe in whatever precepts they deem worthy.

In the courts' view, the principle of "People of the Book," which prohibits the state from recognizing any faith other than Islam, Christianity, or Judaism, is a quintessential aspect of the public order of Egyptian society. The Supreme Court ruling in 1975, which upheld the legality of the ban from 1960 on the Bahai faith, declared that the Egyptian state was only obligated to treat those individuals as equals "who are comparable to each other with respect to their legal status—[that is,] Muslim should be treated as equal to other Muslims, and Christians to other Christians or to Jews, but Christians should not necessarily be treated as equal to Muslims, or Bahais to Christians."[14] The implicit reference in the Supreme Court ruling is the old Islamic maxim, attributed to the prophet Muhammad, that "Islam supersedes and cannot be superseded" (al-Islam ya'lu wa la yu'lu 'alayhi).[15]

This declaration of the essential inequality of Bahais in relation to "People of the Book" contradicts the constitutional guarantee that all Egyptians are equal in the eyes of the law and cannot be discriminated against on the basis of their race, ethnic origin, language, religion, or creed. Interestingly, the Egyptian courts do not reject outright the Bahais' claims to civil and political equality. In a precedent-setting decision in 1983, the SAC ruled in favor of a Bahai litigant who sued the Ministry of Interior for refusing to issue him a national identity card that listed his correct religion, thereby violating his civil and political rights (under Article 46 of Egypt's 1971 constitution).[16]

---

[13] Article 9 of the European Convention, which closely accords with Article 18 of ICCPR, states: (1) Everyone has the right to freedom of thought, conscience, and religion; this right includes the freedom to change his religion or belief, and freedom, either alone or in a community with others and in public or in private, to manifest his religion or belief, in worship, teaching, practice, and observance. (2) Freedom to manifest one's religion or beliefs shall be subject only to such limitations as are prescribed by law and are necessary in a democratic society in the interests of public safety; for the protection of public order, health, or morals; or for the protection of the rights and freedom of others. See www.echr.coe.int/Documents/Convention_ENG.pdf%23page=9.

[14] Supreme Court decision on case no. 7 of the second judicial year, issued on March 1, 1975. Quoted in Pink, "A Post-Qur'anic Religion," 431. Note that the Supreme Court was renamed the Supreme Constitutional Court in 1979.

[15] Cited in the authoritative compendium of hadith, Sahih Bukhari.

[16] Supreme Administrative Court decision on case no. 1109 of the twenty-ninth judicial year, issued on January 29, 1983. All subsequent citations are from a translation of the judgment on file with the author. An earlier judgment, issued by an administrative court in 1948, twelve years before the

The SAC's decision was, however, grounded in a careful distinction between the civil and political status of Bahais and their religious standing in society. In regard to the former, the SAC stated that because "the law requires every citizen who reaches the age of sixteen to obtain an official identity card [that] must state a religion," the appellant, as a citizen of the state, was "entitled to demand his rights under the constitution and the law."[17] From this, the court concluded, "The request to issue an identity card is not a prohibited activity; on the contrary, obtaining one is a duty under the law. The [appellant] cannot change what was written on his birth certificate about his parents' religion, lest it be considered forgery, which is a crime."

In regards to the religious status of Bahais, the SAC argued that even though Islamic governments are allowed to "accommodate non-Muslims with all their differences no matter what their religions are," the shariʿa also prohibits the *public practice* of "anything but the recognized religions, which according to the customs of Muslims in Egypt are only Christianity and Judaism." Apart from the fact that this reading of Islamic history does not concur with the variable status of non-Abrahamic religions in premodern Muslim empires, the SAC's claim that it is merely limiting the *public practice* of Bahai faith (*forum externum*) is in fact entangled with the category demarcated as belief (*forum internum*) and, as I hope to show, defines its substantive meaning—an entwining that the court abjures. While I will elaborate on this issue below, here I want to point out that the SAC decision from 1983, particularly the distinction it established between civil and religious rights, set an enormously consequential precedent for how Bahais fought for their rights in the 2000s.

Recognition and Governance

Egyptian Bahais confronted a fresh set of problems when the government computerized the system that issues national identity cards in 2004. In the past, these documents had been dispensed irregularly and local officials, unaware of the state prohibition, often permitted the Bahai religion to be recorded on identity cards. Digitizing the system produced a crisis when state computer programs did not allow for a "Bahai" entry, thereby alerting local officials to the legal violation.[18] This also led

Bahai faith was banned, had argued similarly that Bahais are not equal to Muslims, Christians, or Jews because they are apostates in the eyes of the shariʿa. For an analysis of this decision, see Pink, "A Post-Qurʾanic Religion," 421–22.

[17] The litigant, a Bahai student, was expelled from the University of Alexandria for failing to produce a national identity card. Subsequently, he took his case to a lower administrative court that ruled against him in 1979. He then appealed this decision in the SAC.

[18] For a comprehensive report on this issue, see Human Rights Watch and EIPR, "Prohibited Identities."

to the Ministry of Interior and its Civil Status Department's (CSD) unprecedented vigilance of the demographic presence of Bahais in Egypt. Several Bahai families had their birth certificates, national identity cards, and other official documents confiscated. Unable to go about their daily business, these Bahais took their case to administrative courts to challenge the actions of the Ministry of Interior and the CSD.[19]

Among these was a case brought by Husam Izzat and his wife, Ranya Rushdie. While their three daughters' and Husam's religious identifications were listed as "Bahai" on their official documents, Ranya's had been left blank. When the family tried to procure passports for travel, the Civil Status Intelligence Unit in Alexandria confiscated their documents without explanation. After failing to get the documents returned, the Izzat-Rushdie family filed a lawsuit in the Court of Administrative Justice against the Ministry of Interior and the CSD for violating their right to religious liberty (Article 46 of the 1971 constitution). On April 4, 2006, the administrative court issued a decision in favor of the Izzat-Rushdie family (hereafter cited as AC 2006a).[20] The ruling drew liberally on the SAC decision from 1983 I discuss above, but also amplified and expanded many of its claims.

What is noteworthy about the AC 2006a judgment and the SAC judgment from 1983 is that they presume that Bahais are entitled to certain rights as Egyptian citizens. The fact that their religion is banned does not automatically annul their political and civil status. As a result, the administrative court ordered the Ministry of Interior to issue the Izzat-Rushdie family identity cards that state their religious affiliation as "Bahai," using the following argument:

> Islamic jurisprudence requires a disclosure that would allow [a distinction to be made] between a Muslim and non-Muslim in their exercise of social life, so as to establish the range of rights and obligations reserved for Muslims that others cannot avail of. . . . The Law of Civil Status no. 143 of 1994 obligates the Ministry of Interior to issue an identity card and birth certificate to every Egyptian that lists his name and religion, [the latter] a requirement of the Islamic shari'a. It is not inconsistent with Islamic tenets to mention the religion on a person's card even though it may be a religion whose rites are not recognized for open practice, such as Bahaism and the like. On the contrary, these [religions] must be indicated so that the status of its bearer is known so that he does not enjoy a legal status to which his belief does not entitle him in a Muslim society.

[19] For an account of these court cases, see ibid., 30–37.

[20] Administrative Court decision on case no. 24044 of the forty-fifth judicial year, issued on April 4, 2006. For a translation of this judgment, see "4 April 2006 Administrative Court Ruling," *Baha'is*, www .bahai.org/persecution/egypt/2006april_en. I use this translation throughout this chapter with some modifications of legal terms and idiomatic phrases.

As this passage makes clear, the *unrecognizability* of the Bahai religion is crucially linked to the *recognizability* of Bahais in civil affairs. In a society where the distinction between Muslims and non-Muslims is central to the distribution of rights and obligations, to *not* recognize Bahais, the court argues, is to contravene the state's ability to govern. The AC 2006a ruling liberally quotes from the SAC decision from 1983, and reiterates the argument that even though non-Muslims in the past were free to hold their beliefs under Islamic empires, this does not mean that Muslims and non-Muslims are equal in the eyes of the state with respect to their rights and obligations. While Christians and Jews putatively fare better in this logic, Bahais have a distinctly lower status in that they are not "People of the Book." As such, they cannot have the same rights as the Christian and Jewish minorities. Consequently, the court concludes that Bahais *must* have their religion recorded on their civil-status documents precisely to preserve their *unequal* status in Muslim-majority Egypt.

While the Islamic contours of this argument are apparent, it is important to recognize how this ruling depends on the distinction between private religious belief and public religious expression and action, as well as on the concept of public order, both of which are shared across the Egyptian and European legal traditions. The AC 2006a judgment provides a historical account of how the right to religious liberty was adopted in the first constitution of Egypt in 1923:

> It is clear from the provisions regarding the freedom of belief in successive Egyptian constitutions that they originated in Article 12 and 13 of the constitution of 1923. The former stipulated that the freedom of belief is absolute, but the latter stated that the state protects the freedom to practice the rites of religions and beliefs in accordance with the observed customs of Egypt, on the condition that they do not violate the public order or morals.

The court reports that the right to religious liberty, when initially proposed by Lord Curzon, the British Minister of Foreign Affairs, applied to "all inhabitants of Egypt [who] may practice, with complete freedom in public or private, the rites of any confession, religion, or belief, provided these rites do not violate the public order or public morals." Members of the Constitutional Committee of 1923 objected to this formulation, the court recounts, on the grounds that "it covered all religious rites," when such freedom should have been limited to "the three heavenly religions: Islam, Christianity, and Judaism." Pursuant to this objection, the right to religious liberty was modified in the 1923 constitution to include two articles, 12 and 13: "The former provided for freedom of belief and the latter . . . for freedom to practice religious beliefs." These two articles were combined into one in the constitution of 1956, which then became Article 46 of the 1971 constitution (on which the AC 2006a ruling is based): "The freedom of belief is absolute and the state protects the freedom to practice religious beliefs and rites in accordance with the customs observed on the condition that they do not violate the *public order and morals*." In the court's reasoning, because Islam is the national religion of the country, it is consonant with the public order of Egyptian society, which in turn gives the state the right to limit the public expression of faiths that Islam does not recognize as legitimate. While I will elaborate on the legal origins of the notion of public order, here I simply wish to point out how intertwined religious freedom is with public-order reasoning in this jurisprudence.

Civil Death?

The AC 2006a ruling quickly went viral, and Bahais, whose faith and legal status were unknown to ordinary Egyptians, burst onto the public scene with force. Some Islamist groups characterized the court ruling as a de facto recognition of the Bahai religion, which, they argued, was a violation of the shari'a. The judgment's defenders cast it as a victory for the civil and political rights of Bahai citizens. For many Bahai activists who had struggled in the anonymity of the bureaucratic maze, the judgment was a welcome relief because it solved an immediate practical problem. The decision of 2006, one might say, brought Bahais into being as particular kinds of religious-civil subjects who were allowed to make a particular kind of claim on the polity.

Despite their long-standing mutual animosity, members of the parliament from the ruling National Democratic Party and the Muslim Brotherhood condemned the decision unanimously and challenged the lower court's ruling in the SAC.[21] A wide-ranging discussion in the media then ensued about the history and presence of Bahais on Egyptian soil. On December 2, 2006, the SAC ruled that the state was prohibited from listing the Bahai faith on identity cards or birth certificates, effectively overturning the lower court's earlier decision and reversing its own judgment from 1983.[22] (The decision is hereafter cited as SAC 2006b.) When compared with the lower court's AC 2006a decision, the SAC provided a strikingly different interpretation of public-order doctrine and refused to recognize the civil status of Bahais.

The SAC begins by affirming the inviolability of the freedom of belief: "It is clear that all Egyptian constitutions guaranteed the freedom of belief and the freedom of religious rites, as they constitute the fundamental principles of all civilized countries. Every human being has the right to believe in the religion or belief that satisfies his

[21] Human Rights Watch and EIPR, "Prohibited Identities," 38.
[22] Supreme Administrative Court decision on case nos. 16834 and 18971 of the fifty-second judicial year, issued on December 16, 2006. I have used a modified version of the following translation: info.bahai.org/pdf/EGYPTSAC_16DEC06_ENGLISH.pdf.

conscience and pleases his soul. No authority has power over what he believes deep in his soul and conscience." The court then moves to limit the *expression* of this belief in public: "As to the freedom of practicing religious rites, this is subject to the limitation . . . of respecting the public order and public morals." The court further argues that because Islamic shari'a does not recognize the Bahai faith, to list it on the national identity cards is a violation of public order: "No data that conflict with or disagree with [public order] should be recorded in a country whose foundation and origin are based on Islamic shari'a."

Several points in this argument are noteworthy. The SAC 2006b ruling construes listing the Bahai religion on state-required identity cards as a manifestation of their religion. This contradicts its own decision from 1983, as well as that of the lower administrative court (AC 2006a) that had permitted the Bahai religion to be listed on the identity cards, precisely as a way to *limit* its open practice and manifestation in public. In SAC 2006b the court appears to be concerned not so much with the manifestation of Bahai practices in the *forum externum* as with the state's recognition of the Bahai faith itself as a *religion*. This implicates the meaning and scope of the *forum internum* and raises issues of status and value, before any question of recognition or limitation on manifestations of religious belief. One important consequence of this elision is that the SAC 2006b decision in fact substantively erases the civil status of Bahais and reduces them to nothing more than heretics or apostates from Islam and, to a lesser degree, from Christianity and Judaism. Unlike the 1983 and AC 2006a judgments, the SAC makes no mention of how a minority whose faith is not recognized is supposed to conduct its affairs. As a leading member of the Bahai community put it, "I am a citizen of Egypt. Even if the state doesn't recognize my faith, you cannot commit me to 'civil death'—I cannot even open a bank account without an identity card. And why would you want me to list myself as a Muslim, Christian, or Jew on the card? Would this not be a lie, and would this not put me in violation of the shari'a or the law?"[23]

Partial Victories?

The SAC 2006b decision was widely condemned by human-rights organizations in Egypt and by international Bahai networks, which mobilized to put pressure on the Egyptian government to redress the discriminatory ruling. Prominent Islamic lawyers in Egypt criticized the decision on different grounds, arguing that it created an impasse in the state's ability to govern effectively because it compelled Bahais to lie about their religion on official documents. This was tantamount to coercing them

---

[23] Ranya Mousa, interview with the author, October 2008, Cairo.

to give up their faith, which is a violation of the Quranic principle, "Let there be no compulsion in religion."[24] It was precisely this contradiction that opened a window for the EIPR to intervene on behalf of another Bahai family whose case was, at the time, pending in a lower administrative court. Since the SAC ruling could not be appealed, the EIPR decided to amend its plea on the Rauf Hindi case from asking the court to allow Bahais to list their religion on their identity cards to requesting that they be able to leave the required field blank (referred to as a "dash"). In an interview, the lead EIPR lawyer for this case commented, "This was a pragmatic decision on our part. We are principally opposed to the requirement that Egyptians have to declare their religious affiliation on state documents. But we knew that we would not win on the basis of such an argument. So we decided to change our appeal to force both the courts and the Muslims to face the contradictions inherent in our system, and to create a space for a different kind of discussion about Bahais, namely, their civil and political status in our country."[25]

The EIPR's strategy worked, and the lower Administrative Court of Justice delivered the following verdict (hereafter cited as AC 2008):[26]

> In keeping with the principle of not forcing any citizen to embrace a divine religion, . . . issuing a national identity card with no space for religion or with a symbol indicating that he does not belong to any of the three divine religions . . . would conform with the law and reality. [Pursuant with the Supreme Court decision of 1975,] the court concludes that the constitutional guarantee of freedom of belief is limited to the followers of the three divine religions and that the exercise of Bahai rites is against the public order [that is] essentially based on Islamic shari'a.

The court emphasized that its judgment did not constitute a "recognition of the Bahai ideology or a way to allow its followers to record it in the space reserved for religion." The judgment was meant to prevent the greater harm that would be visited on "People of the Book" if Bahais listed their religion incorrectly as either Muslims or Christians, since such an act would allow Bahais to insinuate "themselves among the members of the divine religions," which "would present a grave prejudice to the religion that will be recorded incorrectly."

In many ways this ruling is similar to AC 2006a and the earlier SAC ruling from 1983, in that it reinserts the separation between what is construed as a religious requirement to

---

[24] Quran 2:256.

[25] Adel Rafea, chief lawyer for the EIPR, interview with the author, May 2008, Cairo.

[26] Administrative Court of Justice decision on case no. 18354 of the fifty-eighth judicial year, issued on January 29, 2008. All subsequent quotes from the judgment are from a translated copy on file with the author.

deny formal recognition to the Bahai religion and the civil-law requirement to document the true identity of its citizens for governance and regulation. Recall that AC 2006a had argued that while the principle of fairness pertained to the domain of civil law (all Egyptian citizens had the right to a national identity card and the privileges it granted), when it came to religious and doctrinal rulings on the status of the Bahais, the court had no jurisdiction. The AC 2008 judgment follows a similar reasoning in allowing Bahais to leave the religion space blank instead of requiring them to list their correct identity. However, while the AC2006a ruling had run the risk of publicly recognizing the Bahai faith, the AC2008 judgment does not. In so doing, the court appears to close the chasm between the Bahais' civil and political *equality* and their religious *inequality* in the Egyptian polity.

Whereas the AC 2008 judgment made it possible for Bahais to carry on their political and civic life by allowing them to have national identity cards, the blank space rendered them vulnerable to religious discrimination. Because no other religious group has this distinction, their identity cards clearly mark them as Bahais; the empty slot is an indication of their deviation from the Muslim norm and, for some, a sign of their apostasy from Islam. In Egypt's religiously fractious landscape, this is not an easy burden to bear, and it is a reminder that the law can only partially resolve the religious inequalities that permeate the social life of a polity.

Public Order

Public order is a key concept in all the Bahai judgments; it is the basis on which the Egyptian state establishes the distinction between religious and civil acts—the former restricted, the latter permitted—and upholds the prohibition on the Bahai religion even as it simultaneously grants its followers freedom of belief. For many liberal critics, the Egyptian state's use of the concept of public order is casuistic at best, bending a secular legal instrument to justify religious prejudice and intolerance. A closer look at the history of public order and its international trajectory, however, reveals that the Egyptian interpretation is not so foreign to the concept's foundational aims.

The history of public order (*ordre public*) is rooted in nineteenth-century European law, formulated in Article 6 of the French Civil Code, from which it was adopted into the codes of a number of other states.[27] It belongs to conflict of laws jurisprudence and was crafted to resolve contradictory legal ideas and principles of foreign law within a territorially bounded nation-state. As such, public order is an expression of domestic sovereignty and a state's right to reject foreign (or international) laws that it deems unacceptable or contradictory to its own legal system. Initially developed as

---

[27] Husserl, "Public Policy and Ordre Public."

part of private international law, the aim of public order was to help adjudicate "relations among private persons from different states, and [was meant to deal] primarily with commercial and personal status law."[28] *Ordre public* is comparable to "public policy" in the Anglo-American tradition of common law, which, like its French counterpart, is a "manifestation of the sovereign power of the state."[29]

Public order clauses are as much a part of national law as they are of international law, in which their validity is widely accepted and upheld.[30] Public order allows a state to rescind specific terms of international covenants and treaties to which it is a signatory, but which it deems unacceptable given its own legal system, values, and norms. Because public order pertains to national sovereignty and the laws of a particular state, legal historians note, it varies according to time and place. In other words, there is no singular and modular way in which public order is defined in practice; its articulation is contingent and depends upon the principles, values, and laws that a nation-state regards as central to its sociopolitical configuration and collective identity.

Therefore, it is not surprising that in both the European Convention on Human Rights (ECHR) and the International Covenant on Civil and Political Rights (ICCPR), public order figures prominently. Both the ECHR and the ICCPR give signatory and member states a wide margin to limit the right to religious freedom and freedom of speech if their expression is deemed threatening to public order. Article 9 of the ECHR and Article 18 of the ICCPR on religious freedom define public order as consonant with "public safety, health, or morals or the rights and freedoms of others."[31] Article 10 of the ECHR also includes "national security and territorial integrity" as grounds for limiting free speech. Even though these regional and international conventions are binding for states, the public-order clause allows them to suspend these rights. How these "legally permissible" categories of exception are interpreted depends on the nation-state and the values and norms it decrees as worthy of protection.

The Egyptian courts hew closely to this internationally defined conception of public order. Consider, for example, the following passage from the Bahai AC 2008 ruling:

> Considering that the concept of public order has no exclusive
> and inclusive definition, and that it changes from one society
> to another according to the fundamental principles included in

---

[28] Agrama, *Questioning Secularism*, 95.

[29] Husserl, "Public Policy and Ordre Public," 43.

[30] There is some disagreement among legal scholars whether public order applies only to conflicts between national and foreign laws or whether it also applies within domestic law. The majority view holds that insomuch as public order is a measure of the domestic sovereignty of the state to suspend legal norms, it applies equally whether these laws are foreign, international, or national. See ibid.

[31] International Covenant on Civil and Political Rights, www.ohchr.org/en/professionalinterest/pages/ccpr.aspx.

its constitution, legislation, or the customs of the majority of its population, it is clear that the conceptual elements of the public order in Egypt are drawn from the fact that it is a state whose official religion is Islam, which is the religion of the majority of the population, and from the fact that Islamic shari'a is the principal source of legislation. Even though this constitutional provision addresses the legislator, other authorities of the state are [still] bound by it in the fulfillment of their duties. The state of Egypt recognizes three divine religions—that is, Judaism, Christianity, and Islam—and its legislation regulates the religious establishments of only these three religions.

This judgment further notes that the concept of public order is a neutral mechanism that was introduced by the British colonial administrators and enshrined in Article 18 of the ICCPR, which Egypt ratified (in 1982) and is obliged to uphold. However, the court argues that Egypt's compliance with Article 18 of the ICCPR is conditional on "the provisions of the Islamic shari'a," which was made explicit at the time of the "ratification of the covenant." The court therefore concludes that because the public-order clause gives the state the authority to limit the expression of religious beliefs that flout the social and moral order of a given polity, the Egyptian state is within its rights to limit public manifestations of the Bahai religion.

The administrative court's conception of public order is consonant with the global genealogy I trace above in several ways: (1) public order has no necessary definition but changes from society to society, depending upon its legal system and national norms; (2) it is the state's sovereign prerogative to define its scope and meaning; and (3) a sovereign state has the right to rescind specific terms of international covenants that it has signed if they contravene its legal and social norms. Thus, the equivalence the court draws between public order and shari'a principles is *not simply a misuse or misinterpretation of the foundational aims of public order but is constitutive of its conceptual matrix.*[32] As I elaborate below, the European Court of Human Rights (ECtHR) has also produced similar reasoning in a variety of cases, giving states wide leeway to limit expressions of religious beliefs based on public-order considerations. Invariably, in almost all of these cases, public order is defined in accord with majoritarian norms

---

[32] The modern concept of public order is quite distinct from the Islamic notion of *maslaha*, with which it is sometimes confused. *Maslaha*, as it developed in classical Islamic jurisprudence, was meant to answer a specific question: how to discern the divine will in the absence of clear scriptural injunctions. *Maslaha*, therefore, is a method in Islamic jurisprudence by means of which existing shari'a laws may be amended to address particular situations not addressed in law or in the Quran or the hadith. Public order in contrast is aimed at securing the security and strategic interests of the modern state. They belong therefore to two distinct epistemologies. On the historical changes wrought in the concept of *maslaha*, see Opwis, "*Maslaha* in Contemporary Islamic Legal Theory."

that are foundational to national identity, and against which the legitimacy of minority religious traditions is judged.

Subjecting the right to religious liberty to public-order limitations produces an interesting set of conundrums that are symptomatic of a radical ambiguity that haunts the conceptual architecture of the right itself. Drawing upon the Egyptian Bahai decisions, one might say that this ambiguity consists in a genuine oscillation between what exactly constitutes the *forum internum* (religious belief) and what the state should recognize or limit in the *forum externum* (religious expression). Thus, the Egyptian courts' construal of the freedom to have and maintain a *religion* may be read as being subject to the demands of public order in two distinct ways. On one reading, the court can be seen as simply recognizing the freedom to manifest a particular limited category of religious beliefs ("People of the Book") in the *forum externum* (on the grounds that shari'a norms constitute the state's public order). The public-order limit here is not on the manifestation of specific beliefs per se, but on which religious communities are recognized and, therefore, allowed to practice their rituals in public. The implication of this view is that *all* manifestations of religion are subject to state authority and regulation, and they must either be recognized or accept limitation. It is primarily because Islam is the religion of the majority of the population that the state so freely practices and recognizes its rites and rituals. However, this argument, insomuch as it ignores the importance of rites and rituals in the constitution of subjectivity, does not recognize the importance of *religious identity* to the civil status of a citizen.[33]

The question of religious identity suggests another way of reading the Egyptian court rulings. What is most deeply at issue, one might argue, is not the belief-action distinction (as between the *forum internum* and *forum externum*) but the difference between individual belief as an inner dimension of human consciousness and religion as a discursive tradition that undergirds the collective life of distinct communities. This goes beyond public-order limitations imposed on religious rites and rituals. It raises the issue of how the very category demarcated as religious in the *forum internum* is defined in the first place. No matter how minimally we might define religion (as conscience, belief, or experience), it has implications for how collective religious life and identity are lived and practiced. Thus, even a highly individualized and privatized conception of religion (such as a Protestantism) entails a substantive and prescriptive notion of self, sociality, and collectivity that remains unaccounted for in the right to religious liberty.

In what follows, through a close reading of several judgments from the European Court of Human Rights, I want to show how this substantive conception of religion

---

[33] The AC 2006a judgment implicitly recognizes this when it rules that Bahais *should* be allowed to list their religion on legal documents because this would ensure that they do *not* practice their faith publicly.

(often coded as "minimalist") informs the public-order reasoning that European states use to prohibit religious practices they deem threatening to national culture and majoritarian norms. Once again, my aim in turning to this analysis of European rulings is to explicate aspects of the legal-political structure that characterizes secularism, regardless of the identity of a nation-state.

Minority and Majority Religions in the ECtHR

Let me start with the *Lautsi v. Italy* (2011) case, in which Soile Lautsi, a dual Finnish and Italian citizen, sued a public school in Padua on behalf of her two minor sons. Lautsi argued that the compulsory display of crucifixes in the school's classrooms violated her and her children's right to freedom of thought, conscience, and religion protected in Article 9(1) of the ECHR. The Supreme Administrative Court in Italy ruled in March 2005 against Ms. Lautsi, arguing that the crucifix did not have any religious connotation in Italy. Instead, it symbolized Italy's historical and cultural values, which may have had religious origins in the past but did not anymore. Ms. Lautsi appealed this decision in the ECtHR, and in November 2009 the Second Chamber of the European Court ruled that Italy was in violation of Article 9(1) for two reasons: first, the "state's duty of neutrality and impartiality is incompatible with any kind of power on its part to assess the legitimacy of religious convictions or the ways of expressing those convictions"; second, the compulsory display of crucifixes clashed with an individual's "secular convictions" and was "emotionally disturbing for pupils of non-Christian religions or those who professed no religion."[34] The court also argued that the decision to hang a crucifix in a public classroom constitutes an assessment of the legitimacy of a particular religious conviction. In suggesting this, the court implied that the Italian government's decision rested on a normative position *internal* to the *forum internum* (religious belief) and thus was implicated in the category demarcated as religious. The court therefore ruled that Italian public schools could not display crucifixes.

This decision created an uproar in Italy, prompting the Vatican to proclaim, "It seems as if the court wanted to ignore the role of Christianity in forming Europe's identity, which was and remains essential."[35] The Italian government appealed the decision in the Grand Chamber of the ECtHR on January 10, 2010, and was supported

[34] *Lautsi and Others v. Italy*, March 18, 2001, http://hudoc.echr.coe.int/sites/eng/pages/search.aspx?i=001-104040#, para. 31.
[35] "Rulings in Europe and South America Affirm Display of Christian Symbols," *American Daily Herald*, March 27, 2011, www.americandailyherald.com/us-news/religion/item/rulings-in-europe-and-south-america-affirm-display-of-christian-symbols?category_id=147.

by twenty European nations, including Slovenia, Lithuania, and Poland. The Lithuanian Ministry of Foreign Affairs stated, "The use of crucifixes in public in Catholic countries reflects the European Christian tradition and should not be regarded as a restriction on the freedom of religion."[36]

The Grand Chamber of the ECtHR decided to reverse the Second Chamber's decision, agreeing with the Italian court that the crucifix was a "passive symbol" that did not infringe on the beliefs of either Lautsi or her children, who remained free to "believe or not to believe."[37] This shocked many observers of the ECtHR, given that in a series of cases (discussed below) the court had ruled that the Islamic headscarf was a "powerful religious symbol" that, when worn in a classroom, had a proselytizing effect on schoolchildren. In contrast to these earlier rulings, in the *Lautsi* decision, the court concluded that the prominent display of the crucifix in public schools was not an act of proselytization since it had no "influence on pupils comparable to that of didactic speech or participation in religious activities" and did not constitute "an assessment of the legitimacy of a particular religious conviction."[38] Instead, echoing the arguments of the Italian government, the court declared that the crucifix is a cultural symbol that represents the identity of "the Italian civilization" and its "value system: liberty, equality, human dignity and religious toleration, and accordingly also of the secular nature of the state."[39] Consequently, the court ruled that the display of crucifixes in public schools fell within the due margin of appreciation granted to member states to "perpetuate traditions" that expressed their culture and history.[40]

The spokesperson for the Catholic Church welcomed the decision and proclaimed, "To consider the presence of the crucifix in a public space to be against human rights, would be to deny the very idea of Europe. . . . Without the crucifix, the Europe we know today would not exist."[41] The centrality of Christianity to European identity in this formulation is similar to Islam's place in the construction of Egyptian social and state identity, which is echoed in the Egyptian judgments on the Bahais. In both cases, it is the "margin of appreciation" that the public-order clause accords to the sovereign state that *limits or allows* the display of religious symbols in public. As we will see below, whether this identity is secular, Christian, or Islamic, what is consistent across these geographic and legal contexts is the state's ability to define the scope of religion

---

[36] Ibid.

[37] *Lautsi v. Italy*, para. 31.

[38] Ibid., para. 72.

[39] Ibid., para. 15.

[40] Ibid., paras. 68–69.

[41] Benjamin Mann, "European Courts Say the Crucifixes Can Stay in Italian Schools," *Catholic News Agency*, March 18, 2011, www.catholicnewsagency.com/news/european-court-says-crucifixes -can-remain-in-italian-schools/.

and, by extension, its content and meaning in accord with the values of the majority religion at the expense of minorities.

The *Lautsi* decision stands in stark contrast with other ECtHR rulings that involve minority religious traditions in Europe, particularly Islam. Consider, for example, the precedent-setting *Dahlab v. Switzerland* (2001) judgment. This case involved Lucia Dahlab, a public-school teacher and Swiss national who had converted from Catholicism to Islam and took on the headscarf while she was teaching in a public elementary school. When the directorate general for primary education and the Geneva cantonal government prohibited Ms. Dahlab from wearing the headscarf at the school, she appealed this decision in a federal court on the grounds that it violated Article 9 of the ECHR and interfered with the "inviolable core of her freedom of religion."[42] The federal court denied Ms. Dahlab's appeal in November 1997, arguing, "The wearing of a headscarf and loose-fitting clothes remains an outward manifestation which, as such, is not part of the inviolable core of freedom of religion."[43] Ms. Dahlab appealed this decision in the ECtHR, which then ruled that because the Islamic headscarf was a "powerful external symbol" that had the *potential* to affect the convictions of the young children she taught, the Swiss government's prohibition was within its legally permissible margin of appreciation. The ECtHR argued:

> It *cannot be denied outright* that the wearing of a headscarf *might have* some kind of *proselytizing* effect, seeing that it appears to be imposed on women by a precept which is laid down in the Koran and which, as the Federal Court noted, is hard to square with the principle of *gender equality*. It therefore appears difficult to reconcile the wearing of an Islamic headscarf with the message of tolerance, respect for others, and above all, equality and non-discrimination that all teachers in a democratic society must convey to their pupils. Accordingly, weighing the right of a teacher to manifest her religion against the need to protect pupils by preserving religious harmony, the Court considers that, in the circumstances of the case and having regard, above all, to the tender age of the children for whom the applicant was responsible, . . . the Geneva authorities did not exceed their margin of appreciation and that the measure they took was therefore not unreasonable.[44]

Note that even though the ECtHR claims to be only regulating the manifestation of religious beliefs (rather than belief, which is a protected category according

---

[42] *Dahlab v. Switzerland*, February 15, 2001, http://hudoc.echr.coe.int/sites/eng/pages/search.aspx?i=001-22643#.

[43] Ibid., p. 1.

[44] Ibid., p. 15, emphasis added.

to Article 9), it nonetheless makes substantive judgments on what constitutes or falls within this protected category. This requires taking a position on how any set of restrictions will seem from the internal viewpoint of the category itself demarcated as religious. Thus, in the passage above, the ECtHR interprets the Islamic headscarf as a symbol of gender inequality (rather than a religious duty or a marker of piety) that is apparently unacceptable in a "democratic society." Setting aside the objection that all sorts of inequitable gender practices are tolerated in European societies, what is striking about the above reasoning is how the religious interpretation of the veil is repudiated, rendering it instead as an adiaphorous act (irrelevant to religious doctrine), which can then be subject to civic regulation. It mirrors the logic of the *Lautsi* decision, which casts a religious symbol (the crucifix) as a *cultural* object even as it reverses the valuation. Both these decisions (like those of the Egyptian courts) belong to the field of political secularism in that it is the sovereign state that distinguishes between the religious and the civic or cultural valence of an act, on the basis of which it then decides whether the act is worthy of state protection or prohibition. By declaring that the veil is a symbol of gender inequality rather than a religious duty, European states in fact engage in a form of theological reasoning that remains unacknowledged in most scholarly analyses of secularism.

A second notable feature of the *Dahlab* decision is its speculative claim that Ms. Dahlab's wearing of the headscarf had the *potential* to affect the children she supervised: "It *cannot be denied outright* that the wearing of a headscarf *might have* some kind of proselytizing effect." Importantly, as the judgment notes, there was no evidence that Ms. Dahlab had proselytized or promoted her religious beliefs. Nor had the parents or children complained about her headscarf. The ECtHR argued that banning the headscarf was a preemptive act to preserve "religious harmony" and stave off prospective "religious conflict." Commenting on the case, Nehal Bhuta argues that this speculative and "highly abstract analysis is partly facilitated by the court's invocation of the margin of appreciation doctrine, . . . and the way in which [it] is applied betray[s] much about the extent to which Islamic religious practices are understood as an intrinsic or categorical threat to public order and civil peace—regardless of whether the state . . . has demonstrated this to be the case."[45] When compared with the *Lautsi* decision, which posited that Christian values are consistent with democracy, tolerance, and equality, it appears that Christian political theology is just as central to European identity and legal structure as Islamic political theology is to Egyptian identity and legal structure. The difference is that the ECtHR decisions do not include

[45] Bhuta, "Two Concepts of Religious Freedom," 23.

any doctrinal or scriptural citations; instead, Christian values are cast as symbolic rather than substantive, thereby closing the gap between the secular principle of state neutrality and Europe's Christian identity.

The *Dahlab v. Switzerland* ruling set a precedent for the subsequent rulings that the ECtHR issued on the veil, most importantly in *Şahin v. Turkey* (2005) and *Doğru v. France* (2009), both of which upheld the ban on the Islamic headscarf in public institutions (especially schools, as spaces of *laïque* inculcation) on the grounds that it threatened the secular identity of Turkey and France, respectively. Both also reiterated the *Dahlab* assessment that the Islamic veil is incompatible with gender equality, tolerance, and nondiscrimination, which the court characterized as essential features of a democracy.[46] The *Şahin* case involved a student in Turkey who was expelled from medical school for refusing to take off her headscarf, which was at the time banned in public institutions and universities.[47] The Turkish courts rejected Leyla Şahin's challenge on the basis that the veil is a symbol of political Islam and poses a threat to republican values and public order in Turkey. When Ms. Şahin appealed this decision in the ECtHR, the court concurred with the Turkish characterization of the veil as a feature of political Islam (rather than a religious obligation). In doing so, the ECtHR also represented the veil as a threat to the secular identity of the Turkish state and democracy. Once again, the courts engaged in religious reasoning, declaring what was for Ms. Şahin a religious act to be a political one, thus subjecting it to the limitations of public order.

Not unlike the Egyptian Bahai judgments, the ECtHR argued that the prohibition on the veil did not violate Ms. Şahin's religious beliefs because only her actions (*forum externum*) were being limited. The Turkish state, therefore, acted within the "margin of appreciation" to protect public order, public safety, and the rights and freedoms of others.[48] In grounding the judgment in the concept of public order, the Bahai rulings and the *Şahin* judgment are strikingly comparable: in the former, the expression of Bahai identity in public was deemed a threat to the Islamic identity of the state, whereas in the latter the public expression of Islamic beliefs in the form of the veil was understood to pose a danger to Turkey's secular identity. Largely through speculative (rather than evidentiary) claims, the rulings expanded the sovereign powers of the

---

[46] *Şahin v. Turkey*, November 10, 2005, http://hudoc.echr.coe.int/sites/eng/pages/search.aspx?i =001-70956#, para. 3; *Doğru v. France*, April 3, 2009, http://hudoc.echr.coe.int/sites/eng/pages/search .aspx?i=001-90039#, para. 72.

[47] The Turkish ban on headscarves in public schools and government offices was lifted in 2013.

[48] *Şahin v. Turkey*, para. 111.

state to preserve its national identity even as they declared the sanctity of religious belief to be inviolable.

The *Doğru v. France* judgment, issued four years after *Şahin*, involved an eleven-year-old girl, Belgin Doğru, who was expelled from school after refusing to take off her headscarf during her physical-education class. After the Caen Administrative Court denied her parents' appeal in 1999 and the Conseil d'État refused to hear the case, in 2005 Doğru's parents petitioned the decision in the ECtHR as a violation of her right to religious freedom under Article 9 of the ECHR. The court's decision, issued in 2009, starts by foregrounding and quoting circulars from the French ministry of education that laid out the rationale for banning the veil from schools:

> Secularism, a constitutional principle of the Republic, is one of the cornerstones of state education. At school, like anywhere else, an individual's religious beliefs are a matter of individual conscience and therefore free choice. At school, however, . . . keeping with the requirement of respect for pluralism and the principle that the public service shall be neutral, requires that the entire educational community be shielded from any ideological or religious pressure. . . . Accordingly, pupils must refrain from displaying any conspicuous sign, whether in their dress or otherwise, that promotes religious belief. Any proselytizing behavior that goes beyond mere religious beliefs shall be proscribed.[49]

Adhering closely to the *Dahlab* and *Şahin* judgments, the court ruled:

> In France, as in Turkey or Switzerland, secularism is a constitutional principle, and a founding principle of the Republic, to which the entire population adheres and the protection of which appears to be of prime importance, in particular in schools. The Court reiterates that an attitude which fails to respect that principle will not necessarily be accepted as being covered by the freedom to manifest one's religion and will not enjoy the protection of Article 9 of the Convention. . . . Having regard to the margin of appreciation which must be left to the member States with regard to the establishment of the delicate relations between the Churches and the State, religious freedom thus recognized and restricted by the requirements of secularism appears legitimate in light of the values underpinning the Convention.[50]

---

[49] Quoted in ibid., para. 27. Note that the court quotes from the 1989 and 1994 circulars from the ministry of education, which pertain to when Doğru was in school. The French government banned the veil and the display of other conspicuous religious symbols in 2011. For an insightful analysis of the politics behind the French law that banned the headscarf, see Scott, *The Politics of the Veil*.

[50] *Doğru v. France*, para. 72.

In this judgment, the ECtHR implicitly invokes what legal scholars refer to as the principle of general applicability, which allows a state to regulate permitted or protected activities when they conflict with the general laws of a country. Pursuant to this principle, the ECtHR claims that because the general laws of the French Republic are secular, the state can prohibit religious attire in public schools. Note its overlap with the logic of the public-order principle, which gives the state a wide margin of appreciation to decide which values, symbols, and practices are deemed essential to national identity.[51]

Compare this public-order reasoning with the following passage from a much-quoted passage from Egypt's Court of Cassation ruling (1979) that echoes the passage I quoted above from the AC 2008 judgment:

> [Public order] comprises the principles [qawa'id] that aim at realizing the public interest [al-maslaha al-'amma] of a country, from a political, social, and economic perspective. These [principles] are related to the natural, material, and moral state [wad'a] of an organized society, and supersede the interests of individuals. The concept of [public order] is based on a purely secular doctrine that is to be applied as a general doctrine [madhhab 'amm] to which society in its entirety can adhere and which must not be linked to any provision of religious law.[52]

Note that, not unlike in the jurisprudence of the ECtHR, public order trumps individual rights because it secures the collective and moral good of the society, the foundational basis of the modern state. In the following passage, the Egyptian Court of Cassation squares the secularity of the public-order principle with the Islamic identity and laws of the state:

> [The concept of public order] is sometimes based on a principle related to religious doctrine, in the case when such a doctrine has become intimately linked with the legal and social order, deep-

---

[51] The principle of general applicability is also pertinent to American jurisprudence on the First Amendment. Despite the conspicuous absence of a public-order clause in the First Amendment, general applicability works in comparable ways. For example, in *Employment v. Smith* (1990), the Supreme Court ruled that the state could deny unemployment benefits to two Native Americans who were fired for ingesting peyote as part of a religious ritual because that act fell under the state's drug laws and therefore was not protected by the First Amendment. *Employment v. Smith*, April 17, 1990, www.law .cornell.edu/supremecourt/text/494/.

[52] Quoted in Berger, "Public Policy and Islamic Law," 104. Note that Berger uses the term *public policy* instead of *public order*, but I have retained the latter since it gives a more accurate sense of its legal meaning, one that I elaborate in this chapter. The quoted passages are from *al-Mudhakkira al-Idahiyya li-Mashru' al-Qanun al-Madani* (nos. 16 and 26 of the forty-eighth judicial year, issued on January 17, 1979), published as part of the parliamentary Collection of Preparatory Works (*Majmu' al-'Amal al-Tadhiriyya*).

> rooted in the conscience of society [*dhamir al-mujtamaʿ*], in the
> sense that the general feelings [*al-shuʿur al-amm*] are hurt if it is
> not adhered to. The definition [*taqdir*] [of public policy] is char-
> acterized by objectivity, in accordance with what the general ma-
> jority [*aghlab ʿamm*] of individuals of the community believes.[53]

Once again, this conception of public order and the one invoked in the ECtHR's veil rulings are very similar. In the case of France and Switzerland, the European courts ruled that the veil was impermissible because it impinged on the "rights of others" who in turn were described as secular, a term consonant with the national identity of the state in each case. In Egypt, on the other hand, as the above passage makes evident, it is Islam that is represented as the "conscience of the society" and its "general feelings" that may be hurt by practices that do not accord with this national ethos. The public-order doctrine, therefore, allows the state to come to the defense of the rights of the majority (secular or religious) in the name of those it rules.[54] Despite the fact that in one case the identity of the state is Islamic and in the other cases (Turkey, Switzerland, and France) it is secular, they are all exemplary instances of the prerogative of the modern secular state to define national norms in accord with majoritarian religious sensibilities, while at the same time declaring religion to be immune from state intervention.

Freedom of Conscience versus the Rights of Religion

There are three possible objections to the parallels I draw between the jurisprudence of Egypt and that of the ECtHR.[55] First, one could argue that I have ignored a fundamental distinction between Egyptian and European courts: while the former stipulate religious content, the latter merely limit the display of certain religious symbols for the purpose of protecting the rights of others. Consequently, the Egyptian court rulings are far more egregious than the European ones because they pronounce on what "true religion" is. This objection, however, remains blind to the normative conception of religion that informs the European judgments, one that privileges belief and conscience at the expense of practices, rites, and rituals (hence the assumption that banning the veil is not a violation of Islamic beliefs). While it may appear to be minimalist (and

---

[53] Quoted in Berger, "Public Policy and Islamic Law," 104.

[54] This is echoed in the AC 2008 judgment that confirms, "The conceptual elements of the Egyptian public order are drawn from the fact that [Egypt] is a state whose official religion is Islam, which is the religion of the majority of the population, and from the fact that Islamic shariʿa law is the principal source of legislation."

[55] I want to thank Cécile Laborde for drawing my attention to these issues, and to Peter Danchin for discussing these points with me.

thus universal), this conception of religion has a specific Protestant genealogy that does not comport with other religious traditions (particularly the ineluctable relationship many traditions draw between religious belief and its phenomenal forms).[56] The ECtHR presumes this conception of religion against which the deviance of other traditions is measured. The ongoing litigation in Europe around Islamic and at times Jewish practices that do not accord with a privatized conception of religion points to the religious truth internal to European law. It turns out, therefore, that neither the Egyptian rulings nor the European ones are free of normative prescriptions about what religion should be in the public sphere.

A second objection one might raise is that my argument ignores a fundamental difference between the state's denial of the legal existence of a religious group and the state's refusal to accommodate certain religious practices because they contravene its sociopolitical norms. While there is no doubt that there is a difference between the two in that the former pertains to the ontological status of the subject and the latter to his or her actions, it is important to emphasize that the Egyptian courts *do* recognize Bahais as legal subjects, and the court rulings deal precisely with their civil status in relation to their religious identity. The Egyptian court rulings are distinct in that they claim openly that Bahais are unequal to Muslims, whereas the European courts proclaim the minority and majority to be equal in the eyes of the law, even as minority religious practices are subject to greater sanction. We may well prefer the European proclamation to the Egyptian one, but this should not blind us to the majoritarian norms built into the European laws of religious protection.

A final objection one might raise is that the majoritarian tilt of Egyptian and European court rulings is a result not of a prejudice internal to secular liberal law but of its faulty and unfair application. Thus, the right to religious liberty, if implemented properly, would not treat minority and majority religions differently. There is a certain kind of legal formalism that undergirds this argument in that it assumes that the force of law resides not in its normative precepts but in its correct application. Epistemologically speaking, one can separate legal concepts and principles from the social and political institutions from which they emanate. Indeed, insomuch as the correct interpretation of law is presumed to depend on judges and legal bodies, law can be separated from politics. Such an understanding of law has been challenged by a range of legal and political theorists (from Carl Schmitt to Hans Morgenthau).[57] Drawing on these critiques of legal formalism, my analysis in this chapter suggests that the legal grammar of political secularism is neither neutral nor abstract but, as part of the or-

---

[56] On this point, see Mahmood, "Religious Reason and Secular Affect."
[57] See Koskenniemi, *The Gentle Civilizer of Nations*, chap. 6.

ganizing structure of the nation-state, is suffused with the historically specific norms and values that give the nation-state a distinct identity.

The ECtHR is not the only judicial system to consecrate majoritarian sensibilities; European national courts exhibit a similar propensity. For example, the Federal Constitutional Court of Germany upheld the Baden-Württemberg legislation, which bans teachers from wearing Islamic religious symbols in schools while allowing Christian and Jewish ones on the grounds that "the representation of Christian and occidental values and traditions corresponds to the educational mandate of the [regional] constitutions."[58] Similarly, in 1985, the Austrian government prohibited the circulation of a film depicting Jesus, God, and Mary for offending Christian sensibilities, a decision upheld by the national courts and the ECtHR in its *Otto-Preminger v. Austria* (1994) decision. In Britain, the government banned the film *Visions of Ecstasy* in 1989 to prevent "seriously offensive attacks on matters regarded as sacred by Christians."[59] When the director appealed the ban in the ECtHR, the court ruled that Britain had not violated Article 10 on freedom of speech because it had a legitimate reason to ban the film.

Given this history of European rulings, it is easy to chalk them up to a bias in the jurisprudence of the courts "toward protecting traditional and established religions," as Danchin suggests, "and a corresponding insensitivity toward the rights of minority, nontraditional, or unpopular religious groups."[60] Indeed, my own argument may be read in this light as an assessment that denies the possibility that religious minorities could be treated equally in secular liberal polities. This does not, however, capture the argumentative arc of this book. If majoritarian prejudice is one side of secular liberal law, then the other is its promise of civil and political equality for all citizens irrespective of their religious status. Minorities often contest the discriminatory practices of secular law through the same legal instruments that enshrine majoritarian privilege. This constant back and forth—the possibility of prejudice and equality—is highly generative in that it keeps the promise of secular neutrality alive. These two aspects of political secularism are symptomatic of a genuine ambiguity that haunts its praxis—most potently captured in the doctrine of pubic order. As Agrama points out, a certain indeterminacy characterizes all secular liberal polities in that while everyone is equal before the law, the state also aims to uphold "the sentiments and the

[58] Bhuta, "Two Concepts of Religious Freedom," 31.

[59] *Wingrove v. United Kingdom*, November 25, 1996, http://hudoc.echr.coe.int/sites/eng/pages/search.aspx?i=001-58080#, para. 57.

[60] Danchin, "Of Prophets and Proselytes," 275. A wide spectrum of commentators echoes this judgment. See, for example, Evans, *Freedom of Religion under the European Convention*.

values of the majority . . . so long as they have become integral to the cohesiveness of society."[61] Thus, in the name of public order, the state often enacts an exception to its commitment to equality in order to enact *another* norm—namely, the protection and preservation of national culture and values grounded in the sensibilities of the majority.

The indeterminacy that haunts public-order doctrine (as norm and exception), I want to point out, is isomorphic with the ambiguity that characterizes the right to religious liberty. Note that all the court rulings I have discussed here uphold the sanctity of religious belief (*forum internum*), which is supposedly inviolable, while limiting its public expression (*forum externum*). Yet there seems to be a genuine confusion about what exactly the law is seeking to protect in the *forum internum*. Is it the individual who has the right to choose autonomously his or her own beliefs or convictions, religious or not? Or does the law protect the right to have and maintain a certain category of belief, such as conscience or faith, understood in some specified sense as unchosen? Or is it not just individuals but also groups and religious institutions as subjects who have the right to profess and maintain a religious tradition free of sovereign interference?[62]

Most human-rights activists and advocates of religious liberty try to resolve this ambiguity by claiming that a secular state is authorized only to protect the individual's right to conscience and belief, not to smuggle in majoritarian values through invocations of public order.[63] Liberal critics of public-order doctrine recommend doing away with the states' margin of appreciation so as to make the exercise of individual liberty sacrosanct.[64] Others argue that the special status accorded to religion in secular liberal law should be amended. In a coauthored book, Jocelyn Maclure and Charles Taylor propose expanding the individualized conception of religious liberty to include "all

---

[61] Agrama, *Questioning Secularism*, 94.

[62] Danchin, "Islam in the Secular *Nomos*."

[63] For example, in a report submitted to the Human Rights Council by the Special Rapporteurs on Freedom of Religion and Racial Discrimination in 2006, Asma Jehangir and Doudou Diène argued, "International human rights law protects primarily individuals in the exercise of their freedom of religion and not religions per se." Human Rights Council, "Implementation of General Assembly Resolution 60/251 of 15 March 2006 Entitled 'Human Rights Council,'" September 20, 2006, para. 27, www.refworld.org/docid/470b77b40.html. The report acknowledges the general bias built into the laws of various nations that privilege the majority religion at the expense of minority faiths. The Special Rapporteurs argue, however, that this bias cannot be resolved by extending special protections to minority religions.

[64] See, for example, Edge, "The European Court of Human Rights"; and Martínez-Torrón and Navarro-Valls, "The Protection of Religious Freedom." The debate about the proper balance between a liberal state's commitment to protect individual liberty and its duty to secure the social and moral order of a polity has a long genealogy, most famously captured in the Devlin and Hart exchange in the 1960s. See Devlin, "Morals and the Criminal Law"; and Hart, *Law, Liberty, and Morality*.

core beliefs that allow individuals to structure their moral identity," which should receive the same protection as religious liberty does in pluralist democratic societies.[65] This suggestion aims to get around the special protections that religion enjoys in secular liberal societies but that nonreligious values do not. By analogizing religious conviction to other kinds of moral and ethical beliefs, the argument goes, one can remove the bias of the state for religion and, by extension, the values of the majority.[66] These proposals want to make the right to religious liberty more *and* less robust at the same time by bringing a range of beliefs under its protective ambit while shearing away the religious content of those beliefs.

At first glance, this seems to be a neat solution to the majoritarian tilt of religious-freedom law I have discussed in this chapter. Yet on closer inspection, such a proposal fails to resolve the problems that haunt the right to religious freedom, in particular the sovereign prerogative of the state to judge and decide which values are worthy of legal protection. Insomuch as the state's criteria are likely to privilege the norms of the national majority (which the state has a duty to safeguard and protect), then Maclure and Taylor's proposal fails to address the majoritarian bias of the law. Furthermore, in order to judge whether a certain belief is worthy of protection, the state must inevitably involve itself in investigating the substance and sincerity of the belief; this in turn embroils the secular state further into the domain of privacy, which is supposed to be a space of autonomy and freedom.

Insomuch as Maclure and Taylor's proposal consecrates the individual as the bearer of beliefs, it remains caught in a characteristic set of problems that bedevil the right to religious freedom. Consider, for example, the issue of proselytization. Does the right to religious liberty protect this practice because an individual strongly upholds it? If so, how does it infringe upon the rights of the proselytized to maintain *his or her* beliefs without being subject to another person's convictions? The focus on the individual does not get us out of these questions that are at the core of endless court battles, none of which is resolved in an axiomatic or principled manner. Rather, in each case the state decides upon whose rights and which beliefs should take precedence on an ad hoc basis.

The famous ECtHR judgment, *Kokkinakis v. Greece* (1993), captures these dilemmas acutely. *Kokkinakis* was concerned with the Greek government's prosecution of a Jehovah's Witness for proselytism directed at members of the dominant religion, Eastern Orthodox Christianity. The ECtHR, in reviewing this ruling for a potential

---

[65] Maclure and Taylor, *Secularism and Freedom of Conscience*, 89.

[66] A strong proponent of this view is the political theorist Cécile Laborde, who has built a robust theoretical case for why strong nonreligious beliefs should be treated on a par with religious ones. See Laborde, "Protecting Freedom of Religion."

violation of Article 9, decided in Greece's favor that it had a "legitimate aim" in criminalizing proselytism in order to "protect the rights and freedoms of others" (that is, Greek Orthodox Christians). The public disagreement between two of the six jurists who deliberated the case is instructive for the core dilemmas it reveals located at the heart of religious freedom litigation.[67] While Judge Martens criticized Greece's prohibition of proselytization for violating the personal autonomy of the proselytizer by privileging a conception of collective good determined in accord with Greece's national religion, Judge Valticos contended that proselytism itself was "an attack on the religious beliefs of others" and characterized it as a "rape of the beliefs of others."[68]

Departing from most critics of the *Kokkinakis* ruling who saw it as a clash between individualist and collective conceptions of religious liberty, Peter Danchin draws attention to how difficult it was for the court to determine whose right to hold up, "that of the proselytizer or the target of proselytism."[69] Further, he asks, "How is either preference to be reconciled with the 'strict neutrality' of the state?"[70] Danchin's question holds out the possibility of realizing a strictly neutral state that can arbitrate fairly between competing claims. Attempts, such as those of Maclure and Taylor, to make the right to religious freedom more copious are normatively oriented toward this possibility. Yet the material presented in this chapter challenges us to consider what it would mean to give up this possibility and to reckon with the indelibly partial nature of the secular state—to ask, instead, how does the ongoing entwinement of religion and politics open up certain avenues to religious equality while foreclosing others? How do the religious predicates of national identity influence what kind of religious difference is deemed worthy of acceptance and equality?

We cannot answer such questions, however, if we continue to narrowly measure the secularism of Western and non-Western states (more versus less). While there is no doubt that certain nations are more hospitable to religious minorities than others, we should not confuse this with their degree of secularity or presume that secularism itself is equivalent to religious neutrality. Given that secularity entails religion, the task is to analyze how this entwinement conditions our politics. The dilemmas that haunt the exercise of religion in Greece, France, and Egypt are quite analogous. In parsing the similarities and differences between the legal rulings issued in these states, I have aimed to grasp the structurally similar problems that different models of religion-state accommodation manifest.

---

[67] For a detailed discussion of this debate, see Mahmood and Danchin, "Immunity or Regulation?"
[68] *Kokkinakis v. Greece*, May 25, 1993, http://hudoc.echr.coe.int/sites/eng/pages/search.aspx?i=001 -57827#, paras. 9–10.
[69] Danchin, "Of Prophets and Proselytes," 275.
[70] Ibid.

Does this mean that religious freedom is impossible to attain in our modern world? This is not my point, even though it is one that scholars have made recently.[71] I believe that religious freedom, whatever its constraints, is an inescapable part of our present. I do, however, want to invite us to contend with the conditionality of this freedom, its sequestration within a specific political imaginary that cannot make do without the agency of the sovereign state. We cannot but address the state in our quest for political and religious equality, despite its exceptions and constraints. To think with this conditionality is to acknowledge the finitude of our imagination even as we seek to expand its constraints.

[71] See Sullivan, *Impossibility of Religious Freedom.*

Chapter 5

SECULARITY, HISTORY, LITERATURE

U p to this point in the book, I have analyzed secularism as a legal-political discourse that reorders religious life and identity, generating new forms of inter-
communal conflict. In this chapter I want to think about secularity—the shared set of
background assumptions, attitudes, and dispositions that imbue secular society and
subjectivity. Secularity entails a certain judgment about, and appreciation for, what
religion should be in the modern world. Its predicates are found not so much in state
edicts and policies as in culture at large, where they are disseminated, reproduced,
and embodied as sensibilities. We encounter them, for example, in the modern emphasis on individual conscience and experience as the proper locus of religiosity and
in the relative diminution of the phenomenal forms of religion (rites, rituals, attire,
and scriptures).[1] Because secularity exists at the level of sensibilities, its assumptions
are difficult to grasp. However, they often come to the fore when controversies erupt
over works of cultural production that engage religion, such as the fury over the pho-
tograph "Piss Christ," from 1987, by the American artist Andres Serrano, the publication of novels such as *The Satanic Verses* and *The Da Vinci Code*, and the depiction of
the prophet Muhammad in the Danish cartoons in 2006.[2]

In what follows, I explore various aspects of secularity as they emerged in the
Egyptian controversy over the publication of *Azazeel*, an Arabic novel set in the
fourth century, when a doctrinal dispute about the dual nature of Christ tore Christendom apart and eventually gave birth to the Coptic Orthodox Church. Shortly after
the novel's publication, the Coptic Church accused its Muslim author, Youssef Ziedan, of distorting ecumenical disputes to discredit Christianity and foment sectarian
strife (*fitna ta'ifiyya*). While *Azazeel* is not a religiously bigoted text, it does provide a
secular reading of the Christological controversy and delivers a damning critique of

---

[1] On this point, see Mahmood, *Politics of Piety.*
[2] On the "Piss Christ" controversy, see Mitchell, *What Do Pictures Want?*; and on the Danish cartoons, see Asad, Butler, Brown, and Mahmood, *Is Critique Secular?*

the early church for brutally suppressing competing views in order to consecrate its ecclesiastical authority. The novel revolves around a monk's existential struggles between religious submission and individual freedom, often painting clerical leaders as ambitious and heartless. Throughout the novel, *Azazeel* rehearses the familiar secular argument that religion is a human invention created to address man's dilemmas, which, ultimately, it is fundamentally incapable of resolving.

Even though these views resonated with the secular readers of the novel (Muslims and Christians alike), the Coptic Church and many devout Christians found them deeply offensive. The Church tried unsuccessfully to have the novel banned for "defaming the Christian religion" (*izdira' al-din al-masihi*), a crime in Egyptian law, and managed to prevent the production of a film based on the novel. The clerics then followed with a series of publications attacking the novel and the author, Ziedan, who responded with alacrity in writing to defend his position. It is easy to read this standoff as a clash between religious taboos and the right to literary freedom, or as yet another expression of the Christian-Muslim strife that characterizes the Egyptian political landscape. However, I want to suggest that neither interpretation is adequate for understanding the deeper stakes of the *Azazeel* controversy.

The *Azazeel* debate pivoted around two incommensurable understandings of religion: one in which humanity itself provides the values and models of human flourishing against which the contributions of a religious tradition are to be measured and judged; and another wherein human existence must be molded in accord with the dictates of a transcendent god. For humanist scholars engaged in the project of writing a natural history of religion, the crystallization of this opposition and the basis for its overcoming can be traced back to early Christian debates about the dual nature of Christ, as both divine and human. Ziedan's work can be read as a contribution to this project. In *Azazeel*, theological arguments of late antiquity about the human dimension of the nature of Christ are reinterpreted in accord with a humanist reading in accord with a post-Enlightenment critique of premodern religion. From the Coptic Church's point of view, Ziedan's secular evacuation of the divine from the persona of Christ participates in a long-standing Protestant critique of the non-Chalcedonian traditions of Christianity, resurrecting an old wound.

While contrasting conceptions of religion provide an important window into the *Azazeel* controversy, to characterize the two as fundamentally opposed does not do justice to how they are both inflected—albeit in different ways—by a secular episteme. This is evident in the way both Ziedan and the clerics understand scripture as a repository of historical events located in empty, homogenous time. While they offer different interpretations of these events, both subscribe to the secular assumption that for revelation to be persuasive it must be commensurate with historical truth.[3] Thus, it is this secular conception of temporality and history that entangles the author of *Azazeel* and the clerics in the same epistemological world, even as they lock horns and seek to undermine the other's position. This is perhaps not so surprising because, insomuch as secularity is constitutive of the modern condition, its normative assumptions also seed the life world of those who seek to challenge its legitimacy. In what follows, I analyze these implicated and entangled genealogies while simultaneously tracking the oppositions that sustained the *Azazeel* standoff.

Pagan and Christian Itineraries

Azazeel is a work of historical fiction that takes place during a period (319–415 AD) that is foundational to the identity of the Coptic Orthodox Church, two hundred years before Arab Muslims arrived in Egypt. *Azazeel*'s narrative arc is organized around the Christological debate over the divine and human natures of Christ, which eventually resulted in splitting Christendom at the Council of Chalcedon (451 AD) and divided the four sees of the Byzantine empire (Antioch, Alexandria, Constantinople, and Jerusalem). The Coptic Church, along with what came to be known as Oriental Orthodox Christianity, adopted the miaphysite position against the Chalcedonian creed that the Catholic and Eastern Orthodox churches (and later the Protestants) embraced. For taking this stance, Egyptian Christians endured over two hundred years of persecution at the hands of the Byzantine rulers, who sought to exert theological and political control over the Alexandrian See.[4] Though it is difficult to do justice to the complexity of this ancient debate without collapsing important internal distinctions, in general one might say that the Chalcedonian creed (the diaphysite position) subscribes to a dual nature of Christ (human and divine) conjoined in one hypostatic union. The miaphysite view, on the other hand, holds that Christ's humanity and divinity are two aspects of one nature. Given that *Azazeel* not only ventriloquizes the early Christological debate but also takes a partisan position on many of the disputes, it is not surprising that it provoked the ire of the Coptic Church and its lay followers.

The novel's narrative unfolds through the voice of Hypa, an Egyptian monk who travels from Aswan (an ancient frontier town in southern Egypt) to various Christian

---

[3] I do not mean to suggest that this is the only attitude that characterizes a secular attitude to scripture, but that it was one that Ziedan and the Coptic clerics shared.

[4] Oriental Orthodox Christianity (the non-Chalcedonians) comprises the Coptic Orthodox, the Syrian Orthodox, the Armenian Apostolic, the Ethiopian Orthodox, and the Indian Orthodox churches.

monasteries in Akhmim, Alexandria, Jerusalem, Sinai, and, eventually, Aleppo and Antioch. This is a period when Christianity was slowly consolidating itself against the political ambitions of the Roman Empire, as well as a cacophony of beliefs and practices (Jewish, Gnostic, and pagan) that the ascendant church tried to either eradicate or subsume. Versed in multiple languages central to early Christianity—Greek, Coptic, and Syriac—Hypa is a Copt; that is, he is one of the indigenous inhabitants of Egypt who predated Arabs by centuries and embraced Christianity at the time of the apostles, abandoning their pagan gods and mythologies for the truth of the newly ascendant religion. Since its introduction in the first century, Christianity spread quickly in Egypt, and by the third century the Church of Alexandria was regarded as one of the four apostolic sees.

At a time when Alexandria and Antioch competed for importance against Rome (and eventually Constantinople), this was a multicentered world, and the pulls on an energetic and intelligent man like Hypa were many. *Azazeel* is presented as a compilation of his scrolls, which were originally penned in Syriac on papyrus and which survived through the years until discovered by archeologists and rendered in Arabic for the present audience, with an introduction written by the fictive translator. The plot of the novel vacillates between the drama of Christological schisms that threatened to tear Christianity apart and Hypa's own struggles between carnal desire and ascetic monasticism. The title, *Azazeel*, intimates the kind of contention and conflict, both personal and theological, at the heart of the novel. A figure in early Jewish demonology, Azazeel (often spelled Azazel or Azazil in English) is found in various pseudepigraphic texts based on the Old Testament (such as *Apocalypse of Abraham* and *Book of Enoch I*) and appears in later Jewish and Christian demonological lore in various forms. Scholars suggest that Azazeel belongs to two different and competing mythologies of evil: the fall of Adam and Eve, and the revolt of angels in the antediluvian period.[5] They also propose that he was a precursor to Satan in all three monotheistic traditions. In Islam, these two trajectories of evil are preserved in the figure of Iblis, who is cast out of heaven for his refusal to obey God's command to prostrate himself in front of Adam.[6] While the Quran makes no mention of Azazeel, early Sufis (such as Mansur al-Hallaj, d. 922 AD) render him akin to Iblis, emphasizing not so much his ability to incite evil as his argumentative and persuasive abilities to engage the prophets, including Moses and Muhammad.[7] In the novel, when Hypa asks Azazeel

[5] Caldwell, "The Doctrine of Satan"; and Orlov, *Dark Mirrors*.
[6] Notably, in the Quran this occurs after Iblis has been forgiven for enticing Adam to taste the fruit of knowledge (2:30–34 and 38:71–75).
[7] Sells, *Early Islamic Mysticism*, 273–77.

what he would like to be called, he responds, "They're all the same to me—Iblis, Satan, Ahriman, Azazeel, Beelzebub, Beelzaboul."[8] When Hypa then asks for the common meaning of his many names, Azazeel responds, "the antithesis."[9]

In the novel, Azazeel appears as a voice and presence close to Hypa's heart, sometimes even as his conscience, rather than as a presence from without: "Yes, Hypa, the Azazeel who comes to you from within yourself";[10] "I am you, Hypa, and I am them. . . . I am the will, the willer, and the willed."[11] At times enticing Hypa to pursue his desires and at others questioning him when he wants to recoil from theological and existential ambiguities, "Azazeel," Hypa acknowledges, "has strong arguments and he usually wins me over. Or is it that I have emboldened him by tugging him towards myself, as he claims, with my constant hesitation and my chronic worrying?"[12] In the words of Kamal Ghobrial, a liberal Coptic writer and critic, "The novel tells us that Satan (Azazeel) is not a metaphysical entity outside of us, who hatches conspiracies for us day and night, but he is inside of us, the impediment within, [an aspect of] our human disposition from whom it is necessary we do not recoil but confront with courage."[13] In this account the devil and his metaphysical powers are rendered human, properties of a human psyche.

Azazeel is a constant companion to Hypa as he travels far and wide in his search for existential and divine truths in a world located at the cusp of an ascendant Christianity. Hypa carries with him the memory of witnessing the death of his pagan father, when his mother converted to Christianity and conspired with fellow religionists to have her husband killed. After this horrifying event, he leaves home to train at a monastery in Akhmim (a center of pharaonic, Greek, and, later, Christian learning). A young man with many skills, Hypa teaches himself the craft of healing with medicinal herbs and comes to love manuscripts (pagan, classical, Hellenic, and Christian), which he collects clandestinely, absorbing their wisdom even as he strives to become a consummate monk. Over the course of his journey, he indulges in tumultuous affairs with two women, each time turning away to persist in his quest for God.

It is in Alexandria that Hypa encounters the two historical figures at the center of the Christological debate of the period: Patriarch Cyril of Alexandria (c. 376–444 AD)

---

[8] Ziedan, *Azazeel*, 291. All citations of the novel are from the English translation of *Azazeel* by Jonathan Wright.
[9] Ibid., 291.
[10] Ibid., 36.
[11] Ibid., 292.
[12] Ibid., 37.
[13] Kamal Ghobrial, "Maqaraba li-Riwaya Doktor Youssef Ziedan: 'Azazeel,'" *Shaffaf al-Sharq al-Awsat*, August 24, 2008, www.metransparent.com/spip.php?page=article&id_article=4349&lang=ar.

and his nemesis Nestorius (c. 386–451 AD), the Archbishop of Constantinople, whom Cyril succeeded in anathematizing at the Council of Ephesus (431 AD). Through Hypa's eyes, we come to see Cyril (known to Christianity as the "Pillar of Faith" and "Father of the Church") as a cruel and ambitious clergyman who mercilessly persecutes Jews and pagans, key among them the beautiful Greek philosopher and mathematician Hypatia, from whom Hypa takes his name and whose murder by a Christian mob at Cyril's behest Hypa witnesses. Hypa also admires Nestorius and his intellectual predecessor, Arius (anathematized at the First Council of Nicaea in 325 AD). Hypa is critical of Cyril's position on Christ, the divine Word, and the Logos, echoing instead the views of Arius and Nestorius, both of whom are regarded as heretics by the Coptic Orthodox Church.

Literature or Demagoguery?

As *Azazeel* gained wide acclaim in the Arab world, received literary honors, and was translated into multiple languages,[14] the Coptic Orthodox Church claimed that Youssef Ziedan had exploited the Christological schism to impugn the Christian creed and uphold the Islamic view that Jesus was a mere mortal (like the prophet Muhammad). Ziedan was initially surprised at the intensity of the attack. He responded first by defending his record as an ardent supporter of the Coptic faith who, in his capacity as the director of the Egyptian Manuscript Center and Museum, had been hailed by the Church for preserving ancient Coptic manuscripts. As the pressure from the Church mounted, however, Ziedan employed other means of defense, appearing on television and publishing a series of newspaper articles that lambasted the clerics for their inability to appreciate literature and for their obdurate religiosity.

Shortly after *Azazeel*'s publication, a Coptic priest, Abdul Masih Basit, published a short booklet, *The Novel* Azazeel: *Is It Ignorant of History or Does It Falsify History?*, as part of a series on Christian apologetics sponsored by the Coptic Church.[15] Shortly afterward, Bishop Bishoy, one of the most senior and well-respected figures in the Coptic Church, who has been at the forefront of fending off Islamist polemics against Christian doctrine, published a four-hundred-page book, *Response to the Ac-*

---

[14] *Azazeel* was awarded the prestigious International Prize for Arabic Fiction (modeled after the Man Booker Prize) and was quickly translated into multiple languages, including Italian, Hebrew, Greek, and Portuguese. The English translator of the novel, Jonathan Wright, won the 2013 Banipal Translation Prize.

[15] Basit also issued a number of accusations against Ziedan in the media (calling him a terrorist, an inciter to religious hatred, and an atheist), all of which Ziedan denied. Eventually Ziedan brought a libel suit against Basit, which he won in 2011.

cusations in Youssef Ziedan's Azazeel.[16] While not strictly a publication of the Church, Bishoy's book is nonetheless representative of the views of the clerical hierarchy. In the opening pages, Bishoy charges that *Azazeel* is the "worst book ever known to Christianity."[17] He compares it to *The Da Vinci Code* (which the Coptic Church had successfully petitioned the Egyptian authorities to ban in 2006), arguing that it also exploited doctrinal debates to assault Christian beliefs.

While most of Bishoy's charges are similar to Basit's, his text is a more scholarly endeavor, replete with citations to historical works dealing with the period and written in both Arabic and English. What seems to have angered Bishoy most is the novel's depiction of Archbishop Cyril as a brutal and savvy demagogue, as well as its portrayal of Hypa's sympathy for (heterodox) Nestorian views on the nature of Christ. Bishoy's response includes several chapters that present an alternative account of the ecumenical councils at Nicaea and Ephesus, and he launches a sophisticated defense of Cyril's Christological position against Nestorian heresy. It is rare to encounter such a sustained (albeit accusatory) exegesis of early Christian doctrine rendered for a popular audience.

Excerpts from Bishoy's copious response circulated in various forms in the Egyptian, especially Coptic, media. Despite its complexity, *Azazeel* quickly became, for many Copts, synonymous with the attacks they have come increasingly to anticipate from a Muslim majority bent upon excoriating Christian doctrine and practice. Many Coptic Christians I spoke with thought that *Azazeel* was simply a literary version of sermons delivered by fanatical Muslim preachers who attack the truth of the Bible and the divinity of Christ.[18] Others charged that Egyptian Muslims employ a double standard in that it is acceptable for a Muslim to write about Christian doctrinal disputes, while an Egyptian Christian does not enjoy the same privilege in regard to Islam. It is this perspective that Bishop Bishoy foregrounds in his response to *Azazeel*: "What would be the reaction if a person wrote a story that was similar in its falsification and deception (what Dr. Ziedan calls 'literary creation') but in regards to Islam? Will any Muslim, enthusiastic about his religion, accept such a violation of his beliefs, the distortion of Islamic history, the casting of doubt on its traditions and postulates, the insulting of its most respected leading personalities?"[19]

---

[16] Bishoy is the secretary of the Holy Synod of the Coptic Orthodox Church, its highest religious body, and the Metropolitan Bishop of Damietta (an important diocese in Egypt).

[17] Bishoy, *al-Radd 'ala al-Buhtan*, 13.

[18] Among those who engage in this activity on television and in print is the well-known al-Azhar scholar Dr. Zaghloul al-Naggar, who Bishop Bishoy has publicly debated on the television and in print. Against the Muslim invective, there is now an equally vituperative program hosted by a Coptic priest, Zakaria Botros, on a satellite television station aimed at Islamic doctrine and beliefs.

[19] Bishoy, *al-Radd 'ala al-Buhtan*, 14.

Secular Coptic voices, like the prominent public intellectual Karima Kamal, tried to intervene in this debate by pointing out that the clerics' reaction to the novel was based on a fundamental confusion between *literature* and *demagoguery*, a confusion that serves the Church's interests in censoring critical and unorthodox voices, even from within the Coptic community. In the Egyptian daily *al-Badeel*, Kamal writes:

> The outcry around Youssef Ziedan's novel *Azazeel* demands that we pause and ask: Is it within the rights of the Church to be angry and for the Copts to feel hurt? . . . The answer to this question in the absolute [*al-mutlaq*] is one thing and the answer in the context of what is going on in Egyptian society, its religious polarization and bigotry, is another. . . . If we separate ourselves from what is going on in Egypt then it's unimaginable that we would limit writing about Christianity to Christians and about Islam to Muslims. . . . [However,] given the current sectarian climate in Egypt, many Copts are right to say that if an Egyptian Christian were to take up a period in Islamic history as a topic of his novel, the outcry would be enormous and unending![20]

While acknowledging the power of this sentiment, Kamal urges fellow Copts to side with the author's right to freedom of expression:

> Is it possible for us [Copts] to stand in the name of freedom of thought and expression, despite what is happening [to us] in society[?] . . . Should we adopt the [immanent] logic of place, stage, and time or should we adopt the transcendent logic rooted in the desire to overcome these conditions? This is a struggle between . . . the inclination to abide by freedom of thought and creativity and sectarianism and bigotry. . . . How bad would it be if the minority view wins over the despotism of the majority, a minority that wins through reason against a majority steeped in bigotry?[21]

Kamal's invitation to these higher principles was widely echoed by a number of liberal voices, Muslim and Copt alike. It cast the *Azazeel* debate as a battle between the secular principle of freedom of speech and religious prejudice. This view presumes that secular values are themselves bereft of religious precepts and, therefore, can rise above competing religious claims. However, as I hope to show, secularity enfolds within itself a prescriptive notion of what religion should be, propounding a particular interpretation of scripture and theology. These notions permeate not only the novel but also Ziedan's commentaries on the topics of literature, history, and the Christological

[20] Karima Kamal, "Suwal 'Azazil," *al-Badeel*, April 8, 2009, 4.
[21] Ibid.

schism. It is only once we grasp this secularized conception of religiosity the novel propounds that we can begin to comprehend the response it elicited from devout Christians and Coptic clerics. In parsing out this debate, I want to condone neither the Church's call to ban the novel nor the secularist entreaties to freedom of expression. Rather, my aim is to show that the secular is not the neutral ground against which religious objections are staged, but is itself generative of such conflicts.

Hypatia and Cyril: Paragons of Virtue and Vice

One of the most moving chapters in the novel revolves around the ruthless slaughter of the legendary pagan philosopher-mathematician Hypatia in 415 AD at the hands of the followers of Saint Cyril, the Bishop of Alexandra. Cyril is a revered figure in Eastern and Western Christianity, whom the Catholic Church canonized as a saint in 1882. Youssef Ziedan's portrayal of Hypatia accords with a long tradition of Western literary and popular writings that depict Hypatia's youthful beauty and intellect as heroically opposed to the forces of religious dogmatism personified in the figure of Archbishop Cyril. Ziedan sets the stage for Hypatia's murder with a sermon that Cyril delivers at the Caesarium (once a temple built by Cleopatra VII, now a church):

> Children of God, friends of living Jesus. This city of yours is the city of the almighty Lord. Mark the apostle settled here, on its soil lived fathers of the church, the blood of martyrs flowed here and in it the foundations of our faith were built. We have purged it of the Jews, who have been expelled. God helped us to expel them and cleanse our city of them, but the remnants of the filthy pagans are still raising strife in the land. They spread iniquity and heresy around us, and intrude insolently on the secrets of the church. . . . They want to rebuild the great house of idols which was brought down on top of them years ago.[22] They want to revive their abandoned schools, which used to instill darkness in the minds of men. . . . So, children of the Lord, free your land from the defilement of the pagans, cut out the tongues of those who speak evil, throw them and their wickedness into the sea and wash away the mortal sins. Follow the words of the Saviour. . . . Know that our Lord Jesus Christ spoke to us his children in all times when he said: "Think not that I [have] come to send peace on earth, I came not to send peace, but a sword."[23]

[22] Cyrus and his followers purged Alexandria of its Jewish population against the orders of Orestes, the Greek prefect of Alexandria. The "House of Idols" is a reference to the temple of Serapeum, dedicated to the hybrid Hellenic-Egyptian god Serapis and destroyed in 391 AD by Bishop Theophilus, Cyril's predecessor. Chapter 3 of Bishoy's response to *Azazeel* is dedicated to challenging this portrait of Theophilus.

[23] Ziedan, *Azazeel*, 122–23.

Hypa, who is among the sermon's audience, then describes how Cyril's followers rush out of the church to attack pagans and encounter Hypatia riding in her chariot; they pull her down, drag her through the streets, scrape her skin off her flesh, and finally set her on fire. Horrified by the brutality of his Christian brethren, and prodded by Azazeel, Hypa decides to record the events he has just witnessed in this "city of almighty God, the capital of salt and cruelty."[24]

Hypa's rendering of Hypatia's murder is neither unique nor novel. It follows a narrative established by a generation of Protestants and Enlightenment scholars who used Hypatia's murder to launch a broader critique of clerical excess and religious violence.[25] Indeed, Hypatia enjoyed legendary status among such eighteenth- and nineteenth-century liberal critics of ecclesiastical authority as Voltaire, John Toland, Charles Leconte de Lisle, and Edward Gibbon. The title of the deist John Toland's book on Hypatia is representative: *Hypatia or, the History of a Most Beautiful, Most Virtuous, Most Learned and in Every Way Accomplished Lady; Who Was Torn to Pieces by the Clergy of Alexandria to Gratify the Pride, Emulation, and Cruelty of the Archbishop, Commonly but Undeservedly Titled St. Cyril* (1720). In the twentieth century, Bertrand Russell (in *The History of Western Philosophy*) and Carl Sagan (in *Cosmos*) further enshrined this story by championing Hypatia as an early martyr in the battle between scientific rationality and religious obscurantism. More recently, feminists have embraced Hypatia as a pagan prophetess whom the Church sacrificed at the altar of patriarchal monotheism. In these accounts, Hypatia's murder is emblematic of the end of the age of philosophical wisdom and, in Martin Bernal's words, "the beginning of the Christian Dark Ages."[26]

Consider, for example, Edward Gibbon's account in his magisterial *The History of the Decline and Fall of the Roman Empire*:

> Hypatia, the daughter of Theon the mathematician, was initiated in her father's studies; her learned comments have elucidated the geometry of Apollonius and Diophantus, and she publicly taught, both at Athens and Alexandria, the philosophy of Plato and Aristotle. In the bloom of beauty, and in the maturity of wisdom, the modest maid refused her lovers and instructed her disciples; the persons most illustrious for their rank or merit were impatient to visit the female philosopher; and Cyril beheld, with a jealous eye, the gorgeous train of horses and slaves who crowded the door of her academy. A rumour was spread among the Christians that

---

[24] Ibid., 123–29.

[25] These narratives often draw upon Socrates Scholasticus' account of Hypatia's murder in *Historia Ecclesiastica*, written shortly after Hypatia's death in 415 AD.

[26] Dzielska, *Hypatia of Alexandria*, 26.

the daughter of Theon was the only obstacle to the reconciliation of the prefect [Orestes] and the archbishop [Cyril]; and that obstacle was speedily removed. On a fatal day, in the holy season of Lent, Hypatia was torn from her chariot, stripped naked, dragged to the church, and inhumanly butchered by the hands of Peter the reader and a troop of savage and merciless fanatics: her flesh was scraped from her bones with sharp oyster-shells, and her quivering limbs were delivered to the flames. The just progress of inquiry and punishment was stopped by seasonable gifts; but the murder of Hypatia has imprinted an indelible stain on the character and religion of Cyril of Alexandria.[27]

Historian Maria Dzielska offers a critical reading of Gibbon's description of Hypatia's life, suggesting that, like the other writers of this period, he makes cavalier use of earlier chroniclers to launch his critique of pre-Enlightenment religion. Hypatia, Dzielska suggests, was in fact sixty years old, rather than a "modest maid" of twenty-four, who was not opposed to Christianity: "Unlike her contemporary fellow philosophers, [Hypatia] was not a devoted pagan. She did not cultivate Neoplatonic Theurgic philosophy, visit temples, or resist their conversion into Christian churches. Indeed, she sympathized with Christianity and protected her Christian students."[28] Dzielska also challenges the popular consensus that Hypatia's death marked the end of Alexandrian science and philosophy, noting, "The Alexandrian school achieved its greatest success at the turn of the fifth and sixth centuries," long after Hypatia's death.[29]

In Dzielska's view, it was not Hypatia's paganism that bothered Cyril, but her popularity with the Alexandrian elites and the political and intellectual weight she carried with them—particularly with Orestes, the prefect of Alexandria, with whom Cyril was locked in a political battle.[30] Nevertheless, Dzielska suggests, "Cyril must be held to account for a great deal, even if we assume that the murder was contrived and executed by the parabolans [the patriarch's helpers], without his knowledge. For there is no doubt that he was a chief instigator of the campaign of defamation against Hypatia, fomenting prejudice and animosity against the woman philosopher, rousing fear about the consequences of her alleged black-magic spells on the prefect [Orestes], the faithful of the Christian community and the whole city."[31] Note that even though Dzielska does not absolve Cyril, she nonetheless questions the portrayal of Hypatia as a pagan priestess who was opposed to Christianity and valiantly fought its tyranny.

[27] Gibbon, *The History of the Decline and Fall*, 33.
[28] Dzielska, *Hypatia of Alexandria*, 105. For a similar account, also see Wessel, *Cyril of Alexandria*, 53–54.
[29] Dzielska, *Hypatia of Alexandria*, 105.
[30] Ibid., 104; Wessel, *Cyril of Alexandria*, 50.
[31] Dzielska, *Hypatia of Alexandria*, 97; Wessel, *Cyril of Alexandria*, 46.

There is a crucial part of this narrative that Western scholars working on Hypatia's murder overlook, however, and it is one that commands particular weight in the history of Coptic Christianity. Over the course of the eighteenth and nineteenth centuries, as Western Christianity began to construct itself in civilizational terms that had more in common with the late Hellenic world than with the lands where Jesus and his early followers roamed, it also distanced itself from the history of what came to be called non-Latinate Christianity.[32] Hypatia's murder came to symbolize the degenerate character of a specifically "Eastern Christianity," not of Christianity as such. While historians have explored how Enlightenment Christianity ended up distancing itself from its Judeo-Semitic origins,[33] little attention has been paid to how it also cast the history of Oriental and Eastern Orthodox Christianity as alien. The antipathy with which European Christians came to regard their fellow brethren from the "East" is clearly evident in the novel *Hypatia*, published in 1875, which depicts some of the same events as *Azazeel*. Its author, Charles Kingsley (1819–75), was a well-known priest in the Church of England, as well as a popular novelist, an early supporter of Darwin's *Origin of the Species*, and a critic of John Henry Newman. His profile exemplifies the nineteenth-century Protestant who drew a resolute line between the superiority of Western Christianity and the depravity of the Orient. In the epilogue to his novel, Kingsley writes:

> The Egyptian and Syrian Churches . . . were destined to labour not for themselves, but for us. The signs of disease and decrepitude were already but too manifest in them. . . . The races of Egypt and Syria were effeminate, over-civilized, exhausted by centuries during which no infusion of fresh blood had come to renew the stock. Morbid, self-conscious, physically indolent, incapable then, as now, of personal or political freedom, they afforded material out of which fanatics might easily be made, but not citizens of the kingdom of God. . . . The ever downward career of Eastern Christianity went on unchecked for two more miserable centuries, side by side with the upward development of the Western Church.[34]

In Kingsley's view, Cyril and his followers embody the dogmatic Egyptian-Syrian mindset most evident in their intemperate devotion to Egyptian monasticism. Because they once served a useful purpose for the Western Church, "our duty," Kingsley

---

[32] Latinate Christianity is an ideological term of recent coinage aimed at distinguishing Euro-Atlantic Christianity from the Christianity practiced in the non-Western world (including Latin America, the Iberian peninsula, the Middle East, and Africa). See, for example, Taylor's usage of the term in *A Secular Age*.

[33] See Masuzawa, *The Invention of World Religions*, 179–206.

[34] Kingsley, *Hypatia*, xiv.

opines, is "not to sneer at them" but to appreciate what they were able to preserve: "a precious heirloom . . . a metaphysic at once Christian and scientific" that was brought to its fullest potential after it was purged of these old "theoretic monsters" and an "effete Greek philosophy [built] upon Egyptian symbolism."[35] Like Ziedan, Kingsley claims that his novel "closely follows authentic history," although his orientalist condescension finds little resonance in *Azazeel*.[36]

It should come as no surprise, then, that Bishop Bishoy accuses Ziedan of borrowing heavily from Kingsley's *Hypatia*: "If historians like . . . Gibbon were eager to use the death of Hypatia for discourse against Christianity, then there were others [like Kingsley] who were eager to use this murder for their sectarian [that is, Protestant] interests."[37] Bishoy also links these earlier writings with those of such contemporary authors as Carl Sagan, who uses Hypatia's murder as evidence of Christianity's inherent violence and irrationality.[38] Bishoy claims instead that Cyril had nothing to do with Hypatia's murder (the parabolans may have) and asserts that, contrary to popular opinion, she was not a sage but a sorceress who was killed because of her unpopularity.[39] Far more importantly, Bishoy turns the tables on Ziedan and asserts emphatically that it was not the Christians who persecuted the pagans but the reverse, a situation that the novel never mentions.[40]

Bishoy is not entirely wrong in pointing to the violence early Christians suffered at the hands of pagans under Roman rule. But even more central to this sense of persecution is the particular history of Coptic suffering—first at the hands of the Roman Emperor Diocletian in 284 AD (which marks the start of the Coptic calendar with the "Era of the Martyrs") and later, following the Coptic refusal to accept the Chalcedonian creed (451 AD), under Byzantium rulers (the Melkites) for a period of over two hundred years. As a result of this long history, a critical part of the Coptic Church's identity is the valiant resistance that Coptic monks and priests mounted against the imperial governments of Rome and Constantinople. By the time Arab Muslims arrived in 642 AD, the Copts were exhausted by the Byzantine persecution and, according to many historians, welcomed the new rulers.[41] This idea, however, is deeply contested by present-day Copts, given the discrimination they suffer at the

---

[35] Ibid., xv.

[36] Ibid.

[37] Bishoy, *al-Radd 'ala al-Buhtan*, 80.

[38] Ibid., 82.

[39] Bishoy relies on the ecclesiastical historian John of Nikiu to substantiate his claims. Nikiu describes Hypatia as someone who "beguiled many people through [her] satanic wiles" and "started an active 'atheization' of Christian believers." Dzielska, *Hypatia of Alexandria*, 91.

[40] *Watani*, "al-Radd 'ala al-Buhtan fi Riwayat Yusuf Zidan," June 21, 2009, 4.

[41] For this early period of transition in Coptic history, see Mikhail, *From Byzantine to Islamic Egypt*.

hands of Muslims. Bishoy's text, therefore, paints a rather homogenous picture of Coptic persecution from the third century to the present that secures the theme of martyrdom in Coptic ecclesiology.

There is, however, a new twist in this tortured history of European relations with Copts that imparts a fresh charge to the current Christian-Muslim standoff. Pope Shenouda III, known for his political savvy in securing his flock's well-being in a Muslim-majority country, convinced Pope Paul VI to put the old denominational animosities aside. In 1973 they announced their agreement on the "meaning of the Christological formula of Saint Cyril of Alexandria, the famous 'one nature of the incarnate Word.' "[42] Pope Shenouda announced that the past schism was merely a matter of "semantics and terminology," which was secondary to the faith that unites Catholics and non-Catholic churches. This was a momentous event in that it not only settled a long-standing doctrinal dispute, but also laid to rest a century-old conflict over Catholic attempts to gain Coptic converts.

It is this unified Christian identity that Bishoy implicitly invokes when he claims that, insomuch as Cyril's Christology is the essence of Christian doctrine, Ziedan has defamed Christianity tout court by giving voice to Cyril's fourth-century critics (Nestorius and Arius). Bishoy, not surprisingly, downplays the Christian persecution of Copts. To portray Christianity as a unified tradition, he must erase the history of internecine Christian warfare, thus securing a global Christian identity against its current persecutors, the Muslims. Furthermore, in the current climate of confessional polarization, the fact that *Azazeel*'s author is a Muslim can only be read as an act of aggression against a beleaguered minority. Viewed from this perspective, Ziedan opportunistically used the schisms and disputes internal to the Church to cast doubt on the divinity of Christ. Even though *Azazeel* makes no mention of Islam or Arabs, and is in fact concerned with a period in which neither was known to the inhabitants of Egypt, its Coptic audience suspects that its portrayal of the brutality of Christian fathers might discursively level the violence done to them by the Muslim majority. Thus, when a reporter asks Bishoy whether he is angry because Ziedan is a Muslim or because *Azazeel* violates Christian beliefs, Bishoy answers emphatically, "The two together. I will not accept any Muslim explicating Christianity!"[43]

---

[42] This agreement was further sealed in 1991, when bishops from the Greek Orthodox, Armenian, Ethiopian, Syrian, Roman Catholic, and Indian Christian denominations gathered at the Monastery of Saint Bishoy in Wadi Natroun to remove mutual anathemas and to affirm that the Christological mystery could be "expressed in different words and in different traditions though adhering to the same fundamental faith." Meinardus, *Two Thousand Years of Coptic Christianity*, 125–26. See also Kamil, *Christianity in the Land of the Pharaohs*, 200.

[43] *al-Musawwir*, "Anba Bishoy Khomini al-Kanisa: Ghadab al-Muslimin min Salman Rushdie bi-Sabab Ayat Shaytaniyya. Fa-limadha La Naghdib min 'Azazil?," March 25, 2009, 53–54.

History and Literature

The partisan claim that only Christians are qualified to comment on Coptic history became the pivotal point for Youssef Ziedan's response to Bishop Bishoy. The response was published in the leading Egyptian newspaper, *al-Masry al-Youm*, over the course of seven weeks, and the title suggests the tenor of Ziedan's response: "The Lies in the Hallucinations of the Bishop."[44] After stating his public record on combating Muslim violence against Christians in Egypt, Ziedan stresses two issues: the historical veracity of the events on which he based *Azazeel*, and his right as a novelist to render them according to the protocols of literary production. In the beginning of his response to Bishoy, Ziedan asserts, "*Azazeel* is based on actual historical events that are impossible to deny. There is not one historical error in it, no matter how the bishop tries to cast doubt on it."[45] As to the charge that he has meddled in affairs internal to Christianity, he responds:

> How is it that the bishop thinks that the events the novel presents are matters internal to the Church? Is the history of Egypt in the fifth century an internal issue? Is the murder of Hypatia, which cast a shadow on human history for five centuries, an internal issue? Is the Church schism that shook the world and caused people misery to the ends of the earth, leading to the killing of twenty thousand Copts . . . at the hands of a Christian ruler, an internal issue? Is the search for reality [truth] an internal issue? Is an internal issue ever only an internal issue?[46]

Key to the rhetorical structure of Ziedan's argument is the claim that as a human (*insan*) he represents all of humanity: "The novelist [*mu'allif*] is in the end a human being who writes about other human beings."[47] He clarifies this argument in an interview on *al-Jazeera*: "[*Azazeel*] celebrates *insan* . . . . What is this charge about being a Christian or Muslim? I believe in all religions: Christianity, Islam, Judaism."[48] In asserting his humanity, Ziedan seeks to rise above communal boundaries, particularly his Muslim subject-position. Ziedan further buttresses this claim to objectivity by emphasizing his credentials as the director of the Center of Manuscripts. His professional identity was central not only to the defense Ziedan mounted against the Coptic

[44] The term that Ziedan uses here is *matran* (archbishop). Since Bishoy is also referred to as *anba* (bishop), I have retained the latter in my translations in order to be consistent.

[45] Youssef Ziedan, "Doktor Yusuf Zidan Yiktib: Buhtan al-Buhtan fi-ma Yatawahhimhu al-Matran," *al-Masry al-Youm*, July 29–September 9, 2009, http://today.almasryalyoum.com/article2.aspx?ArticleID=221477.

[46] Ibid.

[47] Ibid.

[48] al-Jazeera Channel, "Liqa' al-Yawm," *YouTube*, April 19, 2009, www.youtube.com/watch?v=cPLvuX7X34s.

Church's attack on the novel, but also to the public persona he projects as a valiant custodian of knowledge at a moment when popular interest in it has declined. Ziedan contends that as a historian he is better equipped than "men of religion" (*rijal al-din*) to excavate the past and its true significance for humankind.[49]

At the height of the controversy, Mona Shazli, who enjoyed rock-star status on Egyptian satellite television, interviewed Ziedan on her intellectually inclined talk show *'Ashira Masa'an*. The interview focuses on Ziedan's historical contributions (rather than *Azazeel*), and he holds forth on a variety of topics ranging from the obscure to the popular. When Shazli asks Ziedan why he loves history, he responds, "It is not possible for us to think about what is happening today . . . without seeing how it all began." When she asks him to explain, Ziedan responds, "Let me give you an example: When you argue with people [about historical events] these days they often say, 'So what is the point in the end?' This is wrong! We must understand the origin of a problem." Shazli interjects, "You mean you want to tug at the beginning of a string and see where it leads," to which Ziedan replies, "No! [I mean] without knowing how the root of a narrative got started we cannot get anywhere."[50] In another interview televised on *al-Jazeera*, Ziedan emphasizes a similar theme: "The history I am talking about [in *Azazeel*] is not ancient history but informs the present. . . . I want to [in fact] claim that we will not understand what is happening in our countries today unless we look at aspects of our history that are lost to memory but that we need to examine without bias or sensitivity [*hassasiya*]."[51] In this positivist conception of history, understanding facts is crucial for elucidating the present and for correcting misapprehensions of the past that distort human relations.

Ziedan is not alone in claiming historical accuracy. Over two-thirds of Bishoy's response to *Azazeel* is a refutation of the historical facts he claims Ziedan misrepresents, among them events surrounding the ecumenical councils, statements by various clerical figures, and the exact nature of the Christological schism. Copiously footnoted with scholarly and ecclesiastical works, the document's complexity has been lost in the shrill debate in the media. Indeed, the degree to which the issue of historical veracity is crucial to *both* sides of the debate is striking. This is emblematic, I want to

---

[49] Ziedan faults the bishop for making use of ecclesiastical historians (such as Sozomen and Socrates Scholasticus), calling them "men of religion," and thereby impugning their credibility when compared to the impartiality of a "real" historian. His characterization notwithstanding, Socrates Scholasticus is one of the primary sources of information on that period for a number of modern historians (such as Gibbon, Wessel, and Dzielska).

[50] Dream TV Channel, "al-'Ashira Masa'an Mona al-Shazali Youssef Ziedan Halqa," *YouTube*, November 9, 2010, www.youtube.com/watch?v=zBGMRZO6mso.

[51] Al-Jazeera, "Liqa' al-Yawm."

suggest, of the inordinate weight secular conceptions of history and temporality command in religious narratives today. Note that, despite their disagreement, both Ziedan and Bishoy purport to describe ecumenical events located in *calendrical* (linear, empty, homogenous) rather than *sacral* time, and each posits a distinction between the factuality of events as they "really happened" and their narrative meaning. This distinction is part of the history of the secularization of religion, one in which both religionists and antireligionists came to accept the independence of metaphysical truth (transcendent) from the empirical nature of this world (immanent).

Nineteenth-century exegetical debates of the Bible presumed and amplified this distinction. As historian Hans Frei argues, in the premodern world the question of the factuality of revelation was not distinguishable from its meaning; but as the eighteenth century progressed, the two came to be epistemologically and interpretively separated.[52] It was no longer possible to treat the Bible as a figural narrative within which one's own life was situated; rather, its spiritual meaning had to be distinguished from its historical context, on the one hand, and the imminence of one's life, on the other. This separation between "reality" and "meaning" was crucial, both for the Christian apologists who sought to establish the factual validity of biblical events (hence the search for the "historical Jesus")[53] *and* for the skeptics who used its factual fallibility to cast doubt on divine agency and revelation.[54] Both positions, their antagonism notwithstanding, shared an epistemological world in which the explicative meaning of scripture and its historical or ostensive reference were detached, the former argued in terms of the latter.[55] Both Ziedan and Bishoy occupy this argumentative space, a measure of their common secularity that has become so naturalized that they cannot even recognize it in each other's arguments.

Does this mean that the fundamental disagreement between Bishoy and Ziedan turns upon their interpretation of historical events? Yes and no. Yes, because both subscribe to a conception of history that is necessary to their claim on truth. No, because their disagreement entails two incommensurable understandings of literature and religion that are not so much about history as they are about these very concepts.

---

[52] Frei, *Eclipse of Biblical Narrative*, 5.

[53] Among the first to argue in this vein was David Friedrich Strauss (1808–74), whose *The Life of Jesus, Critically Examined* created a huge outcry when it was first published.

[54] Debates about the Quran in Islam exhibit a similar character, often divided between those who seek to establish the "scientific veracity" of Quranic claims and those who discredit it on the grounds that it is a factually fallible text.

[55] While there are other traditions of biblical exegesis, the path that the historicists charted continues to command allegiance up to the present. For different traditions of biblical exegesis, see Sheehan, *The Enlightenment Bible*; and Shuger, *The Renaissance Bible*.

Ziedan accuses Bishoy of confusing fiction with history, even as Ziedan himself interweaves both:

> [One of] the methodological mistakes . . . Bishop Bishoy makes is that he thinks *Azazeel* is a historical document or formal report of real events or an actual biography of a monk. Even though, to state it most simply, as noted on the cover, it is a novel . . . a novel. But because he is unaccustomed to reading fiction, he is deluded by the artistic illusion mentioned in the beginning of *Azazeel* [told in the voice of the translator of Hypa's scrolls from Syriac to Arabic] and believes it is a book to which he can respond with another book! He would have learned had he inquired into a number of both famous and non-famous literary works and poetry that make recourse to such illusions insomuch as they are a technique of contemporary fictional narrative. . . . The nature of the literary discourse of *Azazeel* escapes the bishop; at the end, *Azazeel* makes man victorious over loathsome violence, which religion uses as a means. It also escapes [the bishop] that the characters [in a novel] are diverse and their positions and thoughts conflict, that when we put words on the tongues of a literary character this does not mean that these necessarily reflect the views of the author.[56]

This is a familiar claim that almost all secular responses to religious critiques of literary works rehearse, replete with the cosmopolitan condescension at play here. Consider, for example, Salman Rushdie at the height of the *Satanic Verses* controversy: "[The writer of] fiction uses facts as a starting-place and then spirals away to explore its own concerns, which are only tangentially historical. Not to see this, to treat fiction as if it were fact, is to make a serious mistake of categories."[57] This is what Ziedan and his defenders also alleged—that Bishoy had made a category mistake between literature and demagoguery, that the unschooled "men of religion" are not capable of deciphering the difference. Yet it seems to me that the claims of history and fiction are more complexly intertwined than this particular trope of literature, with its own protocols of appreciation and critique, allows.

A work of historical fiction recalls a host of images and events that are meant to trigger various kinds of recognition in its audience. Depending on one's location within the social continuum and one's relation to the history invoked, this recognition can evoke different responses, ranging from appreciation to anger to apathy. In other words, a work of historical fiction does not place past events indifferently on a blank canvas but works to induce recognition in its readers, and its success is measured in part by how

---

[56] Ziedan, "Doktor."
[57] Quoted in Asad, "Ethnography, Literature, and Politics," 283.

well it can do so. Among those who recognized themselves in the narrative of *Azazeel* are monks, clerics, and those for whom *Azazeel* voices a critique of the institutional and doctrinal hegemony of the Church. What I want to emphasize here is that insomuch as *both* parties recognize themselves within the historical stock of images, events, and arguments that the novel mobilizes, both reactions squarely belong to the field of literature and its reception. One might be partial to the secular reading of the novel, but that does not mean the other interpretation should be cast as a category mistake.

Finally, here it is important to recall the considerable work in literary studies that points to the nineteenth-century emergence of the novel as a privileged site for the cultivation of bourgeois sensibilities. As a space for the development of the ethical, emotional, and aesthetic refinements championed by this social class, novelistic writing simulated some of the normative functions of religious texts and, thus, contributed to the formation of what I have called secularity. Viewed from this perspective, *Azazeel* does not simply provide an alternative reading of historical debates within Christianity; it also urges its readers to inhabit this history differently, to appreciate it from a secular standpoint and, thus, with a different kind of devotion than that of the clerics. Bishoy's remark that "even a literary work must respect creed" is perhaps best understood as a recognition of *Azazeel*'s solicitation of the secular sensibilities of its audience.

In a thoughtful article, Michael Allan draws attention to the pedagogical, edificatory, and disciplinary aspects of literature that are also resonant in the modern Arabic category of *adab*. In his analysis of a series of canonical figures in literary criticism— Auerbach, Curtius, Welleck, and Said—Allan points to their shared understanding of "literature as the common ground, and a unique manner of reading, appreciating and valuing texts in the articulation of humanism. This humanism . . . presumes the comparability of texts across place and time, united in the homogenizing discourse of world literature. And it is this humanism that presumes the stability of the category of literature—'for its own sake.' "[58]Indeed, on this view, literature has the unique capacity to cut across cultural and historical boundaries, and to articulate fundamental aspects of the human condition. This is precisely what Ziedan claims *Azazeel* sought to capture, embodied in the figure of Hypa, who recoils at the primordial religious violence visited upon humanity. I suggest that this conception of humanity enfolds within itself a secular sensibility that is attuned to appreciating the poesis of "spirituality" at the expense of the doctrinal demands of religion. It is this sensibility, I contend, that upset Bishoy and other clerics the most about *Azazeel*.

---

[58] Allan, "How Adab Became Literary," 193. For a full exposition of how the development of literature in the Middle East is integrally tied to secular forms of knowledge and reading, see Allan, *Shadows of World Literature*.

The Human in the Divine

Among the opinions that Ziedan's characters express that Bishoy finds offensive is the belief—articulated at various points by Archbishop Nestorius ("the heretic"), Hypa, and Azazeel—that Christ was more human than divine. While this position resonates with certain positions in the Christological debate, in *Azazeel* it slips quickly and effortlessly into the claim that religion itself is a human creation. This is a subtle elision, one that fits naturally with the secular ethos of the novel and its audience, but we cannot assume its truth if we are to fully grasp the stakes of this controversy.

The idea that Christ was a man distinct from the divine Word/Logos has a long history in Christianity. Although both Origen of Alexandria (d. 253/254 AD) and Paul of Samosata (d. 275 AD) held this belief, it is most famously associated with Arius (d. 336 AD), an Alexandrian presbyter who was anathematized at the Council of Nicaea in 325 AD, when the Nicene Creed became the doctrinal basis of Christianity. Arius proposed that the Word was autonomous and independent from the essence of God, who was eternal. He also argued that just as the divine Word was distinct from God's essence and beyond human comprehension, so too was the divine Father distinct from the human Son, his wholeness uncontainable by the human form.[59] The fact that Jesus hungered, thirsted, and suffered on the cross was proof to Arius that he was unlike God, whereas Alexandrian Christology claimed that it was not the divine Logos that suffered on the cross but Jesus's flesh. Although the Nicene Creed was meant to seal the fate of this heretical view, it resurfaced almost a hundred years later in the Christology of the Archbishop of Constantinople, Nestorius, who was anathematized at the Council of Ephesus (415 AD) at Cyril's behest.

Historians of this period point out that Nestorius's beliefs were in key ways quite distinct from those of Arius, whom Nestorius, like Cyril, regarded as a heretic.[60] Unlike Arius, who believed that the human essence of Christ was subordinate to the divine Word/Logos, Nestorius advocated that Christ had two natures, human and divine, loosely joined through a single *prosopon*. If to our ears this view sounds similar to current understandings of the human and divine natures of Christ joined in one person, then we are not entirely wrong.[61] Cyril, however, was able to convince the

---

[59] In Arius's well-known formulation, "If the Father begat the Son, he that was begotten has a beginning of existence; and from this it is evident, that there was He when the Son was not." Chidester, *Word and Light*, 46.

[60] Wessel, *Cyril of Alexandria*, 220.

[61] Some historians argue that, ultimately, Nestorius's views are similar to those propounded by Protestants, who nevertheless continue to regard him as a heretic. Others, however, note that Nestorius believed that Christ was the bearer of the Word but not the Word incarnate, which makes his view heretical to all of Christianity. This latter position seems to have prevailed even among those who disagreed with the equation Cyril drew between Nestorius and Arius at the Council of Ephesus.

Council of Ephesus that Nestorius (his actions and words notwithstanding) was no different from Arius, and that Cyril himself was the equivalent of Athanasius, who had saved Christianity from the Arian heresy at the First Council of Nicaea. Susan Wessel characterizes the event in this way:

> When Cyril compared Nestorius to the heretic Arius, he opened a doorway through which the audience saw that Nestorius had made Jesus into a common man. Cyril also implied that he himself was the new Athanasius, the next defender of Nicene orthodoxy. . . . These vivid comparisons, which brought together the qualities of two persons living at widely separated times into a single point in the present, also belonged to the category of types, both biblical and sophistic. By representing events in terms of actions to be imitated, paradigms to be followed, types had strong moral implications. To label one person with the epithet of another implied, especially in the context of the biblical text, that the second person embodied all the significant moral qualities, or deficiencies, of the first.[62]

Cyril also called Nestorius a Jew, and in so doing "invoked the entire Christian corpus of anti-Jewish teachings" and their diminution of Christ's divinity.[63]

In an ironic twist, Ziedan likewise collapses the differences between Arian and Nestorian views, but for reasons quite different from Cyril's. In *Azazeel*, the continuity between Arius and Nestorius is consistently thematized. At his first meeting with Hypa, Nestorius registers his agreement with Arius: "I find . . . the events of [Arius's] life as merely an attempt to purge our religion from the beliefs of the ancient Egyptians about their gods. . . . Arius wanted our religion to worship one God alone. But he sang a song which was unfamiliar in his time, recognizing the mystery of God's manifestation in Christ but not admitting Christ's divinity, recognizing Jesus the son of Mary, a gift to mankind, but not recognizing any divinity other than the one God."[64] He explains to Hypa, "The Messiah . . . was born of man, and humans do not give birth to gods. How can we say that the Virgin gave birth to a god and how can we worship a child a few months old . . . ? The Messiah is a divine miracle, a man through whom God appeared to us. God became incarnate in him to make of him a harbinger of salvation and sign of the new age of mankind."[65] Later, he preaches, "Jesus is human, and his incarnation is a compromise between the Eternal Logos and Christ the human. Mary is the mother of Jesus the human being, and should not be called the mother of

[62] Wessel, *Cyril of Alexandria*, 188–89.
[63] Ibid., 216–17.
[64] Ziedan, *Azazeel*, 39.
[65] Ibid., 33.

201

God. It is not right that she be called Theotokos."[66] When Hypa meets Nestorius again at the end of the novel and on the eve of the Council of Ephesus, Nestorius continues to hold firm in his views. Jesus is not God, he tells Hypa, but his manifestation, "like a hole through which we have been able to see the light of God, or like a signet ring on which a divine message appeared. The fact that the sun shines through the hole does not make the hole a sun, just as the appearance of the message on the signet ring does not make the ring a message. Hypa, these people have gone quite mad, and have made God one of three [the Father, the Son, and the Holy Ghost]."[67]

How are we to understand Ziedan's elision of Arian and Nestorian views? Is it a historical error, as Bishoy charges, or is there something else at play here? I want to suggest that the answer to this question lies in how the Christological debate functions to secure Ziedan's claim that religion is a human creation. The humanity of Jesus that Ziedan ventriloquizes through Nestorius (and by extension Arius) secures for him the figure of *insan* (the human) embattled by the dogmas and duplicities of religious ecclesiasts who want to contain human creativity, imagination, and freedom. It is no accident that Hypa's struggle to be an ascetic monk is fraught with the calling of the flesh, a calling that he both appreciates and resents, battling its force while acknowledging the succor it provides for his soul. The carnal qualities of Jesus that Nestorius emphasizes in the novel—his bowel movements, his thirst, his hunger, and, ultimately, his suffering— are akin to the carnal pulls on Hypa, humanizing Christ in the same way that they humanize Hypa. Note that while this carnality is familiar to humanists of Ziedan's persuasion, it did not concern Nestorius, Arius, or Cyril in the Christological dispute. The issue for them was which aspect of Christ suffered on the cross: the Word or the flesh. The answer to this question had enormous soteriological consequences for how the body of Christ was supposed to mediate man's salvation from original sin.

What I want to draw attention to is how differently the term *humanity* is freighted in the Christological debate than in the version found in *Azazeel*. For Alexandrians like Cyril, to hold that Christ's human nature was separate from his divinity was to jeopardize the conception and practice of the Eucharist as partaking in the divine flesh and blood of Christ. It was this ingestion of divinity that would save Christians from eternal death. For Nestorians (and the Antiochene school more generally),[68] the

---

[66] Ibid., 201–2.

[67] Ibid., 203. Although Bishoy denounces Ziedan for failing to understand important differences between Arian and Nestorian views—differences Bishoy expounds upon at length (*al-Radd ʿala al-Buhtan*, 184–94)—he fails to comment on the fact that it was Cyril who first equated Arius and Nestorius in order to have the latter anathematized. On the differences between the Arian and Nestorian views that Cyril ignored, see Wessel, *Cyril of Alexandria*, 132–33.

[68] This was a school in Antioch, one of the most important cities of the ancient Roman Empire, devoted to the study of theology and biblical exegesis. Nestorius had been a monk at the school before he became the Patriarch of Constantinople.

fact that Christ's divinity and humanity were distinct allowed for a different path to salvation, one that involved emulating Jesus as the ethical exemplar rather than ingesting his person (as in the ritual of the Eucharist).[69] Two different models of human redemption were therefore at stake in this debate about the humanity of Christ, but for *both* sides the fundamental concern was with the Word and its proper relationship to human salvation. In other words, Christ's humanity in the Christological debate shared little with the modern celebration of human agency as the creative force in the world. Rather, the concern with the humanity of Christ was nested in the preordained drama of eschatology, the Last Judgment, and salvation.

In *Azazeel*, assuming Christ's humanity easily slides into claiming that God and religion are human creations, a testament to the creative powers of man's indefatigable imagination. As Azazeel tells Hypa, "In every age man creates a god to his liking, and his god is always his visions, his impossible dreams and his wishes."[70] In a number of interviews and lectures, Ziedan has amplified this position: "The sacred does not exist by itself. It is people's beliefs that endow it with sacrality, which is why what is sacred in one place is not in another. If the sacred existed in itself then all of humanity would accept it so everywhere."[71]

This secular conception of religion as a human feat resonates with a long tradition of humanist writing on religion, among them Ludwig Feuerbach's *The Essence of Christianity*. Feuerbach famously argues that God is a projection of the most distinctive human qualities—reason, will, and love—fueled by the human desire for infinitude when faced with his own mortality: "The divine being is nothing else than the human being, or, rather, the human nature purified, freed from the limits of the individual man, made objective—i.e. contemplated and revered as another, a distinct being. All the attributes of the divine nature are, therefore, attributes of the human nature."[72] Marx expands on Feuerbach's argument to suggest that the liberal state works analogously to religion in that it too becomes the intermediary "to which man [erroneously] confides all his non-divinity and all his *human freedom*."[73] Webb Keane rightfully places this argument within the history of secularization and notes that since Marx and Feuerbach, "the call to self-recognition, traced across historical time, often involves realizing that agency falsely imputed to deities is in fact human. Commonly this story of error disabused is taken to lead inexorably to the secular vision of modernity, replacing gods with humans at the center of the action."[74]

[69] On this point, see Wessel, *Cyril of Alexandria*, 3–4.
[70] Ziedan, *Azazeel*, 290.
[71] Al-Jazeera, "Liqa' al-Yawm." Ziedan repeats this view in an interview in the daily *al-Mussawir*, which Bishoy quotes in his response to *Azazeel*. Bishoy, *al-Radd 'ala al-Buhtan*, 16.
[72] Feuerbach, *Essence of Christianity*, 14.
[73] Marx, "On the Jewish Question," 32.
[74] Keane, *Christian Moderns*, 49.

It is precisely because humans create their gods that these gods embody anthropologically specific characteristics drawn from a particular place and time. This view is extant throughout *Azazeel* in conversations between bishops, monks, and priests. For example, at one point, Bishop Theodore of Mopsuestia (a historical figure in the Antiochene school from which Nestorius hailed) draws parallels between the doctrine of the Holy Trinity and Plotinus's philosophical trinity: while the former, he argues, is no doubt superior, its resonance with the latter testifies to the eternal nature of such questions.[75] Later in the novel, Nestorius reminds Hypa of the similarities between pagan and Christian trinities: "Your ancestors also believed in a holy trinity, made up of Isis, her son Horus and her husband Osiris, by whom she conceived without intercourse."[76] Each period thus endows God with its own cultural meaning and form, making the universal truth of religion sensible to a people in a particular time and place. Such a formulation leaves room for the truth of religion or God to stand (in that it is not nonsensical) while rooting its significance in human imagination and meaning-making capacities.[77]

We can perhaps at this point begin to get a sense of the different meanings of the term *humanity* in Christological debates and in *Azazeel*: in the former, the humanity of Jesus is a medium for God's Word, whereas in the latter, the humanity of Jesus is a symbol of man's capacity to create truth and meaning. The second view wrests power from God and locates it in man. This secular-humanist conception of religion offends Bishoy (as it would Muslims of a similar sensibility) because it fundamentally reverses the epistemological basis of religion: it is not God who creates us, but we who create him. Quoting Ziedan's remarks about the sacred in his response to *Azazeel*, a deeply offended Bishoy can only "leave the reader with these words without any comment."[78]

It is precisely *Azazeel*'s celebration of humanity that appeals to secular Egyptian and international readers of the novel. For critics like Kamal Ghobrial, to foreground the human in this way is not only to celebrate human creativity but also to humanize ecclesiastical power: "I do not believe that what bothered [the clerics] about the novel was its historical veracity [of ecumenical events] but its exhortation to question, to doubt what they present to us as absolute reality. What bothers them is that someone checks what they say and write, and in doing so brings them down from the sky . . . to the earth where the rest of us stand, takes off their godly attire to don human

---

[75] Ziedan, *Azazeel*, 23.

[76] Ibid., 39.

[77] The labor of the anthropologist often consists of analyzing the meaning-making practices that endow gods and revered objects with sacrality.

[78] Bishoy, *al-Radd 'ala al-Buhtan*, 16.

clothing."[79] It seems that in this argument, Ghobrial's Christianity and Ziedan's Muslimness are leveled. What emerges is the universal figure of the author-critic shorn of his creedal accouterments and moorings. Indeed, one might say that in Ghobrial, *Azazeel* has found its ideal reader.

It is not only religiously devout Copts but also orthodox Muslims who contest this conception of religion, popular among secular intellectuals in Egypt today. Its ability to offend, therefore, crosses the Muslim-Christian divide. Indeed, it was not long ago that orthodox Muslims excoriated the Muslim scholar Nasr Hamid Abu Zayd for arguing that the Quran was a human rather than divine creation. The issue in this instance was not the divinity of Christ but that of the Quran; not unlike Ziedan's Coptic critics, those of Abu Zayd charged that he had used medieval Mu'tazilite debates about the nature of the divine Word to propound a humanist conception of religion.[80] Abu Zayd was legally charged with the "crime" of apostasy, leading him to flee to Europe, where he was welcomed for valiantly defending a humanist interpretation of the Quran.[81] Judging from the reception of *Azazeel*, the ability of this humanist conception of divinity to offend Egyptian sensibilities—Muslim and Christian alike—has not lost its potency. For secularists like Ghobrial, these sensibilities are an impediment to dismantling forms of religious power that are in essence this-worldly. For him, as for Feuerbach, to humanize religion is not to delegitimize it but to take a necessary step in its liberation.

Western Christianity enjoys a privileged place in current theorizing about secularism; no other religious tradition, including Eastern and Orthodox Christianity, can claim this kinship. For the French theorist Marcel Gauchet, this filiation goes back to the Christological schism (451 AD) when Western Christendom embraced Christ as a man-god (the human and the divine united in one hypostatic union), and in so doing took "the first decisive step" toward the deconstruction of the hierarchy between the human and the divine.[82] Over time, this nonhierarchical unity of man-god paved the way for a crucial break between transcendence and immanence, temporal and metaphysical worlds—thereby birthing the secular political order.[83] Gauchet concludes, "The god who had been separated and freed from hierarchy was the god who . . . laid the foundation for individual right."[84] The pliability of the dual nature of Jesus Christ is striking in this narrative in that it can facilitate Christian salvation just as

[79] Ghobrial, "Maqaraba li-Riwaya Doktor Youssef Zidan: 'Azazeel.'"
[80] Hirschkind, "Heresy or Hermeneutics."
[81] Agrama, *Questioning Secularism*, chap. 1.
[82] Gauchet, *The Disenchantment of the World*, 126.
[83] Ibid., 151, 153.
[84] Ibid., 160.

it can single-handedly invent secular politics. This pliability, I want to suggest, is the result of the extraordinary power that Western Christianity commands in the modern world, so much so that its history has come to stand in for the history of secularism. Eastern Orthodox Christianity and Oriental Orthodox Christianity are just as alien in such theorizations of the secular as Islam.[85]

Secularity and Secularism

In conclusion, let me briefly address the relationship between secularism and secularity in the making of interreligious conflict. In the preceding chapters, I have argued that secularism as a statist project aims to make religious difference inconsequential to politics while at the same time embedding majoritarian religious norms in state institutions, laws, and practices. Secularity, in contrast, constitutes the epistemological and cultural ground on the basis of which religious claims can be authorized and validated.[86] In this chapter, I have shown how the modern conception of history—as an autonomous mode of inquiry into the positivity of events as they occur in linear time—is a key feature of secularity that has had an enormous influence on how religious truth is interpreted and justified in the modern world. History, of course, does not perform this work alone; individual spiritual experience, for example, has served as an equally important resource in the elaboration of a secular concept of religion (as evident in the works of writers as diverse as Friedrich Schleiermacher, Rudolf Otto, and Carl Jung). However, history was and remains an authoritative discourse for grounding religious claims, as the *Azazeel* controversy demonstrates.

History, in the secular imaginary, is the purportedly neutral ground over which different discursive traditions meet, obliged to translate their specific life worlds into a commensurate form called "religion." Indeed, as a concept, religion reduces a multiplicity of devotional traditions to a standard metric with requisite elements—god, scripture, rituals—that each tradition must supply and embellish with culturally specific hues. It is not surprising, therefore, that in the modern period one finds similar kinds of theological questions posed across traditions: Is the Quran a miracle or is it a human creation? Was the Immaculate Conception, or Moses parting the Red Sea,

---

[85] Charles Taylor's opus *A Secular Age* is an example of this kind of theorizing.

[86] As Hirschkind argues, the boundaries of the categories of the religious and the secular "are continuously determined and reciprocally redefined. . . . Moreover, insomuch as the identity of a secular practice owes to a particular dynamic relation established between these two categories—that every secular practice is accompanied by its shadow, as it were—then the secular will always be subject to a certain indeterminacy or instability. This instability, ensured by the in principle impossibility of bordering off the secular from the religious, is not a limit on secular power but a condition of its exercise." Hirschkind, "Is There a Secular Body?," 643.

reality or myth? Did the god Rama actually live in a specific time and place or is he an imaginary character? All religions are obliged to answer such questions, forced to engage the very epistemological ground that renders their metaphysical claims dubious. Thus in the *Azazeel* debate, complex Christological issues about the nature of Christ had to be reduced to questions such as who did what, when, and for what kinds of worldly reasons.

One might say, at this point, that secularity flattens religious incommensurability, forcing religious traditions to confront one another in the uniform space of history, all equally vulnerable to the questioning power of the secular. This vulnerability was implicit in the Coptic clerics' response to Ziedan's reading of the Christological debate, as they recognized in it a century-old, secular-Protestant condescension leveled at their beliefs. This elicited a robust response from the clerics that could not but mirror the terms of this discourse, even as they fought to articulate a different religious imaginary. The circularity of this debate and the explosive passion it generates characterize not only the *Azazeel* controversy but many others as well. As I pen these words in January 2015, the battle around the publication of cartoons featuring the prophet Muhammad is raging in Europe, resurrected once again after their initial circulation in 2006. Given the iterative nature of such conflicts, it behooves us to recognize that secularity does not provide an Archimedean point from which to objectively assess or resolve such controversies (as conventional wisdom has it). Rather, secularity itself— its epistemic and moral certainty—provides the fuel for the conflict, erroneously described as a standoff between "religious taboos" and "secular freedoms."

EPILOGUE

A fundamental premise of this book is that the conventional distinction between Western and non-Western secularism needs to be fundamentally rethought. As a feature of liberal political rule, secularism characterizes all modern societies. It is embodied in the institution of the liberal state, its laws, and its strategies of governance, making it a necessary feature of modern political rationality. The right to religious liberty, the legal distinction between public and private, the concept of public order, and the demographic category of religious minority are all elements of this political rationality. I have also suggested that while secular concepts and institutions are shared across national contexts, the Islamic legacy of political rule in Egypt (and other parts of the Middle East) tweaks them in particular ways, giving them a specific shape and form. Insomuch as Western Europe is the explicit referent against which I elaborate Egyptian secularism, the two conjoined by a colonial legacy and legal genealogy, a question remains: What is the nature of the relationship between Egyptian and European configurations of secularism? In this short epilogue, rather than summarize the arguments of the book, I would like to reflect on this question.

As I stated in the introduction and have developed throughout the book, a key dimension of secularism is its promise of civil and political equality, irrespective of one's religious affiliation. This promise belongs to a much broader liberal ambition to create an equal-access society wherein each citizen has a direct relationship to the state, in contrast to premodern societies where one's subordination to the sovereign was mediated through one's emplacement within a chain of hierarchical communal relations. As part of the modern social imaginary, this conception of equality has transformed the way people perceive, live, and challenge ascriptive hierarchy. Its global spread does not mean, however, that social and political hierarchies dissolve, but that their legitimacy is subject to increasing scrutiny and challenge (the great exception being inequalities produced by differential access to wealth). As chapter 1 and chapter 2 show, when the ideal of religious equality first emerged, it changed the way relations between Muslims and non-Muslims were lived and experienced in Egypt and the broader Middle East. This liberal aspiration, however imperfectly realized, informs the laws and constitutions of Middle Eastern states, political parties, and reform movements, as well as the struggles of religious minorities against persistent forms of prejudice and exclusion. It is also this aspiration that compels Coptic Christians, Bahais, and European Muslims to make recourse to the courts to contest the various forms of religious discrimination they suffer.

Inequality, however, does not have a generic form; each social and political inequality has a distinct history, institutional locus, and experience. What gender inequality entails in the United States, for example, is quite different than in Egypt (how male-female relations are socially organized, lived, and contested); each, therefore, requires a distinct analytic. Moreover, particular kinds of inequality (racial, religious) strongly inflect other dimensions of hierarchy (class, gender) that permeate a given society, their mutual imbrication producing historically distinct paradoxes and problems. Likewise, despite legal attempts to codify it, the secular aspiration for religious equality takes multiple forms. In this book I have tried to explore the parallel and often contradictory understandings of religious equality in Egyptian society, none of which fits neatly into the straitjacket of legal instruments that are supposed to ensure it. A tension exists, therefore, between the modern aspiration for religious equality and its legally prescribed form precisely because equality itself is an ambiguous concept, its social topography far more varied than what the state mandates it to be.

As I have argued in this book, the principle of religious equality, when the provenance of the state, is subject to majoritarian norms and sensibilities. Consider, for example, how Protestant majoritarian views on Catholicism shaped the American antipathy toward Catholics in the nineteenth century.[1] Similarly, the Egyptian government's stance on the Bahai religion derives in part from its status in Islam as a non-Abrahamic faith, in addition to the geopolitical animosities between Egypt and Israel, where the Bahai spiritual center is located. In comparison, the discrimination against Muslims in France today has been shaped by French colonial history in North Africa, the perceived incompatibility of Muslim cultural practices with French values, and post-9/11 national-security concerns.[2] The threat a minority poses to a given polity may also change over time. This is evident in how European Jews are treated in Western Europe today in comparison to their situation in the mid-twentieth century. Once vilified and demonized in anti-Semitic Germany and France, Jews are now recognized as an integral and valued part of Europe's unique Judeo-Christian heritage. In contrast, Muslims, who were largely ignored in mid-twentieth-century Europe, are now regarded as a threat to its cultural values and lifestyle. In each case, the threat a minority is perceived to pose to national identity and majoritarian norms

---

[1] Gottschalk, *American Heretics*.
[2] Bowen, *Why the French Don't Like Headscarves*; Fernando, *The Republic Unsettled*; Scott, *The Politics of the Veil*.

is distinct—a product of specific religious, social, and political histories—as are the policies devised to deal with this perceived threat.[3] As should be apparent, these inequalities do not map onto the grid of the West versus the non-West and its associated dichotomies: secular/nonsecular, liberal/authoritarian, tolerant/intolerant. Any attempt to institute even a modicum of religious-political equality requires that we pay attention to the specific form religious inequality takes in a given place and time.

The ideal of religious equality, however, is not the purview of the state alone. As an aspect of our modern secular imaginary, it suffuses the desires and aspirations of ordinary people who encounter a variety of impediments in their struggle for its realization. At times, this goal conflicts with the norms and customs of one's own religious community; at other times, competing demands grounded in gender, class, race, or ethnicity require the prioritization of other values that undercut the principle of religious equality; and sometimes the ideal itself may be inconsequential in the face of other pressing demands. The struggle for religious equality, in other words, must be constantly balanced against other political urgencies, desires, and possibilities open to us.

Consider, for example, the decision of some Coptic men and women to bypass the Church's prohibition on divorce and remarriage by converting to Islam, which subjects them to Islamic family-law provisions (see chapter 3). The fact that Islamic family law is somewhat more lax in matters of divorce and remarriage opens up the possibility for Copts to dissolve unhappy marriages by opting out of their membership within the Coptic community (however temporarily). While the subjection of the Coptic minority to majoritarian Islamic legal and social norms is no doubt a condition of their inequality in the polity, their decision to use Islamic family law solves a different kind of a problem. It is one option in a field of unequal alternatives from which they must choose. Their decision to embrace Islamic law, a condition of their *political* inequality, to achieve *civic* freedom (divorce and remarriage) is far from a perfect resolution of the difficulties they face; while it gets them out of one bind, it often results in the loss of valued social relations as well as ostracism from the Church—a loss that is deleterious to their commitments of faith and community.

Let me compare this situation to one that the Muslim minority faced in Europe when a Danish publication ran cartoons of the prophet Muhammad (2006–08). As I have argued elsewhere, what was actually a conflict between incommensurable ways of relating to religious icons, exemplary figures, and semiotic signs quickly dissolved into a legal contestation over the right to freedom of speech and the right to religious liberty.[4] Just as the Danish majority asserted its legal right to "offensive speech" in re-

---

[3] For an excellent analysis of how Muslims have become racialized in contemporary Europe, see Goldberg, *The Threat of Race.*
[4] Mahmood, "Religious Reason and Secular Affect."

sponse to Muslim protests over the cartoons, European Muslims tried to avail themselves of European laws against hate speech. While this provided European Muslims an opportunity to constrain what they perceived to be an onslaught on their religious beliefs, values, and symbols, it also required them to translate their religious grievance into a majoritarian conception of injury rooted in race, ethnicity, and biology, one that has traction in Europe because of the history of anti-Semitism. Ultimately, European Muslims failed to make a successful case for restricting religiously offensive expressions on the model of hate speech, but the temptation remains strong for them to analogize their marginalization in terms of race and ethnicity—two forms of inscription whose violence is legible to the European majority but that remain inadequate to the kind of injury many Muslims experienced.[5] Like Coptic Christians, the Muslim minority in Europe must choose from a variety of unequal options in their struggle for equality; none of the options provides a complete resolution, but they often propel Muslims in Europe onto a different kind of inhospitable terrain.

It turns out that what appears to be an abstract secular principle—religious equality—exists on at least two distinct levels: as a mandate of the modern state and as an aspiration grounded in a historically distinct social experience. As a legal mandate, religious equality depends upon the agency of the sovereign state, which does not simply relegate religion to the private sphere but reorganizes it through its legal and political mechanisms. As an aspiration, religious equality is embedded in the historically grounded sensibilities of the different communities that constitute the social. It is, therefore, not reducible to the actions and policies of the state or its legal edicts. For example, when a fellow citizen discriminates against me, the outrage I feel emanates from a personal sense that this is not right, that I am no different from another and should be treated as such. This sense is not the same as my belief that all citizens are equal before the law.

Moreover, how I react to a discriminatory act depends upon a variety of factors, including my social position, my life experiences, and the avenues I find available at a given moment—all of which determine the action I might pursue, but none of which is reducible to my status as a citizen, equal to others before the law. The secular aspiration for religious equality in everyday life, therefore, should be distinguished from its legal form. One of the greatest paradoxes of political secularism is that by making the state the arbiter of religious equality, it colonizes and often undercuts this socially embedded aspiration. Secularism, in other words, reduces religious equality

---

[5] For example, in 2007 a number of French Muslim associations lost a lawsuit against the editor of the French satirical newspaper *Charlie Hebdo* for republishing the cartoons of the prophet Muhammad (initially published in the Danish daily *Jyllands-Posten*). See Sara Cannon, "French Editor Wins Lawsuit over Publication of Cartoons," Silha Center for the Study of Media Ethics and Law, November 21, 2009, www.silha.umn.edu/news/spring2007.php?entry=199114.

to the politics of rights and recognition, strengthening the prerogative of the state to intervene in and reorder religious life—which, as I show in this book, often results in the exacerbation of religious polarization and inequality.

Secularism as a statist project exerts inordinate power on our political imagination, most evident in our inability to envision religious equality without the agency of the state. It is hard for us to articulate a critique of religious inequality without at the same time calling for the state to become more secular—a call that is erroneously understood to be a demand for the separation of state and religion, but that is, in fact, a call for sovereign power to serve as the arbiter of religious equality. How can we expect the modern state to ameliorate religious inequality when, as I have shown in this book, its institutions and practices hierarchize religious differences, enshrine majoritarian religious and cultural norms in the nation's identity and laws, and allow for religious inequalities to flourish in society while proclaiming them to be apolitical? Can secularity—as a substrate of ethical sensibilities, attitudes, and dispositions—provide the resources for a critical practice that does not privilege the agency of the state? What kind of productive relations might such a critical practice open up between religious majorities and minorities, and between the state and its religious subjects?

Recent events in Egypt and the travesty that followed the 2011 uprising bear witness to the dangers of the secular imperative. In the days immediately following the coup (2013) against President Mohammed Morsi of the Muslim Brotherhood, it was stunning to see how quickly the religious-secular binary crystallized, becoming the singular lens through which people interpreted the immense fluidity and ambiguity of the events they faced. Liberal critics of the Brotherhood claimed that the coup was a necessary (if temporary) step to save the country from an Islamist makeover, whereas the Brotherhood supporters characterized the army and its partisans as secular hypocrites who abandoned democracy when challenged with Islamist victory at the polls. While the Morsi government was certainly incompetent and cavalier, it had no plans or capacity to turn Egypt into a theocracy. The Coptic Orthodox Church and a vast number of lay Christians supported the coup, hailing the military as the savior that would deliver justice to the beleaguered minority and banish the Brotherhood from politics. The army rode in to power on the promise to restore law and order and to cleanse the country of religious "terrorists," as a majority of Egyptians lined up to pledge their allegiance to the junta. In the period since the coup, as the military government has shut down all avenues of political and social dissent, arresting thousands of activists and suspending civil and political liberties, the "rule of law" has emerged again as the phoenix that will save Egypt—not from the Islamists this time, but from military terror. Even for the relatively small group of Egyptian radicals who understand the Russian roulette that the nation was made to play at the time of the coup, it is the promise of the rule of law that keeps hope alive. This hope is symptomatic of our (not just Egyptians') collective incapacity to imagine a politics that does not treat the state as the arbiter of majority-minority relations. Given this context, the ideal of interfaith equality might require not the bracketing of religious differences but their *ethical* thematization as a necessary risk when the conceptual and political resources of the state have proved inadequate to the challenge this ideal sets before us.

BIBLIOGRAPHY

Abul Fattah, Nabil, ed. *al-Hala al-Diniyya fi Masr*. Cairo: Center for Political and Strategic Studies, 1995.

Abu Odeh, Lama. "Modernizing Muslim Family Law: The Case of Egypt." *Vanderbilt Journal of Transnational Law* 37 (2004): 1043–1146.

Afifi, Mohamad. "Reflections on the Personal Laws of Egyptian Copts." In *Women, the Family and Divorce Laws in Islamic History*, edited by Amira Sonbol, 202–15. Syracuse: Syracuse University Press, 1996.

Agnes, Flavia. "The Supreme Court, the Media, and the Uniform Civil Code Debate in India." In *The Crisis of Secularism in India*, edited by Anuradha Needham and Rajeswari Sunder Rajan, 294–315. Durham: Duke University Press, 2007.

Agrama, Hussein Ali. *Questioning Secularism: Islam, Sovereignty, and the Rule of Law in Modern Egypt*. Chicago: University of Chicago Press, 2012.

el-Alami, Dawoud. "Can the Islamic Device of Khul' Provide a Remedy for Non-Muslim Women in Egypt?" *Yearbook of Islamic and Middle Eastern Law Online* 8, no. 1 (2001): 122–25.

Allan, Michael. "How *Adab* Became Literary: Formalism, Orientalism, and the Institutions of World Literature." *Journal of Arabic Literature* 43 (2012): 1–25.

———. *Shadows of World Literature: Religion, Reading, Critique*. Princeton: Princeton University Press, 2016.

Anderson, Benedict. *Imagined Communities: Reflections on the Origin and Spread of Nationalism*. New York: Verso, 2006.

Anghie, Antony. *Imperialism, Sovereignty, and the Making of International Law*. Cambridge: Cambridge University Press, 2004.

Arendt, Hannah. "The Decline of the Nation-State and the End of Rights of Man." In *The Origins of Totalitarianism*, 267–304. San Diego: Harcourt Brace, 1979.

Armanios, Febe. *Coptic Christianity in Ottoman Egypt*. Oxford: Oxford University Press, 2011.

———. "The 'Virtuous Woman': Images of Gender in Modern Coptic Society." *Middle Eastern Studies* 38 (2002): 110–30.

Asad, Talal. "Ethnography, Literature, and Politics: Some Readings and Uses of Salman Rushdie's Satanic Verses." In *Genealogies of Religion*, 269–306.

———. *Formations of the Secular: Christianity, Islam, Modernity*. Palo Alto: Stanford University Press, 2003.

———. *Genealogies of Religion: Discipline and Reasons of Power in Christianity and Islam*. Baltimore: Johns Hopkins University Press, 1993.

———. "Thinking about Religion, Belief and Politics." In *The Cambridge Companion to Religious Studies*, edited by Robert Orsi, 36–57. New York: Cambridge University Press, 2012.

———. "Trying to Understand French Secularism." In *Political Theologies in a Post-Secular World*, edited by Hent de Vries and Lawrence Sullivan, 494–526. New York: Fordham University Press, 2006.

Asad, Talal, Wendy Brown, Judith Butler, and Saba Mahmood, eds. *Is Critique Secular? Blasphemy, Injury, and Free Speech*. New York: Fordham University Press, 2013.

Bahr, Samira. *al-Aqbat fi al-Hayat al-Siyasiyya al-Masriyya*. Cairo: Maktabat al-Anglo al-Masriyya, 1984.

Baring, Evelyn (The Earl of Cromer). *Modern Egypt*. Vols. 1–2. 1908; London: Kessinger, 2008.

Barkey, Karen. *Empire of Difference: The Ottomans in Comparative Perspective*. Cambridge: Cambridge University Press, 2008.

Bashkin, Orit. *New Babylonians: A History of Jews in Modern Iraq*. Palo Alto: Stanford University Press, 2012.

Baubérot, Jean. *Histoire de la laïcité en France*. Paris: Presses Universitaires de France, 2000.

Bayly, C. A. "Representing Copts and Muhammadans: Empire, Nation, and Community in Egypt and India, 1880–1914." In *Modernity and Culture: From the Mediterranean to the Indian Ocean, 1890–1920*, edited by Leila Tarazi Fawaz and C.A. Bayly, 158–203. New York: Columbia University Press, 2002.

Behrens-Abouseif, Doris. "The Political Situation of the Copts, 1798–1923." In Braude and Lewis, *Christians and Jews in the Ottoman Empire*, 1:185–205.

Beinin, Joel. *The Dispersion of Egyptian Jewry: Culture, Politics, and the Formation of a Modern Diaspora*. Berkeley: University of California Press, 1998.

Berger, Maurits. "Apostasy and Public Policy in Contemporary Egypt: An Evaluation of Recent Cases from Egypt's High Courts." *Human Rights Quarterly* 25 (2003): 720–40.

———. "Conflicts Law and Public Policy in Egyptian Family Law: Islamic Law through the Backdoor." *American Journal of Comparative Law* 50, no. 3 (2002): 555–94.

———. "Public Policy and Islamic Law: The Modern *Dhimmi* in Contemporary Egyptian Family Law." *Islamic Law and Society* 8, no. 1 (2001): 88–136.

———. "Secularizing Interreligious Law in Egypt." *Islamic Law and Society* 12, no. 3 (2005): 394–418.

Berman, Nathaniel. "'But the Alternative Is Despair': European Nationalism and the Modernist Renewal of International Law." *Harvard Law Review* 106, no. 8 (1993): 1792–1903.

———. "The International Law of Nationalism: Group Identity and Legal History." In *International Law and Ethnic Conflict*, edited by David Wippman, 25–57. Ithaca: Cornell University Press, 1998.

Bernard-Maugiron, Nathalie. "Divorce and Remarriage of Orthodox Copts in Egypt: The 2008 State Council Ruling and the Amendment of the 1938 Personal Status Regulations." *Islamic Law and Society* 18, nos. 3–4 (2011): 356–86.

Bernstein, Elizabeth. "The Sexual Politics of the 'New Abolitionism.'" *differences* 18, no. 3 (Fall 2007): 128–51.

Bhuta, Nehal. "Two Concepts of Religious Freedom in the European Court of Human Rights." *South Atlantic Quarterly* 113, no. 1 (2014): 9–35.

Bishoy (Bishop). *al-Radd 'ala al-Buhtan fi Riwayat Yusuf Zidan 'Azazil*. Cairo: Dar al-Antun, 2009.

al-Bishri, Tariq. *al-Dawla wa al-Kanisa*. Cairo: Dar al-Shuruq, 2011.

———. *al-Jama'a al-Wataniyya: al-'Uzla wa al-Indimaj*. Cairo: Dar al-Hilal, 2005.

———. *al-Muslimun wa al-Aqbat fi Atar al-Jama'a al-Wataniyya*. Cairo: Dar al-Shuruq, 1980.

———. "Wafa Qustuntin . . . Bayna al-Dawla wa 'al-Idara' al-Kanisiyya." *Wujhat Nazr* 72 (January 2005): 4–9.

Bonfield, Lloyd. "Developments in European Family Law." In *Family Life in Early Modern Times, 1500–1789*, edited by David Kertzer and Marzio Barbagli, 87–124. New Haven: Yale University Press, 2001.

———. "European Family Law." In *Family Life in the Long Nineteenth Century, 1789–1913*, edited by David Kertzer and Marzio Barbagli, 109–54. New Haven: Yale University Press, 2002.

Bowen, John. "Shari'a, State, and Social Norms in France and Indonesia." *ISIM Papers*. Leiden: International Institute for the Study of Islam, 2001.

———. *Why the French Don't Like Headscarves: Islam, the State and Public Space*. Princeton: Princeton University Press, 2010.

Braude, Benjamin. "Foundation Myths of the *Millet* System." In Braude and Lewis, *Christians and Jews in the Ottoman Empire*, 2:55–68.

Braude, Benjamin, and Bernard Lewis, eds. *Christians and Jews in the Ottoman Empire: The Functioning of a Plural Society*. 2 vols. New York: Holmes and Meier, 1982.

———. "Introduction." In Braude and Lewis, *Christians and Jews in the Ottoman Empire*, 1:1–48.

Brown, Nathan. *The Rule of Law in the Arab World: Courts in Egypt and the Gulf*. Cambridge: Cambridge University Press, 1997.

Brown, Wendy. "Finding the Man in the State." In *States of Injury: Power and Freedom in Late Modernity*, 166–96. Princeton: Princeton University Press, 1995.

———. *Politics Out of History*. Princeton: Princeton University Press, 2001.

———. "Tolerance as Supplement: The 'Jewish Question' and the 'Woman Question.' " In *Regulating Aversion: Tolerance in the Age of Identity and Empire*, 48–77. Princeton: Princeton University Press, 2006.

Brubaker, Rogers. *Nations and Nationhood in France and Germany*. Cambridge, MA: Harvard University Press, 1998.

Caldwell, William. "The Doctrine of Satan: I. In the Old Testament." *The Biblical World* 41, no. 1 (1913): 29–33.

Calhoun, Craig, Mark Juergensmeyer, and Jonathan VanAntwerpen, eds. *Rethinking Secularism*. New York: Oxford University Press, 2011.

Castelli, Elizabeth. "Praying for the Persecuted Church: US Christian Activism in the Global Arena." *Journal of Human Rights* 4 (2005): 321–51.

Center for Religious Freedom. *Egypt's Endangered Christians 1999*. Washington, DC: Freedom House, 1999.

Chatterjee, Partha. "The Nation and Its Pasts." In *The Nation and Its Fragments: Colonial and Postcolonial Histories*. Princeton: Princeton University Press, 1993.

Chidester, David. *Word and Light: Seeing, Hearing, and Religious Discourse*. Urbana: University of Illinois Press, 1992.

Christelow, Allan. "The Transformation of the Muslim Court System in Colonial Algeria: Reflections on the Concept of Autonomy." In *Islamic Law: Social and Historical Contexts*, edited by Aziz al-Azmeh, 215–30. London: Routledge, 1988.

Clark, Michele, and Nadia Ghaly. "The Disappearance, Forced Conversion and Forced Marriages of Coptic Christian Women in Egypt." November 2009. http://csi-int.org/pdfs/csi _coptic_report.pdf.

———. " 'Tell My Mother I Miss Her': The Disappearance, Forced Conversion and Forced Marriages of Coptic Christian Women in Egypt II." July 2012. http://csi-usa.org/TellMyMother IMissHer.pdf.

Claude, Inis. *National Minorities: An International Problem*. Cambridge, MA: Harvard University Press, 1955.

Cohen, Mark. "What Was the Pact of 'Umar? A Literary-Historical Study." *Jerusalem Studies in Arabic and Islam* 23 (1999): 100–57.

Cole, Juan R. I. "The Baha'i Minority and Nationalism in Contemporary Iran." In *Nationalism and Minority Identities in Islamic Societies*, edited by Maya Shatzmiller, 127–63. Montreal: McGill-Queens University Press, 2005.

———. *Modernity and the Millennium: The Genesis of the Baha'i Faith in the Nineteenth-Century Middle East*. New York: Columbia University Press, 1998.

Connolly, William E. *Why I Am Not a Secularist*. Minneapolis: University of Minnesota Press, 1999.

Cowan, Jane K. "Selective Scrutiny: Supranational Engagement with Minority Protection and Rights in Europe." In *The Power of Law in a Transnational World: Anthropological Enquiries*, edited by Franz von Benda-Beckmann, Keebet von Benda-Beckmann, and Anne Griffiths, 74–95. New York: Berghahn, 2009.

———. "The Success of Failure? Minority Supervision at the League of Nations." In *Paths to International Justice*, edited by Marie-Benedicte Dembour and Tobias Kelly, 29–56. Cambridge: Cambridge University Press, 2007.

———. "The Uncertain Political Limits of Cultural Claims: Minority Rights Politics in Southeast Europe." In *Human Rights in Global Perspective: Anthropological Studies of Rights, Claims and Entitlements*, edited by Richard Ashby Wilson and Jon P. Mitchell, 140–62. London: Routledge, 2003.

Cuno, Kenneth. "Ambiguous Modernization: The Transition to Monogamy in Khedival Egypt." In *Family History in the Middle East: Household, Property, and Gender*, edited by Beshara Doumani, 247–69. Albany: State University of New York Press, 2003.

———. "Disobedient Wives and Neglectful Husbands: Marital Relations and the First Phase of Family Law Reform in Egypt." In *Family, Gender, and Law in a Globalizing Middle East and South Asia*, edited by Kenneth Cuno, 3–18. Syracuse: Syracuse University Press, 2009.

Dahi, Omar S. "The Political Economy of the Egyptian and Arab Revolt." *IDS Bulletin* 43, no. 1 (2012): 47–53.

Danchin, Peter. "The Emergence and Structure of Religious Freedom in International Law Reconsidered." *Journal of Law and Religion* 23 (2007–08): 455–534.

———. "Islam in the Secular *Nomos* of the European Court of Human Rights." *Michigan Journal of International Law* 32, no. 4 (2011): 675–82.

———. "Of Prophets and Proselytes: Freedom of Religion and the Conflict of Rights in International Law." *Harvard International Law Journal* 49, no. 2 (Summer 2008): 249–321.

———. "Religious Freedom in the *Hosanna-Tabor* Religious Freedom Panopticon." *The Immanent Frame*. March 6, 2012. http://blogs.ssrc.org/tif/2012/03/06/hosanna-tabor-in-the-religious-freedom-panopticon/.

Davis, Stephen. *The Early Coptic Papacy: The Egyptian Church and Its Leadership in Late Antiquity*. Cairo: American University of Cairo Press, 2004.

Davison, Roderic. "The Advent of the Principle of Representation in the Government of the Ottoman Empire." In *Beginnings of Modernization in the Middle East: The Nineteenth Century*, edited by William R. Polk and Richard L. Chambers, 93–108. Chicago: University of Chicago Press, 1968.

———. "The *Millets* as Agents of Change in the Nineteenth-Century Ottoman Empire." In Braude and Lewis, *Christians and Jews in the Ottoman Empire*, 1:319–37.

Deringil, Selim. *Conversion and Apostasy in the Late Ottoman Empire*. New York: Cambridge University Press, 2012.

———. " 'There Is No Compulsion in Religion': On Conversion and Apostasy in the Late Ottoman Empire: 1839–1856." *Comparative Studies in Society and History* 42, no. 3 (2000): 547–75.

———. *The Well-Protected Domains: Ideology and the Legitimation of Power in the Ottoman Empire, 1876–1909*. New York: I. B. Taurus, 1998.

Devlin, Patrick. "Morals and the Criminal Law." In *Morality and the Law*, edited by Richard A. Wasserstrom, 24–48. Belmont: Wadsworth, 1971.

Diamond, Larry, and Marc Plattner. *Democracy and Authoritarianism in the Arab World*. Baltimore: Johns Hopkins University Press, 2014.

Dunn, John. *The History of Political Theory, and Other Essays*. Cambridge: Cambridge University Press, 1996.

Dzielska, Maria. *Hypatia of Alexandria*. Translated by F. Lyra. Cambridge, MA: Harvard University Press, 1995.

Edge, Peter. "The European Court of Human Rights and Religious Rights." *International and Comparative Law Quarterly* 47, no. 3 (July 1998): 680–87.

EIPR (Egyptian Initiative for Personal Rights). " 'Adala al-Shari': Taqrir al-Tahqiq al-Midani fi Ahdath al-'Unf al-Ta'ifi bi-Imbaba Mayu 2011." May 14, 2011. www.eipr.org/report/2011/05/14/1158.

———. "Crimes in al-Amiriyya: Collective Punishment of Copts and Official Sanction for Sectarian Attacks." February 12, 2012. www.eipr.org/en/pressrelease/2012/02/12/1367.

———. "Details of Sectarian Attacks Documented by the EIPR from 10 July to 11 August 2013." August 25, 2013. www.eipr.org/en/content/2013/08/25/1795.

———. "Dimuqratiyya al-Iklirus!: Ru'ya Huquqiyya lil-La'iha Intikhab Baba Iskandariyya wa Batrik al-Kurraza al-Murqusiyya." September 2014. www.eipr.org/sites/default/files/reports/pdf/pope_elections.pdf.

———. "Freedom of Belief and Arrests of Shia Muslims in Egypt." August 1, 2004. www.eipr.org/en/report/2004/08/01/570.

———. "State Security Court Rejects Interior Ministry Appeal of Release Order for Shi'ite Detainees." August 23, 2010. www.eipr.org/en/pressrelease/2010/08/23/964.

———. "Supreme Administrative Court Outlaws Complete Ban on Niqab." June 9, 2007. www.eipr.org/en/pressrelease/2007/06/09/226.

———. "Taqrir al-Ta'ifiyya bi-Madinat al-Khusus wa Muhit al-Katidra'iyya al-Murqsiyya bi-l-'Abasiyya." April 11, 2013. www.eipr.org/pressrelease/2013/04/11/1682.

———. "Two Years of Sectarian Violence: What Happened? Where Do We Begin?" April 2010. www.eipr.org/sites/default/files/reports/pdf/Sectarian_Violence_inTwoYears_EN.pdf.

———. "Unprecedented Spike in Sectarian Violence and Reprisals against Copts; Interim President and Prime Minister Must Protect Egyptians' Lives and Property and Their Houses of Worship." August 25, 2013. www.eipr.org/en/pressrelease/2013/08/25/1791.

Eissenstat, Howard. "Metaphors of Race and Discourse of the Nation: Racial Theory and State Nationalism in the First Decades of the Turkish Republic." In *Race and Nation: Ethnic Systems in the Modern World*, edited by Paul Spickard, 239–56. New York: Routledge, 2005.

Elsässer, Sebastian. *The Coptic Question in the Mubarak Era.* Oxford: Oxford University Press, 2014.

Emon, Anver M. *Religious Pluralism and Islamic Law: Dhimmis and Others in the Empire of Law.* Oxford: Oxford University Press, 2012.

Esmeir, Samera. *Juridical Humanity: A Colonial History.* Palo Alto: Stanford University Press, 2012.

Evans, Carolyn. *Freedom of Religion under the European Convention on Human Rights.* Oxford: Oxford University Press, 2001.

———. "Strengthening the Role of the Special Rapporteur on Freedom of Religion or Belief." *Religion and Human Rights* 1 (2006): 75–96.

Evans, Malcolm. *Religious Liberty and International Law in Europe.* Cambridge: Cambridge University Press, 1997.

Fernando, Mayanthi. *The Republic Unsettled: Muslim French and the Contradictions of Secularism.* Durham: Duke University Press, 2014.

Fessenden, Tracy. *Culture and Redemption: Religion, the Secular, and American Literature.* Princeton: Princeton University Press, 2006.

Feuerbach, Ludwig. *The Essence of Christianity.* Translated by George Elliot. Amherst, MA: Prometheus, 1989.

Fink, Carole. *Defending the Rights of Others: The Great Powers, the Jews, and International Minority Protection, 1878–1938.* Cambridge: Cambridge University Press, 2004.

Frei, Hans. *The Eclipse of Biblical Narrative: A Study in Eighteenth and Nineteenth Century Hermeneutics.* New Haven: Yale University Press, 1974.

Gauchet, Marcel. *The Disenchantment of the World: A Political History of Religion.* Translated by Oscar Burge. Princeton: Princeton University Press, 1999.

al-Gawhary, Karim. "Copts in the 'Egyptian Fabric.'" *Middle East Report* 200 (July-September 1996): 21–22.

el-Ghobashy, Mona. "Constitutionalist Contention in Contemporary Egypt." *American Behavioral Scientist* 51, no. 1 (2008): 1590–1610.

Gibbon, Edward. *The History of the Decline and Fall of the Roman Empire.* Edited by David Womersley. London: Penguin, 1994.

Ginsburg, Tom, and Tamir Moustafa, eds. *Rule by Law: The Politics of Courts in Authoritarian Regimes.* Cambridge: Cambridge University Press, 2008.

Goldberg, David Theo. *The Threat of Race: Reflections on Racial Neoliberalism.* Malden, MA: Blackwell, 2009.

Gorman, Anthony. *Historians, State, and Politics in Twentieth Century Egypt: Contesting the Nation.* New York: Routledge, 2003.

Gottschalk, Peter. *American Heretics: Catholics, Jews, Muslims, and the History of Religious Intolerance.* New York: Palgrave Macmillan, 2013.

Grote, Rainer. "Constitutional Developments in Egypt: The New 2014 Egyptian Constitution." *Oxford Constitutions of the World.* http://oxcon.ouplaw.com/page/egyptian-constitution.

Guirguis, Laure. *Les Coptes d'Égypte: Violences communautaires et transformations politiques, 2005–2012.* Paris: Karthala, 2012.

Guirguis, Magdi, and Nelly van Doorn-Harder. *The Emergence of the Modern Coptic Papacy.* Cairo: American University in Cairo Press, 2011.

Gunn, Jeremy. "Religion after 9-11: When Our Allies Persecute." *Religion in the News* 4, no. 3 (Fall 2001). www.trincoll.edu/depts/csrpl/RINVol4No3/religious%20persecution.htm.

Habermas, Jürgen. "Notes on a Post-Secular Society." *Signandsight.com,* June 18, 2008, www.signandsight.com/features/1714.html.

———. *Time of Transitions.* Cambridge: Polity, 2006.

Habib, Tawfiq. *al-Mu'tamir al-Qibti al-Awwal: Majmu'at al-Rasa'il Musawwara.* Cairo: Tab'a al-Matba'a al-Akhbar li-Masr, 1911.

Haefeli, Evan. *New Netherlands and the Dutch Origins of the American Religious Liberty.* Philadelphia: University of Pennsylvania Press, 2012.

Hallaq, Wael B. "Can the Shari'a Be Restored?" In *Islamic Law and the Challenges of Modernity,* edited by Y. Y. Haddad and B. F. Stowasser, 21–53. Walnut Creek, CA: Altamira, 2004.

———. *Shari'a: Theory, Practice, Transformations.* Cambridge: Cambridge University Press, 2009.

———. "What Is Shari'a?" In *Yearbook of Islamic and Middle Eastern Law.* Vol. 12 (2005–2006), 151–80. Leiden: Brill, 2007.

Halley, Janet, and Kerry Rittich. "Critical Directions in Comparative Family Law: Genealogies and Contemporary Studies of Family Law Exceptionalism." *American Journal of Comparative Law* 58, no. 4 (2010): 753–75.

Hamilton, Alastair. *The Copts and the West, 1439–1822: The European Discovery of the Egyptian Church.* New York: Oxford University Press, 2006.

Hart, H.L.A. *Law, Liberty, and Morality.* Stanford: Stanford University Press, 1963.

Hasan, S. S. *Christians versus Muslims in Modern Egypt.* New York: Oxford University Press, 2003.

Heo, Angie D. "The Bodily Threat of Miracles: Security, Sacramentality, and the Egyptian Politics of Public Order." *American Ethnologist* 40, no. 1 (2013): 149–64.

———. "The Virgin Made Visible: Intercessory Images of Church Territory in Egypt." *Comparative Studies in Society and History* 54, no. 2 (2012): 361–91.

Hirschkind, Charles. "Heresy or Hermeneutics: The Case of Nasr Hamid Abu Zayd." *Stanford Humanities Review* 5, no. 1 (1996): 35–49.

———. "Is There a Secular Body?" *Cultural Anthropology* 26, no. 4 (2011): 633–47.

———. "Religious Difference and Democratic Pluralism: Recent Debates and Frameworks." *Temenos* 44, no. 1 (2008): 67–82.

Human Rights Watch and the EIPR (Egyptian Initiative for Personal Rights). "Prohibited Identities." *State Interference with Religious Freedom* 19, no. 7 (2007): 1–97.

Hunter, Ian. "Religious Freedom in Early Modern Germany: Theology, Philosophy, and Legal Casuistry." *South Atlantic Quarterly* 113, no. 1 (2014): 27–62.

Hurd, Elizabeth Shakman. *Beyond Religious Freedom: The New Global Politics of Religion.* Princeton: Princeton University Press, 2015.

Husserl, Gerhart. "Public Policy and Ordre Public." *Virginia Law Review* 25, no. 1 (1938): 37–67.

Ibn 'Abidin, Muhammad Amin. *Hashiyat Radd al-Muhtar 'ala Durr al-Mukhtar Sharh Tanwir al-Absar*. Cairo: al-Babi al-Halabi, 1966.

Ibrahim, Vivian. *The Copts of Egypt: The Challenges of Modernisation and Identity*. London: Taurus Academic Studies, 2011.

Jackson Preece, Jennifer. "Minority Rights in Europe: From Westphalia to Helsinki." *Review of International Studies* 23, no. 1 (1997): 75–92.

———. *National Minorities and the European Nation-States System*. New York: Oxford University Press, 1998.

Jakobsen, Janet, and Ann Pelligrini, eds. *Secularisms*. Durham: Duke University Press, 2008.

Johansen, Baber. "Apostasy as Objective and Depersonalized Fact: Two Recent Egyptian Court Judgments." *Social Research* 70, no. 3 (2003): 687–710.

Kamal, Karima. *Talaq al-Aqbat*. Cairo: Dar Merit, 2006.

Kamil, Jill. *Christianity in the Land of the Pharaohs: The Coptic Orthodox Church*. Cairo: American University in Cairo Press, 2002.

Karpat, Kemal. "*Millets* and Nationality: The Roots of the Incongruity of Nation and State in the Post-Ottoman Era." In Braude and Lewis, *Christians and Jews in the Ottoman Empire*, 1:141–70.

Katz, Jacob. *Out of the Ghetto: The Social Background of Jewish Emancipation, 1770–1870*. Cambridge, MA: Harvard University Press, 1973.

Keane, Webb. *Christian Moderns: Freedom and Fetish in the Mission Encounter*. Berkeley: University of California Press, 2007.

Kennedy, Duncan. "Savigny's Family/Patrimony Distinction and Its Place in the Global Genealogy of Classical Legal Thought." *American Journal of Comparative Law* 58, no. 4 (2010): 811–41.

el-Khawaga, Dina. "The Laity at the Heart of the Coptic Clerical Reform." In *Between Desert and City: The Coptic Orthodox Church Today*, edited by Nelly van Doorn-Harder and Kari Vogt, 143–67. Oslo: Institute for Comparative Research in Human Culture, 1997.

———. "The Political Dynamics of the Copts: Giving the Community an Active Role." In *Christian Communities in the Arab Middle East: The Challenge of the Future*, edited by Andrea Pacini. Oxford: Oxford University Press, 1998.

Kholoussy, Hanan. "Interfaith Unions and Non-Muslim Wives in Early Twentieth-Century Alexandrian Islamic Courts." In *Untold Histories of the Middle East: Recovering Voices from the 19th and 20th Centuries*, edited by Amy Singer, Christoph Neumann, and Selcuk Aksin Somel, 54–70. New York: Routledge, 2010.

———. "Nationalization of Marriage in Monarchical Egypt." In *Re-Envisioning Egypt, 1919–1952*, edited by Arthur Goldschmidt, Amy Johnson, and Barak Salmoni, 317–50. Cairo: American University in Cairo Press, 2005.

Kingsley, Charles. *Hypatia, or New Foes with an Old Face*. London: J. M. Dent, 1910.

Koskenniemi, Martti. *The Gentle Civilizer of Nations: The Rise and Fall of International Law, 1870–1960*. Cambridge: Cambridge University Press, 2001.

Krasner, Stephen. *Sovereignty: Organized Hypocrisy*. Princeton: Princeton University Press, 1999.

Kugelman, Dieter. "The Protection of Minorities and Indigenous Peoples Respecting Cultural Diversity." In *Max Planck Yearbook of United Nations Law*, vol. 11, edited by Armin von Bognandy and Rüdiger Wolfrum, 233–63. Leiden: Koninklijke Brill, 2007.

Kymlicka, Will. *Multicultural Citizenship: A Liberal Theory of Minority Rights*. Oxford: Clarendon Press, 1995.

Laborde, Cécile. "Protecting Freedom of Religion in the Secular Age," *The Immanent Frame*. April 23, 2012. http://blogs.ssrc.org/tif/2012/04/23/protecting-freedom-of-religion-in-the-secular-age/.

Lambek, Michael. "Kinship, Modernity, and the Immodern." In *Vital Relations: Modernity and the Persistent Life of Kinship,* edited by Susan McKinnon and Fenella Cannell, 241–60. Santa Fe: School of Advanced Research Press, 2013.

Lane, Edward William. *An Account of the Manners and Customs of Modern Egyptians.* Paris: Adamant, 2000.

Laponce, J. A. *The Protection of Minorities.* Berkeley: University of California Press, 1960.

Leiter, Brian. *Why Tolerate Religion?* Princeton: Princeton University Press, 2012.

el-Leithy, Tamer. *Coptic Culture and Conversion in Medieval Cairo, 1293–1524* A.D. PhD diss., Princeton University, 2005.

Liebesny, Herbert J. "Comparative Legal History: Its Role in the Analysis of Islamic and Modern Near Eastern Legal Institutions." *American Journal of Comparative Law* 20, no. 1 (1972): 38–52.

Lindkvist, Linde. "The Politics of Article 18: Religious Liberty in the Universal Declaration of Human Rights." *Humanity: An International Journal of Human Rights, Humanitarianism and Development* 4, no. 3 (2013): 429–47.

———. *Shrines and Souls: The Reinvention of Religious Liberty and the Genesis of the Universal Declaration of Human Rights.* Malmö, Sweden: Bokbox Förlag, 2014.

Locke, John. *A Letter Concerning Toleration.* New York: Hackett, 1983.

Lombardi, Clark B. *State Law as Islamic Law in Modern Egypt: The Incorporation of the Shari'a into Egyptian Constitutional Law.* Leiden: Brill, 2006.

Lombardi, Clark B., and Nathan J. Brown. "Do Constitutions Requiring Adherence to *Shari'a* Threaten Human Rights? How Egypt's Constitutional Court Reconciles Islamic Law with the Liberal Rule of Law." *American University International Law Review* 21 (2006): 379–435.

———. "Translation: The Supreme Constitutional Court of Egypt on Islamic Law, Veiling, and Civil Rights: An Annotated Translation of Supreme Constitutional Court of Egypt *Case No. 8 of Judicial Year 17* (May 18, 1996)." *American University International Law Review* 21 (2006): 437–60.

Maclure, Jocelyn, and Charles Taylor. *Secularism and Freedom of Conscience.* Translated by Jane Marie Todd. Cambridge, MA: Harvard University Press, 2011.

Mahmood, Saba. "Can Secularism Be Other-Wise?" In *Varieties of Secularism in a Secular Age,* edited by Michael Warner, Jonathan VanAntwerpen, and Craig Calhoun, 282–99. Cambridge: Harvard University Press, 2010.

———. *Politics of Piety: Islamic Revival and the Feminist Subject.* Princeton: University of Princeton Press, 2012.

———. "Religious Reason and Secular Affect: An Incommensurable Divide?" In Asad, Brown, Butler, and Mahmood, *Is Critique Secular?,* 65–100.

Mahmood, Saba, and Peter Danchin. "Immunity or Regulation? Antinomies of Religious Freedom." *South Atlantic Quarterly* 113, no. 1 (2014): 129–59.

Maïla, Joseph. "The Arab Christians: From the Eastern Question to the Recent Political Situation of the Minorities." In *Christian Communities in the Arab Middle East: The Challenge of the Future,* edited by Andrea Pacini, 25–47. Oxford: Clarendon Press, 1998.

Makari, Peter. *Conflict and Cooperation: Christian-Muslim Relations in Contemporary Egypt.* Syracuse: Syracuse University Press, 2007.

Makdisi, Ussama. *Artillery of Heaven: American Missionaries and the Failure of Conversion of the Middle East.* Ithaca: Cornell University Press, 2008.

———. *The Culture of Sectarianism: Community, History, and Violence in Nineteenth-Century Ottoman Lebanon.* Berkeley: University of California Press, 2000.

Malik, Maleiha. "Minorities and Law: Past and Present." *Current Legal Problems* 67, no. 1 (2014): 1–32.

Mani, Lata. *Contentious Traditions: The Debate on Sati in Colonial India.* Berkeley: University of California Press, 1998.

Mann, Michael. *The Dark Side of Democracy: Explaining Ethnic Cleansing.* Cambridge: Cambridge University Press, 2005.

Marcus, Jacob Rader. *The Jew in the Medieval World: A Sourcebook, 315–1791*. Cincinnati: Hebrew Union College Press, 1999.

Marshall, Paul, and Lela Gilbert. *Their Blood Cries Out: The Worldwide Tragedy of Modern Christians Who Are Dying for their Faith*. Dallas: Word Publishing, 1997.

Martínez-Torrón, Javier, and Rafael Navarro-Valls. "The Protection of Religious Freedom in the System of the European Convention on Human Rights." *Helsinki Monitor* 9, no. 3 (1998): 25–37.

Marx, Anthony. *Faith in the Nation: Exclusionary Origins of Nationalism*. Oxford: Oxford University Press, 2003.

Marx, Karl. "On the Jewish Question." In *The Marx-Engels Reader*, 2nd ed., edited by Robert Tucker, 26–52. New York: Norton, 1978.

Masters, Bruce. *Christian and Jews in the Ottoman Arab World: The Roots of Sectarianism*. Cambridge: Cambridge University Press, 2001.

Masuzawa, Tomoko. *The Invention of World Religions: Or, How European Universalism Was Preserved in the Language of Pluralism*. Chicago: University of Chicago Press, 2007.

Mazower, Mark. *Dark Continent: Europe's Twentieth Century*. New York: A. A. Knopf, 1999.

———. *No Enchanted Palace: The End of Empire and the Ideological Origins of the United Nations*. Princeton: Princeton University Press, 2009.

McAlister, Melani. "The Politics of Persecution." *Middle East Research and Information Project* 249, no. 38 (2008): 18–27.

McEwan, Dorothea. "Catholic Copts, Riformati and the Capitulations: A Case Study in Church Protection in Egypt." In *Eastern Christianity: Studies in Modern History, Religion and Politics*, edited by Anthony O'Mahony, 499–521. London: Melisende, 2002.

McLeod, Hugh. *Secularization in Western Europe, 1848–1914*. London: Palgrave MacMillan, 2000.

Meinardus, Otto. *Two Thousand Years of Coptic Christianity*. Cairo: American University in Cairo Press, 1999.

Messick, Brinkley. *The Calligraphic State: Textual Domination and History in a Muslim Society*. Berkeley: University of California Press, 1996.

Mikhail, Maged S. A. *From Byzantine to Islamic Egypt: Religion, Identity, and Politics*. London: I. B. Taurus, 2014.

Mills, Alex. "The Private History of International Law." *International and Comparative Law Quarterly* 5, no. 1 (January 2006): 1–49.

Mitchell, Richard. *The Society of Muslim Brothers*. New York: Oxford University Press, 1993.

Mitchell, Timothy, ed. *Questions of Modernity*. Minneapolis: University of Minnesota Press, 2000.

Mitchell, W.J.T. *What Do Pictures Want? The Lives and Loves of Images*. Chicago: University of Chicago Press, 2006.

Mitoma, Glenn. "Charles H. Malik and Human Rights: Notes on a Biography." *Biography* 33, no. 1 (2010): 222–41.

Modern, John Lardas. "Confused Parchments, Infinite Socialities." *The Immanent Frame*. March 4, 2013. http://blogs.ssrc.org/tif/2013/03/04/confused-parchments-infinite-socialities/.

———. *Secularism in Antebellum America*. Chicago: University of Chicago Press, 2011.

Moustafa, Tamir. *The Struggle for Constitutional Power: Law, Politics, and Economic Development in Egypt*. Cambridge: Cambridge University Press, 2007.

Moyn, Samuel. "From Communist to Muslim: European Human Rights, the Cold War, and Religious Liberty." *South Atlantic Quarterly* 113, no. 1 (2014): 63–86.

———. "Personalism, Community, and the Origins of Human Rights." In *Human Rights in the Twentieth Century*, edited by Stefan-Ludwig Hoffmann, 85–106. Cambridge: Cambridge University Press, 2008.

Murqus, Samir. *al-Himaya wa al-A'qab: al-Gharb wa al-Mas'ala al-Diniyya fi al-Sharq al-Awsat; Min al-Qanun al-Ri'aya al-Madhhabiyya lil-Qanun al-Hurriyya al-Diniyya*. Cairo: Merit, 2000.

an-Na'im, Abdullahi Ahmed. *Islam and the Secular State: Negotiating the Future of Shari'a*. Cambridge: Harvard University Press, 2010.

Nakhla Rufila, Yacoub. *al-Tarikh al-Umma al-Qibtiyya*. Cairo: Matba'a Metropole, 1898.

Opwis, Felicitas. "Maṣlaḥa in Contemporary Islamic Legal Theory." *Islamic Law and Society* 12, no. 2 (2005): 182–223.

Orlov, Andrei A. *Dark Mirrors: Azazel and Satanael in Early Jewish Demonology*. New York: State University of New York Press, 2011.

Özsu, Umut. "The Ottoman Empire." In *Oxford Handbook of International Legal History*, edited by Bardo Fassbender and Anne Peters, 429–48. Oxford: Oxford University Press, 2012.

Papaconstantinou, Arietta. "Between *Umma* and *Dhimma*: The Christians of the Middle East under the Ummayads." *Annales islamologiques* 42 (2008): 127–56.

———. "Historiography, Hagiography, and the Making of the Coptic 'Church of the Martyrs' in Early Islamic Egypt." *Dumbarton Oaks Papers* 60 (2006): 65–86.

Pateman, Carole. *The Sexual Contract*. Palo Alto: Stanford University Press, 1988.

Pennington, J. D. "The Copts in Modern Egypt." *Middle Eastern Studies* 18, no. 2 (1982): 158–79.

Pink, Johanna. "A Post-Qur'anic Religion between Apostasy and Public Order: Egyptian Muftis and Courts on the Legal Status of the Baha'i Faith." *Islamic Law and Society* 10, no. 3 (2003): 409–34.

Platt, Nicola Christine. *Democracy and Authoritarianism in the Arab World*. Boulder: Lynne Rienner, 2006.

Pollard, Lisa. *Nurturing the Nation: The Family Politics of Modernizing, Colonizing, and Liberating Egypt, 1805–1923*. Berkeley: University of California Press, 2005.

al-Qattan, Najwa. "*Dhimmis* in the Muslim Court: Legal Autonomy and Religious Discrimination." *International Journal of Middle East Studies* 31 (1999): 429–44.

Quataert, Donald. *The Ottoman Empire, 1700–1922*. Cambridge: Cambridge University Press, 2000.

Rana, Aziz. "Constitutionalism and the Foundations of the Security State." Rapoport Human Rights Working Paper Series. February 7, 2014. http://papers.ssrn.com/sol3/papers.cfm?abstract_id=2392666.

Rehman, Javaid. "Raising the Conceptual Issues: Minority Rights in International Law." *Australian Law Journal* 72, no. 8 (August 1998): 615–34.

Reid, Donald Malcolm. *Whose Pharaohs?: Archeology, Museums, and Egyptian National Identity from Napoleon War to World War I*. Berkeley: University of California Press, 2002.

Reza, Sadiq. "Endless Emergency: The Case of Egypt." *New Criminal Law Review: An International and Interdisciplinary Journal* 10, no. 4 (2007): 532–53.

Robson, Laura. *Colonialism and Christianity in Mandate Palestine*. Austin: University of Texas Press, 2011.

Rodogno, Davide. *Against Massacre: Humanitarian Interventions in the Ottoman Empire, 1815–1914*. Princeton: Princeton University Press, 2012.

Rowberry, Ryan, and John Khalil. "A Brief History of Coptic Personal Status Law." *Berkeley Journal of Middle Eastern Law* 3 (2010). http://scholarship.law.berkeley.edu/cgi/viewcontent.cgi?article=1013&context=jmeil.

Rubin, Gayle. "Traffic in Women: Notes on the 'Political Economy' of Sex." In *Toward an Anthropology of Women*, edited by Rayna Reiter, 157–210. New York: Monthly Review Press, 1975.

Rutherford, Bruce K. *Egypt after Mubarak: Liberalism, Islam, and Democracy in the Arab World*. Princeton: Princeton University Press, 2008.

Salzman, Ariel. "Citizens in Search of a State: The Limits of Political Participation in the Late Ottoman Empire." In *Extending Citizenship, Reconfiguring States*, edited by Michael Hanagan and Charles Tilly, 37–66. New York: Rowman and Littlefield, 1999.

Scott, David. "Norms of Self-Determination: Thinking Sovereignty Through." *Middle East Law and Governance* 4, nos. 2–3 (2012): 195–224.

Scott, Joan Wallach. *Only Paradoxes to Offer*. Cambridge: Harvard University Press, 1996.

———. *The Politics of the Veil*. Princeton: Princeton University Press, 2010.

———. "Secularism and Gender Equality." In *Religion, the Secular, and the Politics of Sexual Difference*, edited by Linell E. Cady and Tracy Fessenden, 25–45. New York: Columbia University Press, 2013.

Scott, Rachel. *The Challenge of Political Islam: Non-Muslims and the Egyptian State*. Palo Alto: Stanford University Press, 2010.

Sedra, Paul. "Class Cleavages and Ethnic Conflict: Coptic Christian Communities in Modern Egyptian Politics." *Islam and Christian-Muslim Relations* 10, no. 2 (1999): 219–35.

———. "Copts and the Millet Partnership: The Intra Communal Dynamics behind Egyptian Sectarianism," *Journal of Law and Religion* 29, no. 3 (2014): 491–509.

———. *From Mission to Modernity: Evangelicals, Reformers and Education in Nineteenth-Century Egypt*. London: I. B. Taurus, 2011.

———. "Imagining an Imperial Race: Egyptology in the Service of Empire." *Comparative Studies of South Asia, Africa and the Middle East* 24, no. 1 (2004): 249–59.

———. "John Lieder and His Mission in Egypt: The Evangelical Ethos at Work among Nineteenth-Century Copts." *Journal of Religious History* 28, no. 3 (2004): 219–39.

Seikaly, Samir. "Coptic Communal Reform, 1860–1914." *Middle Eastern Studies* 6, no. 3 (1970): 246–75.

———. "Prime Minister and Assassin: Boutros Ghali and Wardani." *Middle Eastern Studies* 13, no. 1 (1977): 112–23.

Seligman, Edwin R. A., ed. *Encyclopedia of the Social Sciences*. Vol. 1. New York: Macmillan, 1933.

Sells, Michael. *Early Islamic Mysticism*. New York: Paulist, 1996.

Sezgin, Yüksel. *Human Rights under State-Enforced Religious Family Laws in Israel, Egypt, and India*. Cambridge: Cambridge University Press, 2013.

Shah, Prakash, et al. *Family, Religion, and Law: Cultural Encounters in Europe*. London: Ashgate, 2014.

Shaham, Ron. "Communal Identity, Political Islam, and Family Law; Copts and the Debate over the Grounds for Dissolution of Marriage in Twentieth-Century Egypt." *Islam and Christian-Muslim Relations* 21, no. 4 (2010): 409–22.

———. "Shopping for Legal Forums: Christians and Family Law in Modern Egypt." In *Dispensing Justice in Islam: Qadis and Their Judgments*, edited by Khalid Muhammad Masud, Rudolph Peters, and David Powers, 451–69. Leiden: Brill, 2006.

Shami, Seteney. "*Aqalliyya*/Minority in Modern Egyptian Discourse." In *Words in Motion: Toward a Global Lexicon*, edited by Carol Gluck and Anna L. Tsing, 151–73. Durham: Duke University Press, 2009.

al-Sharif, Muhammed, ed. *'Ala Hamish al-Dustur*. Cairo: al-Maktaba al-Khassa lil-Duktur Nasir al-Ansari, 1938.

Sharkey, Heather. *American Evangelicals in Egypt: Missionary Encounters in an Age of Empire*. Oxford: Oxford University Press, 2008.

———. "Muslim Apostasy, Christian Conversion, and Religious Freedom in Egypt: A Study of American Missionaries, Western Imperialism, and Human Rights Agendas." In *Proselytization Revisited: Rights, Free Markets, and Cultural Wars*, edited by Rosalind I. J. Hackett, 139–66. London: Equinox, 2008.

al-Sharmani, Mulki. *Recent Reforms in Personal Status Laws and Women's Empowerment*. Cairo: American University in Cairo Social Research Center, 2007.

Shea, Nina. *In the Lion's Den: A Shocking Account of Persecution and Martyrdom of Christians Today and How We Should Respond*. Nashville: Broadman and Holman, 1997.

Sheehan, Jonathan. *The Enlightenment Bible: Translation, Scholarship, Culture*. Princeton: Princeton University Press, 2007.

Shenoda, Anthony. *Cultivating Mystery: Miracles and Coptic Moral Imaginary*. PhD diss., Harvard University, 2010.

Shreve, Gene, and Hannah Buxbaum. *A Conflicts of Law Anthology*. Dayton, OH: LexisNexis, 2012.

Shuger, Debora Kuller. *The Renaissance Bible: Scholarship, Sacrifice, Subjectivity*. Berkeley: University of California Press, 1994.

Sills, David L., ed. *International Encyclopedia of the Social Sciences*. Vol. 10. New York: Macmillan and Free Press, 1968.

Skinner, Quentin. "The Empirical Theorists of Democracy and Their Critics: A Plague on Both Their Houses." *Political Theory* 1, no. 3 (1973): 298–99.

Somers, Margaret, and Christopher Roberts. "Toward a New Sociology of Rights: A Genealogy of 'Buried Bodies' of Citizenship and Human Rights." *Annual Review of Law and Social Science* 4 (2008): 385–425.

Sonbol, Amira el-Azhary. "History of Marriage Contracts in Egypt." *Hawwa* 3, no. 2 (2005): 158–96.

Sonyel, Salahi R. "The Protégé System in the Ottoman Empire." *Journal of Islamic Studies* 2, no. 1 (1991): 56–66.

Sorkin, David. "Religious Minorities and the Making of Citizenship in the Long Nineteenth Century: Locating Jewish Emancipation in Some of Its Relevant Contexts." Unpublished manuscript. September 2011.

Stepan, Alfred. "The Multiple Secularisms of Modern Democratic and Non-Democratic Regimes." In Calhoun, Juergensmeyer, and VanAntwerpen, *Rethinking Secularism*, 114–44.

Stevens, Jacqueline. *Reproducing the State*. Princeton: Princeton University Press, 1999.

Strauss, David Friedrich. *The Life of Jesus, Critically Examined*. Translated by Marian Evans. New York: Calvin Blanchard, 1860.

Strauss, Johann. "Ottomanisme et 'ottomanité': Le témoignage linguistique." In *Aspects of the Political Language in Turkey (19th–20th Centuries)*, edited by Hans-Lukas Kieser. Istanbul: ISIS Press, 2002.

Sulayman, Nadia Halim. *Qawanin al-Ahwal al-Shakhsiyya lil-Masihiyyin: Dirasa Tahliliyya Naqdiyya*. Cairo: Center for Egyptian Women's Legal Assistance, 2000.

Sullivan, Winnifred Fallers. *The Impossibility of Religious Freedom*. Princeton: Princeton University Press, 2005.

———. "The World That *Smith* Made." *The Immanent Frame*. March 7, 2012. http://blogs.ssrc.org/tif/2012/03/07/the-world-that-smith-made.

Surkis, Judith. "Code Switching: Conversion, Mixed Marriage, and the Corporealization of Law in French Algeria." Unpublished manuscript. February 1, 2014.

———. "Hymenal Politics: Marriage, Secularism, and French Sovereignty." *Public Culture* 22, no. 3 (2010): 531–56.

Tadros, Mariz. *Copts at the Crossroads: The Challenges of Building Inclusive Democracy in Egypt*. Cairo: American University in Cairo Press, 2013.

———. "Sectarianism and Its Discontents in Post-Mubarak Egypt." *Middle East Report* 41, no. 2 (2011): 26–31.

———. "Vicissitudes in the Entente between the Coptic Orthodox Church and the State in Egypt (1952–2007)." *International Journal of Middle East Studies* 41 (2009): 269–87.

Tambar, Kabir. *The Reckoning of Pluralism: Belonging and the Demands of History in Turkey*. Palo Alto: Stanford University Press, 2014.

Taylor, Charles. *A Secular Age*. Cambridge: Harvard University Press, 2007.

Taylor, Charles, et al. *Multiculturalism and "The Politics of Recognition": An Essay with Commentary*. Princeton: Princeton University Press, 1992.

Tejirian, Eleanor H., and Reeva Spector Simon. *Conflict, Conquest, and Conversion: Two Thousand Years of Christian Missions in the Middle East*. New York: Columbia University Press, 2012.

Tsoukala, Philomena. "Marrying Family Law to the Nation." *American Journal of Comparative Law* 58, no. 4 (2010): 873–910.

Tucker, Judith. *Women, Family, and Gender in Islamic Law.* Cambridge: Cambridge University Press, 2008.

United Nations. "Protocol to Prevent, Suppress and Punish Trafficking in Persons, Especially Women and Children, Supplementing the United Nations Convention against Transnational Organized Crime." 2000. www.uncjin.org/Documents/Conventions/dcatoc/final_documents _2/convention_%20traff_eng.pdf.

Usama, Salama. *Masir al-Aqbat fi Masr.* Cairo: Dar al-Khayal, 1998.

USCIRF (United States Commission on International Religious Freedom). "USCIRF Annual Report 2013—Countries of Particular Concern: Egypt." April 30, 2013. www.refworld.org/ docid/51826efff.html.

US Department of State. "Egypt: 2011 Report on International Religious Freedom." July 30, 2012. www.state.gov/j/drl/rls/irf/2011/nea/192881.htm.

———. "Foreign Military Financing Account Summary." www.state.gov/t/pm/ppa/sat/c14560.htm.

———. "Victims of Trafficking and Violence Protection Act of 2000." October 28, 2000. www .state.gov/j/tip/laws/61124.htm.

van der Vyver, Johan. "Self-Determination and the Right to Secession of Religious Minorities under International Law." In *Protecting the Human Rights of Religious Minorities in Eastern Europe*, edited by Peter Danchin and Elizabeth Cole, 252–94. New York: Columbia University Press, 2002.

Vital, David. *A People Apart: A Political History of the Jews in Europe.* Oxford: Oxford University Press, 1999.

Vogel, Ursula. "Private Contract and Public Institution: The Peculiar Case of Marriage." In *Public and Private: Legal, Political and Philosophical Perspectives*, edited by Maurizio Passerin d'En-trèves and Ursula Vogel, 177–99. London: Routledge, 2000.

Wakin, Edward. *A Lonely Minority: The Modern Story of Egypt's Copts.* New York: William Morrow, 1963.

Warner, Michael. "Sex and Secularity." Unpublished manuscript. April 26, 2011.

Waterbury, John. "Democracy without Democrats?" In *Democracy without Democrats: Renewal of Politics in the Muslim World*, edited by Ghassan Salame, 23–47. London: I. B. Taurus, 1994.

Weiss, Max. *In the Shadow of Sectarianism: Law, Shi'ism, and the Making of Modern Lebanon.* Cambridge, MA: Harvard University Press, 2010.

Wessel, Susan. *Cyril of Alexandria and the Nestorian Controversy: The Making of a Saint and of a Heretic.* Oxford: Oxford University Press, 2004.

White, Benjamin Thomas. *The Emergence of Minorities in the Middle East: The Politics of Community in French Mandate Syria.* Edinburgh: Edinburgh University Press, 2011.

Wiener, Michael. "The Mandate of the Special Rapporteur on Freedom of Religion or Belief—Institutional, Procedural and Substantive Legal Issues." *Religion and Human Rights* 2 (2007): 3–17.

Young, Iris Marion. "A Multicultural Continuum: A Critique of Will Kymlicka's Ethnic-Nation Dichotomy." *Constellations* 4, no. 1 (April 1997): 48–53.

———. *Justice and the Politics of Difference.* Princeton: Princeton University Press, 1990.

Ziedan, Youssef. *Azazeel.* Translated by Jonathan Wright. London: Atlantic, 2012.

Ziyan, Muhammed. *Aqbat al-Mahgar: Suda' fi Damagh Masr.* Cairo: Dar al-Kutb al-Masriya, 2008.

Žižek, Slavoj. *On Belief.* New York: Routledge, 2001.

INDEX

Abdel Nasser, Gamal, 69n6, 77n40, 81–84, 87–88, 129, 152
abduction, alleged, 111–14, 141–45. *See also* Qustuntin; Shehata
abortion, 9, 114, 135
abstraction. *See* formalism; majoritarian bias; norms; promise
Abu Zayd, Nasr Hamid, 138n113, 205
adab. See literature
adultery, 113, 125–26, 129, 138n116, 139n117
affirmative action, 67, 103, 106. *See also* proportionate representation; quota
African Americans, 52, 58
agency: divine, 197, 203; human, 203; state, 28, 180, 211–12; women's, 141
Agrama, Hussein, 118–19, 164, 176–77
ahl al-dhimma, 36–39, 61, 153n6, 155. *See also* People of the Book
ahl al-kitab. See People of the Book
'Alawis, 62, 123
Algeria, 42, 63, 134
American Coptic Association. *See* Coptic diaspora
American Coptic Union. *See* Coptic diaspora
American Federal Council of Churches, 49
American University in Cairo, 46, 91n90
Anghie, Antony, 42–43, 92
Anglicanism, 43, 71, 75, 139n118. *See also* missionaries
anthropology, 23–24, 204n77
anti-Semitism, 8, 55, 57, 64n123, 201, 209, 211. *See also* Jews/Judaism in Europe
apostasy, 44n51, 49, 137–40, 150, 157n16, 161, 163, 205. *See also* Abu Zayd
aqalliyya (minority), 19, 61, 70, 74. See also *millet; ta'ifa; umma*
aqbat al-mahgar (emigrated Copts). *See* Coptic diaspora
Arabic, 47, 77, 81, 100–101, 184, 187, 198–99
Arab Spring. *See* uprising (2011)
Arendt, Hannah, 53, 57
Arius, 186, 194, 200–202

Armenia and Armenians, 41, 44, 74n28, 77. *See also* Eastern Christianity
Article 2 (Egyptian constitutions), 153–55. *See also* constitutional debates
Article 3 (2014 Egyptian constitution), 130. *See also* communal autonomy
Article 4 (1923 Egyptian constitution), 74. *See also* communal autonomy
Article 9 (ECHR), 156n13, 164, 167, 169–70, 172, 179. *See also* religious freedom
Article 10 (ECHR), 164, 176. *See also* freedom of expression
Article 18 (ICCPR), 156n13, 164–65
Article 18 (UDHR), 48–50, 58, 91
Article 27 (ICCPR), 59, 91
Article 46 (1971 Egyptian constitution), 159
Article 149 (1923 Egyptian constitution), 77–79, 154. *See also* constitutional debates
Asad, Talal, 3, 11, 15, 117
authoritarianism, 76, 81, 93, 152, 210; against democracy, 4–6
Azazeel (Ziedan), 27, 181–207

Bahai judgments: administrative court (1948), 156n16; Court of Administrative Justice (2006), 158–63, 166n33; Court of Administrative Justice (2008), 162–63, 173, 174n54; Supreme Administrative Court (1983), 156–59, 161–62; Supreme Administrative Court (2006), 160–61; Supreme Constitutional Court (1975), 156. *See also* Bahais; Egyptian courts; national identity cards; recognition
Bahais, 1, 7, 15–16, 24, 27, 91, 115, 130, 149–71, 175, 209. *See also* Bahai judgments; national identity cards; recognition
Balkans, 62, 64–65
bayt al-ta'a, 133
Bedouins, 69, 73
Bible, 47, 100–101, 125, 127, 187, 197, 201

INDEX

family law: Coptic, 17, 64, 70n12, 113,
123–32, 140; genealogy of, 119–23;
Islamic, 78, 86, 113n10, 123–24, 127n67,
129–30, 133n90, 136–39, 210; nationalization, 118n29. *See also* gender; marriage;
nationalism; secularization; sexuality and
secularism
feminism, 112, 114, 135, 190
Feuerbach, Ludwig, 14, 203, 205
fiction. *See* literature
First Coptic Conference (1911), 69–70
First Nations. *See* Native Americans
formalism, 11, 20, 25, 32–33, 67, 73, 106,
155, 175–76. *See also* majoritarian bias;
recognition; secularism, promise of
forum externum, 56, 150, 155, 157, 161, 166,
171, 177. *See also* religious belief and
practice
forum internum, 56, 150, 155, 157, 161,
166–67, 177. *See also* religious belief
and practice
Foucault, Michel, 147
Fourth Lateran Council (1251), 36n13
France, 4n6, 7, 25, 40, 42–43, 47n63, 52, 55,
62–63, 67n4, 69n9, 71, 79, 119, 122–24,
131, 133–34, 147, 154, 163–64, 172n49,
179, 209, 211n5. *See also* civil code; colonialism; *Dogru v. France (2009)*; *laïcité*;
West and non-West
freedom. *See* communal autonomy; freedom
of expression; individual liberty; religious
freedom
freedom of expression, 164, 176, 188–89
Freedom House. *See* think tanks
Free Officers coup (1952), 73n23, 81, 84n68
Frei, Hans, 197

Gauchet, Marcel, 8, 205
gay marriage, 9, 114, 147. *See also* homosexuality; morality
gender, 12n26, 26–27, 66, 67n4, 133, 147,
155, 169–71, 209–10; secularism and,
114–15, 119, 123, 129, 132–37, 140–41,
146. *See also* sexuality and secularism
Germany, 4n6, 40–41, 52–53, 55, 57n98, 59,
77, 123n49, 131n83, 132, 176, 209
Gibbon, Edward, 190–91, 193, 196n49
global and local. *See* secularism, study of;
universality
Gomʿa, Ali (Grand Mufti), 138
good governance paradigm, 92–94, 98

governance, secular, 1–5, 8–9, 23, 25, 27,
31, 52, 60–61, 68, 81, 87, 105, 117, 128,
134, 147, 151, 155, 163, 208. *See also*
good governance paradigm; political
secularism
Greece, 27, 41, 51, 61–62, 121, 151. See also
Kokkinakos v. Greece (1993)
Greek Orthodox Christianity, 61–62, 121n39,
179, 194n42

Habermas, Jürgen, 8, 22
Halley, Janet, 120, 123
Hatt-i Hümayun (1856), 35n6, 39–41
headscarf, 4n6, 9, 91n90, 132, 134, 147, 168–75
heresy: Christian, 44, 126, 186–87, 200–201;
Islamic, 16, 84, 149, 153, 161. *See also*
apostasy; Christological debates
hermeneutics. *See* interpretation
heterosexuality. *See* family; sexuality
Hizb al-Wafd, 68–69, 73n23, 76–77, 79, 81
homosexuality, 9, 114, 128n71, 147
Hudson Institute. *See* think tanks
humanism, 43, 50n76, 182, 199, 202–5
humanitarianism. *See* interventions
human rights, 8, 16–19, 32, 48–51, 55, 57–59,
66, 86, 88n81, 89, 93–98, 101, 112, 115,
137n106, 142–44, 149, 151, 168, 177. *See
also* European Court of Human Rights;
international law
human trafficking, 143–45
Hypa (protagonist), 183–86, 190, 199–204
Hypatia, 186, 189–93, 195

imaginary, 5, 28, 45, 72, 180, 206–8, 210
immanence, 197, 205. *See also* transcendence
indeterminacy. *See* political secularism
India, 4, 9, 24, 67n5, 69, 73n24, 115n15,
115n16, 124, 153n6
individualization, 12, 17–18, 44, 46–47,
50–52, 55–56, 60, 76, 121, 166. *See also*
privatization
individual liberty, 4–5, 14, 17–18, 20, 44,
46, 49–50, 56, 58, 66–67, 76, 146, 156,
172–73, 177–78, 182, 205. *See also* conversion; formalism; religious liberty
International Covenant on Civil and Political
Rights (ICCPR), 59, 91, 156n13, 164–65.
See also public order; religious freedom
international law, 17, 19, 32, 42–43, 52–55,
57–58, 88–89, 98, 102, 163–64. *See also*
human rights; sovereignty, differential